AWAITING THE MILLENNIAL KINGDOM

By the same author

The Message of the Psalter
An Eschatological Programme in the Book of Psalms

The Songs of Ascents
Psalms 120 to 134 in the Worship of Jerusalem's Temples

Messiah ben Joseph

Jesus: The Incarnation of the Word

How To Be Happy For Ever (No, really!!)

Awaiting the Millennial Kingdom

David C Mitchell

Campbell Publishers
Glasgow Scotland

CAMPBELL
PUBLISHERS
GLASGOW SCOTLAND

CampbellPublishers.com

First Edition. First published in paperback (September 2024)

Paperback ISBN: 978-1916619166

Cover: *Scheidung Abends* (1922) by Paul Klee.

Translations not by the author are from the ESV translation.

Brightmorningstar.org

HOW many years has man been driven
Far off from happiness and heaven?
When wilt thou, gracious LORD, *restore*
Thy wandering church, to roam no more?

Six thousand years are fully past
Since Adam from thy sight was cast;
And ever since, his fallen race
From age to age are void of grace.

When will the happy trump proclaim
The judgment of the martyr'd Lamb?
When shall the captive troops be free,
And keep the eternal jubilee?

Hasten it, LORD, *in every land,*
Send thou thine angels and command:
" Go sound deliverance; loudly blow
" Salvation to the saints below! "

We want to have the day appear!
The promis'd great sabbatic year,
When, far from grief, and sin, and hell,
Your saints in ceaseless peace shall dwell.

'Till then, we will not let thee rest,
Thou still shalt hear our strong request;
And this our daily prayer shall be,
LORD, *sound the trump of jubilee.*

After John Cennick (1718–55)

To Pastor Robert Dodoo of São Paulo, Brazil

Contents

Introduction

THIS BOOK is about the millennial week, the coming end of this age, and the dawn of the Sabbath millennium. In it, I show that we are about to enter the long-awaited times of the messianic age.

Yet, just before I finished this book, in late August, I had a mishap. I was cutting winter logs for our wood-fire and the chainsaw cut through the wood into my leg. I had been wielding this machine for ten years without incident. But there are no smart accidents, and I suppose I just got complacent. In a trice, it cleft my leg to the bone, severing the anterior tibular tendon. Yet God was good. For a start, I could have cut my leg off, but didn't. It was also surprisingly painless and bloodless. In fact, I thought it was just a scratch. I walked up the slope into our house and told my daughter, "I've cut my leg, but it's just a scratch." I pulled aside the lacerated trouser leg to look. She screamed. "That's not a scratch. You need to go to hospital right now." A good neighbour drove me quickly to Brussels Saint Luc teaching hospital, ten minutes from our door. My wife, who is probably the best doc in the world, phoned her colleagues at Emergency to alert them and I was received with *Ooh-la-la-las.* A smiling surgeon told me, *Les tronçonneuses nous donnent beaucoup de travail intéressant.* (Chainsaws give us a lot of interesting work.) Within four hours I was on the operating table. The young surgeon cleaned out the wound and sutured the tendon. Then I was two days lying broken on a hospital bed. To my roommate I croaked the praises of the medical staff and the wonders of modern medicine. *Ah oui,* he replied, *c'est une belle êpoque pour les accidents graves!* (Oh yes, it's a great time for serious injuries!) After I was released from hospital, I was confined to hopping on crutches, rolling on a wheelchair, or sitting with my leg up for six weeks. Six weeks! Unable to walk as summer turned to chill autumn! It loomed ahead dismally. Yet, as the weeks passed, things got better. There was, thank God, no infection. After three weeks, they removed the stitches and the bandage. After four, I was feeling stronger. How I longed for the end of the sixth week and the start of the seventh, when I could stand and walk again! Then I would be restored to freedom and life. That seventh week shone before my eyes like a Sabbath of joy.

The Bible too speaks about six ages of impediment, confinement, and captivity, after which the world will enter a seventh age of liberation, a Sabbath millennium, when the Messiah will return to rule in Jerusalem and creation will enter into the liberty of the blessed sons of God. These six ages, each of one thousand years, began with the creation of Adam and are coming to a close now, in our own time. This millennial week is one way the Bible, the sages of ancient Israel, and the Church Fathers, measured the passing of the ages.

But the Bible and the sages had a second way of calculating the ages of the world. This was by the jubilee cycle, which Moses legislated in Leviticus, a recurring forty-nine-year cycle which also began at Adam's creation and runs to our own time.

These two ancient systems of timekeeping – millennia and jubilees – are, or should be, the basis of all biblical eschatology. They permit us, knowing the times of the jubilee cycle, and knowing the time of the incarnation of Jesus the Messiah, to calculate the date of Adam's creation. More pertinently, they let us calculate the time of the end of our own age, the sixth millennium. With this method we may calculate that the final jubilee year of the sixth millennium begins now, in autumn AD 2024, on 10 Tishri, and ends in autumn AD 2025, at sundown on 29 Elul. Then, on 1 Tishri 2025, we enter the Sabbath millennium, in which the Messiah will return to set up his throne. Yet there may be a transition period between the end of the sixth millennium, in autumn 2025, and the day of the Messiah's longed-for *parousia* in the seventh millennium.

But here is the good news. He is not late. He has never been late. Everything is going according to plan.

David C. Mitchell
Brussels, September 2024

1

Time for the Future

A LONG TIME AGO, in 1993, I was talking to a Baptist friend. We spoke about a project this person was doing which would finish in 1996. "I hope you get it finished before the Lord comes," I said.

One doesn't always know the best thing to say. But, you see, at that time, I was reading about the millennial week, the ancient teaching that this current age will last six thousand years and be followed by the Messiah's thousand-year Sabbath kingdom of peace and plenty. I had heard of it in early Christian teaching. Now I was learning that the rabbis of Jesus's time held to it too. So I found myself asking, "Could the time of his coming really be as easy as counting 6,000 years from creation?" I knew that James Ussher had calculated the creation of Adam in 6004 BC. (His calculations feature in the King James Bible.) And I was discovering that some rabbinic dates of creation were very close to Ussher's. Clearly, adding 6,000 years to 6004 BC gave a date of 1996 in our own time. Could it really be that easy?

So I added blithely, "He's coming in 1996."

My friend felt, I fear, that I was being flippant and replied, with simple candour, "Well, I know he's coming soon anyway."

And he is coming soon. But he didn't come in 1996. He still hasn't come yet, almost thirty years later. Yet I wasn't the first person to hope ahead of time. It seems the apostle Paul hoped the Lord Jesus might come in his time (1 Thess. 4:15–18). But he didn't. The Greek Fathers, who dated creation in 5,500 BC, expected him in the sixth century AD. They got the tribulation all right, from 536 to 549: four years of volcanic winter issued in failed crops, raging famine, and bubonic plague, killing a quarter of the Roman world. But he didn't come. Others expected him in AD 1,000. And many at other times since. But we are still waiting.

MILLENNIA AND JUBILEES

Yet, if we believe the Bible, he is still coming. And every day that goes by brings his coming nearer. And knowing that this age is to last 6,000 years really can help us to know when he will come. Not exactly. But generally. For he who said, "No man knows the day or the hour," also castigated the Pharisees for not being able to read the signs of the times. Those same Pharisees knew full well that Daniel had foretold that the Messiah would come at the end of ten jubilees, or 490 years, from the rebuilding of Jerusalem in the fifth century BC. For almost 500 years they had been counting the jubilees to the appointed time. But they refused to know him when he came.

So hoping to calculate the time of his return is not foolish. If we really know the divine timetable of the ages, we really can know the times of his coming. As for my premature hope that he would come in 1996, it wasn't all Ussher's fault. Ussher was close, probably only a year out. What I didn't know back then was that the calendar of the ages is counted not only in millennia, but also in jubilees, just as Gabriel told Daniel. The overlap of jubilees and millennia adds another twenty-seven years to the calculation.

That brings us, in fact, to autumn 2024 as the beginning of the final jubilee year of the sixth millennium. More precisely, this final jubilee year will begin on 10 Tishri 2024 and run till autumn 2025. It's quite ironic that, having worked on this book for some years, this only became clear to me in the summer of 2024. One is writing a book on the end of the age, just as the age is about to end. But this doesn't render it useless. For a start, the year autumn 2024 to 2025 is not the end of the world, but only the end of the sixth millennium. There will certainly be a transition period into the Sabbath millennium. In fact, since Daniel's prophecy, there are two jubilee cycles interlocking at an interval of eighteen years. That seems to be the transition period. But what is important in all this, as events unfold around us, is that we see that God's plan for the ages is not arbitrary or *ad hoc.* He is not sitting thinking, "When will I send my Son back? I can't make up my mind." Not at all. Everything is happening according to his timetable of the ages which he has known since the beginning (Acts 1:7). If the King hasn't come yet, it is because the times were not fulfilled. And though we cannot know the day, we can certainly recognize the times.

WHY ESCHATOLOGY?

This book is about Eschatology – from Greek *eschatos* or "last" – that is, the theological discipline of what the Bible says about the Last Things, the things that will happen at the end of this age and thereafter. Some resent this fascination with eschatology. They say, maybe, that it's of no practical use. How can eschatology help me feed my kids? How can it solve social injustice or the climate crisis or global poverty? Others object that eschatology is a hallmark of loony cults. They pooh-pooh those who take much interest in it. Anglican theologians are good at this. Bishop Michael Green had no doubts:

> Throughout history, apocalyptic sects in Christianity have played down both cross and resurrection in favour of heightened eschatological expectation. They have developed millennial descriptions, timetables of the Rapture, and geographies of heaven and hell.[1]

Now never let it be said that I disregard the cross. *In the cross of Christ I glory, tow'ring o'er the wrecks of time.* My hope is in the cross. But some theologians cite the cross to suggest that eschatology is a matter for children. I think there are several reasons why they do this. Since the cross and resurrection are historical they feel safe to talk about them. But the return of the Lord is future. Our only basis for talking about the future is prophecy and they are not sure what bits of that to believe or take literally. We cannot expect the Bible to tell us the future, they say. We misread the prophets if we imagine they speak about the future, they say. They say prophets don't foretell, they *forth*-tell; they don't predict the future, they proclaim social justice. They say the Revelation was written not to teach us about the future but to remind the early church that God knows their trials. They think that those who take prophecy too seriously should grow up and talk about the cross and the resurrection.

[1] Green, *Empty Cross of Jesus,* 163.

But eschatology is not a matter for children. It is just as vital as the doctrines of incarnation, atonement, resurrection, ascension, heavenly reign, and the sending of the Spirit. If his incarnation was wonderful, his parousia is no less so. If his affliction was wonderful, his vindication is no less so. Jesus had a lot to say about his return in glory, and whoever relegates it to myth or symbolism, or fails to study what he really meant, is making a bad mistake. The cross may be the head of the Christian faith, but a head without trunk and limbs is not a functioning body. To overstate one truth at the cost of another is to have a lop-sided faith.

Eschatology was the abiding interest of Isaac Newton. Like Ussher, he calculated the date of creation so as to determine the time of the return of Jesus, which he thought would happen in 2060. (I'll explain his calculation later.) Newton's best known work on eschatology is his commentary *On Daniel and the Apocalypse* (1733). But he left many unpublished papers on the subject, including another treatise on the Revelation.[2] A century ago, it was acquired by the polymath and antiquarian Avraham Yahuda. Yahuda showed it to his friend Albert Einstein. Einstein, after studying it, wrote to Yahuda expressing his fascination with Newton's calculations. So those of us who devote time to the study of eschatology can rest assured that we are not in the company of fools.

Newton's comments on prophecy in these unpublished papers are worth considering. He rejects any notion that biblical prophecy is mere encouragement to remind us that God is with us. "The holy Prophesies," he says, "are no other than histories of things to come." (f16r)

He rejects any notion that prophecy cannot be understood. Though it may be hard to understand, diligence in study will make it clearer, especially as the time draws near.

> If they [prophecies] are never to be understood, to what end did God reveale them? Certainly he did it for the edification of the church; & if so, then it is as certain that the church shall at length attain to the understanding thereof. (f2v)
>
> Consider also the designe of the Apocalyps [the Revelation]. Was it not given for the use of the Church to guide & direct her in the right way, And is not this the end of all prophetick Scripture? If there was no need of it, or if it cannot be understood, then why did God give it? Does he trifle? But if it was necessary for the Church then why doest thou neglect it, or how knowest thou that thou art in the right way, and yet doest not understand it? (f3v)

[2] Untitled treatise on Revelation, Section 1.1. (Yahuda Ms. 1.1).

Next, Newton warns of the grave dangers of ignoring prophecy, for those who do so will fall calamitously short in the trials of the last days.

> Indeed, the danger of neglecting prophecy is great. For Daniel spoke clearly of the time of Messiah's coming, but the first-century Jews, by their ignorance of scripture and hardness of heart, failed to discern the signs of the time of his appearing (Matt. 16:3; Luke 19:44).
>
> Consider how our Saviour taught the Jews in Parables that in hearing they might hear & not understand & in seeing they might see & not perceive. And as these Parables were spoken to try the Jews so the mysticall scriptures were written to try us. Therefore beware that thou be not found wanting in this tryall. For if thou beest, the obscurity of these scriptures will as little excuse thee as the obscurity of our Saviours Parables excused the Jews. (f2v)
>
> If God was so angry with the Jews for not searching more diligently into the Prophesies which he had given them to know Christ by: why should we think he will excuse us for not searching into the Prophesies which he hath given us to know Antichrist by? For certainly it must be as dangerous & as easy an error for Christians to adhere to Antichrist as it was for the Iews to reject Christ. And therefore it is as much our duty to indeavour to be able to know him that we may avoyd him, as it was theirs to know Christ that they might follow him. (3r)

Finally, Newton speaks of the great blessings which God bestows on those who study prophecy.

> Lastly consider the Blessing which is promised to them that read & study & keep the things which are written in <5r> this Prophesy. *Blessed is he that readeth & they that hear the words of this Prophesy & keep the things which are written therein, for the time is at hand,* Rev. 1.3. And again to reinforce the invitation to take these things into consideration, the same Blessing is repeated in Ch. 22.7 And does God ever annex his blessings to trifles or things of indifferency? Wherefore be not overwise in thine own conceipt, but as thou desirest to inherit this blessing consider & search into these Scriptures which God hath given to be a guide in these latter times, & be not discouraged by the gainsaying which these things will meet with in the world.

Indeed, there are many blessings attached to the study of prophecy. One of the greatest is, as the apostle John says, "We know that when he appears we shall be like him, because we shall see him as he is. And everyone who thus hopes in him purifies himself as he is pure." (1 John 3:2–3) That is to say, those who ponder the return of the Lord find it has a purifying influence upon the heart and soul and character. Rather than it being an idle hobby, an active hope in the Lord's return is essential to the growth of Christian faith and character.

THE MILLENNIAL WEEK

The ancient prophecy of the millennial week is one of the key subjects of this book. According to this prophecy, our world-age will last seven thousand years. Each thousand years is one day of a millennial week. And so there will be six thousand years of toil and grief, and then, with the seventh millennium, will come the blessed Sabbath of creation, the time of rest and peace, the thousand-year reign of the Messiah in Jerusalem. Here it is, counted in AM (Anno Mundi) years from creation.

Figure 1. The millennial week

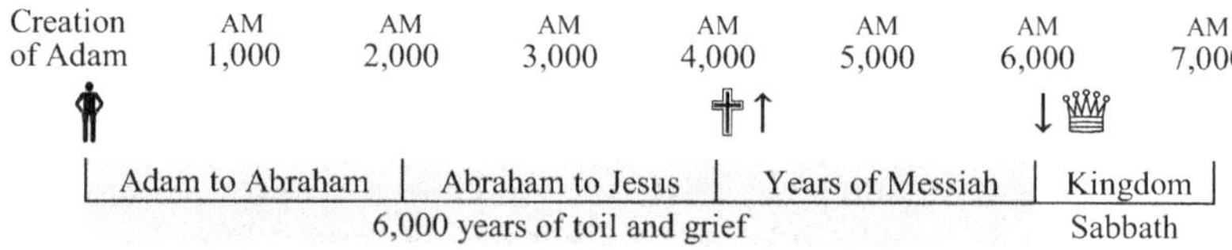

Now you may reply, "I never heard of that ancient prophecy." But you have probably heard of the millennium spoken of by John in Revelation 20. And what is important to realize is that John's millennium is, so to speak, the tip of the iceberg of the millennial week. John's millennium is the seventh Sabbath millennium which follows the six.

But some say it is actually the other way round. John's millennium is not the seventh millennium of the millennial week. On the contrary, John spoke about only *one* millennium and then other people came along and turned this idea into a whole week of millennia.[3] But there are two very good reasons why this cannot be so.

First, we have texts from before the time of the Revelation that speak of the millennial days of creation. The earliest are the Book of Jubilees, 2 Enoch, and the Targum of Hosea. Since these texts already speak of, or allude to, several millennial days, long before the Revelation was written, they cannot be taking their ideas from there. Second, the millennial week appears explicitly in the epistle of Barnabas, from the late first century AD. But it also appears just as explicitly in rabbinic literature only a little later, in the second century. It is unlikely that the Pharisees (Rabbis) or the Nazarenes (early Hebrew Christians) borrowed

[3] So Charles 1913: 2.451n.

such an idea from one another. The Christian and Rabbinic teachings must derive from an older common source. And so again we must accept that this idea was around before Barnabas's epistle and John's Revelation. And so the prophecy of the millennial week does not derive from the millennium of Revelation 20. Rather, the millennium of Revelation 20 derives from the more ancient teaching of the millennial week.

But some say, rightly enough, that patristic and rabbinic teachings are not Scripture. And so, since the millennial week is taught neither in the New Testament nor the Old, it is not a biblical doctrine, and we need not reckon upon it. But I would dispute that the millennial week is not found in the Old or New Testaments. It is found in both, if we know where to look. The evidence is the patristic and rabbinic teachings themselves. Any time we find the same idea in Christianity and Judaism, we must understand that they share the same idea only when both regard it as true. For that to happen, the only explanation is that both saw it as a teaching of the Old Testament scriptures, which were the foundation of the faith of ancient Israel, before that faith split into the Christian Church and the Jewish Synagogue.

So in this book I propose that the millennial week, though not explicitly taught in the Old Testament, is fully implied within it. It was a necessary deduction which the sages of ancient Israel made from their scriptures. It is therefore very much a biblical doctrine. That is why it is also taught, later on, by Jesus and the apostles. And that is why it also appears clearly in the teaching both of the early Church Fathers and of their contemporaries, the Pharisees, whose views are recorded in rabbinic literature. It is a single Old Testament idea inherited equally by the Synagogue and the Church.

I will trace the development of the millennial week through history. In Judaism, it shows an admirable solidity, remaining virtually the same through two millennia. But in Christianity, it falls under the influence of neoplatonism, whose adherents – particularly Origen and Augustine – confused the earthly and heavenly states promised to the faithful. As a result, historical Christian eschatology metamorphoses into a faith with no millennium and no earthly reign of the Messiah. Then it goes through fifteen hundred years of twists and turns as Christian thinkers struggle to reconcile the teaching of the Bible with the errors received from Origen and Augustine. But in this book, we return to the view of the New Testament and the earliest Church Fathers.

The millennial week is implied both in the Old Testament and the New. But we can go further. If we read carefully we will see that all the foundational ideas of New Testament eschatology are not really New Testament ideas at all. All of them – resurrection, rapture, conflagration – derive from the Old Testament. There is almost no distinctive New Testament eschatology. It all derives from the Old Testament. And that is why every element of New Testament eschatology is also reflected in rabbinic Judaism. And that is why the Rabbis can help us understand the New Testament as well as the Old. Both faith traditions received the same beliefs from the ancient scriptures.

THE HISTORY OF ESCHATOLOGY

If the millennial week is the underlying structure of biblical eschatology, it follows that the loss of that structure must lead to biblical eschatology collapsing catastrophically into an amorphous mass of unshapen ideas. And that is exactly what happened when, in the early third century, Origen of Alexandria begat the warped eschatology still held in so many corners of the Church. The millennial kingdom on earth, he said, was merely a fable for the simple. Instead, the disembodied righteous would inherit a heavenly and spiritual kingdom. His follower, Augustine of Hippo, tried to reconcile Origen's extreme teaching with the New Testament. He brought back the resurrection of the body, which Origen had discarded. But there was, Augustine agreed, no future Sabbath millennium. Instead, our current age, the church age, was the long-awaited millennium. At the end of it, there would be a great judgement. Then the saved would ascend to heaven in resurrected bodies and the unsaved depart into eternal torment. Thus they dumped the framework of biblical eschatology in a demolition that lasted for the best part of 1,500 years. Calvin was another who held to this teaching. The Book of Revelation, he said, was incomprehensible, a "wax nose" that one could twist any way one wished. You can't open the treasure-box if you've lost the key.

For 1,500 years, the church tried to understand biblical eschatology without the key. They sought to force the scriptures into a twisted system of their own devising. But the more they stuck to their system, the more they expanded it, the less the scriptures complied. For the word of God does not yield to man-made systems, but only to the God-given framework they had rejected.

It is the millennial week, and the understanding or misunderstanding of it, which leads to all the ideological positions of historical eschatology. These positions give rise to a range of terms that will crop up over and again. We will look at them in detail as we go along. But if we define them now before we set out, we will have a better idea of them as we meet them. They are all linked to different ways of reading the book of Revelation.

The first four terms are about the Book of Revelation as a whole, and about how it relates to our own times.

Futurism is the view of the early Church Fathers. This view sees the first three chapters of the Revelation – the vision and the letters to the churches – as historical, but all the events from the fourth chapter on as taking place at the end of this age, in the years before the return of Jesus.

Historicism appears in early medieval times. It sees the events of the first three chapters of Revelation as symbolically representing seven ages of the church. Then it sees the events from the fourth chapter on as taking place not in the future, but now, in our own time, in the church age, and happening around us. Following this view, Protestants saw the Antichrist as the Pope and the scarlet whore as the Roman Church.

Preterism arose in the early seventeenth century. Preterists think that everything in the Revelation until the end of chapter nineteen was fulfilled in Roman times. Even the coming of Christ, in chapter nineteen, was fulfilled when he judged Jerusalem in AD 70. Only the last three chapters await a future fulfilment. In time, Preterism morphed into Idealism.

Idealism arose in the early twentieth century. This is the view that the events of the Revelation are merely symbolic of the struggle between good and evil but have little correlation to any events on earth, either future or past. Some idealists still accept that this age will end with the coming of Jesus. But others think the world will simply become better as the 'veil' between this world and the spiritual world is lifted and mankind begins to live in the consciousness of God.

These are the four ways to interpret the Revelation. But there are a further four ways of reading the twentieth chapter of the Revelation and the thousand-year kingdom or millennium spoken of there.

Millennialism is the view that Jesus will return in future to set up an earthly kingdom for 1,000 years, as the Old Testament prophets and the Revelation say. This view – also known as millenarianism or chiliasm –

goes hand in hand with the Futurism of the early Church Fathers. In modern times it is more commonly known as Premillennialism, since it asserts that Jesus will return *before* the millennial kingdom.

Amillennialism ('No-millennialism'), also called 'realized' or 'present' millennialism, is Augustine's view that our own present age is the millennium spoken of in the Revelation. Thus there is no millennium still to come. In death, the faithful go to heaven and the unfaithful to hell. Finally, Jesus will return, not to reign on earth, but to raise and judge mankind, to send the righteous and wicked to their allotted places, and to destroy the earth. This goes together with the medieval Historicist view of the Revelation.

Postmillennialism ('After-millennialism') arose in the eighteenth century. It is a variant of Amillennialism. But it sees the end of this age climax into a golden age of worldwide conversion to Christianity and global blessing, as a result of the witness of Christians in the world. Then, at the end of the golden age, Jesus will return to judge and destroy the world and take the faithful to heaven and send the few remaining wicked to hell. This also goes hand in hand with the Historicist view of the Revelation.

Dispensational or *Darbyite pretribulationism* (pretribulational premillennialism) arose in the mid-nineteenth century, in the teaching of J.N. Darby. It is a form of millennialism which believes that Jesus will appear secretly to catch the faithful church up to heaven before the Antichrist begins his persecution. Then, during the time of the Antichrist, Jews and others will be converted to Christ, and will suffer in the Antichrist's Great Tribulation. Then, seven years later, Jesus will return with those raptured earlier to defeat the Antichrist and judge the earth. A variation on it is 'mid-tribulationism' which believes that the Church will remain on earth during the relative peace of the Antichrist's initial rule, but then be taken away before his persecution begins in earnest.

These are the main views historically held by Christians about when and how the kingdom of God is going to take over this world. But, broadly speaking, the great divide between them all is whether or not the twentieth chapter of Revelation gives an accurate "future history" when it says that Jesus will return to rule on earth for a thousand years.

For my part, I answer yes to that question. My view is what is called Historic or Classical Premillennialism. This was the faith of the early Church Fathers, as will become clear in the course of this book.

Where are we going?

Eschatology has undergone a great resurgence in the last century. This was hardly unexpected. The 19th-century church historian Philip Schaff foretold, in his *History of the Apostolic Church*, that, just as each age of the Church makes its own discoveries from the fullness of divine revelation, so the attention of the last days would focus on the last things: death, afterlife, rapture, second coming, and resurrection.

When Schaff wrote he had no idea of the things we would be seeing in the world now. For we live in a time when many sense that the end of the age is at hand, that some great transformation is about to come upon the world. Some of these ideas began in the late nineteenth century when influential Christians and Jews pressed the British Empire to "view with favour the establishment in Palestine of a national home for the Jewish people," as the Balfour Declaration said. This led ultimately to the Declaration of the State of Israel in 1948, the Israeli conquest of Jerusalem in 1967, and the apocalyptic horrors now unfolding in the Middle East.

In the 1970s, Hal Lindsay began to popularize eschatology in books like *The Late Great Planet Earth* (1971), *The 1980's: Countdown to Armageddon* (1980) and *Planet Earth: The Final Chapter* (1999). Since then Christian apocalyptic consciousness has proliferated. Long or short, scholarly or infantile, books on Christian eschatology now abound.

But this is true not only for Christians. Jews too ardently await the coming of the Messiah. Some Israeli politicians believe they are now preparing the way for the soon appearance of the Messiah who will open the way for their dominance of the earth. Claims are made that Benjamin Netanyahu is the Messiah ben Joseph, who will wage war for control of the land, rebuild the temple, and gather in the exiles before the coming of the long-awaited Messiah ben David.

Meanwhile, Muslims await the coming of al-Masiḥ ad-Dajjal, the False Messiah, heading an army of Jews and leading the world astray with miracles. But the Imam Mahdi will rise up against him and defeat the False Messiah, who will finally be slain by Isa (Jesus), who will appear as a Muslim prophet to assist the Mahdi.

But it's not just among religious believers. Expectation of the coming cataclysm is global. Our movies are replete with it: *After The Pandemic, Moonfall, Alien Conquest, Armageddon Tales, 2012 Doomsday, 4:44 Last Day On Earth, Apocalypse Now.* A recent story on Belgium's sedate

RTBF news speaks of how we can discuss with our children the impending *effondrement* (meltdown, collapse) of civilisation.

Nor is this sensationalism. What we see around us – global warming, environmental degradation, mass migration, economic chaos, threats of nuclear war – all lead us to understand that the world cannot continue forever as it now is. Soon we will reach tipping-point. Soon it will all go sky-high. Some vast, unknown, fearful change is about to come upon Planet Earth and all it holds. And we are not ready for that. Probably we will never be ready for that.

Some seek a way to flee the coming cataclysm. They buy land in the farthest corners of the globe – New Zealand or Alaska – where they build homes to withstand the coming meltdown. In fact, the building of these catastrophe-proof homes is a burgeoning industry among the wealthy. The builders tunnel down twenty metres or more into the earth, and construct a concrete-and-lead-encased fortress, safe against nukes and their fallout. Then the standard luxurious dwelling is built on top. If nuclear war should threaten, a lift or staircase takes the lucky one down to the subterranean safe-house. There, equipped with a year or more's food and drink, with all necessary forms of entertainment from bowling allies to movie theatres, the wealthy can sit out the cataclysm and its aftermath until, hopefully, law and order and food supply are restored. Others want to plant colonies on Mars to save the human race. Still others think the idea that you can ever escape is insane optimism. There's no way out, they say. Just accept your inevitable destruction. But some, like you and I, search the future-predicting Bible to gain insight into exactly what is coming. We do not despair at the coming cataclysm. We know it is replete with the good news of our redemption. Salvation from the wrath to come is what God promises his beloved. But the wise will prepare to meet it.

2

Histories of Things to Come

BACK last century, the Finnish composer Jan Sibelius said that writing music was like assembling the pieces of a mosaic that God the Father had thrown down from heaven. Of course, Holy Land archaeologists often do reassemble mosaics in old villas. They may find chunks of mosaic with perhaps fifty or more tesserae (little mosaic pieces) still joined together in the mortar. Other chunks with ten or five or three. But they also find many tesserae lying alone, separate from the mortar in which they lay. Then all the archaeologist's skill is required. He or she must compare the colours of the tesserae, and their shape, and the indentations in the mortar from which they have become dislodged. It's a bit like doing a jigsaw puzzle. The more the pieces look alike, the more acutely must one examine them. But unlike a jigsaw, ancient mosaics don't come in a box with a coloured picture on top to copy.

Old Testament prophecy is a bit like that. Old Ernst Hengstenberg of Bonn, one of the first to read the prophets critically, compared it to a broken mirror. He thought its shattered nature arose because the visions came to the prophet so thick and fast that new visions would appear to him amidst other visions, forcing him to abandon writing one vision and record another. John Sailhamer, on the other hand, sees the prophecies as more like a stained-glass window, with many pieces making up a single picture.[1] But, however we look at it, Old Testament prophecy

[1] Rydelnik & Blum 2019: 48.

comes to us in this fragmentary fashion. Some fragments show a time when the earth will flourish and be fruitful and people will live upon it in peace. Others depict the sufferings and conquest of a righteous king. Others depict the glory of Jerusalem, the resurrection of the dead, the catching up of saints, the destruction of heathen armies, the final defeat of all opposition to Jehovah and his Messiah. But these themes rarely appear altogether. Instead, they appear, sometimes singly, sometimes in twos or threes or fours, like mosaic pieces. Yet all the pieces are visibly related. They belong together. But they have to be reassembled, like a mosaic, or a jigsaw puzzle, or a stained glass window through which the many-angled light streams. And as we assemble them, we discern a story in the events, from one end to the other, so to speak. Certain things will happen first, others next, and others last. All in a preordained sequence.

In this chapter, I'm going to deal with what the Old Testament says about the future. There are good reasons for this. It's true that "The New is in the Old concealed and the Old is in the New revealed." But, in fact, not everything in the Old Testament is fully unpacked in the New. So if we neglect the Old, we may miss part of the total revelation. Further, let's remember that Jesus and the apostles had only the Old Testament, but they were perfectly able to see God's plans for the future with that alone. In fact, if we read the New Testament before the Old, then we may fail to read the Old carefully. We may also fail to see how the Old points forward to the New and how the New is entirely built upon the Old, and so we will risk misunderstanding the New.

So in this chapter we will look briefly at some Old Testament passages that speak about the coming kingdom. Then, in the next chapter, we will reflect on how to put them together to begin to reconstruct the great mosaic of the prophets' picture of the future.

THE REIGN OF THE KING MESSIAH (PSALM 72)

The heading of Psalm 72 says 'Of Solomon' (Heb. *lî-Shlomo*) which can mean either written *by* Solomon or written *for* Solomon (by David). Most ancient interpreters take the second line – a psalm of David written for Solomon – which makes quite a lot of sense.[2] The psalm depicts the ideal of Israelite messianic kingship which Solomon was supposed to live up

[2] See the 3rd-cent. BC Greek Septuagint Bible, the Syriac, the Midrash on Ps. 72 (§2, 6).

to, but could never achieve. And so it has always been read, since long before Christian times, as speaking of the Messiah.[3]

It begins with a prayer that the king be endowed with divine wisdom to rule righteously, to administer justice for the poor, and defend his people from oppression (1–4). He shall rule for ever, like the sun and the moon (5, 15). Like rain, he shall cause righteousness and peace to sprout and flourish (6–7). His kingdom shall extend, first, from the western to the eastern sea, and then from the Euphrates to the ends of the earth. The desert tribes of north Arabia shall bow before him (9). The kings of Tarshish – that is, modern Cadiz, beyond the Straits of Gibraltar – and of the Mediterranean isles, and of Sheba and Seba, that is, south-west Arabia and east Africa, shall bring him tribute (10). All kings and nations shall serve him because of the legitimacy and justice and perfection of his reign (11–14). Because of his just rule people shall bless him and bring tribute all the day (15). In his time, the land shall bear abundant grain and people will multiply like the grass (16). His name and honour shall continue for ever (17). This will be for the glory of Jehovah, who shall do this wondrous thing (18). In fact, Jehovah's glory shall fill the earth in the glory of his messianic king (19). And when all this happens, the prayers of David will be fulfilled (20).

JERUSALEM MOTHER OF THE WORLD (ISAIAH 2:1–4)

Isaiah foresees a time, in the latter days, when the Temple Mount of Jehovah shall be raised up higher than the hills around it and people from all nations shall flow there to worship. In words recalling Psalm 122, they will say, "Come, let us go up to the house of Jehovah, to learn his ways so we may walk in his paths." From Zion shall go forth Torah – divine instruction – for the whole world. And Jehovah shall judge between the nations and settle their disputes. Then they shall beat their weapons into farming implements and there shall be no more war among the nations. So here, Isaiah sees three things. First, Jerusalem is the metropolis of the world. Second, its 'house' or palace or temple is rebuilt in its midst. Third, from that house Jehovah will personally teach all the peoples Torah and communicate his judgements to the nations.

[3] Zech. 9:10 and Ben Sira 44:21 cite v. 8 of the psalm in speaking of the messianic age. Rabbinic texts refer it to the Messiah (Tg. Ps. 72; PRE 14a; NumR 13:14; Midr. Pss. 72.6; Ibn Ezra & Kimḥi *ad loc.*).

PEACEFUL EARTH AND RIGHTEOUS KING (ISAIAH 11:1–16)

A shoot will spring from the stump of Jesse; that is, after the main trunk of David's dynasty has been felled, another branch shall spring from its roots. In other words, Isaiah foresees the termination of Solomon's male line in Josiah's cursed, childless sons, and the raising up of a renewed messianic line, which ultimately sprang from Nathan via Neri to Joseph of Nazareth, the adoptive father, and the blessed virgin Mariam.[4] From this stump shall spring forth the Messiah, gifted by the divine spirit with wisdom and understanding, counsel and might, knowledge and the fear of Jehovah, delighting in the fear of Jehovah, perfect in equitable and righteous judgement, paying the wicked their due sentence of death (vv. 2–5). In his time, savage beasts – wolf, leopard, lion, bear, cobra, and viper – shall become tame. The holy mountain shall be peaceful and knowledge of Jehovah shall flood the earth (6–9). All peoples shall come to the King Messiah to seek his counsel. His Jerusalem palace, where he shall rest untroubled by foes, shall be glorious (10). Jehovah will gather his people from their worldwide dispersion and dry the Gulf of Suez and the Euphrates River to enable their coming (12–16). There shall be no more tribal warfare between Israel's northern and southern kingdoms (13). Instead, they shall quell ancient enmities on every side (14).

This adds to Isaiah's earlier prophecy. The one who shall give Jehovah's counsel to the nations is a king from David's line, perfect in holiness and wisdom. His Jerusalem palace is his 'resting-place' (v. 10, *menuḥato*), a word which evokes the words of Jehovah as he entered his new temple in 959 BC: "This is my resting-place (*menuḥatî*) for ever and ever" (Ps. 132:14). In fact, the king promised to David begins to look like Jehovah himself. He shall regather the scattered Israelites, reunite them in one nation, and bring them peace and security, just as his father David did many years before. The fact that the wild animals shall become docile suggests that a whole new age of creation has begun.

THE DESERT SHALL BLOOM (ISAIAH 32:1–20; 35:1–10)

A righteous king will appear and bring safety (32:1–2). Then the blind will see and the deaf will hear (32:1–3), the ignorant will understand, the

[4] Jer. 22:30; 36:30; Ezek. 21:25–27; Luke 3:27. For a full treatment of these genealogies, see Mitchell 2021, chs. 7 & 8.

foolish will be abased and the righteous exalted (32:3–8). The spirit will be poured out from on high, the desert will become fruitful, forests will grow, and justice and righteousness will abide there (32:15–20).

The deserts shall rejoice and blossom; they shall become verdant and wooded like cedar-robed Lebanon and Carmel, and the oak-forested Sharon plain (35:1–2). Waters shall flow there, and reeds and rushes (35:7). A highway shall pass through it, on which the redeemed Israelites shall return gladly to Zion, and inherit everlasting joy (35:10).

THE GLORY OF JERUSALEM (ISAIAH 60:1–22)

By the time we reach Isaiah 60, we have met with a figure called the Servant of Jehovah. We follow his story from his coming as a just ruler for the earth (42:1–4), through his perseverance and exaltation (49:1–7), his obedience (50:4–9), his disgrace and mortal sufferings for the sins of many, the promise of his resurrection and rule (52:13–53:12), and finally his reappearance, anointed by the Spirit of Jehovah as the liberator and saviour of Zion (61:1–7).

Just before the conclusion of this story, in chapter 60, Isaiah sings this great prophetic song of the future glory of Jerusalem. The city must arise to her destiny, for the glory of Jehovah, like the sunrise, breaks forth upon her. The nations shall come from their darkness to her brightness, which is itself like the rising sun (60:2–3). Then all her scattered children shall return home, bearing the wealth of the nations. Camels shall come from Midian, Kedar, and Sheba – north-west, north, and south-west Arabia – bearing gold and incense and proclaiming the praises of Jehovah.[5] The city shall be rebuilt in beauty with gold and silver, precious timber and stone. All its enemies shall be silenced and its people shall dwell in safety for ever. Jehovah himself shall be its everlasting light.

NEW HEAVENS AND EARTH (ISAIAH 65–66)

In the last chapters of Isaiah's great scroll, he revisits many of his earlier themes. We learn of Jehovah's final plans of judgement and blessing. For the righteous, he will recreate the heavens and the earth and the past

[5] Midian's location was confirmed in 2010, when the name (Madyan) was found in a pre-ninth century BC inscription in the Tayma Oasis (Robin and Al-Ghabban 2017: 363–96).

will be forgotten (65:17). Jerusalem will be the centre of this new world, a place of joy (65:18–19). Its people shall live long in prosperity and blessing (65:20–22). They will bear children, but not to disaster, for they and their children shall be the blessed of Jehovah (65:23). He will swiftly answer their prayers (65:24). The wolf and the lion, as back in chapter 11, shall become mild (65:25). In chapter 66, we learn again that Jerusalem is to be the mother-city of the earth, with overflowing joy, peace, and abundance, and all who love her shall flourish (66:10–14). Finally, we read of a future rebellion against Jerusalem; it is crushed, and the dead bodies of the rebel army lie outside the city (66:24).

LIFE FROM THE DEAD (EZEKIEL 37:14–28)

In the sixth century BC, Ezekiel's account of the valley of dry bones tells how Israel will be raised to life, bone to bone, sinew to sinew, and revived. It speaks both of the national restoration of the "whole house of Israel" and of the physical resurrection of Israel's dead (37:11–14). Then the divided houses of Israel – the tribes of Joseph and of Judah – shall be reunited (37:15–22). They shall be purged of their idolatry and washed of their sins and become again God's people (37:23). David shall be their one king and prince for ever (37:24). They shall be restored to their land and dwell there for ever (37:21–25). Jehovah's sanctuary shall be among them for ever, and all the nations will confess him as God alone (37:27–28).

Ezekiel wrote his prophecy during Israel's exile in Babylon, and his picture of national restoration was partly fulfilled in the return from exile. But it was not completely fulfilled. The tribes of Joseph and Judah were not reunited. Nor did they have one king, but lived under foreign masters. Nor were the dead raised. Yes, the people were regathered and the temple rebuilt. But it was destroyed again, six hundred years later, in AD 70, and the Judahites were scattered into another exile. So Ezekiel's prophecy still awaits its true fulfilment.

But what of the resurrection of these dry bones? Is it all just a picture of Israel's restoration from exile? Or is it more? Does it really speak of the future resurrection of the dead? After all, in the text itself, there is no hint that Ezekiel's visit to the valley is unreal or a dream or a vision. He is carried there bodily and walks among the bones. He speaks as if narrating real events (Ezek. 37.11–13).

In fact, the question of whether Ezekiel's account is true or allegorical is not new. The Israelite sages discussed it long ago.

> Rabbi Judah says: It was truth, a parable. Rabbi Nehemiah said to him: If truth, why a parable; and if a parable, why truth? Rather, in the truth there is a parable. (B. Sanh. 92b)

In other words, the rabbis concluded the event was a real event, but it was a parable foreshadowing things to come. One of the rabbis present, the redoubtable Judah ben Bathyra, even claims to be a direct descendant of the dead whom Ezekiel resurrected.

> Rabbi Eliezer ben Rabbi Jose HaGalili said: The dead whom Ezekiel revived went up to Palestine, took wives and begat sons and daughters. Rabbi Judah ben Bathyra arose and said: I am one of their sons, and these are the *tefillin* which my grandfather left me from them. (B. Sanh. 92b)

The narrator then asks whose the bones were. Several views are offered. They are the Ephraimites who miscalculated the time of the redemption from Egypt. (Rashi adds they reckoned the 400 years of slavery from the time it was told to Abraham, in Genesis 15.13, rather than from the time of Isaac's birth.) They made a premature exodus from Egypt and, going to conquer Gath, they were slain, as recorded in 1 Chronicles.

> Now, who were they whom Ezekiel revived? — Rav said: They were the Ephraimites, who calculated the end [of Egyptian bondage], but got it wrong, as it is written, *And the sons of Ephraim: Shuthelah, and Bared his son, and Tahath his son, and Eladah his son, and Tahath his son. And Zabad his son, and Shuthelah his son, and Ezer, and Elad; and the men of Gath that were born in that land slew them because they came down to take their cattle.*[6] *Then Ephraim their father mourned many days, and his brethren came to comfort him* (1 Chr. 7.20–22). (B. Sanh. 92b)

Or, the narrator continues, they were perhaps Israelites who denied resurrection and were resurrected to prove them wrong; or they were apostate or blaspheming Jews shown mercy; or Jews slain by Nebuchadnezzar on account of their beauty. But every view takes Ezekiel's vision not simply as a prophecy of restoration but as a record of a historical resurrection which Ezekiel saw. And this historical resurrection becomes, in turn, a sign that the God of Israel can and does and will raise the dead.

[6] The view of Keil, *ad loc.*, that 'descend' cannot refer to an Ephraimite incursion from Egypt into Canaan is incorrect. Tell es-Safi (biblical Gath) is surrounded by mountains on three sides. Raiders coming from the mountains would indeed descend on the city.

FIVE KINGDOMS (DANIEL 2)

Daniel's scroll is a series of prophecies, each building on the one before. They forewarn the Israelites of a coming persecution and desecration of the temple by the Greco-Syrian king, Antiochus Epiphanes IV, events which took place from 168 to 167 BC, as recorded in the books of Maccabees.[7] But they also point beyond these times to the last days, and to another king who will arise then.

Given the uncanny detail of Daniel's prophecy of the coming Greek era, many assume the book was written not by historical Daniel in the sixth century BC, but by someone else after the time of Antiochus's persecution, in order to 'predict' events already past. Such a view, however, makes Daniel the prophet to be a fraud. It also allows that Jesus was fooled by this hoax when he said "Daniel the prophet" foretold things to come (Matt. 24:15). Yet there is now abundant evidence in the Dead Sea Scrolls that the Book of Daniel dates from long before the second century BC. Eight manuscripts of Daniel were found in the caves, the earliest being dated palaeographically to the second half of the second century BC, within decades of Antiochus's persecution. These were stored up along with other biblical scrolls. In fact, the copies of Daniel outnumber the scrolls of Genesis, Leviticus, and Isaiah, and were as numerous as Deuteronomy, Kings, and Psalms. So whoever collected these scrolls together must have seen Daniel as a canonical book dating from long before his own time. Further, the Dead Sea scroll 4Q174 (4QFlorilegium) quotes chapters 11 and 12 of "Daniel the prophet" alongside Deuteronomy 33, 2 Samuel 7, Exodus 15, Amos 9, Psalms 1, 2 and 5, Isaiah 8 and 65, and Ezekiel 37. So whoever wrote 4Q174, less than a century after Antiochus's persecution, must likewise have judged Daniel's book to be ancient and canonical.[8]

In chapter two, Nebuchadnezzar dreams of a statue of gold, silver, bronze, and iron, with feet and toes of iron and clay. Daniel interprets this as four kingdoms. They are struck by a heavenly rock which obliterates the four kingdoms and becomes a fifth kingdom filling the whole earth. Later, in chapter seven, the four kingdoms are depicted as four beasts, a winged lion, a bear, a winged four-headed leopard, and a fourth terrifying beast with iron teeth and ten horns. But, as before, all give way to a fifth kingdom, ruled not by savage beasts but by a heavenly son of

[7] 1 Macc 1:43–64; 4:38; 2 Macc 5:11-14, 23-26; 6:1–7; cf. Josephus, *A.J.* 12.5.4 (§253).
[8] See Hasel 1992; E.C. Ulrich 2020: 269-277; Carlson 2020.

man who, with his saints, receives everlasting dominion over all peoples.

Finally, if there were any ambiguity about Ezekiel's vision of the resurrection, there is none in Daniel. The angel describes the resurrection to Daniel, telling him how 'many' shall rise to eternal destinies either of life or of reproach.

> And at that time your people shall be delivered, every one who is found written in the book. And many of the sleepers in the dust of the earth shall awake, some to everlasting life, and some to reproaches and everlasting contempt. (Dan. 12:1–2)

All this will happen at the time when Israel is delivered and all their persecutions cease (12:1, 7).

ABUNDANT HARVESTS (AMOS 9:11–15)

Amos wrote in the seventh century BC, while kings of David's line still reigned in Jerusalem. But he foresees a time when David's 'tent' – that is, his Jerusalem kingdom – will fall but Jehovah will raise it up again (9:11–12). The earth shall be exceedingly fruitful. So abundant shall be the harvest that the reaper shall still be gathering last year's crop when the ploughman comes to sow for the following year. So plentiful shall be the vintage that the hills shall flow with wine (13). Israel's fortunes shall be restored. They will rebuild their cities and plant and sow and eat in abundance (14). They will never again be uprooted from their land (15).

THE DAY OF JERUSALEM (ZECH. 14)

A day of Jehovah is coming when all the nations shall gather against Israel and plunder and ravage Jerusalem (1–2). Then Jehovah will fight against them (3). His feet shall alight on the Mount of Olives and it shall split asunder (4). All the holy ones shall come with him (5). It shall be a unique day to Jehovah, with light at sunset (6–7). Then perennial springs shall flow from Jerusalem, toward the Mediterranean and the Dead Sea (8). Then Jehovah shall be king over all the earth and his name shall be one (9). The surface of the land shall be altered; Jerusalem shall be raised up and secure for ever (10–11). Jehovah will strike the invading nations with confusion and plague: they will slay one another and their flesh will be consumed in an instant (12–13). Their gold and silver shall be taken for plunder (14). Then the survivors of the nations shall go up year by year to worship the King Jehovah of hosts in Jerusalem and keep the Feast of Tabernacles (15). If they do not go up, they shall have no rain (17–19). Then all of Jerusalem shall be holy to Jehovah.

Summary

These are just a few of the many Old Testament fragmentary pictures of a future golden age. But all the visions revolve around a group of common themes. And they develop and become more detailed as the centuries pass.

The righteous King Messiah shall come to rule the earth and set up his kingdom. Then the earth will be renewed and fruitful, the desert will bloom, and harvests and food will be abundant. The scattered people of Israel will be gathered in. They will be attacked, but defended by Jehovah. The dead will rise. The temple will be rebuilt in Jerusalem. All the nations will worship Jehovah there and confess him as the true God. The Messiah will reign there and the city will become the centre and metropolis of the earth. God will create a new heaven and a new earth.

It must be emphasized that these things are to happen upon the earth. They do not happen in the heavens or in some other-worldly or ethereal or allegorical realm. It is this earth that is to become fruitful. The Messiah's foes are earthly foes, and his triumph is an earthly triumph. It is in earthly Jerusalem, in the earthly Holy Land, on the eastern coast of the Mediterranean Sea, that the king is to reign.

These are some of the broad events that the prophets say must happen. What we need to see now is whether we can get any more information on how these events will happen, and especially in what order and when. I imagine that many of you reading this book may agree that the king has already come and died and risen. And I imagine that some may recognize the regathering of the Israelites, in some form, as having happened. But what about the rest? When will these other things happen? Before we turn to that, let's spend a little more time looking at these themes one by one, for they will form the basis of much of our discussion in this book.

3

Themes of the Future

CERTAIN Old Testament passages, then, speak very clearly of a glorious future for the world and human society. So now, in this chapter, we'll try and break down some of what these different passages say into separate themes.

Opinions vary on how many themes of New Testament eschatology first appear in the Old Testament. Many scholars allow that the Messiah, the resurrection of the dead, and the glory of Jerusalem are found there in some form. But they might not see the Antichrist or the catching-up (or rapture) of the saints or the return of the Messiah from heaven. And they might dispute that we can fit all these themes into a sensible sequence. But my view is that every theme of New Testament eschatology can be discerned in the Old Testament. So now we turn to look at them here. This is not just for interest's sake. All these themes, and the sequence in which they occur, will be foundational to our discussion in the course of this book. So we must understand their origins and the bigger issues that surround them. So let's look briefly here at the righteous king and his kingdom, the rebuilding of the temple, the birth-pangs of the Messiah, the Antichrist, and the resurrection of the dead.

THE RIGHTEOUS KING

The first theme is the righteous king who will set up his kingdom over the world. The person and work of the Messiah in the Old Testament is a huge theme we can deal with only briefly here.[1] But he is first foretold in Genesis 3:15. There Adam and Eve are standing amidst the chaos and curses of their disobedience. But Jehovah tells the serpent that the woman will bring forth "her Seed" who will confront the serpent. Since it is "her Seed," not Adam's, there is a hint that this Seed of the Woman will not have the usual human paternity. And this Seed shall strike the serpent's head but the serpent shall strike his heel. And so, in conflict with the serpent, this Seed will suffer, perhaps die, for there was no cure for snake venom in ancient times. But in this showdown, the serpent shall be destroyed.

Later, Jehovah tells Abraham that this Seed will come from him, and through the Seed blessing will be channelled to the world (Gen. 17:7). Then the promise passes to Abraham's offspring. Judah is told that he will rule until a rightful king, Shiloh, comes whom all nations will obey (Gen. 49:10). But we are left wondering whether the coming of Shiloh marks the culmination of Judah's line, or its termination, or somehow both. Later, the Levites are told of a coming righteous priest like Moses whom all Israel must obey (Deut. 18:15–19).[2] And Joseph's tribes are told of a hero who will conquer the world like a mighty aurochs (Deut. 33:17). Later, in 2 Samuel 7, Nathan tells David, by the word of Jehovah, that this king will come from his seed (2 Sam. 7:12–16).

The theme is expanded by the prophets, as we saw in the previous chapter. He will be a shoot who will sprout from the side of David's fallen family-tree (Isa. 11:1; Amos 9:11). He will be perfect in wisdom, in might, in authority, and he will rule the world from Jerusalem. Indeed, he will be a divine man, called Immanuel (God with us) and 'Mighty God', and 'Everlasting Father' (7:14; 9:6).

We learn much more about him in the Psalms. In the first psalm, we learn that he, like Moses's ideal king (Deut. 17:18–19), meditates in the Torah day and night, is separate from evildoers, bears fruit in his time, and prospers in all he does. In the second psalm, we hear the decree of Jehovah that this king, now called the 'anointed' or *mashiaḥ* (Messiah) (2:2), will rule the world from Zion, crushing opposition to his rule. Later, we receive hints of his divine nature. He is addressed as 'God' whose 'throne is for ever and ever' (Ps. 45:6). But this *mashiaḥ* will be

[1] For the beginnings of critical understanding of messianic prophecy, see Hengstenberg 1829 and Delitzsch 1890. For a good modern treatment, see Rydelnik & Blum 2019.
[2] For more on the Shiloh prophecy and the righteous priest, see Mitchell 2021, ch. 3.

'cut off' and his crown defiled in the dust (Ps. 89:38–39). Yet he will return again, anointed as Messiah, like Joseph's conquering aurochs (Ps. 92:10; cf. Deut. 33:17). And, as the eternal priest Melchizedek who appeared to Abraham, he will go forth from the right hand of God to conquer the earth (Ps. 110).[3]

There is also a sub-theme that the coming one must suffer and die before he attains to his throne. After Genesis 3:15 foretells his sufferings, Moses's prophecy to the tribes of Joseph foretells that the Coming One must die the sacrificial death of a firstborn ox before he attains to the majesty of the aurochs (Deut. 33:17). Isaiah speaks at length of a righteous king who will be betrayed to a cruel death for the sins of his people before he receives worldwide kingship (Isa. 53:2–12). Likewise, Zechariah speaks of a Shepherd-King who is stricken so that a sin-cleansing fountain will be released to the world, and who will afterwards return in the power of Jehovah to rule (Zech. 12:10–14:3).[4]

We call this figure the Messiah or, in Hebrew, *mashiaḥ*, that is, the 'anointed' king. But some object to using this title for the promised one within the Old Testament. They say he is not actually called Messiah in the Old Testament, but only in later Israelite literature. But that really depends on how we interpret Psalm 2:2, where the kings of the earth oppose Jehovah and his Anointed (*mashiaḥ*). Some argue that in this psalm the word *mashiaḥ* refers only to King David or to one of his sons and not to a future messiah. And it is true that David and his sons were also 'anointed ones,' quasi-messiahs, shadows of the one to come. But David never subdued all the nations of the world as does the *mashiaḥ* of Psalm 2. And so the psalm must point beyond David to a greater Messiah yet to come. In fact, the Psalms speak frequently of Jehovah's anointed messiah-king.[5] This is because the person who put the whole Book of Psalms together designed it as one collection pointing to the true coming Messiah, who will subdue all nations to the rule of heaven.[6] So when the Book of Psalms speaks of the *mashiaḥ* it ultimately points not to David or to any historical figure but to the coming Messiah. And so there is no good reason why we too can't speak of the Messiah in the Old Testament.

[3] For Melchizedek as an incarnation of the Logos, who is addressed directly in Ps. 110, see Mitchell 2021, chs. 1, 4–5.
[4] For a full treatment of Joseph's dying and rising aurochs, and the slain kings of Isaiah and Zechariah, see Mitchell 2016, chs. 2–3.
[5] Cf. 20:6; 28:8; 84:9; 89:38; 89:51; 132:10, 17.
[6] For the eschatologico-messianic agenda in the Psalms, see Mitchell 1997.

THE RESURRECTION OF THE DEAD

Some say that belief in the general resurrection of the dead is a late idea in the Bible, appearing first in Daniel 12, a passage which some think was written in the second century BC.[7] Yet the idea is much older than Daniel's time.

The Song of Moses. In the mid-second millennium BC, Moses taught this song to the Israelites in the desert of Moab:

> See now that I, I am he, and there is no God beside me.
> I kill and make live; I have wounded and it is I who will heal;
> and none can deliver from my hand. (Deut. 32:29)

The words 'I kill and I make live' are not just a statement that God gives life and takes it away. Rather, as the rabbis say, just as the wounding precedes the healing, so the killing precedes the making live, in order that we may know that, just as the Holy One wounds and heals, so he kills and makes alive again. After all, he who is God alone, from whose hand none can deliver, has perfect power to do this, whether anyone agrees or not.

Hannah's song. Four hundred years later, in the mid-eleventh century BC, Hannah offered her song of praise at the birth of the son who ended her disgrace.[8] She hints back at the words of Moses, but goes further.

> Jehovah kills and makes live;
> he brings down to Sheol and raises up. (1 Sam. 2.6)

She says Jehovah can bring the dead back even from Sheol, the land of the dead. Of course, Hannah is speaking figuratively of her restoration from her own personal hell of barrenness and social disgrace. But presumably she also believed that the Holy One can do just as she said. She speaks, a bit like Ezekiel in our last chapter, of both a figurative and a physical resurrection. And so Hannah became a prophetess and her words were preserved as such by later generations.

The Psalms of the Sons of Korah. Hannah was of the Korahite clan of Levites. And the next voice to utter the hope of resurrection is that of a Korahite psalmist.

[7] As said in the last chapter, I think Daniel's prophecy dates from the 6th century BC.

[8] The two Samuel scrolls must date from before the end of Solomon's reign (c. 931 BC), for they make no mention of the immediately ensuing division of the Davidic kingdom or Shishak's invasion in 925 BC. Since the monarchy is the theme of these scrolls, the only possible reason for the omission of these events is that they had not yet happened.

> But God will redeem my soul from the hand of Sheol
> for he will take me. (Ps. 49:15)

These words are not simply the psalmist's colourful way of saying he hopes for an uptick in his fortunes. The whole of Psalm 49 is a meditation on the futility of heaping up wealth in the face of one's impending death and descent into Sheol. In that context, these words must be taken at their face value. The Korahite psalmist believes that a time is coming when God will bring him up out of Sheol.

Isaiah. In the eighth century BC, Isaiah foretells the everlasting death of Israel's pagan oppressors (26:13–14). Then he says to Israel,

> Your dead shall live – my dead body – they shall arise!
> Awake and sing, dwellers in the dust, for dew of light is your dew
> and earth shall give birth to the shades. (Isa. 26.19)

Once again, this is a testimony to resurrection which only a Sadducee (ancient or modern) could fail to see. The dead, says Isaiah, shall live. Those who dwell in the dust shall awake. The shades shall be reborn from the earth.

Of course, one can add to this the actual resurrections which took place in Old Testament times. Elijah revived the dead (1 Kgs 17:17–23). So did Elisha (2 Kgs 4:32–36). An unnamed man was restored to life on touching Elijah's bones (2 Kgs 13:21). If God has raised people in the past, he can certainly raise many more in the future.

So the Old Testament speaks often of the resurrection of the dead. Some of these sayings can look like a hope for a general revival of fortunes. But ultimately they all hope in One who can revive dead bodies in the time to come. Finally, Daniel, the last to prophesy, clearly foretells a resurrection of the dead from the dust of the earth (Dan. 12:2–3).

Note that this Israelite concept of resurrection is not something the Israelites learned in Egypt. In the Egyptian view of the afterlife, the illustrious departed go to dwell among the stars. But the early Israelite prophecies foretell the return of human spirits to their earthly bodies. Yet later on, Daniel does say the resurrected righteous will become like the stars (12:3). So the Israelite idea of resurrection did develop over almost a thousand years, from the time of Moses to Daniel. And we note that the later prophets of resurrection – Isaiah, Ezekiel, and Daniel – all connect the resurrection with a future deliverance of Israel. That leads to our next point.

THE GATHERING OF THE NATIONS

Another theme of Old Testament eschatology is that God will gather the nations to Jerusalem. But this gathering takes place at two quite different times and for two quite different purposes.

First, the nations gather to make war against Israel. The Israelites, of course, were attacked by enemy nations throughout their history, and the prophets forewarn of these events too. But the prophets speak also of a massive attack that will take place in the far future, in the last days.

Asaphite Psalm 83 foretells a ten-nation confederacy gathered to fight against Israel from every point of the compass (vv. 6–8).[9] The prophecy may draw its inspiration from the four-nation attack against Jehoshaphat, where an Asaphite prophet played a prominent role (2 Chr. 20). Yet biblical history records no such ten-nation attack. And so, since it has not happened, we may conclude that it is still to come. After this attack is defeated, the nations will know that Jehovah is Most High over all the earth (v. 18).

Ezekiel tells of the attack of Prince Gog and his people of the land of Magog on the land of Israel. He will come against a people "gathered from the nations" (38:12), "my people Israel" in the land of Israel (38:14–18) with a vast alliance of nine nations – Magog, Rosh, Meshekh, Tubal, Persia, Cush, Put, Gomer, and Beth Togarmah (38:1–6). But they will be defeated by Lord Jehovah; then the nations will confess that he is God, and a utopian age will follow (38:18–23; 47:1–12). Phrases such as *in latter years/days* (38:8, 16) and *in that day* (38:10, 14, 18, 39:11) make it clear that all this will take place at the end of the age. And, once again, history records no other attack of such dimensions against Israel from the north, nor any such aftermath. Since it has not yet happened, it must be still to come.

Zechariah too foretells an attack against Jerusalem like Gog's attack. The city will be attacked and plundered by "all the nations," and the people taken into exile (14:1–2). But "Jehovah my God will come and all the holy ones with him," and he will defeat the invaders (14:5; 3–15). A new era will begin and Jehovah will rule all the nations (14:6–9). Once

[9] The Edomites were from the south-east, the Ishmaelites from the south-west, the Moabites from east of the Dead Sea, the Hagrites from the north-east, Gebal from either south of the Dead Sea (Pliny's Gebalene) or the north (Byblos [Gebal] cf. Ezek. 27:9), the Ammonites from east of the Jordan, the Amalekites from the southern deserts, the Philistines from the west, Tyre from the north and Assyria from the north-east.

again, since these events have not happened, they must be yet to come.

In addition to these passages, a future massive attack against Israel is foretold also in Isaiah 66:24, Daniel 9:26, and Zephaniah 3:8.

But another gathering of the nations follows the defeat of the alliance. After the invaders have been defeated by the Holy One, all the nations will confess his power and sovereignty, and gather to Jerusalem, bringing tribute and worshipping there with the Israelites (Isa. 2:1–4; 66:12, 18–20; Mic. 4:1–5; Zeph. 3:9). Some from the nations will even be appointed as priests and Levites and dwell among the Israelites (Isa. 66:21; Ezek. 47:22–23). The nations will also worship Jehovah in their own lands (Zeph. 2:11). And all the nations will go up to worship at the Feast of Tabernacles (Zech. 14:16–19).

The Gathering of Israel

Another recurring motif of Old Testament prophecy is the ingathering of Israel. This motif dates from early times. Even before the Israelites entered the Promised Land, Moses foretold that, for their sins, they would one day be scattered from the land, then gathered in again.

> When all these blessings and curses I have set before you come on you and you take them to heart wherever the Lord your God disperses you among the nations, [2]and when you and your children return to the Lord your God and obey him with all your heart and with all your soul according to everything I command you today, [3]then the Lord your God will restore your fortunes and have compassion on you and gather you again from all the nations where he scattered you. [4]Even if you have been banished to the most distant land under the heavens, from there the Lord your God will gather you and bring you back. [5]He will bring you to the land that belonged to your ancestors, and you will take possession of it. He will make you more prosperous and numerous than your ancestors. (Deut. 30:1–5)

Over the years, the Israelites were indeed scattered bit by bit. Some fled famine into neighbouring lands (Ruth 1:1). Some lived in Egypt, at least from the time of Solomon's trading-posts there, if not before (1 Kgs 10:28). Pharaoh Shishak took others captive there (1 Kgs 14:26). By the seventh century BC, the Egyptian Israelites had built their own temple at Elephantine in the Nile. But the Israelites were scattered in many other lands as well. Solomon also had trading posts in Kue (southern Anatolia),

Aram, and among the Hittites (1 Kgs 10:28–29). In the eighth century, the Ephraimites were taken captive by Assyria into north-west Mesopotamia (2 Kgs 17:6). And, by the sixth century, the Judahites were exiled in Babylon and Persia. Obadiah speaks of Judahite exiles in Tsarfat and Sepharad (Odab. 1:20), meaning probably modern France and Spain.[10] And so, by the middle of the first millennium BC, there were Jewish communities in most lands of the Mediterranean and the Near East. Some mingled with the nations. Others remained distinctly Israelite.

But, just as Moses foretold, so all the prophets also proclaimed, that the Israelites would one day be gathered back to the Promised Land. In the eighth century BC, Amos said:

> I will bring my people Israel back from exile. They will rebuild the ruined cities and live in them. They will plant vineyards and drink their wine; they will make gardens and eat their fruit. [15]I will plant Israel in their own land, never again to be uprooted from the land I have given them, says Jehovah your God. (Amos 9:14–15)

And Isaiah said:

> [11]In that day the Lord will set his hand a second time to reclaim the remnant of his people who remain from Assyria, from Lower Egypt, from Upper Egypt, from Cush, from Elam, from Shinar, from Hamath and from the islands of the sea. [12]He will raise a banner for the nations and gather the exiles of Israel; and the scattered of Judah he will ingather from the four corners of the earth. (Isa. 11:11–12)

And the other prophets prophesy in the same vein (e.g., Jer. 29:14; Ezek. 20:41–42; Zeph. 3:10, 19–20).

What's more, a few texts say that the end-time ingathering of Israel will take place in several stages. Zephaniah, for instance, urges the Israelites to gather to Jerusalem before the day of coming wrath (2:1–3). He pronounces judgements on all nations (2:4–15), who are destroyed by the power of God and by the hand of Israel (2:9; 3:6–8). The survivors worship (3:9). And then the Israelites are gathered a second time which, logically, must be a different group from the first one (3:19–20).

Micah paints a similar picture in three distinct oracles. First, Israel's impending capture will be like the pangs of childbirth; but they will be

[10] Sepharad is in Iberia, as the targum's *Hispania* confirms. Tsarfat is more problematic. It was the town near Sidon where Elijah saved the widow and her son (1 Kgs 17:9). Yet it has been the Hebrew word for France since at least early medieval times and Rashi and Radak identify Obadiah's Tsarfat as France.

redeemed from Babylon (4:9–10). Then, many nations are gathered to destroy Israel; but it is Jehovah who gathers them to destruction; Israel will destroy them and devote the plunder (4:11–12). The third oracle looks to the coming of a ruler from Bethlehem; he will be great to the ends of the earth and bring Israel peace; when he appears he will gather another group of exiled Israelites to join those with him in Jerusalem (5:1–3). So in Micah we see the following sequence:

Nations gather against Israel. Israel exiled.	Israel regather.	Nations gather against Israel. Israel triumphs.	Israel's king honoured worldwide. More Israelites gather to him.

Some might think that I am making a narrative out of single prophecies which are really all repeating the same story. But in fact we find this same pattern repeating throughout the prophets, in passages such as Isaiah 27:12–13; 66:18–24; Jeremiah 3:6–18; 4:5–6:30; 23:1–8; Ezekiel 37–48; and Zechariah 9–14.

Israel exiled.	Israel gather.	Nations gather against Israel.	Nations defeated in the time of the Messiah.	Israelites gather with the nations to Jerusalem.

All this is very much Old Testament teaching. For the New Testament, which proclaims salvation for the whole world, has little to say on the destiny of Israel (though see Rom. 11:25–27). But the rabbis always held to an undying hope in redemption from the third exile, that is, the exile following the Roman dispersal of the Judeans, first in AD 70 and then, after the Bar Kokhba rebellion, in AD 132.

Radak, in the thirteenth century, says that this redemption will be a final and everlasting redemption.

> *And I will betroth thee* [*to me for ever*] (Hosea 2:21). This concerns the three exiles of Israel: the exile in Egypt, the exile in Babylon, and this exile which we are in today....And after the third exile they will return in repentance, as it is written, [*in the latter days*] *you will return to the LORD your God* (Deut. 4:30). And he said, *I will betroth thee unto me in faithfulness* (Hos. 2:22), which is what concerns us [in our current exile]: [that is,] in life that will never be removed for ever. (Radak on Hosea)

Rambam, Radak's older contemporary, also says the final gathering of Israel will be in the times of the Messiah.

> The King Messiah will arise and restore the Kingdom of David to its former state and original sovereignty. He will build the Temple and gather the dispersed of Israel. All the laws will be restored in his days as they were of old. Sacrifices will be offered, and the sabbatical years and jubilee years will be observed in all their details as given in the Torah.
>
> Anyone who does not believe in him, or who does not await his coming, denies not only the other prophets but also the Torah and Moses our Teacher. The Torah testifies to him, as it is said: *Then the LORD your God, will bring back your exiles, and he will have mercy upon you. He will once again gather you from all the nations... Even if your exiles are at the end of the heavens, the LORD, your God, will gather you from there, and he will take you from there. And the LORD, your God, will bring you to the land which your fathers possessed* (Deut. 30:3–5). (Rambam, Mishneh Torah, Kings and Wars 11)

THE BIRTH-PANGS AND THE ANTI-MESSIAH

We saw above how Psalm 83, Ezekiel, and Zechariah, foretell a massive attack against Jerusalem in the last days, hinted at also by Isaiah, Daniel, and Zephaniah. Ezekiel calls the leader of this attack Gog and his land Magog. Gog will descend on Israel with his hordes, and devastate the land, but he and his hordes will perish in the land of Israel by fire and brimstone (38:18–39:11).

Daniel too foretells an evil king who in future times will invade Israel and desecrate the sanctuary (8:9–12, 23–25). His words point to the Syrian king, Antiochus Epiphanes, who profaned the temple in 168 BC (11:21–35). But his prophecy changes into a description of an evil ruler who resembles Antiochus only partially (11:36–45). Like Antiochus, he rises suddenly to power, rages against Israel, and bans the divine law. But he shall disregard the gods of his fathers (11:37), whereas Antiochus was an ardent devotee of Zeus, converting even the Jerusalem temple to the worship of Zeus. He conquers Egypt (11:43), which Antiochus never did. He dies in the land of Israel, "between the sea and glorious holy mountain" (11:45), perhaps like Ezekiel's Gog (Ezek. 39:4, 11), but unlike Antiochus, who died in Persia (2 Macc. 1:14–16).[11] Most of all, this new king is to appear at the end-time, just before the resurrection of the dead (12:1). So we must conclude that Daniel is speaking of another Antiochus-like figure who will appear in the last days.

[11] The degree of resemblance to Gog hangs on whether 'the sea' (Ezek. 39.11) is taken as the Dead Sea or the Mediterranean. Most interpreters favour the former.

From these prophecies the Israelites deduced that, in the last days, there would arise an evil king bent on overthrowing the land of Israel and the worship of its God. This figure would resemble Antiochus but be worse still. The time leading up to these events would be marked by accelerating woes, like the pangs of child-birth, a period called the birth-pangs of the Messiah, when there would be a breakdown of all goodness in human civilization to make way for the rising of the evil king.

Already in the Dead Sea Scrolls, a hundred years before the time of Jesus, this evil king is called Malkhi-Resha (Evil King), the counterpart of Melchizedek, the Righteous King. In one text, *The Visions of Amram*, Malkhi-Resha's deeds are wickedness and he dwells in darkness (4Q544, fr. 2.3). In another, *The Blessings Scroll*, he is ritually cursed (4Q280.2). In the great *War Scroll*, he is Belial (the Lawless One), the prince of the kingdom of wickedness and the sons of darkness (1QM 13:2, 11; 16:11; 17:5–6), who will be defeated by Michael the archangel (17:6–7).

We find him too, of course, in the New Testament. Paul speaks of the lawless man whom the Lord Jesus will destroy at his coming (2 Thess. 2:3–8). John speaks of one called Antichrist who is coming, the opponent of Jesus the Christ (1 John 2:18). And John again, in his Revelation, calls him the Beast, prefigured in the historical Nero Caesar, whose number is 666. Soon the Antichrist, a second Nero, becomes a regular theme among the Church Fathers whenever they speak of the future age. In fact, they talk about him so much that the name 'Antichrist' passes into Rabbinic literature, and the rabbis see the Antichrist as a wicked Roman Christian king who oppresses Israel.[12]

JERUSALEM AND THE TEMPLE REBUILT

When the Messiah comes, from David's line (2 Sam. 7:12–16; Jer. 23:5–6), he will rule upon David's throne in Jerusalem, and all nations will obey him (Gen. 49:10; Isa. 9:7; Luke 1:32). Jerusalem will become the metropolis of the world; all nations will bring tribute there; all mankind will worship there; divine instruction will go out from there to all the world; and so the nations will live at peace (Isa. 2:1–4; 11:10; 65:21–23; 66:10–21; Ps. 87; Mic. 4:1–5; Zech. 14:16). A river shall flow from Jerusalem to bless all the lands (Ezek. 47:1–12; Zech. 14:8). The earth will be recreated (Isa. 65:17; 66:22). People will live to a great age in

[12] For more, see Mitchell 2016, chapter 11, and the midrashim there.

prosperity and the earth will be fruitful (Isa. 65:20–23; Amos 9:13–14). There will no more weeping (Isa. 65:18–19). Savage beasts will become docile (Isa. 11:6–8; 65:25).

In 2 Samuel 7:13, the Holy One tells David that his son's throne will endure for ever, and that this son will build a temple for the name of Jehovah. The promise is first fulfilled in shadow by Solomon, who built the first temple in Jerusalem in 959 BC. But the temple was plundered by Pharaoh Shishak, in 925 BC, and later destroyed by the Babylonians in 587 BC. Then the promise was fulfilled in shadow a second time by Zerubbabel, also of David's seed, who built the second temple, destroyed by Rome in AD 70. Since that time, the promise awaits the coming of the Messiah. It is he, called the Branch, who will build the third temple (Zech 6:12 cf. Jer. 23:5). And so Ezekiel describes how, in the last days, Jehovah shall reign in his temple in the midst of Israel forever (Ezek. 43:7), and he describes in detail what that temple will look like (40–48).

The rebuilding of the temple is not a prominent theme in the New Testament, for the New Testament addresses the world rather than the nation Israel. However, Jesus speaks of it in John's gospel (2:18–22), as we shall see in chapter six. But, in Judaism, the building of the third temple by the Messiah is a major theme indeed. It is confessed in the ancient Amidah prayer, which observant Jews pray three times a day, whose fourteenth petition calls for the rebuilding of the temple and the appearance of the Messiah. And Rambam, as we saw above, says of the Messiah that "He will build the Temple."

Summary

So all these themes are found in the Old Testament. None of them appear for the first time in the New Testament. In fact, when the New Testament writers wrote, all these themes were already a well-established part of the future hope of the people of Israel. So the New Testament does not originate any new eschatological ideas, although it does add new information to some of them. All its main themes were foretold by Moses and the prophets hundreds of years before the time of Jesus.

Together, these themes make up the Old Testament's teaching about the future. In other words, the Old Testament doesn't simply foretell the coming of the Messiah (and nothing more), as some Christians have sometimes assumed. Nor does it simply foretell the regathering of Israel (and nothing more), as some Jews have sometimes assumed. Instead, there is a whole sequence of events – gatherings of Israel, the birth-pangs and the wicked king, a gathering of nations against Israel, the defeat of the wicked king, the appearing of the Messiah, the resurrection and the rapture, the coming of the nations to worship, the millennium, the kingdom of God, and the rebuilding of the temple. All these themes appear several times in different parts of the Bible. But we may rightly harmonize them and try to make a broader picture, an eschatological programme, of the things foretold.

In trying to harmonize them like this, we are not assuming too much. For the prophets did exactly the same thing. Look, for instance, at the broad sweep of Isaiah 40 to 66. Isaiah tells how Jehovah will anoint his servant, the Messiah, with his divine Spirit to bring justice and light and a divine covenant to all the nations (42:1–9). He tells how the Messiah will face much opposition and be despised, but that finally all kings will bow before him, and he will gather and redeem Israel and bring salvation to the ends of the earth (49:1–13). He tells how the Messiah will die for the sins of the world (53:1–10) and then rise to worldwide honour (53:11–12). He will gather, comfort, and defend Israel (54:1–17). He will proclaim grace to all the world, even to those who were excluded (55:1–56:8; 61:1–11). Jerusalem shall be glorified and the Israelites gathered in (60:1–22). The earth will be renewed (65:17–25). The kingdom of God shall be established and all the nations shall gather to Jerusalem to worship there (66:8–23). Opposing armies shall be destroyed (66:24).

We find similar eschatological programmes in Ezekiel and Zechariah. Ezekiel tells of the Messiah's coming, his gathering and revival of Israel (34–37), the defeat of Gog and Magog (38–39), the rebuilding of the temple, and the Messiah dwelling in Jerusalem (40–48). Zechariah speaks of the coming king who gathers Israel (9:9–17), is slain, gazed upon and mourned (12:10–14), then reappears to save Jerusalem and bring all the nations to worship him (14:1–21).

Scholars recognize that there are complete programmes of events here. Of Ezekiel they say, "the Gog passage tells a fairly clear and consistent story" with a "loosely strung sequence of ideas."[13] And of Zechariah they speak of "a whole eschatological programme" or "an eschatological timetable" or an "eschatological schema."[14]

[13] Blenkinsopp 1990: 179; Cooke 1936: 407.

[14] Dodd 1953: 64. Smith 1984: 271. Black 1991: 53. For much more on these prophetic

So the Old Testament's teaching about the future points to the King Messiah ruling over a renewed and happy earth from Jerusalem, where the people of Israel are gathered together, the righteous dead are raised, and all the nations come to worship. We must stress that it is *on earth,* and from the earthly Jerusalem, that all these things take place. The only Old Testament passage which points to a heavenly state for the redeemed is Daniel 12:3. From that, we may fairly conclude that there will be a heavenly portion to the lives of the redeemed in the future kingdom. Yet this verse does not nullify the great consensus of the many passages that speak of the earthly kingdom. The earthly kingdom and future heavenly glory must be taken together.

Old Testament teaching about the last things is always programmatic. Therefore they are mistaken who say that eschatological timetables are the domain of loony cults. Eschatological timetables or programmes are the clear teaching of the prophets. Those who see in biblical eschatology only a vague idea that the Messiah may vaguely appear on some vague day simply do not believe the prophets.

What's more, biblical eschatology is calendricized. It gives exact dates. Daniel's famous prophecy of the seventy sevens specifies that it will be 490 years – or ten jubilees – from the going forth of the command to rebuild Jerusalem until the Messiah Prince is "cut off" to bring in everlasting righteousness (Dan. 9:24–26). We know from the Talmud that the first-century Pharisees were well aware that Daniel's prophecy indicated the time of the coming of the Messiah (B. Meg. 3a). They knew he had to come while the temple was standing (Mal. 3:1) and were seized with despair when the temple fell. They said "The time of his coming is past," and pronounced a curse on the bones of anyone who calculated Daniel's prophecy (B. Sanh. 97b). Yet the jubilee cycle, taken together with the teaching of the millennial week, can help us even now to identify the time of his reappearing and the restoration of all things. So it is to the teaching of the millennial week that we now turn.

timetables, see Mitchell 1997, chs. 5–7; 2016, ch. 3.

4

The Millennial Week in the Old Testament

DIRECTLY now we turn to the central theme of this book, that is, the millennial kingdom. This is the ancient belief that the Messiah will bring in his kingdom six millennial days after the creation of the world and that this kingdom will then endure for one millennium, before a whole new age of creation begins. We begin in the creation narrative of Genesis, for it is in Genesis that all the foundations of biblical revelation are laid.

THE DATE OF ADAM'S CREATION

The Hebrew text of the Bible – the Masoretic Text – contains chrono-genealogies from Adam to Abraham, listing the age at which each son was born to his father. This permits us to calculate how many years passed from Adam down to the period of the Israelite kings, whose dates can then be correlated with other historical events in Egypt and Mesopotamia, whose date is securely known. By this means one can, in theory, calculate the date of the creation of Adam. According to the best estimates, this took place, according to the Hebrew Masoretic text, around 6,000 years ago, give or take half a century.

By the sixteenth and seventeenth centuries, when the Hebrew text became available in the university libraries of Europe, the question of the date of the creation of mankind engaged the attention of the greatest minds of the age. Kepler proposed a date of 3977 BC. Newton proposed

3998 BC. Ussher, whose conclusions made their way into the King James Bible, proposed 4004 BC. Many others made similar proposals, most of the dates lying in a seventy-year time-frame between 4020 and 3950 BC. The reason why they could not arrive at an exact date is because one or two points in the narrative are notoriously difficult to calculate. There are questions about Terah's age when Abraham was born, about when Abraham entered the Promised Land, and about the length of the Exodus. These hamper an exact determination of the period from Adam to the Israelite kingdom. Yet, to this day, most modern Bible chronologists still accept that the Hebrew Bible gives a date of creation for Adam between 4020 and 3950 years BC, or around 6,000 years ago. Meanwhile, the medieval Jewish Hillel II calendar now dates Adam's creation at 3761 BC. But earlier Jewish calendars dated his creation closer to the 4,000 BC mark.

Now when we speak of the date of the creation of Adam or of mankind, we are not saying that the world, much less the universe, was created around 6,000 years ago. Nor does the Bible say so. For a start, there is a countless period of time between Genesis 1:1 and 1:2. Nor do we know the length of the first six days of creation. For, as we shall see, they were not solar days. So there is no reason not to accept the best astronomical and geological calculations that the universe dates from around 13.7 billion years ago, and our planet from 4.5 billion. Nor need we deny that there were tool-making, fire-burning hominids before our own species appeared. But what the Bible does give us, as the ancient Jewish interpreters also recognized, is a date for the creation of Adam; that is, a date for the beginning of our own species, about 6,000 years ago. Such a date agrees tolerably well with the rise of the earliest human civilizations: the gradual flowering of the Neolithic Revolution in Anatolia, then Sumer, Egypt, the Indus Valley, the Yellow River Valley, and Mesoamerica. This saw the worldwide emergence of centralized political structures, densely-populated urban centres, hierarchies, division of labour, trade, art, architecture, property ownership, and eventually writing. Such a date also agrees tolerably well with the beginnings of metallurgy, exactly as Genesis records (4:22). In other words, the Bible's date at which our species, Homo Sapiens, emerged is broadly confirmed by the sciences. And, in so far as we can calculate this date from the Bible, it is then that the prophetic and calendrical clock begins its countdown.

GENESIS

In the first chapter of Genesis, we read that God created the heavens and the earth in six days and ceased from his labour on the seventh. But the astute reader will notice that the sun was not created until the fourth day (Gen. 1:16–19). Yet light was created and shone on the first day.[1] And so it should be clear to anyone who reads carefully – and the ancient Israelites read very carefully – that the six days of creation were not solar days.

How can we account for the creation of light before the creation of the sun? The light of Genesis Day One cannot, I think, be simply the light of the primeval explosion of the universe, for when that light was created (v. 3), the earth already existed in an unformed state (v. 2). But the Genesis creation account is earth-centred, and there were periods in earth's history when the sun's light would have been visible, but the sun itself would not. The most important of these is perhaps the period when the earth and sun both formed about 4.5 billion years ago. Earth then collided with another planet in formation, the size of Mars, and the energy from this collision blew Earth's existing atmosphere into space, created our moon, and caused our entire planet to melt. (Portions of this planet, now called Theia, exist as two large 'mantle blobs', one each under Africa and the Pacific Ocean.[2]) As a result, for millions of years, earth was indeed "formless and void" and blanketed in a thick dust cloud. Some sunlight was visible through the thick cloud, but the sun itself was not seen. And so, from the earth-view of Genesis, the creation of light preceded the sun. Thus the creation is not measured in solar days.

God tells Adam not to eat of the fruit of the Tree of the Knowledge of Good and Evil, *for in the day that you eat of it you shall surely die* (2:17). Yet, after eating, Adam lives for 930 years before he dies (5:5). And so the reader must conclude either that God spoke falsely – which cannot be – or that the day within which Adam was to die was also not a solar day. Therefore the opening chapters of Genesis allude twice to a non-solar day. And so one must ask what this other kind of day might be? And how long it is?

Perhaps the second question is easier than the first. Adam and the

[1] The targum Pseudo-Jonathan, to stress that the creation of light occurred after the creation of the world, adds 'immediately' to the text of Genesis 1:3: *And God said, Let there be light to shine upon the world. And immediately there was light.*
[2] Yuan 2023: 95–99.

antediluvian patriarchs die in their tenth century. They never live beyond a thousand years. As a result, we may deduce that the Genesis non-solar day, within which they are to die, equals a thousand years.

As for what kind of day it is, all we can say for sure is that, since it is not a solar day, it is not an earthly day. It is a day measured by some standard which is above the sun and the earth, and so it is a heavenly day or a divine day.

This is confirmed by Psalm 90:4. The heading of the psalm attributes it to Moses. He prays,

> For a thousand years in your sight are like yesterday when it is past,
> and a watch in the night.

Some say that this psalm itself was the origin of belief in the thousand-year divine day. But that all depends, of course, on whether the psalm is older than the Genesis creation account, or vice versa. My view is that both the creation narrative and Psalm 90 come from the hand of Moses. But Psalm 90 is an eye-witness account of the unbelieving Israelites of the Exodus perishing in the desert, and so it seems to be a work from Moses's last days. Meanwhile, it is likely that Moses received the creation account from an older source, from before his own time. And Moses, and the other ancient sages, deduced the one-thousand-year day from the creation narrative. So I suspect that Moses wrote the Genesis creation account before Psalm 90.

Now, let me stress here that, when we read Genesis this way, we are not reading into it something that is not there. On the contrary, we are discerning what is implied in the detail of the text. This is how the sages of ancient Israel read the Bible. And this is how those who followed Moses reached the conclusion that there is a heavenly day which equals one thousand years.

THE MILLENNIAL WEEK

Now something else follows on from the Genesis creation narrative and its one thousand-year day. It's this. Adam and Eve and all their offspring are cursed with hard labour, trouble, and pain for their disobedience. Once again, the attentive reader must ask how long this woeful situation must endure. And once again an answer may reasonably be deduced from Genesis. If God ceases from his labour on the seventh day (2:2–3), and his days are each one thousand years, then it may be that mankind's release from hard labour will come after six divine days, or six millennia. In that case, the seventh millennium from creation will be a time of rest and peace and restoration and blessing, a millennial Sabbath.

And one more thing is implied. If there is a millennial week followed by Shabbat, then there must be another week to follow, just as one week always follows another. The sages agreed that little could be known of this mysterious new week so far in the future. But they assumed it would be greater than the millennial Sabbath. And they gave it a name: *Ha**Olam** Ha**Ba***, the Age to Come.

So there are four ideas inseparably connected. If there is a millennial day, there is also a millennial week. If there is a millennial week, there is a millennial Sabbath. And if there is a millennial Sabbath, there is another millennial week to follow, that is, the Age to Come. And if the millennial Sabbath is a time of restoration and peace, the Age to Come will be greater still, a time of complete re-creation.

Genesis is the sole and sufficient source of all these ideas. They are a simple scaling-up of the Genesis creation week to millennial time. So there is no need to say (as some do) that the idea of the millennial week originated with the Book of Jubilees in the second century BC, or that the Epistle of Barnabas deduced it from the millennial age of Revelation 20. Such hypotheses are quite unnecessary. The millennial week, and all that follows, is implied in Genesis. And, if we have eyes to see, we may find that other Old Testament sages, like Hosea, speak of it too.

Hosea

Hosea says the Holy One will withdraw from idolatrous Israel until they repent, and then, in compassion, he will revive them again.

> [15]I will go and return to my place until they acknowledge their guilt
> and they will seek my face;
> in their affliction, they will earnestly seek me.
> [1]Come, let us return to Jehovah. For he has torn, but he will heal us;
> he has smitten, but he will bind us up.
> [2]He will make us live after two days;
> on the third day he will raise us up
> that we may live before him. (Hosea 5.15–6.2)

Some think that Hosea 6:2 represents Israel's easy, shallow repentance, as if they imagine that the Holy One will forgive them, just like that, literally in two days' time. But if Moses knew a heavenly day is one thousand years, surely Hosea knew that too. Hosea knew the Torah of Moses and Moses's Psalm 90.[3] And, since that is so, is it not likely that Hosea is saying that the Holy One will give the Israelites new life and 'raise them up' after two millennia?

That seems like Hosea is making the Israelites wait a long time for their exaltation. But that depends on the starting date of his two millennia. If they begin in the days of the Patriarchs and the birth of the Israelite nation, then Hosea is saying that their exaltation will arrive some 750 years after his own time.

Or, alternatively, it may be that Hosea means that the day when they will *live before him* is the Shabbat millennium. In that case Hosea is counting from the date of creation and foreseeing the fifth and sixth millennial-days leading to a Shabbat millennium many, many years in the future? Sometimes the prophets see far ahead.

But, either way, if Hosea was acquainted with the Torah of Moses (which he surely was), he would have known how people had been reflecting on these texts for hundreds of years. And so it is likely that he is speaking not of solar days but of the same heavenly days that Moses spoke of. And this, as we shall see, is exactly how later sages, both Jewish and Christian, understood Hosea's words.

SUMMARY

The idea of the one-thousand-year divine day, the seven-thousand-year divine week, the Shabbat millennium, and the following millennial week of the Age to Come, are all implicit in the first chapters of Genesis. The sages of Israel, who studied this text so deeply, deduced these ideas from Genesis in earliest times. Since that is so, we may suppose that Hosea's two or three days until Israel's redemption allude also to millennial days.

[3] For two centuries there has been scepticism about the origin of the Torah. Some date it as late as the 4th century BC. But its exaltation of Joseph and its lower view of Judah suggests it is not a Judahite composition (Gen. 37–50; 49:22–26; Deut. 33:13–17). It must therefore predate the kingdom of David and come from a single source recognized as authoritative by the Judahite and Josephite kingdoms alike.

5

The Millennial Week Between the Testaments

EXITING Old Testament times and entering the Hellenistic period, we turn now to look at how the Israelites thought about the millennial week in the period between the Old and New Testaments. Our four texts here are the Book of Jubilees, the Second Book of Enoch, the Targum on Hosea, and the Biblical Antiquities of Pseudo-Philo.

The Book of Jubilees

The Book of Jubilees was written in the early second century BC, perhaps by a Zadokite, either a temple *kohen* or an Essene.[1] The book counts off the ages of creation in periods of forty-nine year jubilees from Adam to the Exodus. Its writer deduced from Genesis that one heavenly day is 1,000 years, and so Adam, although he lived 930 years, did indeed die in the day he ate the forbidden fruit.

> [29]And at the close of the nineteenth jubilee, in the seventh week in the sixth year thereof [AM 930], Adam died, and all his sons buried him in the land of his creation, and he was the first to be buried in the earth. [30]And he lacked seventy years of one thousand years; for one thousand years are as one day in the testimony of the heavens and therefore was it written concerning the tree of knowledge: *On the day that you eat thereof*

[1] Gurtner 2020: 232–236. Although the bulk of the text now survives in Greek, it was almost certainly written in Hebrew, as Hebrew fragments of about 15% of the text have been found among the Dead Sea Scrolls (Stökl 2006).

> *you shall die* [Gen. 2:17]. For this reason he did not complete the years of this [millennial] day; for he died during it. (Jub. 4:29–30)

The writer does not speak explicitly of a millennial week. But he does speak of a millennial day. So it is fair to assume that he was aware of the idea of a millennial week and its millennial seventh day of rest.

2 Enoch

Later, we find the same idea in *The Book of the Secrets of Enoch* (2 Enoch), which was composed in Greek, probably by an Alexandrian Jew, sometime between 30 BC and AD 65. The book reflects the ideas of pre-Christian Alexandrian Judaism, and particularly of the much older Enoch compendium (1 Enoch), which was composed in Hebrew or Aramaic. There is no evidence that this writer was influenced by Christian ideas.

God speaks about the creation of Adam and paradise and the world, saying:

> 4And I blessed the seventh day, which is the Sabbath, on which he rested from all his works.
>
> 1And I appointed the eighth day also, that the eighth day should be the first-created after my work, and that *the first seven* revolve in the form of the seventh thousand, and that at the beginning of the eighth thousand there should be a time of not-counting, endless, with neither years nor months nor weeks nor days nor hours. (2 En. 32:4–33:1)[2]

It is clear that the days under discussion are millennial days. The seventh millennium Sabbath is followed by the Age to Come in the eighth millennium. The Age to Come will be a period of eternity without any notion of time. So we find here, fully-formed, all the ideas of the millennial week.

The Targum of Hosea

The targums are Aramaic translations of the Bible with interpretational glosses. Their roots lie in the centuries before the Christian era, yet they continued to be supplemented and amended over many centuries. As a result, any chance of determining the date of any passage of a targum must depend on historical clues within the passage itself.

[2] Tr. of Morfill (Charles 1896: 451).

The Targum of Hosea comments on Hosea 6:2, where Hosea spoke of God reviving Israel after two days and raising them up on the third day to live before him. The *meturgeman* – the targum translator – takes this to mean that, after two days of affliction, the dead [of Israel] will be raised at the resurrection at the Messiah's coming.

> He will revive us after two days of consolation,
> which shall be for the dead on the day of resurrection of his coming;
> he will raise us up and we will live before him.[3]

This implies several things. First, he says that after two days will come the day of resurrection. This day of resurrection is presumably a 'third day' (though he does not call it that), and so it can be identified with Hosea's third day. Next, this day of resurrection is a long period of time when Israel will 'live' or flourish. So it is not a solar day. The *meturgeman* knew, of course, that a heavenly day is 1,000 years. So it looks like he sees this long 'day' of resurrection as a millennial day. By that token, the preceding two days must also be millennia. Finally, he says the third-day resurrection will take place on the day of 'his coming.' That must mean the time when the Messiah comes, the messianic kingdom. So the *meturgeman* sees Hosea's three days as three consecutive days of the millennial week, and the third of these days as the day of resurrection when Israel will live before him.

Of course, as I said, the targums are difficult to date. As a result, we cannot know whether this was written before or after the Roman destruction of the Jewish nation in AD 70. If it was written before, then the *meturgeman* may be counting Israel's history, from the time of the patriarchs, as the two millennial days of trouble soon to be gloriously transformed at the imminent resurrection of the dead, perhaps in the fifth day of creation. But, if he wrote after the AD 70 destruction, then it seems he foresees yet two more millennial days of exile for Israel, after which the resurrection will take place at the beginning of the seventh day. This seventh-day resurrection seems to me to be the more likely scenario. (This, as we shall see, is also how many rabbinic sages interpret Hosea's prophecy.) But, either way, the *meturgeman* sees the days of Hosea's prophecy as indicating millennial days of the millennial week.

[3] יְחַיִנַנָא לְיוֹמֵי נֶחָמְתָא דַעֲתִידִין לְמֵיתֵי בְּיוֹם אַחָיוּת מֵיתַיָא יְקִימִינָנָא וּנְחֵי קֳדָמוֹהִי׃

Pseudo-Philo

Pseudo-Philo was the anonymous author of a work called the *Biblical Antiquities*, which records early Jewish traditions about the period from creation to the death of Saul. It survives now only in Latin but was probably written in Hebrew. Views on when it was written differ widely, from the second century BC to the third AD. My view, like many others, is that it was written before the temple's destruction in AD 70.[4] Nothing is known of the author, but there is no evidence that he was Christian. So it is fair to assume that his views are those of pre-Christian Judaism.

In a dialogue between Moses and God, Moses raises the question of how long this age is to last.

> [14]Moses said, "If I may make another request of you, Lord, in accord with the abundance of your mercy, be not angry with me, but show me how much time has passed and how much remains."
>
> [15]And he said to him, "On one side there is a large black cloud, the fullness of a cloud, on the other side a drop from a ladle. But time will fulfil all things. Four and a half [ages] have passed, two and a half remain." (*Biblical Antiquities* 19.14–15)[5]

So Pseudo-Philo says the world will last for seven ages. Seen from the viewpoint of Moses in the mid-second millennium BC, four and a half have passed and two and a half are still to come till the end of the seventh millennium. So, if he sees Moses's time 4,500 years after creation, then he sees creation about 6000 BC. In that case, he sees his own time, 1,500 years after Moses, to be at the end of the sixth millennium. So he expects the Sabbath millennium age to begin soon and to last for 1000 years.

Figure 2. Pseudo-Philo's Seven Millennia

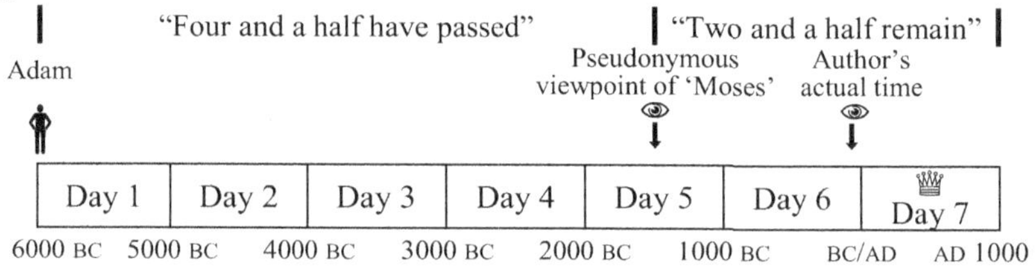

[4] Those who hold a date before AD 70 appeal to the references to ongoing temple worship and priesthood (22:8). Those who hold a later date say the hint of the destruction of the temple (19:7) must have been written after the event, and so the text must date from after AD 70. For early dates see e.g., Murphy 1993:6; Harrington 2012:8 (mid-first century); for the later, see Charlesworth 1981: 170 (c. AD 100).

[5] Jacobson, *Pseudo-Philo*, 1.123.

It's not an easy text. And it's not clear what is his source for the date of creation. It's a date closer to the Septuagint than the Masoretic text.[6] But it's clear that the author believed in seven millennial days of creation. And it seems that, though writing from the viewpoint of Moses in the mid-second millennium BC, he sees himself standing at the dawn of the millennial Sabbath.

Summary

These four texts show that the millennial day was a familiar idea from at least the early second century BC. Although Jubilees speaks only of one millennial day, its author was surely aware that one such day implies a millennial week. Meanwhile, 2 Enoch, the Hosea targum, and Pseudo-Philo all speak clearly of the millennial week. The Hosea targum probably speaks of the millennial Sabbath being the messianic age and 2 Enoch speaks of both the Sabbath and the eighth-day Age to Come. So, as we come to the New Testament, we may safely assume that these ideas were familiar to the New Testament writers, to their readers, and to their contemporaries.

[6] As said above, the date of creation in the Hebrew Masoretic text is about 4,000 BC. But the Greek Septuagint date of creation is about 1500 years earlier. See chapter 9.

6

The Millennial Week in the New Testament

FOLLOWING ON from the intertestamental texts, we come to the books of the New Testament. Only one of them, the Revelation, speaks explicitly of the millennium. However, three others – namely, John's Gospel, the Epistle to the Hebrews, and the Second Epistle of Peter – allude to it. We'll look at them in canonical order.

JOHN'S GOSPEL

In John's Gospel, Jesus is accosted by the temple authorities after he cleanses the temple.

> 18 Therefore the Judeans answered and said to him, "What sign do you show us for these things you do?"
>
> 19 Jesus answered and said to them, "Destroy this temple and in three days I will raise it up."
>
> 20 Therefore the Judeans answered and said, "It took forty-six years[1] to build this temple, and you will raise it in three days?"
>
> 21 He however spoke about the temple of his body. 22 When therefore he was raised from the dead, his disciples remembered that he had said this and they believed the scripture and the word that Jesus had spoken.
>
> (John 2:18–22)

[1] Josephus says Herod began his massive expansion of the second temple in the 18th year of his reign, in 20 BC (*A.J.* 15.380; *B.J.* 5.184–221). So the Pharisees are counting from a start date around 16 BC, perhaps omitting some of the preliminary work.

When Jesus says, "On the third day…I will raise it up," he is certainly alluding to Hosea 6:2. In fact, in saying he is the one who will raise it up, he is equating himself with Jehovah, whom Hosea says will raise Israel on the third day. The Judeans should perhaps have noticed that. But, of course, they take him literally, as everyone always does in John's gospel. How can he rebuild this great temple in two days?

Then John says Jesus's words mean that he was speaking of his body, which was to be raised after three days. But John allows that neither he, John, nor anyone else (except presumably Jesus) knew what he meant at the time (v. 22). Yet, at the time, Jesus was actually talking to the temple leaders about the temple. The dialogue would make no sense at all if Jesus's remarks were deliberately so cryptic that the people he was speaking to could not understand them. (Or do we imagine that Jesus went around making incomprehensible remarks that meant the opposite of what he said?) But, on the other hand, the destruction of the temple is far from hypothetical. Elsewhere Jesus unambiguously and repeatedly foretells its impending doom (Matt. 24:1–2; Mark 13:1–2; Luke 13:35; 19.44; 21:20–44). And so it is only natural that he should speak of its destruction to the temple authorities. Further, it would be strange that he should claim to raise his own body, for elsewhere he always speaks of "being raised" by God. So, if we are to take Jesus's comment at face value, it seems he really was talking about the temple here.

So we must surely concede that when John said, "He spoke about the temple of his body," what he really meant is that Jesus was speaking not only about the temple but *also* about the temple of his body. Negation for the sake of emphasis is a standard Hebraic parlance. Jeremiah says, *For I did not speak to your fathers and I did not instruct them concerning burnt offerings and sacrifices on the day that I brought them out of Egypt.* (7:22) But God did speak to their fathers and did instruct them about these things. What Jeremiah means is, "I did not instruct them *only* concerning burnt offerings and sacrifices, but about other things as well."

In the same way, John is saying that Jesus was speaking not only about the temple in Jerusalem, but also about his body. Why did John not say so? He didn't need to. It was obvious that Jesus was speaking about the temple. What was less obvious was that he was speaking about his body as well.

In fact, we can go further. Jesus is drawing a parallel between his body and the temple. He says that, just as his body will be raised on the third day, so too will the temple be raised on the third day. But his allusion to Hosea points his hearers to understand that he is speaking of millennial days. (His hearers should have understood this well enough from the Targum of Hosea, whose interpretation was now standard by this time.) So Jesus foretells that he, Jehovah, will raise up the temple on the third millennium after its destruction. Indeed, I think he is saying that his resurrection on the third day is a sign that the temple will be rebuilt on the third millennial day. His resurrection will show, for a start, that he is the Messiah. And, of course, everyone knew that the final temple was to be built by the Messiah (Ezek. 43:7; Zech. 6:12 cf. Jer. 23:5). So Jesus is speaking of what the Messiah will do in the messianic age, that is, in the seventh millennium. And Jesus sees this day as the third day from his own time. So it follows that Jesus sees himself standing two millennia before the Sabbath millennium, at the beginning of the fifth millennium from the creation of the world. In other words, he knows it will be around two thousand years until he sets up his messianic kingdom.

Some of the apostles, and perhaps many early Christians, hoped that the Lord would come in their lifetime (1 Thess. 4:17; Jam. 5:7–8; 2 Pet. 3:4). But Jesus taught that his absence would be long. He is the nobleman who went into a *far* country to receive a kingdom and return (Luke 19:12). He is the master who came back after *a long time* to settle accounts (Matt 25:19). Sayings such as Matthew 24:14 and Mark 13:10 about the proclamation of the gospel, and Luke 21:24 about the times of the gentiles in Jerusalem, require a considerable period of time. Peter and Paul might not have imagined that two millennia would elapse. But Jesus, I think, did, and implies as much in this passage.

The Epistle to the Hebrews

The Epistle to the Hebrews dates from before the fall of the temple and the dispersal of the Jewish nation in AD 70 (Heb. 10:11). It is a masterpiece of rabbinic reasoning and argument. Yet, for those uninitiated in such reasoning, it can be difficult. But let us try and follow the argument of chapters three and four.

The author addresses Hebrew believers who are tempted to fall away from faith in Jesus in the face of persecution. He compares their situation to their fathers, the Exodus Israelites under Moses. Their fathers were promised rest but, because of their unbelief, they perished in the desert and did not enter that rest (3:18–19). (Their children, of course, did enter the Promised Land, but that, as he explains later, still did not fulfil the promise of rest.)

Then he says that God entered his own rest on the seventh day of creation (4:3b–4). And so, by implication, God has a place of rest that is available to others, that is, to the faithful (4:6, 11). We begin to see that this "rest" is something greater than the Promised Land.

And therefore, says the author of Hebrews, God spoke, in David's time, of another rest, in Psalm 95, for those who hear his voice (4:7). This cannot refer to the Promised Land, for in David's time, Israel were already living in that land. He explains further:

> For if Iēsous (Joshua/Jesus) had given them rest, God would not have spoken later about another day. There remains then a Sabbath rest (*sabbatismos*) for the people of God. (4:8–9)

He exhorts his Hebrews not to be like their unfaithful fathers, but to strive to enter this promised rest (4:11). Obviously, this cannot mean the Promised Land, for his Hebrew readers are also already dwelling there, before the fall of the temple (7:23–28; 8:3–5; 10:1–11). No, they are to enter the promised rest by enduring in the Christian faith. And so the implication is that the promised rest is in the future and is bestowed by Jesus.

Now, this word *sabbatismos* is unique in the whole corpus of Greek literature up to this time. The usual Greek word for Sabbath is *sabbaton.* But the *–ismos* suffix forms abstract nouns of action or condition or state. So *sabbatismos* is the state of 'being in' Sabbath: a continual extended dwelling in Sabbath rest or 'Sabbathhood.'

This Sabbath rest is related to, but not the same as, the Sabbath rest spoken of in the Ten Commandments. They resemble one another in that each is a seventh period of rest after six of labour. But they differ in that this promised *sabbatismos* is not a single day, but a long period of time that one can enter and dwell in. In other words, the *sabbatismos* of Hebrews must be a Sabbath millennium of rest, in the future, at the conclusion of this age.

There is a further interpretive point here. First, Greek *Iēsous* can mean either Joshua or Jesus, and we may ask whom the author meant here. Most translators think he is drawing a parallel between Joshua and Jesus: just as Joshua led them into the Promised Land, so Jesus will lead them into the Promised Sabbath-Rest. True enough. But the other option is that it refers to Jesus alone. In other words, Jesus is the divine Angel of Jehovah who led the Israelites in the pillar of cloud and fire. He led them through the desert and into the Promised Land, but not into his Promised Rest. Yet now he will grant the Promised Rest to the faithful in the age to come. This, it seems, is how the King James Bible reads *Iēsous*, rendering it as English 'Jesus.' Both translations are reasonable and valid, but the second presents Jesus as the protagonist of Israel's entire story, while earthly Joshua is merely a reflection of the one who is leading in the pillar of cloud and fire.

The Second Epistle of Peter

The Apostle Peter writes as follows in his second epistle:

> 8But do not overlook this one fact, beloved, that with the Lord one day is as a thousand years, and a thousand years as one day. 9The Lord is not slow to fulfill his promise as some count slowness, but is patient toward you, not wishing that any should perish, but that all should reach repentance. (2 Pet. 3:8–9)

Alluding to Psalm 90, Peter equates one day of the Lord with a thousand years. It is this divine timescale, he says, which accounts for the delay in the Lord's return. But he also suggests, of course, that the 'day' of the Lord (v. 10) will not be a solar day but a millennial day. He does not say that there are six thousand years leading up to this millennial day, but it is surely implied. He was a Hebrew, after all, and observed a seven-day week ending in Shabbat. Obviously, the millennial day of the Lord must be the day of Shabbat following a week of six millennial days.

He says something similar in his sermon in Acts 3.

> 19Repent therefore, and turn, that your sins may be blotted out, so that times of refreshing may come from the presence of the Lord, 20and that he may send you the one appointed, Messiah Jesus, 21whom heaven must receive until the times of restoration of all things, which God has spoken of by the mouth of his holy prophets since the beginning.

He connects the return of Jesus and the 'restoration of all things' with 'times of refreshing' from the Lord. The word 'refreshing' (*anapsuxis*) is the same word found in the Septuagint Greek text of Exodus to describe the purpose of the Sabbath.

> Six days shall you do your work, and on the seventh day you shall cease, so that your ox and ass may rest, and the son of your handmaid and the stranger may be refreshed (*anapsuxē*). (Exod. 23:12)

So, Peter's 'times of refreshing' allude to a Sabbath which will begin at the return of Jesus. Taken together with his comments in his epistle, it seems he thought that this Sabbath period would be a millennial day.

The Revelation

The New Testament's clearest teaching on the millennium is in the book of Revelation, written by John (1:1), whom I take to be John the Apostle and Evangelist.[2] Views differ on whether it was written in the time of Nero, in the 60s AD, or of Domitian, in the 90s. Its central evil king, with the number 666, certainly represents Nero Caesar, whose name in Greek, Neron Caesar, by Hebrew numerology (*gematria*) does indeed equal 666. If the earlier date is correct, the Revelation is speaking of Nero in code, during his lifetime. If the latter date is correct, then it is speaking of a Nero-figure to come in future.

Several details point to it being written in or near Nero's time. There are the five kings who have fallen, one who is, and one not yet come (17:9–10). Depending on whether we start with Julius or Augustus Caesar, this makes Nero either the sixth or the deceased fifth king.[3] There is also a reference to the temple apparently still standing in 11:1–2.

Yet, on the other hand, most of the Fathers testify to it being written in Domitian's time, including Hegesippus, Irenaeus, Victorinus, Eusebius, Jerome, Sulpicius Severus, Isidore, and Bede. The testimony of Irenaeus is especially trustworthy, since he was a disciple of John through Polycarp, and came from Smyrna, one of the seven churches of the Revelation. Irenaeus said John saw it "towards the end of Domitian's reign."[4]

[2] Dionysius of Alexandria and Eusebius, who were opposed to an earthly millennium, did not want to credit millennial teaching to the apostle John, and taught that the author was another John. These views are cited to this day. See chapter 10.

[3] Caesars Julius, Augustus, Tiberius, Gaius Caligula, Claudius, Nero, Galba (reigned 6 months, till the fall of Jerusalem) and Otho (reigned three months). Although Augustus was officially the first Caesar, many Romans regarded Julius as founder of the line. It was he who first assumed the right to override the senate, place his head on the coinage, and flood the empire with his image.

[4] *Against Heresies* 5.30.3. Likewise Jerome said that John saw "in the island of Patmos, to which he had been banished by the Emperor Domitian as a martyr for the Lord, an

So deciding the date of the Revelation is no easy matter. However, my feeling, based largely on patristic testimony, is that it dates from Domitian's time.

The Revelation resembles the book of Daniel in so many ways that we should see it as a sibling to Daniel's prophecy. Both books feature revelations from angels to the prophet. Both speak of the coming kingdom of God and his Messiah. Both feature the archangel Michael as a chief protagonist. Both represent kings and kingdoms as beasts and horns. Both speak of periods of days and "time, times, and half a time" (Dan. 7:25; 12:7; Rev. 12:14), that is, three-and-a-half years, alternately given as forty-two months and 1,260 days (Rev. 11:2, 3; 12:6; 13:5; cf. Dan. 12:11–12). And both speak of a ruler who will persecute the saints of God. Daniel foretells the reign of Antiochus Epiphanes. And John, as said, speaks of Nero Caesar, the beast whose number is 666. But in both cases, it seems that this historical figure foreshadows another like him in the future, at the end of the age.

Interpreting the Revelation is no easy matter for it contains much symbolism. As a result, some say that its every detail should be read symbolically, not least the millennium and the two resurrections (20:4–6). Others oppose this, saying all must be taken literally. Yet not even the literalists suggest that the Antichrist will have seven heads (13:1) or that Jesus will appear with a sword coming from his mouth (19:15); nor, I fear, are there any genealogical records to identify modern descendants of Reuben, Gad, or Simeon (7:4–8). So we must balance symbolic and literal interpretation, but lean to the latter.

Likewise, some literalists insist that everything in the book is to be treated as future history happening in sequence. But this too can't be so. Jesus features throughout chapter one to eleven, but his birth is described in chapter twelve (12:1–6). The fall of Babylon is told twice (16:19; 18:1–24) and the victory of the kingdom of God several times (11:18; 14:16–20; 16:17; 19:11–21). One may reply that the earlier accounts are proleptic (looking forward). That is true. But still the narrative jumps ahead and back again. This shouldn't surprise us, for the book of Daniel, the Revelation's older brother, does the same thing. But it means we must balance the sequential against the cyclic nature of the prophecy, always remembering that all is heading toward the climax of the triumph of God.

Apocalypse containing the boundless mysteries of the future." (Against Jovinianus 1:26) For an overview of the case for Domitian's reign, see Hitchcock 2005.

In chapter twenty of his prophecy, John speaks six times of a period of "one thousand years." These years follow the return of the "King of kings and Lord of lords," that is, Jesus the King Messiah, to destroy the beast and his armies and the false prophet (19:11–21). Two good things happen during these thousand years. First, Satan shall be bound; second, the righteous, who did not worship the beast, shall be resurrected and reign with the Messiah for one thousand years (20:2–4). At the end of the thousand years, several other things will happen. Satan will be released for a time; the rest of the dead will be raised; Satan will again deceive the nations into making war against Jerusalem; they shall be consumed with fire; Satan shall be permanently bound, thrown into the lake of fire, and tormented there (20:2–10).

The basic narrative of chapter twenty is clear enough, though why God should think it necessary for Satan to be imprisoned, and then released to work evil again, has given rise to many explanations and interpretations. But we note several things about this millennial kingdom that John describes.

First, it is an earthly kingdom, based in Jerusalem. For, when Satan is finally released and attempts to destroy this kingdom, he gathers the *nations of the earth* to march *across the earth* and to attack the "beloved city" (v. 9) which can only be Jerusalem (cf. Ps. 132:13; 2 Chr. 7:16).

Second, it is not an eternal kingdom but a temporal kingdom, for it lasts a thousand years. However, after the final destruction of Satan, at the end of the thousand years, it has an even greater future, when the New Jerusalem descends to earth (21:2). Yet its first phase is temporary.

Third, since the Messiah is to rule on earth with his saints at this time, this kingdom must be the same kingdom Daniel spoke of, when the Son of Man will rule with his saints (Dan. 7:13–27); that is, Daniel's fifth kingdom of the Rock cut by no human hand which will demolish the four preceding kingdoms of the earth (2:34–45). It is therefore the messianic kingdom, the seventh or Sabbath millennium from the creation of the world.

The millennial kingdom begins and ends with resurrections. The first resurrection, at the beginning of the millennium, consists of those who suffered or died for the name of Jesus, who did not receive the mark of the beast (20:4). They will rule with Jesus the Messiah one thousand years (20:6). At the end of the millennial kingdom comes the second resurrection. It consists of "the rest of the dead," who are raised, and judged according to their deeds (20:5). This is the Bible's clearest description of the double resurrection. Yet it was already implied in Jesus's words about "the resurrection of the righteous" (which implies a resurrection of the unrighteous) (Luke 14:14). And it is taught by Paul in Acts 24:15 and probably in 1 Cor. 15:24, where I suspect *to telos* should mean not "the end" (as in most translations), but rather "the fullness" or "the rest" (of the dead).

> 23 But each in his own order:
> Christ the firstfruits,
> then at his coming those who belong to Christ,
> 24 then the rest (*to telos*),
> when he delivers the kingdom to God the Father after destroying every rule and every authority and power. (1 Cor. 15:23–24)

Further, this idea of a millennial kingdom is not John's invention, as some say. For, as we have seen, long before John's time, texts like Jubilees, the Hosea targum, 2 Enoch, and Pseudo-Philo all spoke of millennial days, the millennial week, and the Sabbath millennium. And as we shall see in the next two chapters, the millennial week was an idea well known to John's contemporaries, both Nazarenes and Pharisees. So John did not invent the idea of the Messiah's millennial reign. It was a well-known idea among first-century Israelites who all drew it ultimately from Genesis. One must conclude that although John speaks only of one millennium, he also knew about the millennial week, and the millennium he describes is the Sabbath millennial kingdom.

7

The Millennial Week in the Nazarene Church

GENERALLY, the term "Nazarene" refers to the early Israelite Christians of the Holy Land, whose native tongues were Hebrew (in Judea) or Aramaic (in the Galilee). It is, in origin, a Pharisaic term for the followers of Jesus, as we see in Acts 24:5. But it helps us distinguish these early Israelite believers from the Greek Fathers who would dominate the church within a few centuries. Two early Nazarene texts witness to belief in the millennial kingdom and the millennial week. They are the Coptic Apocalypse of Elijah and the Epistle of Barnabas.

The Coptic Apocalypse of Elijah

The Coptic Apocalypse of Elijah is an early apocalyptic text. It began as a Jewish apocalypse written probably in first-century BC Alexandria. It seems that this early version was then redacted in Nazarene hands to form this version which now survives only in Coptic. Later, it was redacted by rabbinic hands to form another text, in Mishnaic Hebrew, which Buttenwieser called the Hebrew Elijah-Apocalypse.[1] Some form of the text was known to Origen, who, like Ambrosiaster and Euthalius, ascribes Paul's quote in 1 Corinthians 2:9 to it. In other words, it seems like some form of the Apocalypse was known to Christians of the mid-first century AD, but our surviving Coptic Christian version dates perhaps

[1] For more, see Charlesworth 1976: 95–97 and Wintermute 1983: 722–734.

from the second century. Given the difficulties of dating the text, and its process of growth, we cannot be sure whether this Apocalypse influenced John's Apocalypse, or whether John's influenced this one, or whether both drew from common sources.[2]

The fifth chapter of the Apocalypse describes the Messiah's conquest of the earth.

> On that day, the King Messiah and all his saints will come forth from heaven. He will burn the earth. He will spend a thousand years upon it. Because the sinners prevailed over it, he will create a new heaven and a new earth. No deadly devil will exist in them. He will rule with his saints, ascending and descending, while they are always with the angels and they are with the Messiah for a thousand years.[3] (5:36–37)

So the Messiah's earthly rule will last for a thousand years, in keeping with the general outline of the millennial week and the teaching of Revelation 20. The Messiah will create a new heaven and earth, though exactly when this takes place is not said. (Revelation 21:1 places it at the end of the millennium.) The Messiah, with his saints, will ascend and descend, between heaven and earth, together with the angels.

The Epistle of Barnabas

The Epistle of Barnabas speaks of the destruction of the temple in AD 70 and so must date from after that time. Estimates vary from AD 70 to 130, though an earlier date within this period is likely. The early church accepted the epistle as from the hand of Barnabas, Paul's co-worker, who was also recognized as an apostle (Acts 14:4, 14). Since it is unlikely that they would have accepted it as his if it dated from long after his lifetime, a date of composition between AD 70 and 100 seems reasonable.

The thirteenth chapter addresses the nature of the true Sabbath and then proceeds to speak of the Sabbath millennium of creation, as follows:

> [3]In the beginning of the creation he spoke of the Sabbath. *And God made in six days the works of his hands; and he finished them on the seventh day, and he rested the seventh day, and sanctified it.* [Gen. 2:2]. [4]Consider, my children, what that means: He finished them in six days.

[2] Wintermute 1983:729–730 thinks the Apocalypse borrows from John. He notes the influence of 1 John 2:15 and Rev. 11:8ff upon it, and concludes that, for these Johannine writings to reach Egypt, this version of the Apocalypse dates from after AD 150.

[3] Translation from Wintermute in Charlesworth 1983: 1:753. For the dating, see 721–23.

> The meaning of it is this: That in six thousand years the Lord God will bring all things to an end. [5]For with him one day is a thousand years. For he himself [*i.e.*, Jesus] testified to me (αὐτὸς δέ μοι μαρτυρεῖ), saying, "Behold, the day of the Lord shall be as a thousand years!" Therefore, children, in six days, that is, in six thousand years, shall all things be accomplished. [6]And he rested the seventh day. This means that when his Son shall come, and abolish the times of the lawless one, and judge the ungodly; and change the sun and the moon, and the stars; then he shall truly rest in the seventh day. (Ep. Bar. 13:3–6)[4]

As in earlier texts, after the six millennia from creation, there will follow a Sabbath millennium. But, in this case, the author, perhaps Barnabas, claims that this was taught to him directly by Jesus himself.

The Gnostic Cerinthus

Cerinthus was a first-century Nazarene heretic who was contemporary with and known to the Apostle John. Irenaeus, in fact, says that John wrote his gospel and his epistles specifically to counter the teachings of Cerinthus. It's fair to say that Cerinthus is out of place here beside the orthodox texts of Barnabas and the Elijah Apocalypse. Yet his teachings arose in the same time and place. And, although the apostles squarely rejected him, Cerinthus probably saw himself as a fringe member of the Nazarene community. So I hope the reader will not be offended if I introduce him here, within his historical and geographical context.

Cerinthus had some link to the early Christian heretical group called the Ebionites, and was perhaps their founder. Like the Ebionites, he had a version of Matthew's gospel lacking the infancy narratives of the first three chapters. This truncated gospel enabled him to teach that Jesus was begotten not by the Holy Spirit but by Joseph and Mary, and that the Christ-spirit came upon him at his baptism and left him at his crucifixion. He held to early Gnostic beliefs. He taught that the visible world and heavens were made not by the supreme God, but by a lesser god, the Demiourgos (Demiurge) or 'craftsman.' This lesser god, he said, was quite distinct from the Supreme God and even ignorant of the Supreme God's existence.

However, Cerinthus also taught that there would be a millennium of peace at the end of the age, when people would eat and drink and marry.

[4] My translation, with numeration following the text of the Ante-Nicene Fathers, vol. I. Numeration of the Epistle differs. Some make this chapter 14, others 15.

Earlier church fathers, like Irenaeus, say nothing of his millennial beliefs but simply reject his heterodox beliefs about the Godhead. But later fathers, Dionysius of Alexandria, Eusebius, and Jerome, eating pulse and sworn to chastity, misrepresent his views of the millennium, making it out to be a 1,000-year orgy of unbridled licentiousness. On this imaginary basis they then reject the whole idea of the millennium itself as the carnal creation of Cerinthus's carnal mind. So, justly condemning Cerinthus's Christology, they unjustly condemned his millenarianism by association.

But Cerinthus did not invent the millennium. Like everyone else in first-century Israel, he received it from most ancient tradition. Nor were his imagined millennial activities as reprehensible as they were made out to be. He taught that there would be eating, drinking, and marriage in the millennial time. But Jesus himself taught that there would be feasting in the messianic kingdom. And, as we shall see, several perfectly orthodox fathers who held to millennial beliefs spoke of human reproduction during the millennium. So Cerinthus's Christology and Gnosticism are indeed unorthodox, but his millenarianism seems little different from that of the early orthodox Church Fathers.

8

The Millennial Week in Rabbinic Literature

NOW the Pharisees oppose Jesus and the apostles, and how they go head to head over and over again is told to us in the New Testament. But of course the Pharisees discussed many of the same things that the New Testament talks about. They too were waiting for the Messiah and the kingdom of God. They too believed in a coming tribulation under an evil king, a coming resurrection of the dead and judgement of the world, and in Paradise, Gehenna, and immortality. They too believed that the history of the world was mapped out over seven millennia and they too hoped for the messianic kingdom at the beginning of the seventh millennium. In fact, to read the New Testament without being aware of what the Pharisees thought, sometimes feels like hearing only half the conversation. But if we want to know what the Pharisees did say about these things, then the place where we find it is in Pharisaic, that is, rabbinic literature.

THE MISHNAH

The Mishnah, compiled by Rabbi Judah the Prince in the late second century AD, lists the psalms sung in the temple on each day of the week.

> On Shabbat they sang, *A psalm, a song for the day of Shabbat* (Ps. 92), that is, *A psalm, a song,* for the future to come (*le'atid la<u>b</u>o*), for the day that will be wholly Shabbat of rest for life everlasting. (M. Tam. 7:4)

Here the title of Psalm 92 is taken as indicating not merely the weekly Shabbat, but a future day which will be a great Shabbat of everlasting life. The words can only indicate the great Sabbath of the seventh millennial day.

THE BABYLONIAN TALMUD

The Babylonian Talmud was compiled in Babylonia in the mid-fifth century AD. In tractate Sanhedrin the rabbis list the sorrows that will be in the world prior to the coming of the Messiah. Then they turn to the subject of how long this present age of sorrows will last.

> R. Katina said: Six thousand years shall the world be, and one [thousand, it shall be] desolate [*ḥaro<u>b</u>*], as it is said, *And HaShem alone shall be exalted in that day* [Isa. 2:11].
>
> Abaye said: Two [thousand shall it be] desolate, as it is said, *After two days will he revive us: in the third day, he will raise us up, and we shall live in his sight* [Hos. 6:2].
>
> It has been taught in accordance with R. Katina: Just as the seventh year is one year of release in seven, so is the world: one thousand years out of seven shall be of release, as it is said, *And the Lord alone shall be exalted in that day* [Isa. 2:11]; and it is further said, *A Psalm, a song for the Sabbath day* [Ps. 92:1], meaning the day that is altogether Sabbath; and it is also said, *For a thousand years in thy sight are but as yesterday when it is past* [Ps. 90:4].
>
> Tanna debe Eliyahu taught: The world is to exist six thousand years. Two thousand: chaos. Two thousand: Torah. Two thousand: days of the Messiah.[1] || But for our iniquities, which have been many, they [the years] have gone which have gone. (Sanh. 97a/b)[2]

Rav Katina was a Babylonian rabbi who taught in the late third century. He says the world shall exist six thousand years and in the last thousand it shall be desolate. The later sages debated what he meant by 'desolate.'[3] But they generally agree that it points to a time of the desolation of the wicked heathen kingdoms. After all, Katina continues by saying that HaShem alone shall be exalted in that day. So 'that day' must be the day

[1] *Y'mot ha-mashiaḥ* (not *y'mei ha-mashiaḥ*) is rabbinic standard. But cf. Deut 32.7.

[2] A parallel passage at R.H. 31a repeats the comments of Kattina and Abaye verbatim.

[3] Meiri (preface to Pirkei Avot) says the one thousand years of desolation are the sixth millennium or else the destruction of wickedness in the Shabbat millennium. Rashba, *Teshuvot HaRashba* 1.9, and Abravanel, *Yeshuot m'shiḥo* 1.1, say the world will return to primordial chaos; Baḥya b. Asher, on Num. 10.35, says it applies only to part of the world. Rambam says it is not to be taken literally (*Moreh nevukhim* 2.29).

when HaShem rules the earth; that is, the time of the seventh millennium messianic kingdom. This is confirmed by the third section which elucidates Rav Katina's teaching. The one thousand years that he called 'desolate' are also described as 'release' or 'fallow'; that is, the land and its people shall cease from exertion, as in a sabbatic year. The citation of Psalms 92:1 and 90:4 confirm that this refers to the Sabbath millennium.

The next comment is from Rav Abaye, head of Pumbedita Academy in Babylonia in the early fourth century. Quoting Hosea, he speaks of two 'days' of desolation before God will raise and revive Israel. Abaye thus endorses the view that we saw earlier in the Targum to Hosea and John 2; namely, Hosea's 'two days' mean Israel will be humbled for two thousand years, and then they *will live before him* (Hos. 6:2). Of course, the time when Israel will live before him must be the messianic kingdom. And Abaye is speaking two and a half centuries after the destruction of Jerusalem and the temple. So he means that Israel's desolation and disgrace will last two thousand years, and then will come the Sabbath millennium. In this he concurs with the words of Jesus in John 2:19.

Finally, Tanna debe Eliyahu (The Teachings of Elijah) comes from the *yeshiva* of Rav Anan in the early third century. But its Hebrew tongue suggests that it arose in the Holy Land before the end of the second century. (Rabbinic discourse in the Holy Land changes from Hebrew to Aramaic in the late second century AD, as the children of the rabbis driven from Jerusalem became more fluent in Aramaic than Hebrew.) In other words, this text is an anonymous oral teaching of tannaitic times (AD 50–200), preserved in the school of Rav Anan, and dating from a century or more before the time of Katina and Abaye.

This teaching of 'Elijah' outlines the history of the world as six thousand years. The first two thousand years are chaos; the next two thousand are of Torah; and the next two thousand are the days of the Messiah. However, it is said that the Messiah has not yet arrived because of Israel's iniquities.

This same teaching is interpreted further in the tractate Avodah Zarah 9a. Here, the older tradition – the first paragraph – is cited in Hebrew and is followed by commentary in Aramaic.

> The Tanna debe Eliyahu taught: The world is to exist six thousand years. Two thousand: chaos. Two thousand: Torah. Two thousand: days of the Messiah. But for our iniquities, which have been many, they [the years] have gone which have gone.

> The two thousand years of Torah, from whence [are they reckoned]? If from the giving of the Torah [at Sinai] till now, there is not [time enough] for all these years. For, if you examine, there were two thousand plus a part of the [third] thousand [from the creation of the world until Sinai].
>
> But [instead, it is reckoned] from *the people they acquired in Haran* (Gen. 12.5). For we have a tradition that Abraham at that time was fifty-two years old. (B. AZ 9a)

That is to say, the rabbis knew the giving of the Torah at Sinai took place in the middle of the third millennium Anno Mundi. Therefore the years of Torah could not be dated from Sinai, for that would be two and a half thousand years from creation. Rather, they are reckoned from the fifty-second year of Abraham's life, who was born in AM 1948 and turned fifty-two in AM 2000. (This is, incidentally, the date given for Abraham's birth in Seder Olam Rabbah, the 'Great Book of the World-Age.') And it was at that age that Abraham acquired bondsmen in Haran and began to instruct them in the way of God. Thus the 2,000 years of Torah began in AM 2001, and so the six thousand years are as follows:

> Two thousand years of chaos (AM 1–2000). Creation to Abraham's fifty-second year.
> Two thousand years of Torah (AM 2001–4000). Abraham to the Messiah.
> Two thousand years of the Messiah (AM 4001–6000).
> But the Messiah has not come because of their iniquities.

Finally, at the beginning of the Talmud, in Berakhot 34b, we find a teaching on the *Olam HaBa,* the Age to Come. As is clear from the text, that age is to follow the messianic kingdom. But only God knows the mysteries which shall be revealed in that time.

> R. Yoḥanah said, All the prophets did not prophesy except about the days of the Messiah. But, about the Olam HaBa [it is said], *No eye has seen, God, apart from you* (Isa. 64:4). (B. Ber. 34b)

The Jerusalem Talmud and Sifrei Devarim

Tractate Berakhot 14d of the Jerusalem Talmud (and its close parallel in Sifrei Devarim 11.22) contains the following passage:

> Said Rabbi Shimon ben Laqish: In *Megillat Ḥasidim* they found written:

> 'On the day you forsake me, I shall forsake you two days.'[4] [It is like] Two people went, one from Tiberias and one from Sepphoris, and met at a certain shelter. They had only parted and each one went one mile, and they were separated two miles. Or a woman sat and waited for a man. All the time that he intended to marry her, she sat and waited for him. When he put her out of his mind, she went and married another.

The phrase, "On the day you forsake me, I will forsake you two days," looks like an allusion to Hosea 6:2. Given how Hosea's words are interpreted in the Targum on Hosea and in Bavli Sanhedrin 97a, it seems fair to see here the expectation that Israel will be rejected for two thousand years; then they will be revived on the third day, that is, on the Sabbath millennium. Then follow two parables. The first says that if two people walk a mile in opposite directions, they are soon two miles apart. In other words, if Israel forsakes the Holy One for one day, he will forsake them in the other direction, and there will be two days' distance between them, that is, two millennial days until their reconciliation. The second suggests that Daughter Jerusalem waited for the Messiah to come and redeem her, but when he did not come, she gave herself to another.

MIDRASHIC LITERATURE

Bereshith Rabbah, the Midrash on Genesis from the fourth or fifth century, contains a midrash on Genesis 3:8. After Adam has been sentenced to die within one day, the ministering angels look down on him at the end of the day and ask, "Is he still walking?" The Holy One explains to them about Adam's punishment and death.

> Said the Holy One, blessed be He, to them: *Le-ruaḥ ha-yom* ['in the cool breeze of the day'] [means] *Le-revaḥ ha-yom* ['A day's respite']. Behold, I will give him life for a day. For thus I spoke to him: *For in the day that you eat it, you shall surely die* (Gen. 2:17). Now you do not know whether that means one day of Mine or one day of yours. But behold! I will grant him one day of Mine, which is a thousand years, and he will live nine hundred and thirty years and leave seventy for his children. For this is what is written, *The days of our years are threescore years and ten* (Ps. 90:10). (Gen. R. 19.8)

That is, Adam's lifetime of 930 years, added to the seventy years

[4] No scroll by the name of Megillat Ḥasidim is known elsewhere (Leiman 1974: 348).

promised to his descendants, make up one divine day of 1,000 years.[5]

An ancient Hebrew midrashic text, cited by Hulsius simply as 'Pesikta', speaks of the Messiah redeeming the world after 6,000 years:

> The Holy One brought forth the soul of the Messiah, and said to him, Are you willing to be created and to redeem my sons after 6,000 years? He replied, I am. God replied, If so, you must take upon yourself chastisements in order to wipe away their iniquity, as it is written, *Surely our sicknesses he has carried* [Isa. 53.4]. The Messiah answered, I will take them upon me gladly.[6]

From the same period, the midrash Aleph Beth presents the scenario where God says to Satan at the judgement, "Six thousand years you slandered the works of my hands to me all the day long." (8:1). That is, Satan slandered mankind to God from the creation of Adam until the start of the seventh millennium, when Satan will be judged.

Pirkei de Rabbi Eliezer, from the eighth century, compares the sanctity of the seventh age of creation with the seventh day of the week and with the sabbatic year of the seven-year agricultural cycle, legislated in Exodus 23:10–11 and Leviticus 25:2–7 (cf. 26:34–35).

> The Holy One, blessed be he, created seven aeons [millennia]. And of them all he chose only the seventh aeon. Six are for going out and coming in, but one of them is "wholly Shabbat of rest for life everlasting" (M. Tam. 7:4).
>
> [The Holy One, blessed be He, created seven years, and of them all He chose only the sabbatic year.]
>
> The Holy One, blessed be he, created seven days. And of them all he chose only the seventh day, as it is said, *And God blessed the seventh day and sanctified it* (Gen. 2:3).[7]

Elsewhere, Pirkei de Rabbi Eliezer speaks of Adam's 930 years and

[5] A similar teaching is later found in the twelfth-century midrash on Numbers, BaMidbar Rabbah, where Adam's lost seventy years are given to David. "Seventy…alludes to the seventy years which Adam deducted from his total number of years and gave to David ben Yishai. Adam should have lived a thousand years; as it says, *For in the day that you eat of it, you shall surely die* (Gen. 3:17), and a day of the Holy One, blessed be he, is a thousand years; as it says, *For a thousand years in thy sight are but as yesterday when it is passed, and as a watch in the night* (Ps. 90:4)." (Num. R. 14.12)

[6] Hulsius (1653: 328). Prof Ulmer (the authority on Pesikta Rabbati) advises me that the passage is not found in any known text of Pesikta Rabbati, nor of Pesikta deRav Kahana, nor Pesikta Zutarta. Yet it gives the impression of being from a rabbinic source, and its language resembles Pesikta Rabbati §36–37. It may be from a lost manuscript of that text. Prof. Ulmer also suggests it may be from a "mystical (remotely in the Zohar)" text.

[7] §19; fol. 23b–24a. (Friedlander 1916: 141).

David's seventy years making a divine day. And it tells how one hour of the Holy One is eighty-four years, and so one of his days is 1,000 years.[8]

Another eighth-century midrash, *Asereth Melakhim* (*Ten Kings*), tells of ten kings who will rule from one end of the earth to the other.[9] The ninth king is the Messiah, who will usher in 1,000 years of peace for Israel, until the Holy One, the tenth king, will rule in the Age to Come. This is all interpreted in line with Hosea's two and three days.

> The Ninth King. This is Messiah ben David who will rule from one end of the earth to the other, as it is said, *And he will rule from sea to sea and from the River to the ends of the earth* (Ps. 72:8). And Israel will dwell in peace one thousand years, and they will eat Behemoth, Leviathan, and Ziz of the fields.[10] And at the end of a thousand years they will be gathered for judgement, as it is said, *After two days he will revive us; on the third day he will restore us, that we may live before him* (Hos. 6:2). This is the day of judgement. Blessed is the one who is acquitted upon it. [And then the Holy One, blessed be he, will reign, and he is the tenth king.[11]] The Holy One, blessed be he, acquit us upon it, together with all Israel. Amen and Amen.

The midrash *Nistarot Rav Shimon ben Yoḥai* (*The Mysteries of Rav Shimon ben Yoḥai*) is also from the eighth century.[12] It sees the Messiah appearing and reigning for 2,000 years, an idea perhaps derived from the Talmud teaching that there would be two thousand years of Messiah (cf. above, Sanh. 97a/b; AZ 9a). The author identifies this with Hosea's two days, which will culminate in the third day of universal judgement.

> And the temple, which is prepared in the fourth heaven, which Moses, peace upon him, saw in the Holy Spirit,[13] will descend, built-up, from the heavens.... At the end of 2,000 years, the Holy One, blessed be he, sits on his judgement throne in the valley of Jehoshaphat. Thereupon the heavens and earth gradually wear away, and the sun is abashed and the moon ashamed, and the mountains will be removed so that they do not remind Israel of their sins. On the third day the gates of Gehenna open in the Valley of Joshua and the gates of the Garden of Eden in the East, as it is said, *After two days he will make us live* (Hos. 6:2): these are the

[8] §18, fol. 22b; §7, fol. 8b; §28, fol. 33 (Friedlander 1916: 128, 49, 201).

[9] Text in Eisenstein 1915: 2.466 (Heb.); Mitchell 1997: 344 (Heb.); 2016: 206 (ET).

[10] Leviathan is a fabulous water-beast, Behemoth a fabulous land animal, and Ziz a fabulous bird.

[11] Eisenstein 1915: 2.466 gives this reading in a footnote.

[12] Text: Jellinek, *BHM* III.78–82 (Heb.); Mitchell 1997 (Heb.): 332; 2016: 198 (ET).

[13] Moses saw heavenly antitypes of cultic items at Exod. 25.9, 40; 2 Bar. 4.5. For the heavenly Jerusalem, temple, and altar in *Zebul,* the fourth heaven, see B. Hag 12b.

> days of the Messiah which are 2,000 years. *On the third day* (Hos. 6:2): this is the day of judgement. Woe to all who die on that day!

This *darshan* hoped for the inauguration of a two-thousand-year period of the 'days of the Messiah' to be followed by the day of judgement. But his time-frame isn't clear. Perhaps he expects the Messiah at the start of the fifth and sixth millennial days, with the day of judgement to fall on the seventh millennium.[14] Or perhaps more likely he looks forward to the Messiah reigning through the sixth and seventh millennia. (This, as we shall see, was the view of Ramban in the thirteenth century.) In that case, he would see the day of judgement at the start of the eighth millennial week, in the Age to Come, just as in Revelation 20:5–11.

The 11th-century Midrash Vayosha on Exodus 15:18 is similar.[15] Hosea's two and three days are cited once again. The Holy One raises the dead at the end of the Messiah's 2,000-year reign, which is followed by the Day of Judgement, when the idolatrous heathen nations will be judged and Israel saved.

> After that, Messiah ben David will come, as it is said: *And behold with the clouds of heaven one like a son of man* (Dan. 7:13), and it is written afterward, *He will have authority and royal dignity* (Dan. 7:14). He will kill Armilus the wicked, as it is said: *He will slay the wicked one with the breath of his lips* (Isa. 11:4).
>
> Then the Holy One, blessed be he, will gather Israel, who have been dispersed here and there, as it is said: *I will whistle for them and I will gather them, when I have redeemed them, and they will be as numerous as they were before* (Zech. 10:8). And hung in Jerusalem will be seventy-two precious stones which will shine from one end of the world to the other, and the nations of the world will come to that light, as it is written: *Nations will come to your light, and kings to the brightness of your rising* (Isa. 60:3). The Holy One, blessed be he, will lower the temple from heaven – the same one which the Holy One, blessed be he, showed to Moses, as it is said: *You will bring them and plant them upon the mount of your inheritance; the place which you made for your dwelling, O Lord;* [*the sanctuary, O Lord, which your hands established*] (Exod. 15.17). Israel shall dwell there for two thousand years, and they will eat Leviathan.
>
> At the end of the two thousand years, the Holy One, blessed be he, will sit upon a throne of judgement in the Valley of Jehoshaphat. Thereupon the heavens and the earth will be displaced and the sun and moon ashamed, as it is said: *The moon will be ashamed, and the sun abashed* (Isa. 24:23). Where do we learn that judgement will be pronounced on the third day? As it is said: *After two days he will make us live; on the*

[14] See above B. AZ 9a; B. Sanh. 97a; and, in the next chapter, Ep. Barn. 15.
[15] Text: Jellinek, *BHM* I.55–57 (Heb.); Mitchell 2016: 216–217 (ET).

> *third day he will raise us up and we shall live before him* (Hos. 6.2): this is the Judgement.
>
> The Holy One, blessed be he, will bring every nation and tongue and say: 'What did you serve in the world that has departed, and whom did you worship?'

This *darshan* is writing toward the end of the fifth millennium of the Hillel II calendar which dates Adam's creation in 3761 BC.[16] He likely sees the 2,000-year messianic reign falling on the sixth and seventh millennia, and the Day of Judgement on the eighth-day Age to Come, at the start of the next millennial week.

The Zohar

The Zohar is the foundational text of the Jewish mystical tradition called Kabbalah. It was compiled in the late thirteenth century by Moshe ben Shem Tov de León, perhaps from older sources. It speaks several times of the sixth millennium and the ensuing Shabbat. At the end of the sixth millennium, Israel will be redeemed from their long exile.

> Rabbi Shimon began and said: *And I will remember my covenant with Ya'akov* (Lev. 26:42). This refers to the exile of the sons of Israel. While in captivity, they will be redeemed by the power of the [sixth] letter Vav [in Ya'aqov], that is, in the sixth millennium. Through the letter Vav, their exile is ended. (Zohar, Vayera 1:119a; §476)

At the end of the sixth millennium, the Holy One shall unite the new and old souls – referring perhaps to the resurrection – and those inscribed for life shall inhabit Jerusalem.

> Happy all those who shall remain in the world at the end of the sixth millennium and enter Shabbat. Because that is a day for HaShem alone on which to effect the union of new souls with old souls in the world, as it is written: *And it shall come to pass, that he that is left in Zion, and he that remains in Jerusalem, shall be called holy, everyone that is written for life in Jerusalem* [Isa. 4:3]. (Zohar, Vayera 1:119a; §483)

Signs of the coming redemption shall appear from the 600th year of the sixth millennium.

> In the 600th year of the sixth thousand, the gates of wisdom on high and

[16] The modern Jewish calendar is attributed to the Nasi Hillel II in the year AD 359. But it codified four centuries of earlier Pharisaic calendar changes, and continued to be modified until at least AD 924.

> the wellsprings of lower wisdom will be opened. This will prepare the world to enter the seventh thousand, just as man prepares himself toward sunset on Friday for the Sabbath. (Zohar 1:117a; §445)

The 600th year of the sixth millennium in the Jewish Hillel II calendar is the year 1840 in the Gregorian calendar. Hasidic authorities note how the sixth century (1741 to 1840) saw the rise of Hasidism, under the Baal Shem Tov (1698–1760), the industrial revolution, and the desire to found a Jewish settlement in Palestine. The years from AM[J] 600 onward (1841 to 1940) saw the *Memorandum to Protestant Monarchs of Europe for the restoration of the Jews to Palestine* published in the Colonial Times (1841) and the increasing fulfilment of the Zohar's prediction that Jews would return from exile to the Holy Land, a movement culminating in the declaration of the State of Israel in 1948.

The Rishonim

The *rishonim* – the early medieval rabbis – speak frequently of the millennial week and its Sabbath. Rashi (1040–1105) comments on the above-mentioned talmudic passage, Sanhedrin 97a/b:

> *And two thousand [are the] years of the Messiah.* After the 2000 [years] of Torah, Messiah should have come to end the exile and remove servitude from Israel. *But for our iniquities, which have been many,* the Messiah came not at the end of the 4,000 years, and there has gone forth what has gone forth, and he is delayed from coming.

He makes similar comments on the passage from Avodah Zarah, exclaiming how much time has now passed without the Messiah coming.

> Two thousand: days of the Messiah. But for our iniquities, which have been many, they [the years] have gone forth. From the last two thousand years, how much has gone forth! And the Messiah has not come. (Rashi on AZ 9a)

Like his predecessors, Rashi treats Hosea's 'days' as millennial ages that must pass before the rebuilding of the temple.

> *He will revive us from the two days* (Hos. 6:2): He will strengthen us from the two retributions which have gone over us from the two sanctuaries that were destroyed. *On the third day* – with the construction of the third Temple – *he will raise us up; from the two days:* From the two ages that have passed over us; *on the third day:* In the third age.

In other words, Rashi expects two ages to pass and then the third temple will be built at the beginning of the third millennium from the destruction of the second temple in AD 70. Since the builder of the third temple is understood to be the Messiah, it means his kingdom will arrive at the beginning of the third millennium from the destruction of the temple. This, of course, is the same view as we saw in the Targum on Hosea and in Jesus's words in John 2.

Ramban, in his Torah commentary, written in Jerusalem between 1268 and 1270, speaks frequently about the millennial week. In his lengthy comments on Genesis 2.3, he says:

> *And God blessed the seventh day and sanctified it* (Gen. 2.3). The six days of creation are all the days of the world, for its entire existence will be six thousand years. That is why they said: "A day of the Holy One, blessed be he, is a thousand years" [citing Gen. R. 19.8].

He draws parallels between the first three days of creation and the lives of Adam, Noah, and Abraham. He then notes that there must be a transition period between each millennium.

> Know that from the time twilight falls it is already considered as the following day. Therefore, the subject of every "day" begins somewhat before it, just as Abraham was born at the end of the second thousand years. And you will see similar examples for each and every day.

He draws further parallels between the fourth day of creation and the first and second temples, and between the fifth day and the period of Israel's exile under the rule of the nations. Then he expects the Messiah to appear in the sixth day, the day of the creation of man, that is, in the second century of the sixth millennium.

> This is the son of David, who was formed in the image of God, as it is written, *And behold, there came with the clouds of heaven, one like unto a son of man, and he came even to the Ancient of Days, and he was brought near before him. And there was given him dominion, and glory, and a kingdom* (Dan. 7:13-14). This will take place one hundred and eighteen years after the completion of five thousand years.

That is to say, if Ramban was following the Hillel calendar, which was widely accepted among Jews by his time, he was expecting the Messiah in the Gregorian year AD 1358, some two generations after his own time. So he saw the sixth millennium as the time of the Messiah and the seventh millennium as the Age to Come (Olam HaBa):

> The seventh day, which is Shabbat, alludes to the Olam HaBa, "which will be wholly Shabbat of rest for life everlasting." [M. Tam. 7.4] And God guard us during all the days and set our portion with his servants, the blameless ones.[17]

On Exodus 21, he comments on the six years of service of a bondsman as follows:

> *If you buy a Hebrew bondsman* (Exod. 21:22). He [God or Moses] began the first ordinance with the subject of a Hebrew bondsman, because the liberation of the servant in the seventh year contains a remembrance of the Exodus from Egypt, mentioned in the first commandment, as he said, *And you shall remember that you were a bondsman in the land of Egypt, and HaShem your God redeemed you; therefore I command you this thing today* (Deut. 15:15). It also contains a remembrance of the work of creation, like Shabbat. For the seventh year signals to a servant a complete rest from the work of his master, just as the seventh day of the week does. There is also a seventh amongst the years, which is the jubilee, for seven is the chosen of days, and of years, and of *shemittot* [sabbatic cycles]. And they all point to one thing: the secret of the [seven] days of the world-age, from *bereshith* (in the beginning; Gen. 1:1) till *vayekhulu* (and they were finished; Gen. 2:1).

So Ramban, like *Pirkei de Rabbi Eliezer* §19, is saying that God has built the time-structure of the world in sevens. Just as he chose the seventh day of the week as Shabbat, so he chose the seventh or sabbatic year as *shemittah*, and the seventh *shemittah* as the *shnat yovel* or jubilee year.[18] But greatest of all is the seven days of the world-age, which reflect the seven days of creation, as they appear in Genesis from the first to the seventh day. Thus there is a continual pattern of recurring sabbaths, from the Sabbath day to the Sabbath millennium. By analogy with the seven days of creation, the seven ages of the world will culminate in the Shabbat age. In the same way, at his comments on the sabbatical year (Lev. 25:2), Ramban says, "The secret of the years of the world is alluded to in this place." He makes many other such remarks to the same effect, citing also similar opinions of Rashi and Ibn Ezra.

[17] Ramban proposes the same view of a messianic sixth millennium and a seventh millennium Age to Come in his *Sha'ar HaGemul* 58, a treatise on death, the post-mortem state, and the resurrection.

[18] See Ex. 23:10–11; Lev. 25:2–7 for the sabbatic year and Lev. 25.8–17 for the jubilee.

The Samaritans

The Samaritans expect the Messiah, whom they call the Taheb – that is, the 'restorer', or 'returner', or 'converter' (of the nations) – to appear at the six-thousandth year from creation, the beginning of the seventh millennium of the world's history.[19]

The Taheb will come at the beginning of the Shabbat millennium and introduce the happy millennial age of Ridhwan.[20] Like the Samaritan patriarchs, Joshua and Joseph, he will live 110 years.[21] Like Joshua, he will conquer seven nations and rule the earth from Shechem. But he is mortal, and will die as a mortal, like Joseph and Joshua.[22] But after the age of Ridhwan, the resurrection of the dead will take place at the start of the Age to Come at the beginning of the eighth millennium. Then the Taheb will be foremost among the resurrected.

Tribulation

The Rabbis all agree that the period before the Messiah comes will be marked by times of social chaos and suffering. This period they called the "Birth-pangs of the Messiah." It is discussed in tractate Sanhedrin.

> R. Johanan said: In the generation when Ben David comes, sages will be few in number, and as for the rest, their eyes will fail through sorrow and grief. Multitudes of trouble and evil decrees will be promulgated anew, each new evil coming with haste before the other has ended…
>
> R. Judah said: In the generation when Ben David comes, the synagogue will be for harlots, Galilee in ruins, Gablan lie desolate, the Sanhedrin wander from city to city, receiving no hospitality, the wisdom of scribes in disfavour, God-fearing men despised, people be dog-faced, and truth entirely lacking…The School of R. Shila said: He who departs from evil will be dubbed a fool by his fellow-men…
>
> R. Nehorai said: In the generation when Messiah comes, young men will insult the old, and old men will stand before the young; daughters will rise up against their mothers, and daughters-in-law against their mothers-in-law. The people shall be dog-faced, and a son will not be abashed in his father's presence. (97a)
>
> Ulla said: Let him [Messiah] come, but let me not see him. Rabbah said likewise: Let him come, but let me not see him…Abaye asked

[19] Thomson 1919: 196.
[20] Montgomery 1907: 242.
[21] Montgomery 1907: 244–49; Thomson 1919: 193–96.
[22] See Crown 1967: 70–85; 1989: 266–92.

> Rabbah: What is your reason [for not wishing to see him]? Shall we say, because of the birth pangs of the Messiah? But it has been taught, R. Eleazar's disciples asked him: "What must a man do to be spared the pangs of the Messiah?" [He said,] "Let him engage in study and benevolence; and you, Master, do both." (98b)

The Messiah will not come until after the tribulation. No one imagined that anyone would be taken heavenward to be spared these pains. Nor would there be any way to avoid them on earth unless it be, as Rabbi Eleazar taught, by Torah study and benevolence.

Summary

The millennial week with its seventh-millennium Sabbath age is an idea perfectly familiar to the rabbinic sages. They see the Genesis creation narrative as the true source of this idea. They see implied in the Genesis narrative not only the thousand-year divine day, but also the seventh-millennium Shabbat of rest and the eighth-millennium Age to Come. They also associate the millennial week with the *shemittah* or sabbatical year legislation, and with Hosea 6:2 and Psalm 90:4 and 92:1.

They did not borrow this idea from Christian sources, whether from Revelation 20 or anywhere else. They did not need to, for it was plain enough from Genesis. And it is clear, from the Book of Jubilees and the Targum to Hosea, that the idea of the millennial week was quite familiar before the Revelation was written. So there need be no doubt that the Rabbis saw the Torah as the ultimate source of this teaching.

They did not completely agree on what to expect in the seventh millennium. The Mishnah, followed by Pirkei deRabbi Eliezer and Ramban, see it as "wholly Shabbat of rest for life everlasting." But there was also a minimalist view that life would continue as normal except that the Messiah would free Israel from foreign oppression: "The only difference between the present age and the messianic age is that the oppression of kingdoms will cease." (B. Ber. 34a/b)

Again, they do not always agree on how each stage of redemption fits in with the millennial week. Many, following the Talmud, say the messianic age should have begun at the start of the fifth millennium, but he did not come. Others expect his rule in the seventh millennium and the Day of Judgement to take place at the end of that age. Later, others expect him to rule in the sixth millennium, and the seventh to be the Age to Come. Yet others expect him to rule through the sixth and seventh millennia, followed by the Day of Judgement in the Age to Come, at the start of the eighth millennium. But, in general, all agreed that the plan of the ages was based on the pattern of a millennial week, and that the seventh, Shabbat millennium was the immediate goal of creation.

Among modern Orthodox Jews, it is now widely held that the seventh millennium will be the awaited messianic age.[23] In the Hillel II calendar, almost eight hundred years of the sixth millennium have now elapsed and just over 200 years remain till the Sabbath millennium, which will begin in the Gregorian year AD 2239. Yet, just as the Zohar hoped for the gates of wisdom to be opened in the 600th year of the sixth millennium, just as Ramban spoke of transition periods between the millennia, so too many modern Jews hope for the seventh millennium to dawn in our own time. Recently, the Jerusalem Post (10 June 2022) expressed the view that it is now 12:45 on the sixth-day afternoon and one must prepare expectantly for Shabbat. If this all seems 200 years premature, they reply the Messiah could arrive as the sun begins to wane on the sixth day (PdRE 33). Behind it lies, perhaps, the suspicion that the Hillel II calendar is slow. For it is clear enough that Abraham lived 4,000 years ago, and David 3,000, and we are now at the end of the sixth millennium. And so Shabbat preparation is busily underway. Hasidic Jews strive to rebuild the temple in its place in our own time. The Temple Institute in Jerusalem has prepared a golden menorah, vessels, and robes for the new temple. They have identified *kohanim* of Aaronite descent and trained a Levitical choir. They have bred and may soon sacrifice the tenth red heifer, which, they say, will usher in the messianic era. Three prominent rabbis, Menachem Schneerson, Yitzhak Kaduri, and Moshe Ben Tov, are said to have informed Benjamin Netanyahu that he has been chosen to hand over the Israeli state to the Messiah.

They believe that, in this coming Shabbat, the entire Jewish people will be gathered back to the Holy Land, the royal dynasty of King David will be restored, Jerusalem and the Third Temple will be rebuilt, the temple service, the yearly sabbatic cycle, the jubilee year, and the Sanhedrin will all be restored, and the whole world will turn to God in a

[23] Other streams of Judaism – Progressive, Liberal, and Reformed – have given up belief in the coming of the Messiah, yet continue to believe in a "messianic" age in which the Jews will hold the place of eminence. One Progressive rabbi recently wrote, "although we have abandoned belief in the Messiah, we have (at a liturgical and official level, at least) maintained a belief in a messianic age" (Jacobi 2007: 115).

form of the Jewish faith. Nor are those engaged in this struggle at all dismayed by the opposition they face. For did not the Rabbis always teach that the years leading up to the coming of the Messiah would be turbulent years of strife and trouble?

9

The Millennial Week in the Ante-Nicene Fathers

IT'S TIME now to see what the rabbis' Christian contemporaries, the early church fathers, were saying about the millennial week. We find that the Ante-Nicene fathers – who lived before the Council of Nicaea in AD 325 – mostly held the same views on this subject as the rabbis. But there were two important differences.

First, since their Messiah had come and ascended heavenward, leaving a promise to return and rule, they looked forward to the seventh millennium beginning not with his first coming, but with his second coming.

Second, they mostly read a different Bible with a different date of creation. The early church was divided from the beginning into two groups. There were Hebrew-Aramaic Nazarenes, mostly reading Hebrew scriptures similar to the Hebrew Bible we know. These Hebrew scriptures, which the rabbis read too, place the creation of Adam around 4,000 BC. But, within a century or so, most of the fathers were Greek speakers. They read the old Greek Bible, the Septuagint, translated in Alexandria, Egypt, in the third century BC. The Septuagint extends the life-spans of the antediluvian patriarchs by some 1,500 years. As a result it dates the creation of Adam around 5,500 BC.[1] Therefore the Greek Fathers who

[1] There are two competing dates. The Alexandrian reckoning placed the Incarnation in AM 5490 and the Byzantine reckoning placed it in AM 5509 (or 5508 after Heraklius). They therefore expected the sixth millennium to begin in AD 490 or 508/9 respectively. See de Lange 2007:274–284 for more on the year AD 500 in Byzantine hopes.

dominated the early church felt they would not have long to wait for the seventh millennium. For according to the Septuagint, it would begin around AD 500, This is a hope we find expressed repeatedly in their writings.

Since the majority of Christians outside Palestine spoke Greek, this Septuagint date of creation ruled the early church until Jerome translated the Hebrew scriptures into Latin in the late fourth century. In time, this Latin Vulgate translation became known among the Latin church leaders and they began to adjust their date of creation accordingly. However, the Greek-speaking churches continue to use the Septuagint date of creation to this day.

So now we turn to see what the fathers, Greek-speaking or otherwise, have to say on the subject of the millennial week.

PAPIAS

Papias, bishop of Hierapolis, was born in the mid-first century in south-western Anatolia. As Irenaeus, Eusebius, and Jerome relate, he was a disciple of the Apostle John and a contemporary of the daughters of Philip the Evangelist, with whom he had conversed; he had also learned the teaching of the apostles Andrew, Peter, Philip, Thomas, James, and Matthew, from their disciples.[2] Papias wrote a tractate called an *Exposition of the Sayings of the Lord*, of which fragments survive in the writings of Irenaeus and Eusebius.

Now Eusebius was a staunch opponent of millennial teaching, and no admirer of Papias. But he describes Papias's views as follows:

> He says there will be a millennium after the resurrection of the dead, and that there will be a bodily reign of Christ upon this very earth. (History 3.39.11–12)

Jerome, another non-fan of Papias, describes his views in the same way.

> This Papias is said to have promulgated the Jewish tradition of a millennium, and he is followed by Irenaeus, Apollinarius and the others, who say that after the resurrection the Lord will reign in the flesh with the saints. (Illustrious Men 18.)

A later source, Anastasios of Sinai, in the seventh century, says that Papias taught that the six days of creation imply a millennial week.

[2] Irenaeus, Against Heresies 5.33.4; Eusebius, History 3.39; Jerome, Illustrious Men 18.

> Taking occasion from Papias of Hierapolis, the illustrious, a disciple of the apostle who leaned on the bosom of Christ, and Clemens, and Pantaenus the priest of the Alexandrians, and the wise Ammonius, the ancient and first expositors, who agreed with each other, who understood the work of the six days [of creation] as referring to Christ and the whole Church.[3]

Irenaeus cites Papias's *Exposition of the Sayings of the Lord*, describing the wonders of the millennial age.[4]

> The predicted blessing certainly belongs to the times of the kingdom, when the righteous shall rule when they rise from the dead. Then the creation, renovated and set free, shall bear fruit abundantly with all kinds of food, from the dew of heaven, and from the fertility of the earth: as the elders [*ie*, Papias and Polycarp] who saw John, the disciple of the Lord, related that they had heard from him how the Lord used to teach in regard to these times, and say: The days will come, in which vines shall grow, each having ten thousand branches, and in each branch ten thousand twigs, and in each true twig ten thousand shoots, and in each one of the shoots ten thousand clusters, and on every one of the clusters ten thousand grapes, and every grape when pressed will give five and twenty metretes of wine. And when any one of the saints shall lay hold of a cluster, another shall cry out, "I am a better cluster, take me; bless the Lord through me." In like manner [the Lord declared] that a grain of wheat would produce ten thousand ears, and that every ear should have ten thousand grains, and every grain would yield ten pounds of clear, pure, fine flour; and that all other fruit-bearing trees, and seeds and grass, would produce in similar proportions; and that all animals, eating [only] the produce of the earth, should become peaceful and harmonious among each other, and be in perfect subjection to man.
>
> And these things are borne witness to in writing by Papias, the hearer of John and companion of Polycarp, in his fourth book; for there were five books compiled by him. And he says in addition, Now these things are credible to believers. And he says that when the traitor Judas did not believe them, and put the question, "How then can things about to bring forth so abundantly be wrought by the Lord?" the Lord declared, "Those who shall come to these [times] shall see." (Irenaeus, Against Heresies 5.33.3–4)

[3] Papias, fragment IX. Roberts and Donaldson, *ANCL*, 1.447.

[4] Papias's language about the abundance of the grape vine resembles 2 Baruch 29:5 which is usually said to date from the late first or early second century, that is, from the time of Papias himself. Both may draw from a common source, perhaps from a saying of Jesus.

Justin Martyr

Justin Martyr (c. 100–165) wrote his *Dialogue with Trypho the Judean* as the record of his discourse with an eminent rabbi – perhaps Rabbi Tarfon HaKohen – which took place in Ephesus where they had fled from the Roman purge following the Second Jewish Revolt in AD 132. The debate therefore took place around AD 135 and was written down by Justin some years later. Justin admits to Trypho that there are some 'so-called' Christians who deny the resurrection and the messianic age and teach instead that their souls will ascend to heaven. But, he says, Trypho should not consider these to be true Christians. All orthodox Christians, he insists, believe in a millennial kingdom in the city of Jerusalem.

> For even if you yourselves have ever met with some so-called Christians, who yet do not acknowledge this – but even dare to blaspheme the God of Abraham, and the God of Isaac, and the God of Jacob – who say that there is no resurrection of the dead, but that their souls ascend to heaven at the very moment of their death, do not suppose that they are Christians, any more than if one examined the matter rightly he would acknowledge as Jews those who are Sadducees, or similar sects of Genistae, and Meristae, and Galileans, and Hellenians, and Pharisees, and Baptizers (pray, do not be vexed with me as I say all I think), but that though called Jews and children of Abraham, and acknowledging God with their lips, as God himself has proclaimed, yet their heart is far from him. But I, and all other entirely orthodox Christians, know that there will be a resurrection of the flesh, and also a thousand years in a Jerusalem built up and adorned and enlarged, as the prophets Ezekiel and Isaiah, and all the rest, acknowledge. (Dialogue §80)

Justin quotes the Septuagint text of Isaiah 65:22: *For as the days of the tree of life shall be the days of my people.* Isaiah, he says, is pointing to Adam's death which occurred less than 1,000 years after eating of the other tree, the Tree of the Knowledge of Good Evil. But the Tree of Life would have allowed him to live at least 1,000 years. Thus a day with the Lord is one thousand years. And so the Messiah shall rule a thousand years in Jerusalem and then the general resurrection shall take place.

> Now we are of the opinion, I said, that by these words, *For according to the days of the tree of life shall be the days of my people, the works of their toil shall long endure* [LXX Isa. 65:22], he means a thousand years in a mystery. For as it was said to Adam that *in the day in which* he *should eat of the tree*, in that he should die, we know that he did not fill up a thousand years. We understand also that the expression, *a day of the*

> *Lord is as a thousand years* [2 Pet. 3:8], coincides with this. And, further, a man among us named John, one of the apostles of Christ, prophesied in a revelation made to him that they who have believed our Christ will spend a thousand years in Jerusalem, and that afterwards the universal, and, in one word, eternal resurrection of all at once, will take place, and also the judgement. And this too our Lord said: *They shall neither marry, nor be given in marriage, but shall be equal to angels, being children of God (that is) of the resurrection* [Luke 20.35]. (Dialogue §81)

Irenaeus

Irenaeus (c. 130–c. 200), Bishop of Lyons in the late second century, was a disciple of Polycarp, the disciple of John the apostle. In his book, *Against Heresies*, Irenaeus spoke of the millennial week as follows.

> For in as many days as this world was made, in so many thousand years shall it be concluded. And for this reason the Scripture says: *Thus the heaven and the earth were finished, and all their adornment. And God brought to a conclusion upon the sixth day the works that he had made; and God rested upon the seventh day from all his works* [Gen. 2:2]. This is an account of the things formerly created, as also it is a prophecy of what is to come. *For the day of the Lord is as a thousand years* [2 Pet. 3.8] and in six days created things were completed. It is plain, therefore, that they will come to an end at the six-thousandth year. (5.28.2–3).

He identifies the seventh day of rest with the kingdom that Christ will establish after he defeats the Antichrist.

> But when this Antichrist shall have devastated all things in this world, he will reign for three years and six months, and sit in the temple at Jerusalem; and the Lord will come from heaven in the clouds, in the glory of the Father, sending this man [Antichrist] and those who follow him into the lake of fire; but bringing in for the righteous the times of the kingdom, that is, the rest, the hallowed seventh day; and restoring to Abraham the promised inheritance, in which kingdom the Lord declared *that many coming from the east and from the west should sit down with Abraham, Isaac, and Jacob* [Matt. 8.11]. (5.30.4)

When the Messiah returns, it is in Jerusalem that he shall reign.

> Then again, speaking of Jerusalem, and of his reigning there, Isaiah declares, *Thus says the Lord: Happy is he who has seed in Zion, and servants in Jerusalem. Behold, a righteous king shall reign, and princes shall rule with judgement* [Isa. 31:9; 32:1]. (5.34.4)

In that time, "the Lord shall remove evil men and the righteous shall multiply upon the earth" in great joy and bounty (5.34.2). He then gives many examples from scripture to prove that the resurrected dead shall live on the renewed earth. To Abraham and his seed was promised the earth, but how can he receive the earth if he dwells in a heavenly place (5.32.1)? The disciples will drink anew of the fruit of the vine, but how can they do so in heaven, for the fruit of the vine is a thing of the earth (5.33)? And he gives many other proofs of the same kind.

Irenaeus, like Justin, was opposed to certain teachers who said that the redeemed would not rise to live on the earth, but that they would pass from death to the heavens. He explains their beliefs further.

> Since, again, some who are reckoned among the orthodox go beyond the pre-arranged plan for the exaltation of the just, and are ignorant of the methods by which they are disciplined beforehand for incorruption, they thus entertain heretical opinions. For the heretics, despising the handiwork of God, and not admitting the salvation of their flesh, while they also treat the promise of God contemptuously, and pass beyond God altogether in the sentiments they form, affirm that immediately upon their death they shall pass above the heavens and the Demiurge, and go to the Mother (Achamoth) or to that Father whom they have feigned. Those persons, therefore, who disallow a resurrection affecting the whole man, and as far as in them lies remove it from the midst [of Christian belief], how can they be wondered at, if again they know nothing as to the plan of the resurrection? (5.31.1)

The false teachers that Irenaeus is opposing hold recognizably Gnostic views. They say that this lower world is the work of the Demiurge, the lower deity. Their hope of salvation is to pass from this world to the imagined higher mother or father creator deity. He suggests that these people, 'though reckoned among the orthodox' have derived their teaching from heretics, maybe Cerinthians, Marcionists or Valentinians, and have wandered into error. He then explains further the "plan for the exaltation of the just." The different stages of salvation – from this world, through the millennial kingdom, into the future – are a process by which the righteous are taught to partake in the divine nature.

> Inasmuch, therefore, as the opinions of certain are derived from heretical discourses, they are ignorant of God's dispensations, and of the mystery of the resurrection of the just, and of the kingdom which is the commencement of incorruption, by means of which kingdom those who shall be worthy are accustomed gradually to partake of the divine nature. And

> it is necessary to tell them concerning those things, that the righteous must first receive the promised inheritance which God promised to the fathers, and reign in it, when they rise again to behold God in this creation which is renewed. And then the judgement shall take place afterwards. (5.32.1)

Irenaeus says, then, that the seventh millennium will be the kingdom inaugurated by the Lord at his coming, when he shall appear to destroy the brief rule of the Antichrist and rule from Jerusalem to fulfil his promise that the righteous shall reign on the earth. This millennial reign is an intermediate period in which the righteous are prepared for fuller participation in the divine nature. He says, like Justin, that this is traditional Christian orthodoxy and that any other view is heretical.

Clement of Alexandria

Clement of Alexandria (150–215) was Origen's tutor in the Catechetical School at Alexandria. Like Origen, he was committed to reconciling the Christian faith with Platonism. But unlike Origen, Clement saw the history of the world as being in seven ages. Speaking of the Levitical priest who had to purify himself seven days for attending to his dead near-relative, he compares this to "the seven days, the period in which creation was consummated" and to "the time…which through the seven enumerated ages (*periodôn*) returns to the chiefest rest." (Stromata 4.25)

Tertullian

Tertullian (160-220), born in Carthage in modern Tunisia, and educated in Rome, was converted to Christianity in his forties. He taught about the millennial kingdom in his treatise, written around AD 208, against the Gnostic heretic Marcion. In it, he speaks of a kingdom on earth "before heaven," that is, before the saints ascend to live in the heavens. This earthly kingdom will begin at the resurrection and will last for a thousand years in the divinely-built city of Jerusalem here on earth.

> But we do confess that a kingdom is promised to us upon the earth, but before heaven, only in another state of existence; inasmuch as it will be after the resurrection for a thousand years in the divinely-built city of Jerusalem, let down from heaven [Rev. 21:2] which the apostle also calls *our mother from above* [Gal. 4:26]. And, saying that our *politeuma*, or

citizenship, is in heaven [Phil. 3:20] he means that it is really a heavenly city. Ezekiel knew of this [Ezek. 48:30–35] and the Apostle John beheld it [Rev. 21:10–23].

> We say that this city has been provided by God for receiving the saints on their resurrection, and refreshing them with the abundance of all truly spiritual blessings, as a recompense for those which in the world we have either despised or lost; since it is both just and God-worthy that his servants should have their joy in the place where they have also suffered affliction for his name's sake. (Against Marcion 3:25)

During the millennium, the saints will be resurrected in order, according to their worth. At the end of the millennium, the world will be destroyed in fire, and the righteous will be transformed into the substance of angels and will inherit the heavens.

> Of the heavenly kingdom this is the process. After its thousand years are over, within which period is completed the resurrection of the saints, who rise sooner or later according to their deserts, there will ensue the destruction of the world and the conflagration of all things at the judgement. We shall then be changed in a moment into the substance of angels, even by the investiture of an incorruptible nature, and so be removed to that kingdom in heaven of which we have been speaking…
>
> What appears to be probable to you, when Abraham's seed, after the primal promise of being like the sand of the sea for multitude, is destined likewise to equality with the stars of heaven? [Gen. 22:17] Are not these indications both of an earthly and a heavenly actuality? When Isaac, in blessing his son Jacob, says, God give you of the dew of heaven, and the fatness of the earth [Gen. 27.28], are there not in his words examples of both kinds of blessing? Indeed, the very form of the blessing is in this instance worthy of notice. For in relation to Jacob, who is the type of the later and more excellent people, that is to say ourselves [the Christian church], first comes the promise of the heavenly dew, and after that of the fatness of the earth. So are we first invited to heavenly blessings when we are separated from the world, and after we find ourselves obtaining earthly blessings also. (Against Marcion 3.24)

Therefore Tertullian, like Irenaeus, sees the earthly millennium as a preparatory period for the saints until their exaltation to the heavenly city after the millennial kingdom.

Africanus

Sextus Julius Africanus (c. 160–240) was a Christian chronographer and historian who was born in Jerusalem. He wrote his *Chronography*, a history of the world, in the early second century. In it, he calculates, from the Septuagint date of creation, that Jesus was born after 5,500 years of the world's history.

> For why should I speak of the three myriad years of the Phœnicians, or of the follies of the Chaldeans, their forty-eight myriads? For the Jews, deriving their origin from them as sons of Abraham, having been taught a modest mind, and one such as becomes men, together with the truth by the spirit of Moses, have handed down to us, by their extant Hebrew histories, the number of 5,500 years as the period up to the advent of the Word of salvation, that was announced to the world in the time of the sway of the Cæsars. (*Chronography,* Frag. 1)

Admittedly, Africanus does not say that the messianic age is to begin after 6,000 years. But it is likely that he shared this view with the other Fathers who counted the ages according to the Septuagint chronology.

Hippolytus of Rome

Hippolytus (c. 165–236) was bishop of Rome in the early third century. According to Photius, he was a disciple of Irenaeus and acquainted with Origen.[5] In 234, Hippolytus wrote a *Chronicon* or world-history where he says there will be six thousand years until the thousand-year Sabbath, which is the fulfilment of the type of the regular weekly Sabbath.

> 4. For as the times are counted from the foundation of the world, and reckoned from Adam, they set clearly before us the matter with which our inquiry deals. For the first appearance of our Lord in the flesh took place in Bethlehem, under Augustus, in the year 5,500; and He suffered in the thirty-third year. Six thousand years must be completed in order that the Sabbath may come, the rest, the holy day *on which God rested from all his works* (Gen. 2:2). For the Sabbath is the type and emblem of the future kingdom of the saints, when they *shall reign with Christ*, when he comes from heaven, as John says in his Apocalypse. For *a day with the Lord is as a thousand years* (2 Pet. 3:8). Since, then, in six days God made all things, it follows that six thousand years must be fulfilled. And they are not yet fulfilled, as John says: *Five are fallen; one is,* that is, the sixth; *the other is not yet come* (Rev. 17:10).
>
> 5. In mentioning the other, moreover, he specifies the seventh, in which there is rest. But someone may be ready to say, How will you prove to me that the Saviour was born in the year 5,500? Learn that

[5] Photius, Bibliotheca, Cod. 121.

> easily, O man; for the things that took place of old in the wilderness, under Moses, in the case of the tabernacle, were constituted types and emblems of spiritual mysteries, in order that, when the truth came in Christ in these last days, you might be able to perceive that these things were fulfilled. For he says to him, And you shall make the ark of imperishable wood, and shall overlay it with pure gold within and without; and you shall make the length of it two cubits and a half, and the breadth thereof one cubit and a half, and a cubit and a half the height; which measures, when summed up together, make five cubits and a half, so that the 5,500 years might be signified thereby.
>
> 6. At that time, then, the Saviour appeared and showed His own body to the world, (born) of the Virgin, who was the ark overlaid with pure gold, with the Word within and the Holy Spirit without; so that the truth is demonstrated, and the ark made manifest. From the birth of Christ, then, we must reckon the 500 years that remain to make up the 6,000, and thus the end shall be. (*Hexaëmeron*, Fragment 2.4, 6 on Daniel)

Hippolytus follows the Septuagint dating of creation at 5500 BC. (He is unique, as far as I know, in seeing this date prefigured in the dimensions of the ark.) Writing in AD 234, he therefore believed the messianic age was due to appear some two hundred and sixty-six years after his own time.

Nepos of Arsinoë

Nepos, Bishop of Arsinoë (Faiyum) in Egypt, wrote a book, in the mid-third century, called *Refutation of the Allegorists*, defending millenarian teaching against the Origenists. Nepos's work is lost. But from Eusebius we know that Nepos argued for the literal sense of the millennial kingdom in the Revelation, and that all the brethren in the district of Arsinoë adhered to his views. Eusebius relates how, after Nepos's death, Pope Dionysius of Alexandria travelled to Arsinoë, 300 kilometres south, to hold a three-day conference with the presbyters of Arsinoë to dissuade them of Nepos's views (History 7.24). Dionysius was, by his own account, mild in his reproach, out of respect not only for the presbyters, but also for Nepos, whom he regarded as a worthy scholar and hymn writer. Initially, the presbyters of Arsinoë would have none of it and repeatedly cited Nepos's book to refute Dionysius's arguments. Schism loomed. But, at length, says Dionysius, he persuaded one of their leaders, Coracion, to leave off Nepos's teachings, and the others duly followed.

Dionysius then returned to his palace and wrote a two-volume work,

On the Promises, in which he recounts how he persuaded the men of Arsinoë to toe the line. He lays out the arguments he presented to them, namely that the Revelation was written not by John the Apostle but by one John the Presbyter, and that the idea of a millennium of delights sprang from the carnal delusions of the heresiarch Cerinthus.

Commodianus, Victorinus, Methodius

Commodianus the poet (c. 200–270) speaks of the millennium in his great didactic poem, *Instructiones:*[6]

> After a thousand years the nations are delivered to Gehenna, and he who made them what they were [*ie,* Satan] is burnt up with them (§42).
>
> They shall come also those who overcame cruel martyrdom under Antichrist. And they will live for all time and receive blessings, because they suffered evils. And for a thousand years they will marry and beget [children]... The evil man is imprisoned in torment because of the righteous; but God will take away all evils from the thousand years (§43).

Victorinus of Pettau (d. 304) was also a chiliast, according to Jerome. Confirmation of this can be seen in his short commentary on the creation, where he writes: "The true Sabbath will be in the seventh millennium of years, when Christ will reign with his elect." Yet it seems that later, as opinion swung away from the millennium, he changed his mind. Perhaps he had been reading Dionysius's *On the Promises,* for his commentary on Revelation 20 blames Cerinthus for the millennium.

> Therefore they are not to be heard who assure themselves that there is to be an earthly reign of a thousand years; who think, that is to say, with the heretic Cerinthus. For the kingdom of Christ is now eternal in the saints, although the glory of the saints shall be manifested after the resurrection.

It is perhaps the millennial teaching in his earlier works which explains the disappearance of most of them, censored either by his own hand or by others.

Methodius (d. 311), Bishop of Olympus in the early fourth century, was Platonist enough in some of his ideas, especially on celibacy. But he opposed Origen's rejection of the millennium, and continued to advocate it. In his *Symposion* or *Banquet of the Ten Virgins,* he wrote:

[6] Some versions number these sections as §43 and 44. The text will be found in 41–44, of Migne, *PL* 5:231f.

> When this world will be terminated at the seventh thousand years, when God shall have completed the world, he shall rejoice in us. (9:1)

He sees the seventh age foreshadowed in the seventh-month Feast of Tabernacles. On this basis, he expects believers to live a life of 1,000 years in the "bodily tabernacle" – that is, in bodily form – in the true Sabbath of the millennial kingdom, after which they will be raised to heavenly dwellings.

> For I also… celebrate with Christ the millennium of rest, which is called the seventh day, even the true Sabbath. Then again from thence I, a follower of Jesus, *who hath entered into the heavens* (Heb. 4:14)…not continuing to dwell in tabernacles – that is, my body not remaining as it was before – but, after the space of a thousand years, changed from a human and corruptible form into angelic size and beauty. (9:5)

Lactantius

Lucius Caecilius Firmianus (250–325), dubbed Lactantius for his milk-sweet orations, was a Latin rhetor at the Byzantine court, an adviser to the Emperor Constantine and tutor of his son, Crispus. His systematic theology, *Divine Institutes*, was inscribed to, and studied by, the Emperor himself. In it, Lactantius writes at length about the Sabbath millennium.

> Let the philosophers, who enumerate thousands of ages from the beginning of the world, know that the six-thousandth year is not yet completed, and that when this number is completed the consummation must take place, and the condition of human affairs be remodelled for the better, the proof of which must first be related, that the matter itself may be plain. God completed the world and this admirable work of nature in the space of six days, as is contained in the secrets of Holy Scripture, and consecrated the seventh day, on which he had rested from his works. But this is the Sabbath day, which in the language of the Hebrews received its name from the number, whence the seventh is the legitimate and complete number. For there are seven days, by the revolutions of which in order the circles of years are made up; and there are seven stars which do not set, and seven luminaries which are called planets, whose differing and unequal movements are believed to cause the varieties of circumstances and times.
>
> Therefore, since all the works of God were completed in six days, the world must continue in its present state through six ages, that is, six thousand years. For the great day of God is limited by a circle of a thousand years, as the prophet shows, who says, *In your sight, O Lord, a thousand*

> *years are as one day* [Ps. 90:4]. And as God laboured during those six days in creating such great works, so his religion and truth must labour during these six thousand years, while wickedness prevails and bears rule. And again, since God, having finished his works, rested the seventh day and blessed it, at the end of the six-thousandth year all wickedness must be abolished from the earth, and righteousness reign for a thousand years; and there must be tranquility and rest from the labours which the world now has long endured. (*Institutes* 7:14)

He holds to a date of creation in 5,500 BC and expects the seventh millennium to begin around AD 500. (He would have calculated this from the Septuagint or one of the Old Latin translations.)

> I have already shown above, that when six thousand years shall be completed this change must take place, and that the last day of the extreme conclusion is now drawing near… Those teach, who have written respecting the times, collecting them from the sacred writings and from various histories, how great is the number of years from the beginning of the world. And although they vary, and the amount of the number as reckoned by them differs considerably, yet all expectation does not exceed the limit of two hundred years. (*Institutes* 7:25)

When the thousand years begin, the righteous will be raised to life.

> The dead will rise again, not after a thousand years from their death, but that, when again restored to life, they may reign with God a thousand years. For God will come, that, having cleansed the world from all defilement, he may restore the souls of the righteous to their renewed bodies, and raise them to everlasting blessedness. (*Institutes* 7:22)

The Son of God will come and set up his kingdom, where the risen righteous shall rule over the surviving mortals.

> The Son of the most high and mighty God shall come to judge the quick and the dead, as the Sibyl testifies and says: *For then there shall be confusion of mortals throughout the whole earth, when the Almighty himself shall come on His judgement-seat to judge the souls of the quick and dead, and all the world.*
>
> But he, when he shall have destroyed unrighteousness, and executed his great judgement, and shall have recalled to life the righteous, who have lived from the beginning, he will live among men a thousand years, and will rule them with perfect justice. Which the Sibyl proclaims in another place, as she utters her inspired predictions: *Hear me, you mortals; an everlasting King reigns.*
>
> Then they who shall be alive in their bodies shall not die, but during

> those thousand years shall produce an infinite multitude [of children], and their offspring shall be holy, and beloved by God; but they who shall be raised from the dead shall preside over the living as judges. (9:24)

Then, at the end of the millennium, there will be a revolt against the Messiah's reign, as is said of Gog and Magog in Revelation 20:2–9.

> At the beginning of the sacred reign, the prince of the devils will be bound by God. But when the thousand years of the kingdom, that is, seven thousand of the world, shall come to an end, he will be released again. Coming from his prison, he will go and gather all the nations, which shall then be under the dominion of the righteous, that they may make war against the holy city. An innumerable company of the nations shall gather together from all the world and besiege and surround the city. Then the final anger of God shall come upon the nations, and utterly destroy them. (*Institutes* 7.26)

He equates this revolt with Gog and Magog's invasion of the land of Israel, described in Ezekiel 38, where the fallen army's weapons shall provide fuel for seven years.

> The mountains shall be filled with carcasses, and the plains shall be covered with bones; but the people of God during those three days shall be concealed under caves of the earth, until the anger of God against the nations and the last judgement shall be ended.
>
> Then the righteous shall go forth from their hiding-places, and shall find all things covered with carcasses and bones. But the whole race of the wicked shall utterly perish; and there shall no longer be any nation in this world, but the nation of God alone. Then for seven continuous years the woods shall be untouched, nor shall timber be cut from the mountains, but the weapons of the nations shall be burnt; and now there shall be no war, but peace and everlasting rest. (*Institutes* 7:26)

Lactantius was the last great advocate of millenarian belief. Yet his views were already becoming eclipsed in his own time. And it was two fourth-century bishops who hastened the downfall of millenarianism.

Marcellus and Apollinaris

In the mid-fourth century, Marcellus of Ancyra (d. 374) became known for teaching that the kingdom of Christ "would have an end," by which he meant that Christ's kingdom would end after his millennial reign on earth. This in itself was not heresy; it was simply millenarianism. But

Marcellus was also an eager opponent of Arianism. So eager, in fact, was he to stress the divinity of Jesus that he overstepped the mark and taught a form of Modalism; that is, that the Father, Son, and Spirit are not three different Persons but three different modes of operation of the one God. Thus he taught that God was originally one Being, but at Creation the Logos and the Holy Spirit went forth from the Godhead, making the Trinity; yet, at the consummation, the Logos and the Spirit will return to the Father, and the Godhead will again become an undivided unity; then the kingdom of Christ would have its end, for the Christ would cease to exist as a separate Being. For this teaching, Marcellus was deposed by the First Council of Constantinople in AD 336. And millenarianism, already waning in popularity, became tainted by association with him.

Apollinaris, Bishop of Laodicea (d. 382) was another opponent of Arianism whose zeal led him over the line of orthodoxy. He taught that Jesus did not have a rational human soul, but that his soul was replaced by the Logos. This implied that the Logos, in the man Jesus, had not assumed human nature in its entirety. This in turn implied a form of Docetism; that is, the view that Jesus was not truly human but only human in appearance. Full-blown Docetism had already been rejected by the Council of Nicaea in AD 325 on the basis that Jesus could not save mankind if he were not truly a man. So Apollinaris's modified Docetism was duly condemned by the Second Council of Constantinople in AD 381. Apollinaris, however, is said to have been a millenarian. His writings on the subject are lost. But Basil of Caesarea, Epiphanius, and Jerome all testify to his beliefs in this matter.[7] And so, as with Marcellus, millenarian views were again tainted by association with heresy.

THE END OF CHILIASM

Two millenarian timetables were yet to appear. In 397, Quintus Julius Hilarianus wrote his *Chronology or Book Concerning the Duration of the World.* In it, he relates that the age will endure six thousand years. Then, following the Septuagint date of creation, the end of these ages will occur in 498, when Christ will establish his kingdom and rule for 1,000 years.

A few years later, around 404, Sulpicius Severus of Aquitaine, a disciple of Martin of Tours, published his *Chronica* of the world. He says

[7] Basil, Epist. 263:4; Epiphanius, Haeres. 70:36; Jerome on Isa. 18; *De vir. ill.* 18.

that God created the world nearly 6,000 years ago and he expects the current age soon to give way to the kingdom of Christ, as foretold in Daniel's interpretation of Nebuchadnezzar's dream (1:2; 2:3).

These two chronographers mark the end of the period of millenarian belief, which was already largely displaced by the teachings of Origen, Jerome, and Augustine. And from this time on, the millennial kingdom found no champion among the theologians of the western church.

WERE THE ANTE-NICENE FATHERS REALLY MILLENARIAN?

It has been long acknowledged that the early Fathers held to millenarian beliefs.[8] Yet, recently, some defenders of the magisterium – the traditional Augustinian teaching of the Roman Church and its Protestant successors – have argued otherwise. They propose that the millenarianism of the early Fathers has been overstated. In reality, they say, non-millenarian views were also widespread and were also recognized as orthodox.

The foremost champion of this view is Charles Hill.[9] Hill, it should be noted, was Professor of New Testament at the Reformed Theological Seminary, a body which subscribes fully to Augustinian and Calvinist amillennialism. He points out, rightly enough, that Justin and Irenaeus recognized that there were those in their time who did not accept millenarian beliefs. But he suggests that Justin and Irenaeus accepted such views as orthodox. But that is simply not true. Justin said:

> For even if you yourselves have ever met with some *so-called* Christians, who yet do not acknowledge this – but even dare to blaspheme the God of Abraham, and the God of Isaac, and the God of Jacob – who say that there is no resurrection of the dead, but that their souls ascend to heaven at the very moment of their death, *do not suppose that they are Christians.* (Dial. Try. §80; my italics)

And Irenaeus says of non-chiliasts:

> Since, again, some who are *reckoned among the orthodox* go beyond the pre-arranged plan for the exaltation of the just, and are ignorant of the methods by which they are disciplined beforehand for incorruption, they thus entertain heretical opinions. (*Against Heresies* 5.31.1; my italics)

[8] See Fairbairn in Blomberg and Chung 2009: 110–13.
[9] Hill: 2001.

Irenaeus further stresses that such heretical teachers should be correctly instructed that there must first be a kingdom in this world.

> It is necessary to tell them concerning those things, that the righteous must first receive the promised inheritance which God promised to the fathers. (*Against Heresies* 5.32.1)

Likewise, Lactantius states that belief in the millennial kingdom "is the doctrine of the holy prophets, which we Christians follow." (*Institutes* 7:26)

Hill further suggests that chiliasm imploded because of a fatal tension between New Testament teaching on the blessed afterlife and standard millenarian belief, as he sees it, of the soul dwelling in Hades until the first resurrection. He concludes: "Christian hope of union and fellowship with Christ after death was too strong for the chiliastic eschatology to flourish ever again in its original form."[10]

Of course, the New Testament does speak of a place of happiness for the righteous immediately after death (Luke 24:43; Phil. 1:23). So do the Fathers. Yet they do not call this place Hades.

Clement of Rome taught that, after death, the apostle Peter went to "his appointed place of glory" and Paul "unto the holy place" (1 Clem. 4:5–6). And all the righteous shall go to a place prepared for them.

> All the generations from Adam unto this day have passed away: but they that by God's grace were perfected in love dwell in the abode of the pious; and they shall be made manifest in the visitation of the rule of God. For it is written, *Enter your chambers for a very little while until my anger and my wrath shall pass away* (Isa. 26:20) and I will remember a good day and will raise you from your tombs. (1 Clem. 50:2–3)

Tertullian, speaking of the parable of the rich man and Lazarus in Luke 16, emphasizes the "great gulf" fixed between *inferus* (the lower region, or Hades) and the abode of the righteous in Abraham's Bosom. For the rich man had to lift up his eyes through "a vast immensity" to behold Lazarus. And therefore Lazarus was not in Hades but in quite a different region.

> "Hades," I take it, means one thing, and "Abraham's bosom" another… This region, therefore, I call Abraham's Bosom. Although it is not in heaven, it is yet higher than Hades, and is appointed to afford an interval of rest to the souls of the righteous, until the consummation of all things

[10] Hill 2015.

> shall complete the resurrection of all men with the full recompense of their reward. (*Against Marcion* 34:11:13)

Hippolytus of Rome speaks of how the righteous, at death, are led away from the darkness of Hades to a place of light, called Abraham's Bosom.

> The just are guided to the right hand, and are led with hymns, sung by the angels appointed over that place, unto a region of light, in which the just have dwelt from the beginning of the world...with whom there is no place of toil, no burning heat, no piercing cold, nor are any briers there; but the countenance of the fathers and of the just, which they see always, smiles upon them, while they wait for that rest and eternal new life in heaven, which is to succeed this region. This place we call the Bosom of Abraham. (*Discourse to the Greeks Concerning Hades* 3)[11]

Irenaeus rejects the idea that the righteous at death go immediately to the heavens. But he doesn't say they go to Hades. Instead, like Lazarus, they go to Abraham's bosom.

> The Lord has taught with very great fullness...in that narrative which is recorded respecting the rich man and that Lazarus who found repose in the bosom of Abraham...that each class [of souls] receives a habitation such as it has deserved, even before the judgement. (*Against Heresies* 2.34.1).

And, again, the souls of disciples shall go to a place allotted to them by God, there to await the resurrection.

> For just as the Lord went into the midst of the shadow of death, where the souls of the dead were, yet afterwards arose in the body, and after the resurrection was taken up, it is clear that the souls of his disciples also, upon whose account the Lord underwent these things, shall go away into the invisible place allotted to them by God, and there remain until the resurrection, awaiting that event; then receiving their bodies, and rising in their entirety, that is bodily, just as the Lord arose, they shall come thus into the presence of God (*Against Heresies* 5.31.2).

In other words, the early Fathers saw no tension between the scriptures and their millenarian beliefs. They did not think the righteous awaited the resurrection in Hades. Rather, they departed to Abraham's Bosom or Paradise until the resurrection of the body in a renewed earthly kingdom.

Other opponents of millenarian belief argue that millenarianism was condemned by the Church Councils, either of Constantinople (381) or

[11] The *Discourse to the Greeks Concerning Hades* was formerly attributed to Josephus. It is now believed to be the work of Hippolytus.

Ephesus (431). But not only do the texts of those councils not condemn belief in the millennium, there is, in fact, not one hint that the millennium ever arose as a topic of discussion in those councils, or in any other.[12] The Councils of Constantinople did condemn Marcellus and Apollinaris, but it was for their Christology, not their millenarianism.

SUMMARY

The majority of Church Fathers until the Council of Nicaea, and some after it, believed that the current world-age would last six millennia and be succeeded by a Sabbath millennium when the Messiah would reign on earth. Among them were Barnabas, Papias, Justin, Irenaeus, Clement of Alexandria, Tertullian, Africanus, Hippolytus, Nepos, Commodianus, Victorinus, Methodius, Lactantius, Quintus Julius Hilarianus, and Sulpicius Severus. The foremost of them – Justin, Irenaeus, and Lactantius – regard belief in the Sabbath millennium as an essential part of orthodox belief. Marcellus of Ancyra and Apollinaris of Laodicea held to the same doctrine, but were condemned for trespassing the bounds of orthodoxy in regard to their beliefs about the nature of the Son.

Even Jerome, no millenarian, admits the primacy of millenarian faith. Of condemned Apollinaris, he says, "Not only men of his own sect, but also a very great multitude of our people follow him in this point only" (i.e., in his millenarianism, not his heresy); and again, "Such beliefs we hold not, yet neither do we condemn them, because a multitude of churchmen, and even martyrs, have spoken them."[13]

Church historians too have long recognized this. Philip Schaff wrote,

> The most striking point in the eschatology of the Ante-Nicene age is the prominent chiliasm, or millenarianism, that is, the belief of a visible reign of Christ in glory on earth with the risen saints for a thousand years, before the general resurrection and judgement. It was indeed not the doctrine of the church embodied in any creed or form of devotion, but a widely current opinion of distinguished teachers, such as Barnabas, Papias, Justin Martyr, Irenaeus, Tertullian, Methodius, and Lactantius.[14]

[12] Lacunza (tr. Irving) 1827: 1.61–65 is eloquent on this matter of millenarianism never being condemned by any Church Council. See too Gumerlock 2004: 83–95.
[13] Jerome on Isa. 18; Jer. 19.
[14] Schaff, 2:614.

Likewise, Adolf Harnack said,

> That a philosopher like Justin, with a bias toward the Hellenic construction of the Christian religion, should nevertheless have accepted its chiliastic elements, is the strongest proof that these enthusiastic expectations were inseparably bound up with the Christian faith down to the middle of the 2d century.[15]

These millenarian views of the early church can be summarized in the following stages.

1. This age will last 6,000 years from the creation of Adam to its end.
2. At its end, Antichrist will arise and rule for three and a half years.
3. Jesus will return in majesty and slay the Antichrist.
4. He will raise the righteous dead and catch up the living saints in the first resurrection.
5. He will judge among the nations and bring peace. His kingdom will last a thousand years, throughout the seventh millennium.
6. At the end of that millennium, the rest of humanity will be raised to judgement, reward or punishment, in the second resurrection.
7. There will be a new age, a new heaven and a new earth.

Drawing as they do from the same ancient Israelite spring, it is no surprise that patristic millenarian views resemble rabbinic views in many ways. But, as said, they differ in some particulars. First the rabbis looked for the first coming of the Messiah, while the Fathers looked for his second coming. Second, the rabbis, following their Hebrew scriptures, dated creation to around 4,000 BC, but the Fathers, with their Greek scriptures, placed creation around 5,500 BC. Third, the rabbis hoped for an exalted place for the Jewish people in the millennial kingdom. But the Fathers did not, seeing in the destruction of Jerusalem and its temple in AD 70 the punishment and final rejection of the Jews for their unbelief. Thus Tertullian rejects any notion of the revival of Jewish statehood and applies Bible prophecies of Israel's resurgence to the church.

> As for the restoration of Judea, however, which even the Jews themselves, induced by the names of the places and countries, hope for just as it is described, it would be tedious to state at length how the figurative interpretation is spiritually applicable to Christ and his church. (Against Marcion 3:25)

In this, the Fathers differed from many modern premillennialists who,

[15] Harnack, *Encyc. Brit.* 9th ed. 16:316.

beginning with Joseph Mede in the seventeenth century, see an end-time restoration of the Jews foretold, either in their conversion, or in the re-establishment of a Jewish state.

Irenaeus, Tertullian, and Lactantius all speak of a greater, heavenly age which will follow the millennial kingdom, an age equal to the eighth millennium of 2 Enoch and the *Olam HaBa* (Age to Come) of rabbinic literature. They therefore see the millennium as a preparatory period to train the righteous for the greater age to come. Irenaeus says that even the Jerusalem of the millennial age is but an image of the one which is to descend thereafter (Against Heresies 5.35.2).

Some Fathers add yet further details to the millenarian schema. Irenaeus, Commodianus, and Lactantius speak not only of earthly fruitfulness but of human marriage and reproduction during the millennium, ideas they drew from Isaiah 65:17–25. In this matter, their views seem to have differed little from those of Cerinthus.

So deeply embedded was the idea of the millennial week in the thought of the early church that even Augustine, when he replaced the earthly reign of the Christ with a heavenly kingdom, still subscribed to the idea that the heavenly kingdom would follow after six millennia of creation. To this heavenly kingdom we now turn.

10

The Rise of Amillennialism

JUST as the third century dawned, another view began to emerge. This looked not for a coming millennial kingdom on earth, but rather expected the present age, the church age, to last one millennium. In this millennial church age, the Lord would call the souls of believers to heaven through death, until, at his second coming, he would judge the world and destroy it completely. This view – which denies that the Messiah will return and rule on earth for a thousand years – is now called 'Amillennialism.'

The seeds of this view lay, as we shall see, in Greek thought. There were evidently some who held such views even in the second century, when Justin Martyr spoke of "some who are called Christians who say there is no resurrection of the dead, and that their souls, when they die, are taken to heaven" (Trypho 80). In the early third century, Gaius, a Roman presbyter who rejected the writings of the apostle John, denounced the millenarianism of the equally-heretical Cerinthus (Eusebius, History 3.28). It was this Gaius who prompted Hippolytus's defence of the six ages of creation which we saw in the previous chapter. However, the most ardent adversaries of the millennium were yet arising. We turn now to their story.

The Catechetical School of Alexandria

Alexandria, at the mouth of the Nile, was the greatest city of Hellenic civilization. Greek in culture and in language, and of huge population, its famed library and *museon* made it the international epicentre of wisdom and learning. A place of astronomers, geographers, poets, historians, mathematicians, philosophers, and physicians, it was a proud city: proud of its learning and culture, its influence and wealth, and its multicultural mix of Egyptian, Greek, Roman, and Jewish civilization.

Its million-strong Jewish community was as remarkable as anything in the city. It grew in the rich ground of two quite different cultures: Jewish monotheism and Greek rationalism. From the first, it inherited the revealed Scriptures, Torah observance, and Jewish ethnic identity. From the second, it inherited the Greek philosophic and aesthetic tradition with its emphasis on individual action and thought. Alexandrian Jews felt little tension between these two extremes. They were as proud of their Jewish heritage as of their Greek culture, and they creatively modernized and applied their scripture and tradition to their environment. In the third century BC they produced the first ever complete translation of the Hebrew scriptures, the Greek Septuagint Bible. Their philosophers, Aristobulus and then Philo, expounded Hebrew scripture and tradition in terms of Pythagorean and Platonic philosophy.

It was in this great city that Mark the Evangelist, himself a Jew of north African birth, arrived in the middle of the first century. There he set up a catechetical school, the first theological institute of the ancient world. By the second century, this school was teaching not only Christian scripture and theology, but also philosophy, mathematics, medicine, rhetoric, and logic. In the latter part of the second century, it flourished greatly under the direction of Pantaenus (*fl.* 170–200), a converted philosopher deeply-versed in Platonism, Stoicism, and Judaism. Pantaenus was succeeded by his student, Clement, another converted philosopher. The goal of Pantaenus and Clement was to glean the good from the various systems of belief – Egyptian, Jewish, Pythagorean, Platonic, and now Christian. They taught that, just as the law of Moses was given to prepare the Jews for the gospel, so philosophy was given to prepare the Greeks. Hence their teaching sought to express the Christian faith in Greek philosophical terms.

But translating the Christian faith from Hebrew to Greco-Roman culture was not straightforward. There were major differences in the two world-views. And the Alexandrians' attempts to reconcile them have influenced Christian thought to this day.

The Israelite world-view saw creation as fundamentally positive. God had made the world very good (Gen. 1:31). And so Jews looked forward to the full renewal of creation in the days of the Messiah. Greek culture, on the other hand, was imbued with a deep pessimism about the created world, seeing it as a place of suffering, sickness, defilement, decay, and death. Platonism, in particular, saw this world as an unreal and corrupt shadow of a heavenly world of perfect forms. The world, its events and history, is of no consequence. Happiness was to be found only in escape from the world to the heavenly sphere of incorporeal, immortal souls. Any notion of a bodily resurrection in this world was a most unattractive proposition.

Of course, Platonism had to ask why the good God would create a bad world. By way of answer, by the late first century, it was already synthesizing not only with Christianity, but also with Zoroastrianism and Mithraism to form the potent cocktail of beliefs we now call Gnosticism. The Gnostics saw the heavenly spheres as the work of the good creator, while this lower earth was said to be the work of the Demiurge or 'craftsman' (*demiourgos*), a meaner spirit altogether. Some Gnostics identified the Demiurge with the God of the Jews and the Old Testament, and even with Satan, thus setting the New and Old Testament in stark opposition. Such a view inevitably influenced the Christian Platonists. It coloured their thoughts on the incarnation. Jesus, as representative of the higher god, could not be truly human in flesh, but only seem to be so. Thus arose docetism. It led also to a complete denigration of the material world, its relations and history – including the biblical account of creation and the history of Israel.

Meanwhile, they witnessed the low estate of the Israelite nation. The Second Jewish Revolt of AD 132 had been efficiently crushed by Roman legions. The surviving Judeans had been banished from Jerusalem on pain of death. A few clung on in Yavneh as the small, self-appointed, Pharisaic Sanhedrin under Gamliel II. But the rest were scattered throughout the world. The Holy Land was now inhabited largely by Christians. Many of them were the descendants of Galilean Israelites whose families had been Christian for a hundred years and more, since the time of Jesus. Others, like Origen, Eusebius, and Jerome, were immigrants of Greco-pagan background. By the second century, the Fathers accepted that the Jews had been rejected by God for their rejection of Christ. This view was confirmed, in the fourth century, by the Christian conversion of the Roman Emperor. The land and city of the

Jews had been given to the Greek-speaking Christian kingdom. If there was a kingdom of God on earth, it was now in Constantine's Byzantium, with the Holy Land under the administration of Greco-Roman Christian bishops. The evangelists and apostles had spoken Greek. The Fathers therefore saw it as perfectly fitting that Christian theology should now be framed in Greek rather than Israelite language and terminology.

Origen

In the year 185, a boy called Origen was born in Alexandria to Christian parents. His father, seeing the boy's studious demeanour, provided him with a good education, sending him to the Catechetical School. When he was seventeen, a fierce local persecution broke out against the Alexandrian church. His father was imprisoned and martyred. According to Eusebius, Origen would gladly have joined him, had not his mother hidden his clothes. The family's property was confiscated and Origen began teaching to support his mother and six brothers.

When Clement retired from his post in the Catechetical School, Origen took up Clement's duties, and was confirmed in this office by the Patriarch Demetrius a year later. He devoted himself to the scriptures and to the teaching of a 'Christian philosophy.' His lecture-room increasingly attracted pagans who, converting at his teaching, became confessors and martyrs, whom Origen accompanied on the road to their bloody triumphs.

Recognizing the need to augment his education, Origen continued his studies, especially in philosophy, under Pantaenus. He then left his post as catechist and set himself up as a Christian rhetor and philosopher, teaching students who flocked to him from all over the Mediterranean world.

In these years, there arose, between Origen and his student Plotinus, a belief-system that is now called Neoplatonism, a synthesis of Platonist and Christian belief, with flavours of the ancient Egyptian afterlife. Whereas, for the Platonist, the higher world was the eternal, real world of perfect forms and ideals, for the Neoplatonist the higher world became the Kingdom of Heaven, where the souls of the righteous would ascend after death. Such ideas had been part of the background heretical noise since Justin's time, but now Origen taught them as the new orthodoxy in the Alexandrian Catechetical School.

Origen's fame grew. Young men flocked to his lectures. Young women too. Lissom, starry-eyed darlings from all over the Med, gazing up at him with unfeigned adoration. That was a distraction every day. It wasn't any easier by night. What was a man to do? Origen knew. Never one for half-measures, he called in a physician to castrate him.[1] This agreed (as he thought) with Jesus's teaching that *there are eunuchs, who have castrated themselves for the kingdom of heaven's sake. He that can receive it, let him receive it* (Matt. 19:12).

In the ancient world, populated with slaves and eunuchs, castration was a routine surgical intervention. One way was to make an incision in the scrotum, sever and remove the testes, and suture the wound. Another was to bind the scrotum with a tourniquet until blood supply ceased and the testicles atrophied and fell off. Either method was fairly safe. Of course, there was also total emasculation, the removal of all the genitalia, usually for punishment or total subservience. That was more dangerous. It is not clear which process Origen underwent, though simple castration is the more likely. Either way, he became infertile and void of sexual desire. Those lissom beauties tempted him no more. Needless to say, it was a course of action one might live to regret. And, later on, he did regret it. Even if one had no plans to marry, it had other drawbacks. But for now he resumed life in his new capacity as a eunuch.

Yet Origen's bishop Demetrius was not pleased with him. How he responded to Origen's philosophico-theological innovations is not clear, but he certainly saw Origen's popularity as a direct threat to his own authority. Meanwhile, Origen made increasing demands to be ordained as a presbyter (priest). But Demetrius was utterly opposed. And he had perfect grounds for opposition: the priesthood was closed to eunuchs (Deut. 23:2).

Now, if Anastasios of Sinai is believed, Origen's teacher Pantaenus still held to the traditional view of the millennium. So did his classmate, Ammonius. But, over time, Origen had other ideas. His Neoplatonic philosophy, the idea that earthly life is but a shadow of the higher heavenly life, had much to do with this. Yet there were other reasons too, which arose as a result of his moving to Caesarea in the Holy Land.

[1] Eusebius's account of Origen's castration (*History* 6.8) was once universally accepted. Yet modern authors dispute its veracity, seeing it as a slander put about by Demetrius to justify his refusal to ordain Origen. They say that Origen's repudiation of castration in his commentary on Matt. 19:12 means he never did any such thing. Yet it may be that he is admonishing others from following in his steps.

It was another persecution in Alexandria, in 215, which drove him to Caesarea. There he was warmly received by the bishops of Jerusalem and Caesarea, who invited him to preach in their churches even though he was not a priest. When Demetrius of Alexandria heard of this, he was furious. "Send back my catechist!" he thundered. Origen returned. But Demetrius still refused to ordain him. And so, around 231, Origen returned to the Holy Land again. And there, eunuch though he was, he was ordained by Theoctistus, bishop of Caesarea, and he stayed in that city.

In Caesarea, his influence as a teacher continued to grow. He set up there a library and a school, based on the Alexandrian model, where he expounded Christian truths through Platonic philosophy and Socratic reasoning. Again, pagans and Christians from all over the Mediterranean flocked to hear his teaching. He also began, at the relatively mature age of forty-five, to publish his first major works. The most important of these was his *On First Principles,* the first ever attempt at a systematic theology. In fact, in the twenty years from 231 to 251 he published a prodigious body of work, without parallel in patristic literature, adding up to at least 2,000 works (though Epiphanius claimed as many as 6,000). Many of these he produced by dictation, for which task he is said to have kept seven stenographers employed.[2]

In Caesarea, he also met with some who spoke of the millennial kingdom in the most unreconstructed terms. There would be, they said, masters and slaves, just as in this present age. There would be feasting and drinking. There would even be – horror! – marriage and child-bearing. It is likely that those who held such views were Nazarene Judeo-Christian groups. Such views, based on passages like Isaiah 60 and 65:17–25 and Zechariah 8:20–23, had always been part and parcel of Jewish belief about the days of the Messiah, along with the expectation that all the nations would serve the Jews. But for Origen, ascetic, celibate, world-rejecting, and non-Israelite, such views were carnality and sensualism, going against everything he believed about the spiritual life. For Judeo-Christians to claim that the despised Jews would rule over him in the age to come was intolerable.

He became an increasingly zealous opponent of the whole idea of a millennium. The gospel message of an earthly kingdom of God had to

[2] Epiphanius, *Adv. Haer.* 65.3.4, says that he was supported in this, presumably in later life, by Ambrose of Milan.

be understood spiritually and allegorically. The true kingdom would not be a material kingdom on earth, but a kingdom of souls in the heavenly realm.

Meanwhile, his vast written output and his forthright expression made his ideas extremely influential. But his rock-star status led to a growing hubris. And his torrent of words could not help but contain much at odds with, or in addition to, biblical teaching. In line with Plato, he said that the soul was immortal; individual souls had always existed and always would; all would ultimately be saved, even Satan. He said the coming of the Christ would not be in one earthly place, but that he would appear at once to all. He maintained that the Father, Son, and Spirit were three gods. He rejected any future restoration for the Jews; their conspiracy against Jesus had merited the destruction of their city and nation and the blessings offered to them had passed to the Christians.[3] He rejected any idea of this world being a good creation, and dismissed the Genesis creation narrative as mythology. He denied the earthly resurrection of the dead, saying we have our bodies temporarily as a divine punishment because of our fall in a former purely incorporeal existence, but "the need of bodies will cease. And if it ceases, bodily matter returns to nothing, as formerly also it did not exist."[4] Everything in the Bible was to be understood allegorically, through the lens of Platonism. Rightly did Jerome call him "our allegorist."

One may seek to excuse his errors on the basis that he lived before the great ecumenical councils. But, even before Nicaea, tritheism and denial of the resurrection were no acceptable part of the Christian faith. As Schaff says,

> He can by no means be called orthodox, either in the Catholic or in the Protestant sense. His leaning to idealism, his predilection for Plato, and his noble effort to reconcile Christianity with reason, and to commend it even to educated heathens and Gnostics, led him into many grand and fascinating errors.[5]

Later generations corrected some of his errors. But his notions about soul-immortality, his denial of an earthly millennium, and his teaching that the Kingdom of God was a heavenly kingdom only, these ideas stuck. And, due to the great influence of his writings, millenarianism

[3] Against Celsus, 4.22.
[4] De Principiis, 2.3.3.
[5] Schaff, *History*, II. 790.

gradually disappeared in the churches both of the east and the west. Of course, there were some, like Nepos and Lactantius, who did all they could to combat his influence. But eventually they were overwhelmed. Great changes and weighty authorities were poised to advance the amillennial cause.

THE CHRISTIAN KINGDOM

In 312, the Emperor Constantine (*r.* 306–337) became a Christian. His court historians, Eusebius and Lactantius, relate that, on the eve of the battle of Milvian Bridge, outside Rome, Constantine had a vision with the words *In hoc signo vinces* (In this sign, conquer) and the sign of the cross (according to Eusebius) or the *chi-rho* symbol (according to Lactantius).[6] The next day, his adversary, Maxentius, fell into the Tiber in his armour and drowned, and the opposing army was dispatched. In the following year, Constantine issued the Edict of Milan which declared tolerance for Christianity throughout the empire. Although not baptized until on his deathbed – a common practice at the time – it is said the emperor was outspoken about his devotion to the Christian faith.

> This God I invoke with bended knees, and recoil with horror from the blood of sacrifices, from their foul and detestable odours, and from every earth-born magic fire: for the profane and impious superstitions which are defiled by these rites have cast down and consigned to perdition many, nay, whole nations of the Gentile world. (Eusebius, *Life of Constantine*, 4:10)

Native cults and religions were still permitted. But Constantine favoured Christians. He endowed funds to build basilicas and extend their lands. He returned confiscated Christian property, placed Christians in high office, and exempted clergy from taxes. Meanwhile, his devout mother, Helena, toured the Holy Land, identifying the sites of the life of Jesus and building churches upon them. In 325, he called the bishops to the Council of Nicaea, where he was acclaimed as God's chosen king, Christ's representative on earth, and the supreme patron of the church. As head of the church and of the empire, he issued imperial dictates to promote unity of Christian belief throughout his domains.

For the church, Constantine's conversion changed everything. Before

[6] The *chi-rho* or christogram (☧) is the first two Greek letters of *Christos* superimposed.

it, the Christian presbyter or bishop survived between periods of reluctant toleration and sporadic outbursts of sharp persecution in which he was an immediate target. He was aware of the cost of the cross he bore and hoped in the coming of Jesus to overthrow his foes. But now, suddenly, ecclesiarchs found themselves in places of eminence and power, with no real threat, except perhaps from other members of the clergy. They were the new imperial aristocracy. Ecclesiastical eminence now allowed a man to gain wealth, fine clothes, chariots, palaces, and servants, the reputation of being a philosopher and an intellectual, and access to power and royalty. Their ecumenical councils now met at leisure to argue over fine theological differences. Ambitious young men from all over the empire now began to strive for leadership in the church.

This had a far-reaching effect upon views of the millennium. The church had been waiting for a righteous kingdom that would endure for 1,000 years. But now many bishops and priests believed that the millennium had arrived in Constantine and his successors. Perhaps there was no millennium yet to come.

The emperor's conversion also reinforced the Christian narrative about the Jews. Since the Romans destroyed Jerusalem in AD 70, Christians had seen the Jews as rejected by God in favour of the church. The narrative was now confirmed. The Roman Empire who destroyed the Jews was now the Christian Empire. In Jewish and in Christian eyes the two were one. At Nicaea, the emperor severed the connection which some Christians still observed between Easter and the Jewish Passover.

> It appeared an unworthy thing that in the celebration of this most holy feast we should follow the practice of the Jews, who have impiously defiled their hands with enormous sin, and are, therefore, deservedly afflicted with blindness of soul… Let us then have nothing in common with the detestable Jewish horde; for we have received from our Saviour a different way. (Eusebius, *Life of Constantine*, 3:17)

The emperor and bishops felt increasingly justified in censuring and suppressing the Jews, who were forbidden from owning Christian slaves.

There was a brief hiatus, between 361 to 363, when Constantine's nephew, the Emperor Julian, 'the Apostate,' attempted to turn the empire back to philosophy and the worship of the old gods. He even started to rebuild the Jerusalem temple in order to enlist the support of the Jews. But he soon died in battle with the Persians at Samarra and his changes were swept away. His successors, briefly Jovian and then Valentinian, dismissed Julian's court philosophers and sophists, restored the bishops to their former estate, and returned the empire to the Christian faith. This status quo would endure, in one form or other, until modern times. Bishops still sit by right in Britain's House of Lords.

EUSEBIUS

Origen, on his death, bequeathed to the church in Caesarea his large library, which added greatly to the prestige of the school he had founded there. Not long after, a young man from Beirut, Pamphilus, became a tutor and librarian in the school. He had earlier studied in Alexandria, and was a disciple of Origen. His labour brought such growth to the school in Caesarea that it began to rival Alexandria for status. This Pamphilus counted among his pupils a young man called Eusebius (c. 260–340) who was also an ardent Origenist. In 313 or 314, just after the Emperor's conversion, Eusebius became bishop of Caesarea and the first historian of the church.

In his *History of the Church*, Eusebius writes of Origen's life and teaching with great devotion. This devotion expressed itself particularly in a vigorous opposition to any idea of an earthly millennium. The story begins in the third book of the *History*, where he apparently accepts that John the apostle was the author of the Revelation with its millennial teaching, saying, "the apostle and evangelist John" was confined on Patmos where he wrote about the number of Antichrist's name in "what is called the Revelation of John." He cites Irenaeus, that it was written in the reign of Domitian (3.18.1–3).

But, later in the same third book, Eusebius suggests, on the authority of Gaius of Rome and Pope Dionysius of Alexandria, that the Revelation is the work of the gnostic arch-heretic Cerinthus.

> At the time under discussion, tradition tells us, another heretical sect was founded by Cerinthus. Gaius, whose words I quoted earlier, in the Dialogue attributed to him, writes this about him:
>
> "Cerinthus also, by revelations purporting to have been written by a great apostle, presents us with wondrous tales which he falsely claims were shown him by angels. He says that after the Resurrection the Kingdom of Christ will be on earth, and that fleshly humanity will dwell in Jerusalem, once more enslaved to lusts and pleasures. And in his enmity towards the Scriptures of God, and to lead men astray, he foretells a period of a thousand years given up to wedding festivities.

> "Dionysius again, who was bishop of Alexandria in my own time, in the second book of his *On the Promises,* makes statements about the Revelation of John on the basis of ancient tradition. He then refers to Cerinthus in the following terms:
>
> "This Cerinthus, the founder of a sect called Cerinthian after him, wished to attach a name commanding respect [the name of John] to his own creation [*ie,* the Revelation]. The doctrine he taught was this: Christ's Kingdom would be on earth. And, being devoted to the pleasures of the body and altogether sensual in his nature, filled the city of his dreams with those things which he desired, namely, the delights of the belly and sexual passion, that is to say, in eating and drinking and marrying, and (or to call these by what he thought more respectable names) in festivals and sacrifices and the slaying of victims, under the guise of which he thought he could indulge his appetites with a better grace." (3.28.1–5)

Eusebius then turns to undermine the testimony of Papias, who claimed that both Jesus and John spoke of a coming earthly kingdom. He cites Papias's own account as follows:

> I enquired into the words of the presbyters, what Andrew or Peter had said, or Philip or Thomas or James or John or Matthew, or any other disciple of the Lord, or what Aristion and the presbyter John, were still saying. (*History* 3.39.4)

Eusebius takes this to mean that there were two Johns in Asia Minor, both buried in Ephesus, namely, John the apostle and John the presbyter. On this basis, Eusebius proposes that Papias was not a disciple of John the apostle at all but rather of this alleged 'John the presbyter' (3.39.5–6). Of course, it should have been clear enough that Papias was not speaking of two Johns. It's clear from his words that by 'presbyter' he means the apostles. The reason he mentions John twice is because John, unlike the other apostles, was still alive and "still saying."

Eusebius then says that Papias, being not a disciple of the Apostle John, but a man of low intelligence, invented the millennium, and so led Irenaeus and other unthinking church leaders astray.

> The same historian [Papias] gives also other accounts, which he says he received from unwritten tradition, likewise certain strange parables and teachings of the Saviour, and other things mythical. In these he says there would be a certain millennium after the resurrection, a bodily reign of Christ on this very earth; which things he appears to have imagined, as if they were authorized by the apostolic narrations, not understanding

> correctly those matters which they spoke of mystically. For he seems to have been very small of intelligence, to judge from his books. But it is partly due to him that the great majority of churchmen after him took the same view, relying on his early date; like Irenaeus and several others, who clearly held the same opinion (History 3.39.11–13).

In his seventh book, Eusebius once again denies that the Book of Revelation, with its millennium, could ever have sprung from John the apostle. He again quotes Dionysius of Alexandria, as he related his attempts to dissuade the presbyters of Arsinoë from their devotion to the millennial views of Nepos. He reports Dionysius as having said:

> Some of our predecessors rejected the book [Revelation] and pulled it entirely to pieces, criticizing it chapter by chapter, pronouncing it unintelligible and illogical, and the title false. They say it is not the work of John nor is it a revelation at all, since it is heavily veiled by its thick curtain of incomprehensibility: so far from being one of the apostles, the author of the book was not even one of the saints, or a member of the church, but that Cerinthus, who founded the sect which was called after him the Cerinthian, desiring reputable authority for his fiction, prefixed the name [of John]. (History 7.25.1–2)

Thus Eusebius approves Dionysius's view that Cerinthus was author of the Revelation. He says, with Dionysius, that this view was held by their predecessors. But these "predecessors" remain nameless. Indeed, one would have been hard-pressed to name them. For Justin, the Muratorian Canon, Irenaeus, Clement of Alexandria, Tertullian, Hippolytus, and Origen himself, all accepted John the apostle as author.[7] He even rejects Irenaeus's testimony about Papias, although he elsewhere praises Irenaeus as a faithful witness to apostolic tradition.[8] He equally rejects Irenaeus's and Justin's testimony to the millennial reign. It's a tangled web indeed. But such was the fruit of his fervent devotion to Origen's heavenly kingdom of incorporeal souls and his desire to undermine belief in an earthly kingdom of the Messiah. When one considers the solemn warnings that close the Revelation, one must wonder how his disembodied soul is faring in the Neoplatonic heaven, whose ardent efforts were directed not to remove words from the book, but to remove the whole book from the church.

[7] The Muratorian fragment was found in Milan in the 18th century by Ludovico Muratori. The ms dates from the 8th century, but its text is from the second half of the 2nd century, referring to the papacy of Pius I (140–155) as "recently in our time".

[8] History 3.23.2; 3.26.2; 3.39.

But Eusebius had more than words on his side. After meeting the Emperor Constantine at the Council of Nicaea in 325 BC, he followed up with an adulatory *Life of Constantine*, wherein he recorded the story of Constantine's conversion as he had learned it from the Emperor himself. This earned him the position of court bishop and adviser to the Emperor. Under the influence of the learned Eusebius, Constantine imbibed Origen's amillennial views on the future age. Meanwhile Lactantius, ten years Eusebius's senior and working in the same palaces, taught the Emperor and his young Prince Crispus about the millennial reign. History doesn't record what words the two men exchanged as they passed in the courts of holy Constantinople. But the presence of both views so close at hand to the Emperor may be the ultimate explanation why Eusebius did not succeed in having millenarianism banned at the Council of Nicaea.

JEROME AND THE ORIGENIST CONTROVERSY

Jerome was born in Stridon, in Dalmatia, sometime in the mid-340s AD. In his youth, he went to Rome to study rhetoric and philosophy. There he roamed freely amid the great city's brothels and taverns. But he was tormented with guilt over his doings. So, skirts having been chased, he decided it was time he should be chaste. He converted to the Christian faith and was baptized in his early twenties. Desiring to live a life of penance he first lived as an eremite in the Syrian desert. Then he returned to Rome where he served as secretary to Pope Damasus I and devoted himself to writing tracts extolling virginity and excoriating human sexual reproduction. This had the happy effect of gathering to him a devoted group of Roman noblewomen, who looked to him as their spiritual father. Egged-on by their admiration, he castigated the secular clergy of Rome for their carnality. But, in 385, on the death of Damasus his patron, the castigated clergy bit back, accusing him of impropriety with the patrician widow Paula. To quell rumours, Jerome and Paula, with her daughter, Eustochium, packed their suitcases and quit Rome for the Holy Land. He settled in the monastery at Bethlehem, supported by Paula who, with her wealth, enlarged the monastery and had Jerome appointed abbot there. She also established a convent in the city where she assumed the role of abbess. Jerome visited the libraries of Origen and Eusebius at Caesarea, and became a great admirer of Origen.

But Epiphanius, bishop of Salamis in Cyprus, was rather less of an admirer of Origen and set out to oppose Origenism in its native soil, in Palestine and Jerusalem. In the early 390s, he asked Bishop John II of Jerusalem to condemn Origen as a heretic. John declined. Then Epiphanius sent a monk named Atarbius to tour Jerusalem's monasteries and ask the brothers to sign a denunciation of Origen's teachings. In Bethlehem, the almoner Rufinus, Jerome's friend and Bishop John's right hand man, refused to see him. But Jerome listened to Atarbius's arguments and became an ally of Epiphanius.

Epiphanius became increasingly outspoken against Origen. In his treatise, *Against Heresies* (395) he denounced eighty sects and belief-systems that he deemed heretical. Most of them receive a couple of paragraphs. But section 65, devoted to Origen, runs to hundreds of pages. Epiphanius censures him as an orthodox Christian corrupted by Greek philosophy, whose teachings were gnostic and gave rise to Arianism. He particularly condemns his subordinationist view of the Trinity, his doctrine of the pre-existence, fall, and ultimate universal salvation of all souls, including Satan, and his denial of bodily resurrection.

Since Bishop John would not come on his side, Epiphanius became increasingly critical of him. In 394, he preached in Jerusalem, delivering a denunciation of Origenism which was plainly aimed at John. John retorted that afternoon with a sermon against anthropomorphism, a term with which Origenists stigmatized their accusers. A few days later John published a confession of faith. Yes, he admired some of Origen's teachings, but everyone should know that he was a trinitarian Christian. Epiphanius could find no fault with it. But he still wanted John to submit to his demands. He began openly denouncing him in sermons and tracts. He ordained Jerome's brother as a priest within John's own diocese. He wrote an open *Letter to John,* condemning his Origenist views, which he circulated among the bishops and monks of Palestine, with another letter urging them to break communion with John. He urged Jerome to break communion with John, which Jerome duly did.

Jerome then joined the fray. Making the most of Paula's connections, he wrote a treatise to her son-in-law, the senator Pammachius, entitled *Against John of Jerusalem*, detailing Origen's heresies. Then he wrote more of the same in his letter *Against Rufinus.*

Bishop John did not reply. Instead, he wrote an apologia to Pope Theophilos of Alexandria. Theophilos duly wrote to Jerome ordering him to desist and to show proper obedience to his bishop.

But down in Alexandria, Theophilos (*r.* 385–412) had troubles of his own. He may have been Athanasius's successor, but he was no great theologian, and he had always been more or less happy with the Origenist doctrines he had been taught. So too were the majority of his clergy. But a significant minority of his monks was now reading Epiphanius's tracts and pressing Theophilos to denounce Origenism.

While Theophilos was pondering how to respond, he heard a rumour that one of his presbyters, Isidore, had secretly received a very large sum of money from a wealthy benefactor. What was worse, the wealthy benefactor, knowing Theophilos, had made Isidore swear never to tell Theophilos about the gift. Theophilos was incensed at this slur on his probity. The money was surely his. Yet Isidore, honouring his oath, resisted Theophilos's command to hand it over. What could Theophilos do? When clerics seek to destroy one another, the nearest weapon is always an accusation of heresy. So Theophilos duly accused Isidore of being led astray by the heresies of Origen. This was not a good move, as most of the Alexandrian presbyters were Origenists and they flocked to the defence of their hero. Theophilos had no option but to raise an army and slay them. The numbers are disputed. But to this day the Greek Orthodox Church remembers annually the 10,000 presbyters and monks slain by Theophilos. The survivors, led by the four handsome "Tall Brothers," fled to Constantinople and there appealed to the archbishop, John Chrysostom.

At this, Jerome, hearing of Theophilos's bloody crusade against the Origenists, saw an opportunity to regain his favour, and wrote him an adulatory missive:

> The whole world glories in your victories. An exultant crowd of all nations gazes on the standard of the cross raised by you at Alexandria and upon the shining trophies which mark your triumph over heresy. Blessings on your courage! Blessings on your zeal! (Epistle 86)

This astute move regained him Theophilos's support. With Theophilos as his new ally, Jerome was freer than ever to denounce his bishop.

In 401, Theophilos called the Synod of Alexandria and there condemned Origen as the "hydra of all heresies." But, in Constantinople, Chrysostom was horrified by the Tall Brothers' tales of Theophilos's misdeeds. He had the Emperor Arcadius summon Theophilos to a synod in Constantinople to explain himself concerning his persecution of the Origenists. Theophilos came in pomp with a grand retinue of suffragan bishops and enlisted the aid of the empress, who disliked Chrysostom, and turned the tables. He accused Chrysostom of Origenist heresies and secured his condemnation and banishment at the Synod of the Oak (403). Having won his battles, Theophilos returned to Egypt, happy once again to receive and ordain Origenists and Platonists as before.

It's an all-too-familiar tale of clergy behaving badly. But the upshot of it all was to take the shine from Origen's teaching. Origenism was no longer untouchable. Many now agreed that it was unscriptural in at least some things. Jerome turned to refuting many of Origen's ideas, particularly his ideas on the resurrection. After all, the resurrection was clearly a scriptural teaching, even if Jerome couldn't see how to fit it in to neoplatonic belief in a heaven of souls. Yet he swallowed Origen's amillennialism hook, line, and sinker. He was, after all, every bit as ascetic and obsessively celibate as Origen had been. Following Eusebius, he made Papias out to be the inventor of the millennium. Sitting, presumably, with the words of Dionysius or Eusebius before him, he distinguishes between John the Evangelist and John the Presbyter. Yet he mentions this to no good effect, for he himself believed that John the Evangelist composed both the Gospel and the Revelation.[9]

> [Papias] said, "I considered what Andrew and Peter said, what Philip, what Thomas, what James, what John, what Matthew or anyone else among the disciples of our Lord, what also Aristion and the elder John, disciples of the Lord had said, not so much that I have their books to read, as that their living voice is heard until the present day in the authors themselves."
>
> It appears through this catalogue of names that the John who is placed among the disciples is not the same as the Presbyter John whom he places after Aristion in his enumeration. This we say moreover because of the opinion mentioned above, where we record that it is declared by many that the last two epistles of John are the work not of the apostle but of the presbyter.
>
> He [Papias] is said to have published a *Second coming of Our Lord* or *Millennium*. Irenaeus and Apollinaris and others who say that after the resurrection the Lord will reign in the flesh with the saints, follow him. Tertullian also in his work *On the hope of the faithful*. Victorinus of Petau and Lactantius follow this view. (*De Vir. Ill.* 18)

[9] See his comments in *De Vir. Ill.* 9.

In his old age, he became more adamant. In his commentary on Daniel (407), he said, "The saints shall never possess an earthly kingdom, but only a heavenly. Away, then, with this fable about a millennium!" (On Dan. 7:17–18). And in his commentary on Isaiah (410), he lays out his thoughts on the matter in full. He says there are still those who endorse millennial views. But he dismisses the views of Irenaeus, Tertullian, and Lactantius, and applauds Pope Dionysius's refutation of it. A literal interpretation of the millennium is, he says, a carnal and Judaizing doctrine. The millennium must be interpreted spiritually.

> I am not unaware of how great is the diversity of opinions among human beings, I do not say concerning the mystery of the Trinity, the correct confession of which is the ignorance of knowledge, but concerning other ecclesiastical dogmas, namely, about the resurrection and the state of souls and of human flesh, concerning how the promises of future things ought to be interpreted, and in what manner the Apocalypse of John should be understood, which if we interpret it literally, one would have to Judaize. If we explain it spiritually, as it was written, we shall seem to go against the views of many: of the Latins, Tertullian, Victorinus, Lactantius; of the Greeks, to pass over the others, I shall mention only Irenaeus, Bishop of Lugdunum, against whom the very eloquent Dionysius, pontiff of the Church of Alexandria, writes a fine book, mocking the fable of a thousand years, and the golden and bejewelled Jerusalem on earth, the restoration of the temple [Rev. 21:10–22], the blood of the sacrificial victims, Sabbath rest, the injury of the circumcision, marriage, births, children, upbringing, splendid banquets, the servitude of all the Gentiles; and on the other hand, wars, armies, and also triumphs, the killing of the vanquished, death of the hundred-year-old sinner [cf. Isa. 65:20].
>
> I do not envy these people, if they love only the world, so that they have desired earthly things even in the kingdom of Christ, and in addition to the abundance of foods and the gluttony of the throat and the belly, they look for those things which are below the belly. The Apostle Paul says of them, "Food is for the belly and belly for food, but God will destroy them both" [1 Cor. 6:13], and, "The kingdom of God is not food and drink" [Rom. 14:17]; and the Lord and Saviour says, "You are in error, knowing neither the Scriptures nor the power of God; for in the resurrection they shall neither marry nor be married, but they will be like the angels" [Matt. 22:29–30]. (Jerome on Isa. 18)

By the last decades of Jerome's life, in the early fifth century, millenarianism was completely eclipsed in all the churches of east and west.

AUGUSTINE OF HIPPO

Augustine (354–430) was born to Latin-speaking parents in Hippo, in modern Algeria. His mother was a Christian; his father a pagan who repented on his death-bed. From his earliest studies of philosophy, Augustine held to Platonist ideas of the immortality of the soul, even writing a treatise on the subject in his teens. He went to Carthage in his mid-teens, where he became first a student and later a teacher of rhetoric. As a student, he ran with the wild young men of the city, delighting in the licentiousness of its pagan festivals. However, before long, he took a local girl as his concubine, to the dismay of his mother who wished him to make an honourable marriage to a woman of wealth. But this nameless young woman may have helped to tame his excesses; he claimed that during their relationship he was faithful to her. They had a child together, a son called Adeodatus.

Also in Carthage, from at least the age of nineteen (373), or earlier, he was drawn to Manicheism, the creed of Mani from Sassanid Babylon. Mani had grown up among the Judeo-Christian Elkasaites of Mesopotamia, but had turned their faith into a new religion of his own. He claimed it was a form of Christianity. But in reality it was Zoroastrian Gnosticism which named Christ as its Gnostic saviour. Manicheism viewed the world as a struggle between two opposed, eternal, cosmic forces: good and evil, light and darkness, God and matter.[10] The human soul is composed of light, but is trapped in the darkness of the material lower world. Christ is the saviour who can liberate the particles of light in the soul and let them escape to the realm of eternal light. Mani saw the Old Testament as the work of the lower deity, the Gnostic Demiurge or Persian Ahriman. But he accepted the New Testament – or parts of it – as emanating from the Father of Greatness, equivalent to Persian Ahura Mazda.

For the Manichees, everything from the lower world was tainted. The first human couple were the fruit of the cannibalism and copulation of demons. Thus sexual desire was both the primordial sin and the punishment for sin, procreating itself by means of copulation. Human sexuality was synonymous with darkness and the works of the lower deity. Those who indulged in it remained trapped by the Demiurge. Food and drink were also tainted. But the Manichean priests could convert food and

[10] For more on Manichean cosmology and its view of concupiscence, see van Oort 2020.

drink to particles of light by eating and drinking. And so the *auditores* (hearers) were required to supply the Manichean *electi* (clergy) with food and shelter, for which service they earned merit for the liberation of their souls. The *auditores* were also required to be zealous missionaries.

Augustine was a good disciple. He brought the *electi* their food and drink and, within a few years, won at least eight of his friends to this faith. Of course, life with a concubine hardly followed Mani's teachings. Yet Augustine continued to live with his woman. But it seems that he conformed to the Manichean requirements of abstinence, for they had no more children. But after years of devotion to the Manichees, Augustine became disenchanted with them. His given reason for this is that he had found the Manichean clergy, ostensibly liberated from sexual desire, to be secretly occupied with their own concubines. He also found the Manichean bishop, Faustus of Mileve, to be an ignorant man who could answer questions only by empty slogans.

But he had other reasons. The Manichees were clearly determined to exclude him from their clergy and keep him on the neophyte rung of *auditor*. That did not suit a man of Augustine's ambitions. Second, and no less important, the imperial Edict of Thessalonica, in 380, decreed Nicene Christianity to be the only lawful religion of the Roman empire. Being on the wrong side of the emperor suited his ambitions even less. He began to distance himself from the Manichees. In 382, an imperial edict proscribed Manicheism on pain of death. Augustine promptly and sensibly ceased from the Manichees, yet he continued to maintain a few old Manichean friends.

In 383, taking his little family with him, he went to Rome, where he hoped for better things. But he became ill, almost to death, upon his arrival. Then he found the city disappointing. The glories of the empire had moved east to Constantinople. The Romans treated foreigners disdainfully. And his students of rhetoric were unwilling to pay, forcing him to survive on the largesse of friends. He was just about to return to Carthage when those old Manichean friends introduced him to Symmachus, the Prefect of Rome. Symmachus was an old-school pagan, resentful of the Christianization of the empire and the dominance of the clergy. He had been tasked to find a professor of rhetoric for the imperial court in Milan. And, being glad to find that Augustine was not a Christian, he recommended him for the post.

He was duly accepted and arrived in Milan in late 384. Now that he had a proper job, his mother appeared on the doorstep, determined to secure for him the honourable marriage she had always sought. A girl from a wealthy family was soon found and pledged to him in marriage. And so his concubine, now an impediment to his marriage, was sent weeping on a ship back to Carthage. But since his new betrothed was still young – probably only eleven years old – and the marriage could not be consummated for two years, he took to himself another concubine as a stop-gap.

One of the most influential people in Milan was the bishop, Ambrose, who happened to be the cousin of his Roman mentor Symmachus. Augustine began listening to Ambrose's sermons with a professional rhetor's ear. He was surprised to find that, for Ambrose, substance was more important than style: rhetoric took a back seat to the message. Augustine found this strangely impressive and he began to listen to the message. At the same time, his recommendation by Symmachus, and his new status in the imperial court, gave him unique access to Ambrose, and he frequently conversed with him on the faith. But the great obstacle to his conversion was his fondness for women, which he saw as something inherently sinful. This was certainly due more to his training in Manicheism than to Christian teaching. Marriage was no impediment to Christian conversion. But celibacy was becoming the norm for Christian clergy. No married man could attain prominence within the church hierarchy. And Augustine, if he were to become a Christian, would be a prominent Christian.

And so, finally, in AD 386, on reading the Epistle to the Romans, he decided to put behind him "chambering and wantonness." He dismissed his second concubine, severed his betrothal to his young bride-to-be, and was baptized by Ambrose into the Christian faith to live the life of celibacy that was essential to achieving high position in the Church. He returned to Africa in 388 and settled there, with some friends, on his deceased parents' estate to live a monastic life of fasting and prayer. In 391, he was ordained priest and, in 395, became bishop of Hippo.

The Fall of Rome and Millennial Reassessment

In 410, Rome fell to the Goths and the Roman world was turned upside down. The pagans blamed the city's fall on the spread of Christianity and the influence of its priests. Augustine was concerned to answer these accusations in his greatest work, *City of God.* But, under the pressure of these events, his views on the millennium were changing.

The few millenarians who still remained followed the Greek Septuagint dating of creation. As a result, they were expecting the millennium to appear around the year AD 500. They saw the fall of Rome as the beginning of the end times and said the redemption was drawing nigh. Augustine too had formerly believed in a coming millennium, but now he saw these ardent hopes for the dissolution of the empire as something destabilizing and looked for a way to reframe them. At this point he was influenced by Tyconius, another African theologian, who argued not only that there would be no earthly millennium, but that the two resurrections spoken of in Revelation 20 are quite different in nature, for one is spiritual and the other physical.

This led to Augustine's final position on eschatology in the last chapter of *City of God.* He realizes that the millennium of Revelation 20:1–6 is indeed the seventh millennium from creation, following six millennia of toil. He admits that he too formerly believed that there would be a millennial reign of Christ on earth. But now, he says, he has changed his mind because of descriptions of the millennial kingdom where the resurrected enjoy all kinds of carnal pleasures, like eating and drinking way too much.

> Those who, on the strength of this passage, have suspected that the first resurrection is future and bodily, have been moved, among other things, specially by the number of a thousand years, as if it were a fit thing that the saints should thus enjoy a kind of Sabbath-rest during that period, a holy leisure after the labours of the six thousand years since man was created, and was on account of his great sin dismissed from the blessedness of paradise into the woes of this mortal life, so that thus, as it is written, *One day is with the Lord as a thousand years, and a thousand years as one day* (2 Pet. 3:8), there should follow on the completion of six thousand years, as of six days, a kind of seventh-day Sabbath in the succeeding thousand years; and that it is for this purpose the saints rise, that is, to celebrate this Sabbath. And this opinion would not be objectionable, if it were believed that the joys of the saints in that Sabbath shall be spiritual, and consequent on the presence of God; for I myself, too, once held this opinion. But, as they assert that those who then rise again shall enjoy the leisure of immoderate carnal banquets, furnished with an amount of meat and drink such as not only to shock the feeling of the temperate, but even to surpass the measure of credulity itself, such assertions can be believed only by the carnal. They who do believe them

> are called by the spiritual Chiliasts, which we may translate literally by the name Millenarians. (20:7)

Thus, since millennial belief is carnal, Augustine proposes the solution he borrowed from Tyconius. He says, the *first resurrection* (Rev. 20:6) "is temporal and spiritual and allows no second death"; that is, it is not a bodily resurrection at all but a resurrection of the soul in mercy, the spiritual rebirth of believers to faith in God through baptism. But the *second resurrection* (Rev. 20:13) is "not spiritual but corporeal and is to be at the end time"; that is, a bodily resurrection at the last judgement, at the end of time, which will send "some into the second death, others into that life which knows no death."[11]

As for Satan being bound during the thousand years (Rev. 20:1–4), Augustine takes this to mean that Satan is bound from Christ's first coming to his second. That does not mean that Satan cannot still deceive and attack the saints and the Church. Yet he is bound when people are converted from unbelief to faith. Nor can he seduce them to destruction. And such conversions shall continue until the end of time, at the end of the thousand years.[12]

During the thousand years when the Devil is bound, the saints also reign for a thousand years (Rev. 20:6). Thus, the two periods are identical and signify the span between Christ's first and second coming. Therefore the millennium is the age of the Church and of the Christian kingdom under the governance of its kings and bishops, through whom Christ rules on earth through the church. The struggle between Christ and Satan, the saints and the wicked, wages continually. But those who are converted to Christ, particularly the hierarchs of the Church, triumph over Satan and rule with Christ in this age. Thus, even the invading Goths are no threat to the kingdom of Christ, for they too can be (and were) converted to the faith. Then the age will be completed with the second coming of Christ, which will be followed by eternity.[13] In the conclusion to his great work, speaking of the Perpetual Sabbath of Eternal Rest, Augustine then ties these ideas to the millennial week. He calculates five ages from the creation of the world; he and his readers now find themselves in the middle of the sixth age; after this will come the true heavenly Sabbath, which will ultimately be followed by an eighth eternal day.

[11] City of God, 20:5–7.
[12] City of God, 20:8.
[13] City of God, 20:9.

> This Sabbath shall appear still more clearly if we count the ages as days, in accordance with the periods of time defined in Scripture, for that period will be found to be the seventh. The first age, as the first day, extends from Adam to the deluge; the second from the deluge to Abraham, equalling the first, not in length of time, but in the number of generations, there being ten in each. From Abraham to the advent of Christ there are, as the evangelist Matthew calculates, three periods, in each of which are fourteen generations – one period from Abraham to David, a second from David to the captivity, a third from the captivity to the birth of Christ in the flesh. There are thus five ages in all. The sixth is now passing, and cannot be measured by any number of generations, as it has been said, *It is not for you to know the times, which the Father has put in his own power* (Acts 1:7). After this period God shall rest as on the seventh day, when he shall give us (who shall live on the seventh day) rest in himself.
>
> But there is not now space to treat of these ages; suffice it to say that the seventh shall be our Sabbath, which shall be brought to a close, not by an evening, but by the Lord's day, as an eighth and eternal day, consecrated by the resurrection of Christ, and prefiguring the eternal repose not only of the spirit, but also of the body. There we shall rest and see, see and love, love and praise. This is what shall be in the end without end. For what other end do we propose to ourselves than to attain to the kingdom of which there is no end? (22.30)

Augustine, then, seems to have hoped that Christ would appear around the year AD 1000. But, of course, that year too passed without any such appearing. But his comment that the sixth millennium "cannot be measured by any number of generations" covered any embarrassment for his followers. They were happy to keep taking the continually-expanding sixth age as the times of the Church Age.

By this allegorical reading of Revelation 20, Augustine developed all the central elements of the amillennial view. There would be no millennial reign of Jesus on the earth and no bodily resurrection before it. Rather, the millennium is the Church Age, followed by a single judgement to eternal bliss or eternal doom, and the destruction of the material world as the blessed are translated to the Neoplatonic heaven. This view spread through the whole church. Under its pervading influence, belief in the millennial reign of Jesus on earth rapidly vanished altogether.

JULIAN OF ECLANUM

The triumph of Augustine's views is the more tragic because, even in his lifetime, he had eloquent critics. His younger contemporary, Julian, Bishop of Eclanum in southern Italy (c. 380–454), knew Augustine well. Julian's father was on good terms with him. But Julian was a different kind of bishop. For a start, he had been married. (He became a priest after the death of his beloved wife.) He was learned in the scriptures and well-versed in Greek, of which Augustine was ignorant. He taught that sexual desire and sexual activity were a gift of God for procreation.

Julian was also familiar with the teachings of the Manichees. And he accused Augustine, based on Augustine's view of sexual desire and the sexual transmission of original sin, of being still a Manichee, and of infecting the entire church with Manichean doctrine.

> If the Ethiopian will change his skin or the leopard its spots, only then will you be able to cleanse yourself from the Manichean mysteries.[14]

Indeed, Julian's claims seem not unreasonable. Even after Augustine's conversion, his opinions resembled Mani's. Both speak of sexual desire in a negative way: it is sinful, a punishment for sin, and sin is propagated through it.[15] The same holds true in other teachings, whether the eternity of the soul, or the grossness of matter, or the rejection of an earthly kingdom. Despite Augustine's public opposition to the outlawed Manichees, he seems to have remained secretly Manichean in thought all his life.

But Augustine was a more successful self-publicist than Julian. His *Confessions* were the purplest thing going in the Latin monasteries; his enormous literary output evoked awe. Julian, on the other hand, is mostly forgotten. And so Augustine's influence has been enormous in the history of Christian thought. He is the pre-eminent 'Doctor of the Church.' His teachings form the basis of the magisterium and regulate the lives of millions of churches to this day. Some of his teachings are valuable – on the Trinity, on grace, on government and just war – though he was not the only one saying these things. But in many ways his influence over Christian thought was malign. He is the chief architect not only of the rejection of the millennium in favour of the Platonist heaven of souls, but of the unbiblical doctrines of clerical celibacy, the sinfulness of sexual desire, the sexual transmission of original sin, and the eternal

[14] Julian, as cited by Augustine, *Op. imp. c. Iul.* 4:42.
[15] For a fuller discussion, see van Oort 2020.

punishment of the damned. To this day, such views are a stumbling block to believers and unbelievers alike. But they spring not from scripture. They are the effluence of Augustine's Origenism and Manicheism.

THE END OF THE MILLENNIUM

In the end, three things conspired to cancel belief in the millennium of Revelation 20: allegorical interpretation, the conversion of Rome, and the failure of the seventh millennium to appear in AD 500.

Allegorical interpretation sprang from Alexandria and its son Origen. His allegorism allowed him to rewrite completely the message of the scriptures in line with Platonism, the chief philosophy of the Hellenic world. For Platonism, the soul was an immortal entity distinct from and purer than the mortal body, but all matter was inherently gross and unspiritual, especially the body's requirements of food, drink and sexual propagation. The earth, the material creation, was destined only for annihilation. Thus the Christ would never set up an earthly kingdom. His kingdom, and the kingdom of his saints, could only be spiritual in nature. For Origen, clasping this philosophy to his heart, nothing was off bounds, whether the goodness of creation, or the denial of bodily resurrection, or the Messiah's return to earth, or an earthly millennial kingdom. By allegorical reinterpretation he rejected them all. And although successive church councils condemned the worst of his errors, his rejection of the millennial kingdom was never condemned. Some, like Nepos and Lactantius, strove against it. But Nepos was posthumously outpunched by Dionysius of Alexandria, who taught that the Revelation was written by Cerinthus. And Lactantius was sidelined by Eusebius.

The second pillar in the rejection of the earthly millennial kingdom was the conversion of the Emperor Constantine to the Christian faith. Under the rule of Constantine and his sons the earthly kingdom of Christ had already arrived. And, since the true kingdom of the Christ was now accepted to be a neoplatonic heavenly kingdom, the view naturally arose that Christian Constantinople would be followed, at 'the end of time,' by the great judgement of God and the heavenly kingdom of the saints. But, for now, the earthly kingdom of Christ had arrived in Roman Constantinople. Any belief in a future earthly millennium was a carnal error of the despised and rejected Jews, whose conquest and subjugation by Rome was God's judgement upon them. Everything Jewish was therefore rejected, whether the Hebrew scriptures, or rabbinic interpretation. If the Fathers had known Hebrew, or had been willing to listen to rabbinic interpretation with its high value on the plain sense of scripture, they might have warded off the influence of allegorical Platonism. But their contempt for defeated Judaism led them to despise all these things. The alienation of the Jews was as much a tragedy for the Church as it was for the Jews themselves.

Eusebius, Jerome and Augustine promoted this new creed. Eusebius advanced it in his *History of the Church*, amplifying Dionysius's unholy fancy that the Revelation was written by Cerinthus. Jerome and Augustine lent their hands to the task, nailing down the coffin of the earthly millennial kingdom and raising up the neoplatonic heaven of souls. They are hailed as doctors of the church. But they seem more like those whom the apostle foretold, who forbid marriage and demand abstinence from foods that God had created to be received with thanksgiving, denying the goodness of God's created world and captive to pagan philosophies (1 Tim. 4:1–4).

The third pillar was the Fathers' adherence to the Greek Septuagint text of the Old Testament. It was, after all, the text (more or less), which Jesus and the apostles appeared to have quoted.[16] It had to be inspired by God. And so they swallowed it as unassailable truth, including its totally divergent dating of the creation of the world at 1500 years before the Hebrew Masoretic text. This led them to believe that the seventh millennium would arrive around AD 500. But what arrived first was the Edict of Thessalonica (380) and the Promulgation of the Theodosian Code (439), which made Christianity the official religion of the empire. The Roman Christian empire, and its church hierarchy, was now the kingdom of God on earth. It was to last, they said, for 1,000 years, from the birth of Christ, during which period the millennium of Revelation 20 would be fulfilled. The first resurrection was the spiritual rebirth of the faithful; the second resurrection was the resurrection of all the dead *simul et semel* – together at one time – at the return of Jesus in judgement.

The resurrection of the flesh held a special position. They came within a whisker of being like those Justin spoke of, "who are called

[16] I say, "appeared to have quoted" because the NT cites the OT in Greek, in versions similar to the LXX, giving the appearance that Jesus quoted the Greek text. But, in reality, when Jesus spoke with the Pharisees, he would have cited the Hebrew text. He probably did the same with the disciples, even though they conversed in Aramaic, for Galilean Israelites would have known the Hebrew Torah from their synagogues.

Christians...who say there is no resurrection of the dead, and that their souls, when they die, are taken to heaven; do not imagine that they are Christians" (Trypho 80). But, in the end, the bodily resurrection remained, due perhaps to the influence of the oldest creeds. But it was not a resurrection body to live on earth. Instead, the dead were to be raised in bodily form for the one judgement of all flesh. Then the wicked would be tormented bodily in eternity. Meanwhile those who passed successfully through the judgement would go bodily into the neoplatonic heaven of souls where bodies seemed largely superfluous.

Such were the forces that led to the rejection of the hope in the earthly millennial messianic kingdom so widely testified to by the prophets and so clearly taught in John's Revelation. Now even the glorious conqueror of Revelation 19, called "King of kings and Lord of lords," was no longer Jesus, but the Archangel Michael, for it was unthinkable that Jesus should ever again put foot on this putrid earth. He had come once. Why would he come again? Instead – in a scenario drawn from Joel 3 and Matthew 25 – Jesus would return from heaven and sit on his heavenly throne, suspended in the air amidst the clouds above the Valley of Jehoshaphat. He would raise the dead and mete out eternal life to the righteous on his right hand and damnation to eternal torment to the wicked on his left.

This was the new orthodoxy. It was, it's fair to say, a mistake anyone could make, if they were rewriting the Bible according to Platonism and Manicheism, and dazzled by earthly riches, and reading a Bible with a distorted chronology. It penetrated to the very heart of Christian theology and metastasized through the whole body of the Church. From the fourth century until almost the seventeenth, the belief that there would be no earthly reign of the Messiah reigned supreme. It persists into our own century.

> I think we should boldly affirm that the millennium symbolizes the whole period between the first and second comings of Christ...There is no mention here of a millennium 'on earth'; the millennium is a reign with Christ 'in the heavenlies'.[17]

[17] Stott 2001: 231.

11

The Decline of Amillennialism

KEEP in mind then, that for well over 1,000 years – from the fourth century until the seventeenth – the denial of the earthly kingdom of the Messiah ruled virtually unopposed. Jesus was not coming back to rule on earth. God's plan for the earth was its destruction on the Day of Judgement.

The sixteenth-century Reformers appealed for a return to scripture. Yet they too were devotees of Augustine. They reasserted Augustine's amillennialism in the Augsburg Confession of 1530, which flatly rejected any earthly rule of the saints as a Jewish superstition.

> XVII. *Of Christ's return to judgement.* Also they ["Our Churches"] teach that at the Consummation of the World Christ will appear for judgment, and will raise up all the dead; He will give to the godly and elect eternal life and everlasting joys, but ungodly men and the devils He will condemn to be tormented without end.
>
> They condemn the Anabaptists, who think that there will be an end to the punishments of condemned men and devils. They condemn also others who are now spreading certain Jewish opinions, that before the resurrection of the dead the godly shall take possession of the kingdom of the world, the ungodly being everywhere suppressed.

As they said, there were various Anabaptist groups who asserted a literal reading of the millennium of Revelation 20. In 1534, they tried to set up the millennial kingdom on earth in Münster in Alsace. They were a wild bunch, seizing property, subjecting all to forced rebaptism, and practising polygyny, which they defended from Matthew 22:30. The

Bishop of Münster raised an army and besieged the city. Thereupon, the rebel leader, Jan Mathys, believing he was a second Gideon, marched out against them with twelve hapless men who were promptly slain. John of Leiden then proclaimed himself king and took sixteen wives, apparently executing one who refused his advances. After much further disorder within the city, the rebellion was crushed, and the rebels slain and hung out for the ravens. (The victorious Bishop then tried to introduce Lutheranism within his see, as a ploy to marry and legitimize his eight children, but failed.) To the external observer, none of this looked much like the kingdom of Christ on earth nor did much to recommend the millennialist cause.

So, a little later, John Calvin censured "the chiliasts, who limited the reign of Christ to a thousand years" (*Institutes* 3.25.5). And again, a century later, the Anglicans, of Roman Catholic ritual and Calvinist theology, taught in their Westminster Confession (1648) that there would be a single resurrection of the righteous and the wicked to a single judgement, whereupon the righteous would go to eternal life in the heavens, the wicked to eternal torments (32 & 33). The Larger Catechism explains it more fully.

> Answer: Immediately after the resurrection shall follow the general and final judgment of angels and men; the day and hour whereof no man knows, that all may watch and pray, and be ever ready for the coming of the Lord.
>
> Answer: At the day of judgment, the righteous, being caught up to Christ in the clouds, shall be set on his right hand, and there openly acknowledged and acquitted, shall join with him in the judging of reprobate angels and men, and shall be received into heaven, where they shall be fully and forever freed from all sin and misery; filled with inconceivable joys, made perfectly holy and happy both in body and soul, in the company of innumerable saints and holy angels, but especially in the immediate vision and fruition of God the Father, of our Lord Jesus Christ, and of the Holy Spirit, to all eternity. And this is the perfect and full communion, which the members of the invisible church shall enjoy with Christ in glory, at the resurrection and day of judgment. (Westminster Larger Catechism, Answers 88 & 90)

All these confessions rejected any earthly reign of Jesus. Instead, the Lord would return, judge the world, send the unrepentant to everlasting hell and take the righteous to the neoplatonic heaven.

Historicism

Throughout the amillennial period, the church tended to interpret the Revelation in the same way the Israelites had always read Daniel's vision of the four kingdoms; that is, they saw it as a prophetic overview of the entire history of the world. This is generally called a 'historicist' interpretation of Revelation. (It is not to be confused with 'historic' or 'classical' premillennialism.) The rise of Islam fitted neatly into this historicist view. Muhammad was the false prophet and the Saracens, making war on Jerusalem, were the Antichrist. Pope Innocent III made use of this in urging the Fourth Crusade of 1202.

But with the ferment of the Reformation, and Rome's opposition to it, the Reformers tended instead to see the Pope as the Antichrist, and the worldly Roman Catholic Church as the Whore of Babylon, the persecutor of the saints, riding on the back of the secular authority. The first to identify the Pope with the Antichrist were apparently the Waldensians, in their early twelfth-century confession.

> We believe that after this life, there are only two places, the one for the saved, and the other for the damned, the which two places we call Paradise and Hell, absolutely denying that Purgatory invented by Antichrist and forged contrary to the truth. (Morland Confession §9)

All the Reformers took the same line. The Westminster Confession of 1646, for instance, said:

> There is no other Head of the Church but the Lord Jesus Christ, nor can the Pope of Rome, in any sense, be head thereof, but is that Antichrist, that man of sin, and son of perdition, that exalteth himself in the Chuch against Christ and is called God. (§25.6)

Together with this historicist interpretation, the Reformers also held to the "day-year" theory of Daniel where the 2,300 days of Daniel 8:14 and the 1,290 days of Daniel 12:11 represent a corresponding number of years ending in their own time, which was the time of the end.

But these historicist readings were inescapably subjective, on at least two levels. First, they were based on the temporal viewpoint of the reader. Christians have often tended to think they are living in the last days. And so the timescale of the Revelation became elastic as each generation located its own successive period in the final cataclysmic chapters. Over four centuries, historicists – Luther, Calvin, the English

Puritans, the Millerites, the Jehovah Witnesses, and the Mormons – all interpreted the endpoint of the book as being in their own time and shifted the start date of the 1,290 and 2,300 days to various significant points in early medieval times. Some dated it from the Code of Justinian in 534, others from some point in the Muslim conquests, from 622 onwards, still others from the Donation of Pepin in 756.

But it was subjective too in whom it saw as the persecuting Antichrist and Whore and the persecuted saints. In time, Protestants also became quite adept at riding the Beast of secular authority and crushing those of differing beliefs. But they still saw the monsters of the Revelation within the Roman church.

Naturally enough, Catholic theologians were not entirely happy with the idea of the Pope being the Antichrist and the Roman Church the scarlet Whore. To cut the ground from under the Protestant stance, they came up with two alternatives: Futurism and Preterism.

FUTURISM

Futurism was the brainchild of the Jesuit Francisco Ribera (1537–1591). He had drunk deeply of the writings of the Ante-Nicene Fathers and his view was really the revival of their belief that the Tribulation and the Antichrist would appear just before the return of Christ. But it was a view that had not been heard in over 1,000 years. In his commentary on Revelation, published a year after his death, Ribera proposed that only the first three chapters of the Revelation applied to ancient, pagan Rome; the rest of the book referred to a future period of a literal three-and-a-half years, just before the coming of Christ. In this future time, the Roman Church would indeed fall away. But it would not fall away *because* of the Pope. Rather it would fall away *from* the Pope into apostasy. At this time, the Antichrist would arise. He, as the Fathers said, would be a Jew who would rebuild the temple in Jerusalem, receive the worship of the Jewish people, and rule the world for three and a half years, claiming divine power, persecuting the church, and wreaking havoc on mankind, until his demise at the coming of Christ.

Ribera's futurist reading of the Revelation managed to break any link with the reader's own time and to place the fulfilment of the Revelation in the period before the coming of Christ. This took the heat off the Protestant accusations against Rome. Yet his views did not win Rome's immediate approval, since they denied Augustinian amillennialism along with the prevailing historicist interpretation of the Revelation, with its 'day-year' theory that the 1,260 days represented 1,260 years. But within a few decades, Cardinal Bellarmine took up Ribera's ideas, steering Catholic interpretation of the Revelation toward future unfulfilled events, to defend against Protestant charges against the papacy.

PRETERISM

The counterpart to Ribera's Futurism was Preterism, proposed by another Jesuit, Luis del Alcázar of Seville (1554–1613), whose commentary on Revelation, like Ribera's, was published posthumously, in 1614. Alcázar's variation on Ribera's approach was to move the split point between past and future much nearer to the end of the book. He proposed that everything up until the end of chapter nineteen had already been fulfilled in Roman times, and that only the last three chapters awaited a future fulfilment. Even the coming of Christ in chapter nineteen had already been fulfilled, when he came in judgement to destroy Jerusalem in AD 70. (This was not so hard to swallow as it seemed, since amillennialists, desiring that Christ should not actually touch the earth, had long made chapter nineteen's "King of kings" to be Michael the Archangel.) Since almost everything had been fulfilled in the first century, nothing was now expected in the future except the establishing of the kingdom of Christ which he identified, of course, with the amillennial judgement and heavenly kingdom.

In time, preterism divided into two streams: Partial and Full. Partial preterists see all of Revelation already fulfilled except the return of Christ and the judgement of the world. Therefore they still await the return of Christ to earth, as described in Revelation 19. Meanwhile, Full preterists, holding to Alcázar's view, see all the prophecies of Revelation already fulfilled, including the return of Christ to earth (when he came to judge Jerusalem in AD 70). They await only his sudden appearing for the universal judgement of the world and the ensuing eternal state.

Preterism still has its supporters, of whom the foremost is Kenneth Gentry. Yet there are serious objections to the preterist view. First, Preterism only makes sense if the Revelation were already written prior to AD 70.[1] If it were later, John was in the incongruous position of writing

[1] Gentry 1989, dates it to AD 65–66.

a prophecy to warn the church against things that had already happened. Yet, as we saw in chapter six, the evidence for the composition of the Revelation being before AD 70, in Nero's time, is not conclusive.

But a second objection is even more damning. Preterists maintain that all the prophecies of the Revelation were fulfilled in the first century. But all the evidence is that these prophecies were never understood in this way at that time nor for centuries after. If prophecy is given by God for the age for which he intends it, how strange that no one in the first century saw these prophecies applying to their own time, when alone they would have been useful. Instead, all the early patristic writers affirm with one voice that the Revelation concerns a future time, and they hand down to us the teaching of the Antichrist to arise in the last days.

Joseph Mede's Historicist Premillennialism

After Ribera, the next mover of a return to premillennialism was Joseph Mede (1586–1639), a tutor of Greek at Cambridge. In his *Clavis Apocalyticae* (1627), Mede upheld Justin Martyr's view that a literal view of the millennial kingdom of Christ is the ancient faith of the Church. But his view differed in two things from the view of Justin and the early Fathers.

First, unlike Ribera, he still clung to the medieval historicist reading of the Revelation, seeing the events of the Revelation as happening in his own time. There was no Antichrist or Tribulation to come. The corrupt papacy was still the Antichrist and its oppressions were the Tribulation. As a result, he saw the 1,260 days of Revelation as day-years until the downfall of the papacy. And so, with start dates of 394, when Nicene Theodosius defeated the pro-pagan Eugenius, or the sack of Rome in 410, he came up with dates of 1654 to 1716 for the end of Antichrist's reign.

Second, based on Romans 9 to 11, he argued that the Jews would be miraculously converted to the Christian faith before the appearance of Christ to inaugurate the millennium. This was not an idea much spoken of by the Fathers.

Mede's work influenced many. In England, Thomas Goodwin, John Milton, Henry More, Isaac Newton, and William Whiston followed him. Working with the day-year principle, Newton and Adam Clarke calculated that Christ would return in 2016, that date being 1,260 years after the Donation of Pepin (756), which invested royal status upon the Pope. Newton also considered that the date might be calculated from the coronation of Charlemagne in 800, giving an end date of 2060.

In France, Mede influenced the Huguenot Pierre Jurieu. In America, Increase Mather, who had studied in Ireland and ministered in England, was also persuaded by Mede. In 1669, he proposed that Christ would come to inaugurate the millennium, at which time the Jews would be converted, and a long period of blessing would come upon the earth:

> That which presseth me so, as that I cannot gainsay the Chiliastical opinion, is that I take these things for Principles, and no way doubt but that they are demonstrable. 1. That the thousand apocalyptical years are not passed but future. 2. That the coming of Christ to raise the dead and to judge the earth will be within much less than this thousand years. 3. That the conversion of the Jews will not be till this present state of the world is near unto its end. 4. That, after the Jews' conversion there will be a glorious day for the elect upon earth, and that this day shall be a very long continuance.[2]

In Germany, Mede's ideas were taken up by J.A. Bengel (1687–1752). Bengel taught that the papal Antichrist would be overthrown in 1836, that is, 1,290 days after the sack of Rome by Totila in 546. The overthrow of the papacy would usher in two separate millennia, the first on earth, followed by the judgement, and then the second in heaven. The Moravians learned this from Bengel and, in turn, passed it on to John Wesley.

Thus Mede's book brought about a new dawn for premillennialism on both sides of the Atlantic, with a schema now including the conversion of the Jews, their restoration to Palestine, the resurrection of the dead, and the thousand-year rule of Christ, all to be followed by a final apostasy and a final confrontation between good and evil. But all this was still based on a historicist reading of the Revelation and still calculated the time of the end by the day-year principle.

The French Revolution gave a tremendous boost to the day-year principle. The slaughter of priests, overthrow of all civil order, and exaltation of paganism, shocked the whole civilized world. Many were convinced that the events in France were the beginning of the awaited tribulation and Napoleon was the Antichrist. The events of 1792 to 1793 – the abolition of the monarchy and execution of Louis XVI – fell 1,260

[2] Mather 1669: Author's Preface to the Reader, folio 4.

years after the Code of Justinian (534) which granted spiritual supremacy to the Pontiff in perpetuity. Following Daniel 12:11–12, many awaited the 1,290 days (to fall in 1823) and the 1,335 days (in 1868) to usher in the millennial kingdom. One writer described the prevailing mood in the first half of the nineteenth century:

> Everything rung, and was connected with the revolution in France; which, for above 20 years, was, or was made, the all in all. Everything, not this thing or that thing, but literally everything, was soaked in this one event.[3]

Postmillennialism

In the meantime, another view arose, now called Postmillennialism. It was foreshadowed in the teaching Joachim of Fiore (1135–1202) who taught that history would exist in three ages analogous to the Persons of the Trinity. The Age of the Father was the time of the Old Testament, when man was taught to obey the divine law. The Age of the Son began with the birth of Jesus, when man became a son of God. The Age of the Holy Spirit would see the earth transformed into an earthly Paradise, a time of universal love, but ruled not by Christ, but by the priestly Order of the Just. Joachim expected this Age of the Spirit to begin in 1260.

But the chief architect of true postmillennialism was an Anglican divine, Daniel Whitby (1638–1726), who first published his views in his New Testament commentary of 1700. Whitby saw that the Bible spoke of a time when the earth would return to a blessed state. He could not reconcile this with the traditional Augustinian view of earth continuing in its present form until its judgement and destruction. So he proposed that, before the Second Coming of Christ, there would be a conversion of the world, a great golden age of the Church, which would usher in a worldwide time of righteousness, blessing, and peace. This would happen as the result of the outpouring of the Holy Spirit, which would be the 'first resurrection' of Revelation 20:5. This golden age might not be a literal thousand years, but it would endure for a long time. In this outpouring of the Spirit, said Whitby, all opposing forces would fall

[3] Henry Cockburn 1856: 1.79. Cockburn, later Scotland's Solicitor General, was connected with the events surrounding Edward Irving (see chapter 12). He was counsel for Hugh Bailie MacLean in his trial before the General Assembly in 1831, when MacLean brought about his own condemnation by failing to heed Cockburn's admonitions to silence (Brown 1887: 265).

before the preaching of the gospel. Jews and 'Mahometans' would turn to Christ. Christ's kingdom would come and the earth would be restored, all before Christ returned for the day of judgement.

But, in reality, postmillennialism was simply another version of Augustinian amillennialism. As in Augustinian amillennialism, the Church Age was the millennium. It would be ruled, not by the King Messiah, but by bishops and divines. As in Augustinian amillennialism, Satan would be bound in the Church Age. But now he would be even more bound in the golden age before the appearing of Christ. Yet they allowed the possibility of a revolt from grace, followed by tribulation, in the period just before the Second Coming, as in Revelation 20:7–9. And as in Augustinian amillennialism, the final appearance of Christ would signify the end of the world, in a cataclysm of resurrection, judgement, destruction, and eternal destinies in heaven or hell.

There were things about Whitby that should have made his views distasteful to the Reformed tradition. He tended towards Arminianism and Arianism (though he confined the latter to his journals). Yet his optimistic hope of better things yet to come, was immensely influential. It spread widely in Britain. It appeared in Jennen's libretto to Handel's *Messiah* (1741), where the preaching and triumphs of the gospel (§37–43) are followed by *Hallelujah* as "the kingdom of this world is become the kingdom of our God and of his Christ" (§44); then comes the Day of Judgement and the Resurrection (§47–48) and finally the acclamation of the Messiah (§53). And it was an earthly kingdom *before* the coming of Christ that Isaac Watts envisaged in his paraphrase of Psalm 72.

> Jesus shall reign where'er the sun
> Doth his successive journeys run;
> His kingdom stretch from shore to shore
> Till moons shall wax and wane no more.

Postmillennialism then crossed the Atlantic to America where it was taken up by Jonathan Edwards and Samuel Hopkins.

It's an ill wind that blows no good. And postmillennial optimism did much good. It inspired a bold and vigorous faith that transformed Britain and America. It lay behind the Great Awakenings in America. It inspired the missionary zeal of William Carey and David Livingstone, and the social crusades of Wilberforce, the Clapham sect, and Shaftesbury. Within Protestantism, it remained a powerful drive of evangelism right through to the early twentieth century, until the carnage of two World Wars largely shattered any hopes that the world was moving toward any golden age of faith. Yet it has adherents to this day, who see its truth proven in its role in evangelizing the world. Indeed, wherever Christians still work to implement biblical ethics in society we can still see a post-millennial optimism that hopes to convert the world to Christ's cause.

Yet, for all its good works, it contains errors serious enough that it should have been doubted earlier than it was.

First, it flies in the face of the scriptural testimony that the world will get worse, not better, before the Lord returns. The Parable of the Weeds shows that good and evil will grow side by side until the end (Matt. 13:36–43). The Parable of the Net shows that the end-time harvest will draw up both the righteous and the wicked and separate them (Matt. 13:47–50). The Lord Jesus says, "For as were the days of Noah, so will be the coming of the Son of man" (Matt. 24:36). That is, he will come in days like Noah's when *the wickedness of man was great in the earth and every intention of the thoughts of his heart was only evil continually* and *all flesh had corrupted its way* (Gen. 6:5, 12). Again, the Lord asks, "Nevertheless, when the Son of Man appears, will he find faith on earth?" (Luke 18:8) It is a question which invites a negative response or else there would be no point in asking it. And he says that the day of his coming shall be like a snare to all who dwell on the earth (Luke 21:34–35); that is, it shall not be an event that mankind hopes for and welcomes, but a thing of destruction to those unprepared. Again, Paul speaks of the Day of the Lord coming like a thief in the night, bringing sudden, inevitable destruction upon those who imagine themselves at peace (1 Thess. 5:2–3). And he speaks of a great apostasy and the rule of the lawless man before the coming of the Lord (1 Tim. 4:1; 2 Thess. 2:3–8). The Revelation speaks of the unholy threesome of the beast, the false prophet, and the Babylonian whore, who will tyrannize the earth prior to Jesus's return.

At heart, postmillennialism remains an amillennial position, which does not take seriously the Bible's teaching that the Messiah will rule the earth from Jerusalem. Indeed, it minimizes the importance of the Lord's return in saying that it is ultimately the Church who will save the world. And, as freedom to read and interpret the Bible for oneself grew in the nineteenth century, and as wider education and better libraries gave more access to the writings of the early Fathers, it was inevitable that others would turn to a more literal understanding of those texts that speak of the earthly messianic kingdom.

Lacunza and Futurist Premillennialism

While the English-speaking world was counting the day-years to the end of the Antichrist's reign, Manuel de Lacunza (1731–1801), a Chilean Jesuit, was reading Ribera. Deeply distraught at the suppression of the Jesuits by the Holy See, and seeing in it a portent of the end, he devoted himself to a life of secluded examination of the scriptures. After almost twenty years, he completed in 1790 the three volumes of his *La venida del Mesías en gloria y majestad*, which he presented in the pseudonym of a Hebrew Christian, Juan Josafat Ben-Ezra, in correspondence with a priest, Christophilus. But the work failed to obtain the royal patronage he sought, and was not printed during his lifetime. However, it circulated in manuscript throughout the Spanish dominions until, in 1810, it was secretly published in Cadíz. Then an 1816 Spanish edition appeared in London, before the work was condemned by the Inquisition in 1819 and proscribed by Pope Leo XII in 1824. Yet none of this reduced its popularity and it continued to be published secretly within the Spanish dominions and in Paris and London. In 1827, it appeared in an English translation by Edward Irving.

Lacunza's book is a work of eloquence and erudition, running to almost eight hundred pages in Irving's translation. His persona of a converted Jew shows great sympathy with the Jewish people and deep understanding of Jewish messianic beliefs. Like Ribera, he says that the Revelation pertains wholly to the time immediately before the coming of the Lord.[4] He asserts the ancient belief that Jesus shall return in glory to reign on earth, and all people shall know and adore him. To this he adds that, following Gentile Christian apostasy, the Jews will finally be converted to their Messiah, and worship him, bringing "life from the dead" (Rom. 11:15). In this Gentile apostasy, even the papacy will become corrupt and persecute true believers. They will do this in league with the Antichrist who will claim to be the Messiah and do remarkable wonders. Many Jews will turn to him, and he will proclaim himself to be God and, for three and a half years will persecute the church. But Jesus will appear and destroy him. The Lord will judge the living, convert the

[4] Lacunza (tr. Irving) 1827: 1:200–201.

Jews, raise the righteous dead, and inaugurate his 1,000-year earthly kingdom of peace and justice and oneness of faith and language. Then, after the earthly kingdom, the dragon will once again be loosed to deceive the world, but he will be defeated; and then Christ will raise all the individuals of Adam's race to the last judgement. Lacunza rejects the Augustinian idea that the world is to be consumed by fire and destroyed at the return of Christ.

Lacunza's futurist views therefore represent a full return to the historic premillennialism of the Church Fathers, including his seeing the 1,260 days of Daniel and Revelation as a literal three-and-a-half years. But he adds to them, and to Ribera, the matter of the conversion of the Jews at the end of the age. What's more, he adds the idea, based on Daniel 12:11, that, after the return of Jesus in judgement, there will be a 45-day period of "commotion, perturbation, and agitation of our globe," during which the wicked will be annihilated but the righteous preserved.[5]

Le Vice Anglais

Alcázar's Preterism was taken up in England by Thomas Hayne (1645) and Joseph Hall (1650) who also claimed that the prophecies of the Book of Daniel had all been fulfilled by the first century. Since then, Preterism has been in vogue more in England than elsewhere. By the twentieth century, it had morphed into the Idealism which became so prevalent in Anglican theological education, as noted in chapter one. In this view, gone is any idea that Bible prophecies are, as Newton said, "histories of things to come." Instead, the prophecies of Revelation arose perhaps from the cataclysm of Jerusalem's fall in the first century, but are now symbolic of the continual struggle between good and evil. They foretell no particular earthly events, except perhaps the return of Jesus, though not all agree even on that.

The foremost modern exponent of such views is the former Bishop of Durham, N.T. Wright. It is sometimes said, especially when it comes to eschatology, that it is easier to learn what Wright doesn't believe than what he does believe. He strongly opposes what he says is the average Christian view, the amillennial view that we die and go to heaven, a view which he attributes to Lessing and the Enlightenment more than to Origen and Plato. He also speaks dismissively of "dispensationalism,"

[5] Lacunza (tr. Irving) 1827: 2:250.

by which he seems to include all forms of premillennial belief. He rightly says that the rapture is "not about saved souls going up to heaven" but that 1 Thessalonians 4 is about going out to meet the Lord in the air – "whatever Paul thought would be the objective corollary to that" – and coming back, but "even if you want to take 1 Thess. 4 moderately literally" (which he doesn't), we don't stay in heaven but escort the Lord back to earth.[6] Instead, he says, the truth is that the New Jerusalem comes to earth (omitting any mention of the intervening millennial reign of Rev. 20), uniting heaven and earth. Therefore the promises of God are about the renewal of the earth, not about Jesus coming to destroy the earth. A biblical eschatology has to talk about the new heavens and the new earth. He thinks that talk of Jesus's return in power and judgement, in Matthew 24, may refer to the AD 70 destruction of Jerusalem.

But, he says, the great transformation has already taking place at the cross and the resurrection, and in our regeneration. So he speaks of the appearing of Jesus rather than the coming of Jesus. For Jesus is not coming from a far place, but rather the curtain that separates the divine world from our earthly experience will be drawn aside so that the earth will be infused with the presence of Jesus and the divinity of God. He does not say whether this drawing aside of the curtain, this unveiling, will be swift or slow. Will Jesus suddenly be revealed to the world, or will there be a dawning process of God-consciousness that will transform the world? He says, "I don't deny that I believe some future event will result in the personal presence of Jesus within God's new creation."[7] But for now we await the eventual lifting of the veil between our world and the life of God. All this suggests that he is not expecting Jesus to return on the clouds in power and glory to break the power of the Antichrist and set up his millennial kingdom on Zion.

I hope I have done Wright no wrong in this brief summary. As said, his eschatology is not the clearest. Even the ever-gracious John Stott, who was no literalist in things eschatological, was at a loss over what Wright meant.

> Tom Wright alludes many times to the climax and consummation of history. But he reverses the direction of Christ's 'coming' from 'a downward cloud-borne movement' to his exaltation from earth to heaven, involving his vindication. Does this mean that the personal,

[6] Wright 2001.
[7] Wright 2001.

> visible, and glorious parousia of Jesus Christ has been completely dissolved into apocalyptic imagery?[8]

Of course, we may raise the same objections to Wright's Idealism as we did to simple preterism. First, it depends on a pre-AD 70 date for the Revelation, which goes against patristic testimony. Second, at the time when the Revelation was written, and for 1500 years after, no one ever read it the way Wright does. More broadly, his disregard of the plain meaning of prophecy about the glorious, bodily return of Jesus is deeply concerning. With the Church of England in such bondage to these ideas, it is small wonder that it finds itself in the straits it now does.

SUMMARY

So now there are three ways of reading the Revelation – Historicism, Preterism, and Futurism. All three would remain influential in their respective circles. Historicism still has followers in the Reformed tradition. Preterism briefly served its role in deflecting the Reformers' accusations that the Pope and his minions were the Antichrist and the scarlet Whore, and lives on in Idealism. Yet it was the Futurism of Ribera and Lacunza which was to prove most influential of all, in the part it played in the nineteenth century's rediscovery of premillennialism.

[8] Stott 2001: 115.

12

Dispensational Pretribulationism

LACUNZA's book, as said, was published in London, in the Spanish tongue, in 1810. There, in 1825, an unnamed missionary brought it to the attention of a Scots preacher called Edward Irving (1792–1834) who was making a great name for himself in early nineteenth-century London.

EDWARD IRVING

Irving was appointed minister to the Church of Scotland in London in 1822. Soon he was the cynosure of the great city, and aristocracy and royalty flocked to hear "The Caledonian Prodigy." Irving held to the premillennial, historicist views of Joseph Mede and his preaching was given to Medean exposition of prophecy. The 1,260 day-years of Daniel and Revelation, he taught, were fulfilled at the French Revolution in 1792. He counted Daniel's 1,290 years as pointing to 1823 and declared that year to be one of great significance. Yet it came and went without great incident.

Then he learned about Lacunza's futurist interpretation of the Revelation, that the entire book, save the first three chapters, speaks only of the last three and a half years before the return of the Lord. He was intrigued. He began taking Spanish lessons, and, in the early summer of 1826, on a sabbatical in Scotland, translated Lacunza's book and furnished it with a 192-page preliminary discourse. He wrote:

> His book is the finest demonstration of the orthodoxy of the ancient system of the millenarians which can be imagined; indeed I may say perfect and irrefragable, I never expect to see an answer to it, nor do I believe an answer will ever be attempted.[1]

Irving admits that he still takes the historicist viewpoint that the 1,260 days of Revelation (and the 1,290 days of Daniel) are day-years. He adds that both the 1,260 years and the 1,290 years are now passed and that the Lord will come after Daniel's 1,335 days, in 1868. But he concedes that Lacunza is persuasive and allows that there may also be a literal three and a half year rule of Antichrist once the allotted number of day-years is fulfilled.[2] He admits that although he formerly held postmillennial views, he now rejects them: the world can never be converted to the church, for the two are at continual war. The church must hope entirely for Jesus's return and earthly rule.[3]

Then Irving outlines three 'dispensations' of salvation history. First was the 'local' dispensation of the Israelite kingdom, typologically prefiguring the millennium; second, the spiritual dispensation of the church; third, the universal and real dispensation of the millennium (which the first dispensation had prefigured). This would be inaugurated by the conversion of the Jews to Christ, then Jesus would rule from Zion with his government of risen saints. Thus he saw the second dispensation – the church – as a hiatus between the first and third dispensations, that is, between typological national Israel and its fulfilment in the millennial kingdom.

Irving had already begun to gather around him a coterie of wealthy gentlemen interested in prophecy. In 1826, Henry Drummond, a banker, together with Hugh Boyd M'Neile, a bold Irish-Scots preacher, hosted a prophecy conference at Drummond's stately home in Albury Park, Surrey, where they discussed prophecy for seven hours a day. Irving was one of the leading lights there, propounding a premillennialist reading of scripture with insights from Lacunza. Those who attended began to style themselves 'the students of prophecy' and published *The Morning Watch or A Quarterly Journal of Prophecy.* These conferences continued annually until 1830 when their spirit flew across the Irish Sea, where Theodosia Lady Powerscourt, another Irving admirer, who had attended

[1] Lacunza (tr. Irving) 1827: 1:xxvi.
[2] Lacunza (tr. Irving) 1827: 1:xxix-xxx, lii.
[3] Lacunza (tr. Irving) 1827: 1:vii–viii.

the 1827 Albury conference, began hosting similar prophetic conferences in her palatial residence near Dublin from 1831 to 1833.

In 1828, Irving published his own mature thoughts on the coming of the Lord in *The Last Days: A Discourse on the Evil Character of These Our Times*. Christ, he said, would appear to the Jews and through them destroy all anti-Christian nations, evangelize the world, and rule in the millennium. This would take place in 1868, being 1,335 years from Justinian's exaltation of the See of Rome and 75 years – that is, 1,335 minus 1,260 – from the French Revolution.

In the summer of 1828, Irving preached in the church of John McLeod Campbell in Row in Dunbartonshire, Scotland, and brought back to London a young assistant, A.J. Scott, who helped him from 1828 to 1829. Scott challenged the cessationist claim that the miraculous gifts of the Spirit had ceased at Pentecost, and persuaded Irving to his views. And so Irving, adding yet another radical doctrine to his pulpit, began to teach that the apostolic spiritual gifts had disappeared from the church because of its carnality and worldliness, and looked forward to their reappearing in the approaching last days.

He was also teaching on the incarnation. In March 1827, some of his congregation were shocked at his reference to the human nature of Jesus as "sinful flesh." He meant that Jesus received his human nature from his mother, whose human nature was that of Adam after the fall. (The only alternative was the Catholic doctrine of Mary's Immaculate Conception, which Protestants rejected.) Therefore, since the Son of God came in real flesh, his flesh was the flesh of fallen humanity. Of course, he was sinless in thought, word, and deed. But his sinlessness was due not to his flesh, but to the sanctifying work of the Holy Spirit within him, in which matter he provided a pattern for the believer's life.

But rumours spread. An Anglican priest, Henry Cole, attended an Irving sermon in October 1827 and asked afterwards what he meant by calling the flesh of Jesus "that sinful substance." Irving explained. But Cole published his account of their conversation, condemning Irving's views as heretical. This sparked an ongoing tract war between the two, and Irving's name fell under suspicion of heresy. Determined to set the matter straight, he published his response in *The Orthodox and Catholic Doctrine of our Lord's Human Nature* in 1830.[4]

[4] He wrote three tracts in his defence: the third was *The Opinions Circulating Concerning Our Lord's Human Nature, Tried by the Westminster Confession of Faith* (May 1830).

After Scott's departure, in 1830, Irving took on a new assistant, an Aberdonian called David Brown. He too had read Mede and tended to premillennialist views, but he was a sagacious man, in no hurry to stir up controversy. On the matter of Irving's Christology, he recalled that Irving loved the Lord and that his views were orthodox, but he saw well that the opening words of *The Orthodox and Catholic Doctrine* were ambiguous enough to sustain the accusations against him.[5] Terms and words had been chosen carelessly and his views could be read as Nestorian. Despite his admiration for Irving, he wondered whether his mind was "getting off its balance."[6]

In the spring of that year, reports arrived of an outbreak of charismatic tongues and prophecy in Port Glasgow around the church of John McLeod Campbell in Row. Irving welcomed the news of these events, seeing in them his anticipated restoration of apostolic gifts in the last days, and he longed for their manifestation in London. As a result, in the spring of 1831, amidst an outbreak of cholera, Irving held meetings in his church every morning from 6:30 to 7:30, attended by up to 1,000 people, praying for an outpouring of the Spirit and restoration of the apostolic gifts as they had appeared in Glasgow. Select guests then followed Irving home for breakfast. At one of these breakfasts, Miss Emily Cardale, from Glasgow, and others burst into "utterances" in English.[7] Later, in April, her mother, Mrs Cardale, spoke in tongues and prophesied at the early prayer meeting.

Meanwhile, in May of 1831, the General Assembly deposed three ministers associated with Irving's ideas.[8] The saintly John McLeod Campbell of Row in Dunbartonshire, who had endorsed the charismatic outbreak in Port Glasgow, was condemned for teaching "universal pardon," although he did not teach salvation apart from faith.[9] A.J. Scott, Irving's assistant from summer 1828 to 1829, was deposed for opposing the Calvinist doctrine of limited atonement. And Irving's disciple, Hugh MacLean, was deposed for teaching, "The Sinfulness of Christ's Human Nature." Irving's closest colleagues were coming under attack for Irvingite doctrines. Brown suspected that the Kirk was closing in on him.

[5] Brown 1887: 264.
[6] Brown 1887: 259.
[7] Brown 1887: 267–269.
[8] Brown 1887: 262.
[9] Brown 1887: 262. The "Row Heresy" and the Kirk's persecution of John Campbell remained a live issue for years. See McGregor 1950: 281–301.

In September 1830, he was summoned before the Presbytery of London. The deep-considering Brown, seeing the lives of some involved in the prophetic manifestations, now judged that they were not of divine origin. He confided as much to Mrs Irving on the evening before Irving was to appear before the Presbytery. Yet, the next day, Irving boldly informed the Presbytery that his teachings and the prophetic manifestations were in line with the Westminster Confession. The Presbytery were not convinced. In November 1830, they ruled that his teachings were heretical. Yet they lacked the authority to depose him. His elders defended him and he continued ministering.

But even his elders and trustees were divided over the growing place of the tongues and utterances. Many objected. But Irving said he could not oppose the Holy Spirit. The board of trustees ruled that these phenomena should not appear in the Sunday morning services, but the prayer meeting attendees pushed for their inclusion. Irving was caught between. Some months later, he was preaching on Sunday morning, when Miss Hall, a governess, stood up during the sermon, hurried to the vestry, and began prophesying aloud in tongues. The congregation, overhearing this, was thrown into confusion. Irving explained that this was the reappearance of the tongues of 1 Corinthians 14. And from then on, he permitted these manifestations. Services were punctuated with outbreaks of tongues, visions, and prophecy. An outburst of tongues would be greeted by cheers from one side and cries of "Silence!" from the other. The board of trustees demanded the chaos stop.

How this Scotch madness was viewed by the Londoners can be imagined. *The Times*, on 29 October 1831, warned "sensible people who frequent the Caledonian Chapel – lately converted into a miracle shop – that these follies are contagious." Irving defended it as the gifts of the Spirit, but the board of trustees brought it to the Presbytery.

The Presbytery considered it an embarrassment to the Scottish Church. They had listened with growing concern to reports of Irving's hubris and folly. There was his unsparing criticism of the church, his translating and endorsing of Jesuit books teaching the earthly rule of Christ, his heretical views on the human nature of Christ, and now his adoption of the Port Glasgow madness. On 2 May 1832, they judged him to be in violation of the order of worship for the Church of Scotland by allowing interruptions by the laity. They deemed him unfit to minister and ordered his removal from ministry. The next day, those who came for morning prayer found the church locked. Later that month he was condemned and defrocked by the Edinburgh General Assembly.

With 800 charismatics from his church, Irving repaired to a rented facility on Newman Street, there to explore the full restoration of New Testament spirituality in Spirit baptism, tongues, and prophecy. They called their new assembly the Catholic Apostolics. The front platform of the church was laid out in six levels as an expression of its authority structure. At the top level were the Apostles. At the second level sat the Prophets. The third, fourth, and fifth levels were for the Elders, Evangelists and Deacons in descending order. The bottom level was reserved for Irving, who received the title "Angel," from Revelation chapters two and three. Yet Irving's role seems to have been more token than real; leadership was in the hands of the apostles. Irving preached on the full restoration of the gifts of the Spirit, including healing. Healing was a Christian's right. No one with faith need be stricken by sickness.

In March 1833, the Church of Scotland Presbytery who had ordained Irving, in his hometown of Annan, charged him with heresy regarding his doctrine of the "sinfulness of our Lord's human nature," and condemned him. A month later, despite all prayers for healing, Irving lost his son to sickness. Weighed down by sorrow, by the burden of the new church, and broken by blame on all sides, his prayers were now for his own health. But these too went unanswered. He died of tuberculosis in December 1834, at the age of forty-two. His last words were, "If I die, I die unto the Lord. Amen." It is possible that the mental imbalance of his last years was a prodromal symptom of the tuberculosis bacterium.

THE GLASGOW OUTPOURING

We spoke of the outbreak of "prophecies" in Glasgow which manifested itself in Irving's church, and of the condemnation of the ministers who supported it. We must now retrace a little the story of these events. It's a fascinating tale, especially if (like me) your ancestry is deeply connected to that city which, in the nineteenth century, was the second city of the British empire. Scotland in the 1800s was a uniformly Christian country, with Presbyterian institutions, universities, and schools. The Highland clearances of 1750 to 1850 had driven hordes of "bare-arsed highlanders" (in David Hume's phrase) – landless Campbells, McDonalds, McLeods, McKays – to seek work in the great bustling commercial city and its environs, as shipbuilders, tanners, weavers, spinners, and all other trades of the day. Many were rough on the outside, no foes to whisky. But they were pious within. They had to be, in the face of life's brevity before the scourges of poverty, malnutrition, and deadly disease – polio, cholera, smallpox, diphtheria, tuberculosis – that lashed the land.

The dominant influence on Scottish civic life, far from the London parliament, was the Church of Scotland. But many were unhappy with it. Their especial grievance was the fact that ministers were appointed not on learning or sanctity, but on the patronage of wealthy landowners. This eventually led to a split in the church in the following decade – the Great Disruption of 1843 – led by Thomas Chalmers, in whose Glasgow church Irving had first ministered, and by Irving's former assistant, David Brown.

In 1826, John McLeod Campbell pastored the parish of Row (now Rhu) on the Gareloch in the Clyde Estuary, north-west of Helensburgh. He was a classicist and a devoted reader of the Fathers. And, in contrast to the hard, damning Calvinism of much of the Scottish church, he preached the love of God and the humanity of Christ. Thousands came to his services. Irving preached there in the summers of 1828 and 1829 and left his own mark upon the congregation. Campbell's assistant, A.J. Scott, as we saw, returned to London with Irving.

Five miles south-east of Row, at Port Glasgow over the River Clyde, lived a family of McDonalds who had visited Campbell's church in Row. In 1830, the twin brothers, James and George, thirty years old, worked as shipbuilders to support their three sisters, including fifteen-year-old Margaret.[10] Margaret was bed-ridden and ailing. But, in February, she received what she called an "outpouring of the Spirit." Through this, and through her reading of the scriptures, she began to speak of the apostasy of the church and of the Lord's imminent return. She prophesied that the Lord, when he came to judge the world, would catch up the faithful few first to spare them from his judgement, but that worldly people would have to endure the tribulation. By these 'worldly' people, she meant worldly Christians, that is, nominal Presbyterians and the few Catholic churchgoers.

By April, doctors had given up all hope of Margaret's recovery and she was drawing near to death. But, on 14 April, 1830, despite her frailty, she began powerfully praising and prophesying in the Spirit, and ended

[10] McPherson 1973: 72–73.

by praying that her brother James would be anointed by the Holy Spirit. James then said, "I have got it." After some minutes of silence, he turned to Margaret and said, "Arise and stand upright." He took her by the hand and she arose, healed of her sickness.[11]

The next day, James wrote to another bed-ridden young woman, one Mary Campbell in the nearby town of Fernicarry, telling her likewise to "Arise and stand upright." On reading his letter, she too was healed. Now this Mary Campbell had already begun speaking in unknown tongues some two weeks before, on March 28. Then, two days after Margaret's healing, her brothers, first George and then James, also began speaking in tongues. Shortly after, Margaret herself began speaking in tongues.

At news of these events, a revival of prayer and praise broke out in towns across the West of Scotland. Many came from Scotland, England, and Ireland, to visit Margaret and hear her testimony, and the house was full every day. Her emphasis, and that of her brothers, was always the coming of the Lord. As one visitor said, "The burden of all they say is – that the Lord is near, near at hand."[12] A young doctor, Robert Nolan, recorded that she spoke of a two-stage coming of the Lord.

> The power of the Holy Ghost rested upon her for several successive hours...here we first see the distinction between that final stage of the Lord's coming, when every eye shall see Him, and His prior appearing in glory to them that look for him.[13]

Among these charismatics, Margaret's views about a two-stage return of the Lord became widely known.

Not everyone was sympathetic, of course. Most Church of Scotland clergy were opposed to this outbreak of enthusiasm. The McDonalds' own parish minister denounced them from the pulpit.[14] Soon the national press weighed in against the "fanatics." Proud Edinburgh's proud *Scotsman* pronounced, on 2 June, 1830:

> One might suppose that the superior intelligence of even the lower population of Scotland would at once have buried these absurdities in ridicule and contempt. But no! even a clergyman has been sucked into the Gareloch whirlpool of blasphemy, and is preaching and teaching the new creed, and encouraging the workers of miracles with all his might. Next

[11] McPherson 1973: 63.
[12] McPherson 1973: 65.
[13] Norton, cited in McPherson 1973: 47.
[14] McPherson 1973: 80.

> we are told that a writer to the signet has given the right hand of fellowship to the presumptuous spinster of "the tongues"; and (tell it not in Gath!) it is a fact that the wiseacres of Cambridge University have had their wits employed in decyphering the sayings of Miss Mary [Campbell], and have absolutely pronounced the "new tongues" to *resemble* Chinese! Gramercy!

On 18 June, the *Glasgow Herald* wrote in similar vein:

> The public have already been made fully acquainted with the miracles of speaking in unknown tongues and writing in unknown languages—the miraculous healing of the sick, and the attempt to make the lame walk without crutches—and other affected doings, equally insane and ridiculous.

But not all the clergy were opposed. The Reverend John Cardale witnessed the events, and believing them to be the work of God, began to encourage them among his own congregation. His wife began speaking in tongues and repeating prophecies like those of Margaret McDonald. In Spring 1830, the Cardales were in London, and on 30 April, Mrs Cardale uttered a prophecy about the coming of the Lord in Irving's church. This, it seems, was the 'woman's utterance' in Irving's church, which Samuel Tregelles said was the origin of the pretribulation rapture teaching. Cardale and his family became dedicated supporters of Irving.

In September 1830, the prophecy journal of the Albury Park conferences, *The Morning Watch,* edited by Irving, reported these events along with an explanation of Margaret McDonald's prophecies that there would be a two-stage coming of the Lord. It distinguished between the 'epiphany' of Christ and his 'advent' or 'parousia', the former issuing in the resurrection and the rapture, the latter being his public appearing in judgement. The saints caught up to heaven in the rapture would be sheltered from judgement in some 'little sanctuary.'

John Nelson Darby

John Nelson Darby was a young Anglo-Irish Anglican cleric. In the mid-1820s, he led some Irish peasantry from Catholicism to Anglicanism. His archbishop insisted that the converts swear allegiance to King George. But Darby – despite his oath of allegiance to the Sovereign and the Bishop – was unwilling to comply. In 1827, he fell from a horse and spent some months recuperating. During this time, he concluded that clerical leadership of any form was unbiblical. That year, he helped to found in Dublin a community of 'Brethren' for 'the breaking of bread.'

In 1830, when the Port Glasgow outpouring took place, Darby went to see it first-hand, being sent by some of the Brethren, in company with another Anglican cleric Benjamin Wills Newton. This was apparently in response to the report in the September *Morning Watch.* Twenty-three years later, he reported what he saw in his book, *The Irrationalism of Infidelity* (1853). The McDonalds invited him into their home. There he heard James McDonald speak and sing in tongues for about fifteen minutes, after which Margaret rose to give an interpretation. Darby was bemused by the proceedings, remembering their misquotations of scripture. But he says nothing whatsoever of Margaret McDonald's or anyone else's views of the coming of the Lord. This is surprising, for all acknowledge that this was a constant theme of these meetings. Despite the fact that he does not mention it, it is hard to believe that he heard nothing of the subject, either from the McDonalds or from others.

By 1831, Darby had moved to England and formed an assembly in Plymouth together with Benjamin Wills Newton. The two became increasingly critical of the Anglican Church and eventually left it. With money from a wealthy adherent, George Wigram, they bought a chapel in Plymouth, which was open to Christians of any stripe for fellowship, prayer, praise, and communion, and called themselves the Plymouth Brethren. From the beginning, they stressed biblical prophecy, eschatology, and the soon coming of the Lord. Their eschatology was a mix of historicist and futurist, seeing the climactic events of the book of Revelation as awaiting their fulfilment in the end times.

In October that year, Darby, along with some 400 other evangelicals, attended the first prophecy conference hosted by Lady Powerscourt at Dublin. The accounts of the conference have recently been found and published.[15] Darby and Irving were both there. The chairman, Robert Daly, and other guests championed a pretribulation rapture, just as it had appeared in Irving's *The Morning Watch* more than a year before, in September 1830.[16] But Darby condemned it as "an absurdity," saying, "the grand tribulation of the latter days will fall upon the Jews – the

[15] Notebooks recording eye-witness accounts of the 1831 Powerscourt conference have emerged recently and been made public by Tom Chantry. See Fazio 2020.
[16] Rowdon 1967: 16.

church will be sifted."[17] Newton fully agreed. After all, if the church was to be raptured before the tribulation, who would the Antichrist persecute?[18] At this time, Darby was still wedded to "day-year" interpretation, saying, "the 1260 days most unequivocally mean years…all arguments against it are totally astray."[19]

Yet it seems that, by December, Darby was himself speaking of a pretribulation rapture. And by 1833, at the third Powerscourt conference, with Irving and Daly absent, Darby had changed his tune entirely. History, he said, was a series of divine dispensations – seven in number – running from creation till the millennial kingdom. He argued that there would be a "great parenthesis of prophetic time" between the 69th and 70th weeks of Daniel's prophecy. In this "parenthesis" fell the church age, a 2,000-year "postponement" of the divine plan for Israel, which began at Pentecost and will end at the Rapture. For God has two distinct peoples, and two distinct plans and destinies for them. God, in a move unforeseen by the prophets, had put on hold his promises for Israel until the church age was complete. Most of the scriptures, he said, including the four gospels, apply only to Israel. But the church is a mystery of which Paul alone speaks. Therefore some key eschatological texts, like Matthew 24, apply only to Israel and have nothing to say to the church. He proposed that, at the end of the church age, Christ would come secretly and invisibly to rapture the church heavenward seven years before the coming of the Antichrist and the tribulation. After the removal of the church, the divine plan for Israel would recommence. The people of Israel would undergo great tribulation. (This neatly answered the objection about whom the Antichrist would persecute if the church were raptured.) But from them would step forth the 144,000 Jewish virgins who would proselytize the world (Rev. 7:1–8). Then, finally, Christ would come, visibly and publicly, with all his saints, and judge the Antichrist, and save the Jews and others converted during the tribulation, and bring all the saved into the millennial kingdom.

Newton, who was Darby's junior by eight years, had thus far allowed Darby to treat him as his disciple. But when Darby started airing these views, Newton was appalled, and said so. Darby's dispensationalism and secret rapture was, he said, "the height of speculative nonsense."[20] It was

[17] Powerscourt Notebooks, ii.4–5.
[18] Coad 1968: 129.
[19] Powerscourt Notebooks, i.37.
[20] Ladd 1956: 41.

clear from Scripture, Newton said, that the rapture would be public and after the tribulation. On Darby's theory about the "great parenthesis of prophetic time" and the postponed seventieth week of Daniel, he said, "The secret rapture was bad enough but this was worse."[21] He utterly rejected Darby's notion that the prophecies of Matthew 24 relate not to all Christians but only to the Jews after the secret rapture of the church. All God's people, Newton said, whether Gentile or Jewish Christian, are one.

Darby did not take kindly to such dismissal of his views. He retaliated by challenging Newton over a Plymouth member, Francis Newman – the younger brother of John Henry Newman – who had begun to express unitarian views. Newton had allowed him to remain in the Plymouth assembly, hoping that he would be restored. But Darby excommunicated Newman, overriding Newton. Newton, in protest at Darby's assuming authority to do any such thing, resigned as presiding elder of the Plymouth assembly. Yet Newton was highly respected by the Plymouth congregation and his influence there continued. The affair presaged what were to become abiding traits of Brethren assemblies: first, the tension between Christian holiness and the desire to welcome all; and, second, the question of who makes the rules in a society of equals. In time, these issues led to the multiple fracturing of the movement into many degrees of Open and Exclusive Brethren.

A deeper immediate rift was averted by Darby's taking himself to Switzerland to establish Brethren assemblies there. Eventually, through his followers, he established congregations in Switzerland, France, Germany, Italy, Sweden, and Holland, ultimately producing a new Darby Bible translation in each country. But in 1843, he returned to Plymouth, where the assembly had now built a larger chapel and numbered over 1,000 members. Darby immediately censured Newton and the Plymouth congregation for their formal recognition of elders, which, he said, ran counter to the priesthood of all believers. He was also critical of Newton's book, *Thoughts on the Apocalypse*, and devoted himself to writing a book condemning it. Then he returned to Switzerland.

In 1845, at the threat of revolution in Geneva, he returned again to Plymouth to "battle for the soul of Brethrenism." He again criticized them for their appointment of elders and their view that each assembly should be autonomously ruled by such elders. Seeing himself as "more

[21] Rowdon 1967: 96–97.

equal than others," he demanded that they submit to his views on these matters. When they refused, he exited the Plymouth fellowship and, persuading Wigram to give him the use of a chapel in Raleigh Street, set up a rival assembly there. He enlisted others to his side, persuading the assembly in Rawthorne Street, London, to excommunicate Newton.

In 1847, Darby's followers claimed to have detected a whiff of heresy in Newton's earlier rebuttal of the incarnational views of Edward Irving. There Newton had allowed that Christ had suffered 'Adamic' sufferings – hunger, pain, and the frailties of a mortal body – before the crucifixion. Darby condemned this as heresy. Newton withdrew his pamphlet for reconsideration. But Darby was unsatisfied. He demanded that Newton make a full repentance for this alleged sin and acknowledge the justice of Darby's accusation. Not a few agreed with Henry Groves that Darby was "bent on ruling." But Newton, wishing to avoid division, left Plymouth and the Brethren and moved to London, where he set up an independent congregation. There he taught futurist, post-tribulation pre-millennialism, as taught by the Ante-Nicene Fathers.

But Darby couldn't leave him alone. In 1848 he accused him of being inspired by Satan, just as Irving was.

> I have not the least doubt (from circumstances I have heard lately of the authenticity of which I have not the smallest question) that Mr. Newton received his prophetic system by direct inspiration from Satan, analogous to the Irvingite delusion.[22]

Finally, Darby was left unopposed as the Brethren kingpin and duly excommunicated all other assemblies who would not condemn Newton's 'heresy.' But Newton was defended by the most prominent evangelical leaders of the day, including Charles Spurgeon, George Müller, and Samuel Tregelles. Spurgeon utterly rejected Darby's views as mistaken on eschatology and heretical on the doctrine of the atonement.

> With a diligence never exceeded, and a subtlety never equalled, they [Darby and his followers] are labouring to seduce the members of our churches to the subversion of the truth.[23]

Condemning Darby's "new Bible," he said, "I hold him to be outside the Church of God on earth, being outside what represents it in London. I

[22] Irving, "A Plain Statement of the Doctrine on the Sufferings," 109 (16).
[23] Spurgeon 1869:1.

am bound by Scripture to count him so."[24] Müller said, "The time came when I had to either part from my Bible or part from John Darby. I chose to keep my precious Bible." He recorded in his diary that Darby appeared at his door seeking to bring Müller's Bristol Brethren back into the Darby fold. Müller's words to him were, "You have acted so wickedly in this whole affair, that many things have to be looked into before we could be really united again." He and Darby never spoke again.

The origin of Darby's views

Some maintain that Darby's eschatological views came to him during his recovery from his riding accident. They resist the idea that Irving or the Port Glasgow tongues had any influence on him. Walvoord wrote:

> Any careful student of Darby soon discovers that he did not get his eschatological views from men, but rather from his doctrine of the church as the body of Christ, a concept no one claims was revealed supernaturally to Irving or Macdonald… The often-repeated charge that Darby secured his pretribulationism from Edward Irving has never been actually documented. One can hardly account for the wide acceptance of pretribulationism by Plymouth Brethren, who are devoted students of the Bible, to the offering of this view by a person who had no reputation for orthodoxy.[25]

Yet Walvoord was wrong about Irving's influence on Darby not being documented.[26] Harold Rowdon and Roy Coad, both British Brethren men who knew heaps more about Darby and the Brethren than Walvoord ever did, had already written of it in the 1960s. Rowdon says that Darby was influenced by the September 1830 article in Irving's *The Morning Watch,* which distinguished between the 'epiphany' of Christ and his 'advent' or 'parousia.'[27] Coad says plainly that from Irving "Darby had adopted the doctrine of 'the secret rapture of the saints.'"[28] In 1971, Murray's *Puritan Hope* noted that "All the salient features of Darby's scheme are to be found in Irving," from his general millenarianism to the specifics of the pretribulation rapture and the end of the Gentile

[24] Spurgeon 1874: 22.
[25] Walvoord 1976: 47–48. On the same topic, see Ice 2016.
[26] McPherson 1973, 1974, 1975; cf. also 2000.
[27] Rowdon 1967: 16.
[28] Coad 1968: 128.

dispensation.[29] In 1973, McPherson's *The Unbelievable Pre-Trib Origin*, and its later versions, documented Darby's dependence on Irving and the Glasgow charismatics in detail. Perhaps Walvoord was unaware of all of them. (Though, to be honest, pretribbers have always sought to dismiss McPherson.) But their sources and research were solid, and McPherson, who was a journalist, investigated the original Scottish sources in great detail. Let's look briefly at a few of the facts.

Darby certainly read Irvingite publications. In a paper called *Reflections Upon the Prophetic Enquiry,* he speaks of reading Irving's Preliminary Discourse to Lacunza, and alternately praises Irving and condemns his "great carelessness."[30] In December 1830, he published an article in the Irish *Christian Herald* called, "On Days Signifying 'Years' in Prophetic Language," in which he proposed that "earthly things were the Jews proper portion" but "the church was a system of grace and heavenly hopes."[31] This language is straight from Irving's Preliminary Discourse to Lacunza, where Irving speaks of "dispensations both Jewish and Gentile" relating respectively to "earthly things" and "heavenly things."[32]

Further, in this 1830 paper, we can see that Darby's ideas are by no means in their final form. He still defends the day-year theory and speaks of the church suffering in the tribulation. It therefore seems that, at the time of writing, Darby's views had been influenced by Irving but he had not yet adopted the idea of the pretribulation rapture, nor the futurist view of the Revelation so crucial to his mature views.

In the same month, December 1830, Irving also published an article, in *The Morning Watch,* saying:

> My conviction, then, is, that our dispensation, since Christ, is altogether an interjected and intercalated period; during which the members of the church that is to be glorified are in succession forming until the body shall be completed: and, this done, this period proper to the sons of God is ended, and the ways of God in governing men in flesh, which for this object were suspended, resume their wonted course. When the Spirit hath united all Christ's members to the Head; when the number of the elect rulers is completed, and the spouse made out of his spiritual substance; then the sons of God are manifested in and under the Head, to take the

[29] Murray 1971: 200.
[30] Darby 1829.
[31] Darby 1830: 211.
[32] Lacunza (tr. Irving) 1827: 1:x.

> rule over the world in flesh, which is now governed as it was at the first, and brings out the perfection of holiness. My idea is, that not the Old-Testament but the New-Testament dispensation hath an end: and then the other resumes its course, under Christ and his bride, which is his Church.

This is so similar to Darby's view of the church as an intercalation in the divine plan for Israel that the similarities cannot be accidental. It was evidently another Irving idea that Darby borrowed.

We know too that Darby spoke with Irving, for he wrote in 1844 that, "at least fourteen years" before he "insisted on these very things with Mr. Irving."[33] That points to 1830. Irving was in Dublin in September of that year, as a guest at the home of Lady Powerscourt, who had arranged for him an intensive preaching and lecturing tour and introduced him to prominent Irish evangelicals with an interest in prophecy.[34] Darby appears to have been in Ireland at the same time, and is known to have been acquainted with Lady Powerscourt. So it is likely that they met then. It is also possible that they met on one of Darby's trips to London, perhaps when he was there in May 1830. Both were also present at Powerscourt in October 1831, when Darby trashed Robert Daly's views on the pretribulation rapture. On as many occasions as he did meet Irving, they would have had ample opportunity to exchange ideas.

THE SPREAD OF DARBY'S TEACHING

Darby's pretribulational views had little uptake in England and Europe outside Darby's Exclusive Brethren churches. But, between 1862 and 1868, he travelled throughout the United States and Canada, and then again, between 1870 and 1875. Since America was still largely in the grip of postmillennialism, the biblical realism of Christ's earthly kingdom and the futurist interpretation of the Revelation was electrifying for many. And since the only version they had ever heard of this message was Darby's pretribulationism, they welcomed it. D.L. Moody took up these ideas and spread them through his preaching. In 1886, he founded the Chicago Evangelization Society (later the Moody Bible Institute), which was dispensationalist from the outset. In 1909, one of Moody's

[33] Darby 1844.

[34] Oliphant 1862: 2.149–53. Fazio 2020: 8. Irving was back in London by 13 Oct., for he wrote a letter with "London" as his address on that date (Oliphant 1862: 2.151.

assistants, Cyrus I. Scofield (1843–1921), published a reference Bible whose King James text was furnished with Darbyite dispensationalist notes. This had a huge circulation and influence, selling a million copies in the USA in twenty years, making Scofield wealthy. It led L.S. Chafer, in 1924, to found another dispensationalist institution, Dallas Theological Seminary. These institutions, through their graduates and publications, converted tens, perhaps hundreds, of millions of American evangelicals to Darby's dispensationalism.

More was to come. In 1963, Finis J. Dake, a Pentecostal dispensationalist of chequered history, issued yet another dispensationalist reference Bible to spread Darby's gospel among Pentecostals. Hal Lindsey's *Late Great Planet Earth* (1970), which foretold that the rapture, tribulation, and second coming would take place in the late 1980s, was the best-selling non-fiction book in the United States throughout the 70s and well into the 80s. In 1979, it became a film narrated by Orson Welles. Bigger still was the 'Left Behind' series of apocalyptic thrillers by Tim LaHaye and Jerry Jenkins. A series of sixteen books, forty kids' novellas, five movies, and a PC game, it details the exploits of a group of young people 'Left Behind' at the Rapture, who are then converted to the Christian faith and work to save the world under the tyranny of a Romanian Antichrist. LaHaye then went on to set up the Pre-Trib Research Center, a body for promoting pretribulation dogma, run by pretribulation scholars, lavishly funded by public donations.

The result of this outpouring of sensationalist unscriptural prophecy was that almost every person in America was influenced, one way or another, by these ideas. People in historically amillennial churches – Catholics, Presbyterians, Episcopalians – learned more of Darby's eschatology than of the teachings of their own church, and swallowed it without pausing to examine it. It was influential in the wider English-speaking world and, in translation, far beyond. Christians worldwide now hoped for the sudden, secret appearing of Christ at any unheralded moment to rapture them to heaven. Never before in the field of human communication had there been such a triumph of marketing over content.

DIVIDING THE WORD OF TRUTH

As we have seen, Darby's contemporaries – Newton, Spurgeon, and Tregelles – denounced his views as erroneous. As these views began to spread in early 20th century America, many warned against this novelty. Philip Mauro, a notable Brethren lawyer and former dispensationalist, said Scofield's Bible was "modernism, moreover, of a very pernicious sort, such that it must have a 'Bible' of its own for the propagation of its peculiar doctrines, since they are not in the Word of God."[35] Mixing the Bible with Scofield's commentary was, he said, a "mixture of the precious and the vile" and he derided its claim that "there can be no adequate understanding or rightly dividing of the Word of God except from the standpoint of dispensational truth."[36]

"Rightly dividing the Word of Truth" became the favourite maxim of Darby's movement – hijacking Paul's phrase in 2 Timothy 2:15. By this they meant apportioning different Bible periods and texts to Darby's system of dispensations, deciding what applies to Israel and what to the Church. But, in effect, his system divides many things that God has joined together.

First, it divides the coming of the Lord. Instead of one advent, there were now two: first, a secret, invisible, coming of Christ to take away faithful Christians in the pre-tribulation rapture; then a second public coming, at the end of the tribulation, when he will take those converted during the tribulation: converted Jews, nominal Christians, and others.

Second, it divides the rapture. Now there was to be not one but two catchings-up. In the first, the Lord will not be seen by the world, but he will catch the church heavenwards. In the second, when he appears publicly, he will raise up those who were not caught up the first time.

Third, it divides the resurrection. Instead of there being two resurrections, one of the righteous and one of the unrighteous, as scripture says, there were now three resurrections; first, the rapture at which the righteous, living and dead, are resurrected, caught up, and transformed; second, the first biblical resurrection, at which the tribulation saints and saved Jews and Old Testament saints are transformed; and third, the second biblical resurrection of the remainder of people to judgement.

Fourth, it divides the people of God. Foundational to Darby's view is that the Church is a different people from the Old Testament saints. Therefore, the bride at the Marriage Supper of the Lamb, will be only the church, not the Old Testament saints, nor the tribulation saints, nor the converted 144,000 Israelites, who fall into a different category of later

[35] Mauro 1928: 9.
[36] Mauro 1928: 6.

"guests" at the wedding.[37] So Moses and the prophets will not get to sit at the marriage supper with the church. The supper will take place with only part of the bride (i.e., part of all the saved) present.

Fifth, it divides the teaching of the church. Of course, church teaching has often divided on many matters. But Darby introduced a whole new subject of contention in proposing a doctrine with no proven antecedent of any kind in 1800 years of church history, except perhaps for desperate Fra Dolcino in the fourteenth century.[38]

Sixth, it divides the judgement of God. Mark Hitchcock, a prominent pretribulationist, lists no less than seven different judgements, with supporting Bible verses for each one: the judgement seat of Christ for Christian believers (2 Cor. 5:10); the judgement of Old Testament believers (Dan. 12:1–3); the judgement of tribulation saints (Rev. 20:4–6); the judgement of Jews alive at the second coming (Ezek. 20:34–38); the judgement of Gentiles alive at the second coming (Matt. 25:31–46); the judgement of Satan and the fallen angels (Rev. 20:10); the judgement of the unrighteous at the Great White Throne (Rev. 20:11–15).

Finally, it divides even the dispensationalists, for they diverge upon almost every detail. Even among classical dispensationalists there was no consensus on the number of dispensations. But now there is classical, revised, and progressive dispensationalism, along with ultradispensationalism, divided into Acts 28 and Mid-Acts dispensationalism. They disagree on Israel and the church. Classical dispensationalists say the present church age is a "parenthesis" in God's plans for Israel, which have temporarily been placed on hold; there is only one "new covenant" and it is for Israel. Others minimize the parenthesis and see believing Jews and non-Jews as one. Some see two covenants, one for Jews, one for Gentiles; others see one covenant for both; still others see three covenants, one for Gentiles, one for current believing Jews, and one for future believing Jews. Nor is there any agreement on the time of the rapture. Some defend Darby's view: the Lord will rapture the church seven years before the tribulation begins. Others are now "mid-trib," saying the church will be raptured before the tribulation gets too bad, perhaps after three and a half years. Others say the church will be raptured before the wrath of God, but not during the Antichrist's tribulation. They disagree over when the church is raptured in the Revelation. Some say it must be

[37] Hitchcock 2012: 226.
[38] See chapter 15.

after Revelation 3, for the church is not mentioned again until chapter 20. Others say the church is caught up in chapter 11 or 12. To defend these views, they say that Revelation's frequent references to the "saints" cannot possibly mean the church; they can refer only to the "tribulation saints," that is, Jews and others who become believers after the rapture.

SUMMARY

Darby borrowed his pretribulation rapture and dispensationalism from Edward Irving. Irving in turn was influenced by Lacunza, and, to some degree, by the enthused women of the Glasgow outpouring, Mrs Cardale and Margaret McDonald. Darby initially rejected Irving's ideas publicly. But once Irving was defrocked, discredited, and ailing, Darby made these ideas known as his own new insight into scripture, and denounced Irving as Satanically inspired. The most prominent Christian leaders in Great Britain rejected Darby's teachings, but Americans imbibed them eagerly as an alternative to the prevailing postmillennialism. From the United States his teaching spread like wildfire.

Darby proclaimed that he had been given a revelation to "rightly divide the Word of Truth." But in fact he divided the coming of the Lord into two comings, the rapture of the saints into two raptures, the two biblical resurrections into three resurrections, God's one flock into two peoples, one of which was uninvited to the marriage supper of the Lamb. After separating from the Anglicans over a matter of church order that he had pledged to obey, he divided the Plymouth Brethren over his desire to be first. It is said that he greatly loved the poor and was loved by them. But the poor did not question his authority or his beliefs. The Brethren historian Roy Coad, sums up Darby as follows:

> Darby was a complicated and immense personality. Psychologically, he was obviously abnormal: but so have been many geniuses. It would be trite to see his deplorable actions only as the fruit of a subconscious drive for power: but such power as he sought would bring him little fame and less fortune. Somehow, beneath it all, there was also the force of a genuine and intense devotion to Christ. Darby's tragedy was that his actions, in their result, could only bring dishonour on the Name he loved.[39]

As for Irving, he seems to have been a man of great heart. By the grace of God, he died before he could amplify his errors any further. As

[39] Coad 1968: 161.

for the Glasgow charismatics, the healings may well have been real, and they seem to have loved the Lord, but they were no more infallible than anyone else. As for Darby, he spent his life peddling this "speculative nonsense," as B.W. Newton called it, across two continents, as if it were the gospel itself, and filled the world with the noise of it.

But a charge of false prophecy hangs over all of them alike – Irving, the Irvingites, the Glasgow outpouring, Darby and the Brethren. They all taught that the coming of the Lord was imminent. But they were mistaken. Two centuries have passed and he still has not come. Few now give any credence to Irving. But millions still hang on Darby's false system as their infallible guide to future redemption.

One might ask, in reply, if Darby's teaching actually does any harm? Is it not good that we should wait expectantly for an any-minute coming of the Lord? But false doctrines are never harmless, and this one has its own dangers.

First, if Christians are taught that the Lord will catch them up before tribulation arises, they are likely to lose faith if tribulation does fall upon them. No one wants to endure persecution. But the Bible never teaches freedom from it. On the contrary, "In the world you will have tribulation" (John 16:33). Teaching freedom from tribulation makes for shaky faith.

Second, dispensationalism teaches that there may yet be opportunity for repentance and salvation after the coming of Christ, both for unrepentant Gentiles and unrepentant Jews. This has no biblical basis. From what we know, there is no such second chance. Such a doctrine offers false hope to the unrepentant.

Third, dispensationalism overturns biblical teaching on the Church and Judaism. It teaches that the Jews are still God's favourite people and that the Church, instead of being God's master-plan since the beginning, is a divine afterthought, a thing unknown to the prophets. Some dispensationalists even seem to offer hope of salvation to Jews simply by virtue of their being Jewish. But that is not at all consistent with the New Testament.

13

The Rapture

MANY object to the Rapture on the basis that it is not biblical. This is not really true. Rapture – from Latin *raptus* – means 'snatching' or 'seizing' or 'taking.' And the Bible says that, when Jesus comes, his people will be "caught up in the clouds" to meet him in the air (1 Thess. 4:17). So, although the word 'Rapture' does not appear in our English Bibles, the idea does. Like the words Incarnation or Trinity, it's a genuine biblical idea, though the word is not found in the Bible.

Others think the Rapture is a Dispensationalist invention. But it's not. It's taught in the New Testament. But its origins, as ever, lie in Genesis. Some Israelites held to such a hope before Christian times, as ancient texts show. And the idea appears also in rabbinic and patristic literature. We'll trace the Rapture from the beginning, into the New Testament, into the teaching of the early church and rabbinic literature.

Enoch

The first rapture occurs right at the beginning of the Bible, in the fifth chapter of Genesis. We read how Enoch the patriarch walked with God, then "he was not, for God took (*laqaḥ*) him" (Gen. 5:24). This contrasts with all the other patriarchs. The brief summaries of their lives, in Genesis 5, close with the words, "And he died." But not Enoch. The author of Hebrews sums it up,

> By faith, Enoch was taken, not seeing death. And he was not found because God had taken him. (Heb. 11:5)

Of course, it doesn't say exactly where God took Enoch. But since God did take him, he must have taken him towards himself. Any other direction would not have been 'taking', but 'sending' or 'dismissing.' Genesis, of course, assumes that God's dwelling is in the heavens (Gen. 11:5–7; 19:24; 22:11). And, in the Bible, the heavens are above the earth, where the stars are. So it seems that this is where God took Enoch.

That's all we learn from Genesis. But later texts expand on Enoch's journey and destination. The Enoch books – 1, 2, and 3 Enoch, dating from about 300 BC through to Roman times – tell us how Enoch goes up through the ten heavens to the throne of God, passing the third heaven or Paradise on the way, where the Garden of Eden is located with its roots in the earth. The Book of Jubilees, from the second century BC, tells a similar story, with Enoch taken to God's presence in the Garden of Eden. So they all agree that God took Enoch heavenward.

Now it's worth pointing out what a remarkable idea this is. In ancient eastern thought, human beings do not ascend to heaven, either alive or dead. They live on earth and, at death, they descend to the underworld of Sheol. Even the righteous do not go to heaven. At best, they "sleep with their fathers." For Enoch to be taken up toward God is something really unusual. Yet, for the author of 1 Enoch, Enoch doesn't completely lose touch with the world. For he gets a visit from his son Methuselah who comes to ask him about the auspicious signs surrounding the birth of his grandson Noah (1 Enoch 106–108).

So the taking of Enoch in Genesis stands as an example or paradigm. This is what God is like and this is what God does. He takes those who walk with him into the heavens. He has done it in the past and can do it in future. The verb used in Genesis 5:24 for 'take' is *laqaḥ*. It's the ordinary everyday Hebrew word for taking, say, a kingdom or a wife or anything else. But here it is used in a particular sense of God taking a person heavenward to himself without that person dying.

ELIJAH

The next person God takes is Elijah. At the end of his earthly labours, after standing up against the cohorts of Baal, he is taken to heaven, courtesy of a fiery chariot.

> [3]The company of the prophets at Bethel came out to Elisha and asked, "Do you know that Jehovah is going to take (*laqaḥ*) your master from you today?"
> "Yes, I know," Elisha replied, "but do not speak of it."...
> [11]As they were walking along and talking together, suddenly a chariot of fire and horses of fire appeared and separated the two of them, and Elijah went up to heaven in a whirlwind. [12]Elisha saw this and cried out, "My father! My father! The chariots and horsemen of Israel!" And Elisha saw him no more. (2 Kgs 2:3, 11–12)

Once again, the verb 'take' (*laqaḥ*) describes God's action (2:3, 5, 9). God does the taking. It is not something Elijah conjures up. But those who are in touch with God – Elijah, Elisha, and the prophets of Bethel and Jericho – know what's about to happen. They've had a divine premonition (2:2). In fact, Elijah already had a reputation as one who gets snatched away by the spirit of Jehovah (1 Kgs 18:12). Then God takes Elijah directly into the heavens. His disciples search far and wide for him, but he is not seen again on earth.

The intriguing coda to this tale is that Elijah, like Enoch, doesn't lose touch with the earth. For Elijah ascended in the reign of Jehoshaphat, who was succeeded by his son Jehoram. But, some five years or so after his 'taking up,' Elijah ends a letter to Jehoram, rebuking him for his idolatries and fratricides and foretelling his downfall and humiliating death (2 Chr. 21:12–15). Does this mean that Elijah didn't die, but was just 'taken' to another corner of the land? Some think so. They say Elijah (and Enoch) did actually die and did not ascend to heaven. They point out that Jesus says, "No one has ever gone up to heaven" (John 3:13) and that Hebrews says, "These all died [including Enoch] in faith" (Heb. 11:13). Yet Hebrews itself says that Enoch was taken up to heaven (Heb. 11:5). And the gospel accounts of Elijah's appearance at the transfiguration suggest that there was something unusual about his removal (Matt. 17:3–4, Mark 9:4–5; Luke 9:30–33). So we must allow that 'none' and 'all' are exaggeration as they not infrequently are in Scripture, as when Obadiah says that there is no nation or kingdom where Ahab has not sought Elijah (1 Kgs 18:10).

So Elijah, like Enoch, ascended into the heavens. And again, this is a very striking thing. Mortals do not ascend to heaven. They descend to Sheol. But Elijah is taken up to the heavenly realms of God. And we are left again with an example of what God may do to those who love him.

KORAHITE PSALMS 48 AND 49

Sometime in the tenth or ninth century BC, around the time of Elijah or a little earlier, the Korahite singers sang of how what happened to Enoch would one day happen to others also. Their psalms must be read against the background of their clan history, as it is told in Numbers 16.

Their forefather, Korah ben Izhar, was wealthy and proud. This, say the rabbis, was because he had been Pharaoh's treasurer, or because he had found Joseph's treasure hidden in Egypt.[1] He resented the eminence of his kinsman Moses, and led a rebellion against him. He was followed by Dathan, Abiram, and two hundred and fifty prominent Israelites. But Jehovah defended his servant Moses. The earth split and opened its mouth and swallowed Korah alive into the underworld of Sheol. Dathan and Abiram too, with their wives and children, were swallowed alive by Sheol. And the two hundred and fifty were consumed by fire.

Later, we read of Korah and his followers that *They became a sign* (Num. 26:10). And if we ask what they became a sign of, the answer must surely be: "They became a sign of those whom Sheol would swallow and fire consume." But then the text informs us that the sons of Korah (unlike those of Dathan and Abiram) did not die (Num. 26:11). Presumably, they too became a sign: a sign of those who are saved from cataclysmic judgement.

Against this background, Psalm 49 is a Korahite meditation on the futility of heaping up earthly wealth when the future of all mortals is to be swallowed up in Sheol, the world of the grave. But the psalmist speaks of his own hope for the future.

> But God will redeem my soul from the hand of Sheol
> For he will take (*laqaḥ*) me. (Ps. 49:15)

The psalmist believes that God will 'take' him to himself. Just as God took Enoch and Elijah, so he will take him. Even if he should go down into the underworld, God will redeem him from the 'hand' and the realm of Sheol. It seems he believed in a linked resurrection and rapture. God will take him upwards from the grave.

If we then read the preceding Korahite psalm, Psalm 48, in the light of Psalm 49, we see something similar.

[1] Pes. 119a; Sanh. 110a; PRE (Friedlander 1916: 398); Est. R. 7.4; Exod. R. 31.3; Eccl. R. to 5.12; for Korah's wealth, see also Josephus, *A.J.* IV.2.4; Midr. Ps. on 49.7-8, 17; Quran, Sura 28.76-82.

> This God is our God for ever and ever
> He will carry us above death (*hu' y'nahagenu 'al-mut*) (Ps. 48:14)

Translators have always found the last part of this verse difficult. Even in the third century BC, the translators of the Greek Septuagint seem to have read the last words, *'al-mut*, as *alamot* or 'ages.' So they translated it as "He will shepherd us in the ages"; that is, he will shepherd them for ever and ever.

Modern Bible translations, on the other hand, offer other translations:

> He will be our guide even unto death. (KJV)
> He will lead us until death. (NASB)
> He will be our guide even unto death. (RSV)
> He will be our guide even to the end. (NIV)
> He will guide us forever. (ESV)

Now 'guide us' is a reasonable translation for *y'nahagenu*, though it rather means to 'lead,' as a shepherd leads his flock (Exod. 3:1; Isa. 11:6; Ps. 80:1). So the Septuagint got that right. Or it can even mean to 'carry away,' as one carries away spoil or captives (Gen. 31:18; 1 Sam. 23:5; Job 24:3; 1 Sam. 30:2).

But *'al* does not mean 'until' or 'unto'. It means 'upon' or 'over' or 'above'. ('Until' would be *'ad.*) And so those who want to read *'al* as 'until' are indulging in unjustifiable textual emendation of *'al* to *'ad.*

Finally, despite the NIV, *mut* means 'death', not 'the end', The NIV is perhaps following the Septuagint here, as if in despair at understanding the Hebrew. But there is no reason to despair of the Hebrew. It is perfectly clear: He will carry us above death.

So all these translations erroneously say that God will guide the Korahite and his people *until* death (or 'the end'). Does this mean he will stop guiding them when they are dead? But the true sense of the words is really quite the opposite. It is that God will carry them over and beyond death, just as he carried the sons of Korah over Sheol in the wilderness when the earth opened its mouth and swallowed their father alive.

So it's not clear why the translators feel they have to emend in this way. It's true that the verse can be hard to grasp if one does not consider the story of Korah's rebellion. But I suspect the translators have subscribed to the popular misconception that the Hebrew scriptures say little on the redemption of the faithful after death. Unfortunately, such presuppositions quite often colour Bible translation.

So, the plain sense of Psalm 48:14 is not such a puzzle, especially if we see it in the light of the other Korah psalms. In Psalm 46, the psalmist speaks of not fearing when the earth gives way and melts and the mountains fall into the sea (46:2, 6). In Psalm 49:15, he says God will redeem his soul from the power of Sheol. And, in Psalm 48:14, he says God will carry 'us' over or above death. In other words, he believes that, on a coming cataclysmic day, God will lift his people up above Sheol, the gaping realm of the dead, and take them to himself.

As in Psalm 49, he seems to see resurrection and rapture as one event. But this time he speaks of God carrying 'us' over death. By 'us' he means perhaps his Korahite clan or even all faithful Israel. But here, for the first time, we begin to see belief in a general catching-up of all the faithful.

DEUTEROCANONICAL TEXTS

Since the 'taking' of the faithful is found here in the Old Testament, we should not be surprised to find it in other Israelite literature dating from before, or around the same time as, the New Testament.

Sibylline Oracles 2.165–166. The Sibylline Oracles are five books of Greek texts, mostly of Jewish or Nazarene origin, but perhaps with pagan elements too. Josephus knew and cited parts of the Oracles as prophetic texts in the first century AD, though we cannot assume that he had the full collection of texts that we possess.[2] Modern scholarship tends to see the first and second books of the oracles as originating from a Jewish or Nazarene hand in Asia Minor sometime between 30 and 70 AD.[3] In the second book of the Oracles we find:

> The taking-up (*sunaíresis*) is near when some deceivers,
> in place of prophets, approach, speaking on earth. (Sib. Or. 2.165–6)

This 'taking-up' or 'catching-up' sounds like the same event spoken of by the Korahites long ago, and by the New Testament authors a little after the time this text was written. The sign that the taking-up is about to happen will be the appearance of false prophets. That, of course, is a familiar characteristic of the end-times in the New Testament also (cf. Matt. 7:15–23; 24:4–5, 11, 24; Acts 20:29–30; 2 Tim. 3:13).

4 Ezra 6:25–26. The Apocalypse of Ezra was written in the aftermath

[2] Ant 1:4:3 [118] citing Sib. Or. 3:101–110.
[3] Collins 1983: 331.

of the Roman destruction of Jerusalem in AD 70 by a Pharisaic Jew trying to make sense of the catastrophic loss of temple and statehood.[4] He describes the convulsions that are yet to overwhelm the world in the future time of the Messiah. Then he says,

> And it shall be whosoever shall have survived all these things that I have foretold unto you, he shall be saved and shall see my salvation and the end of the world. And they shall see the men who have been taken up (*et videbunt qui recepti sunt homines*), who have not tasted death from their birth. Then shall the heart of the inhabitants [of the world] be changed and be converted to a different spirit. (4 Ezra 6:25–26)

So 'Ezra' foresees a time when certain people shall be taken up without ever 'tasting death,' that is, without ever having died. Then these people shall appear to the world; that is, having been taken up, they shall reappear from heaven. But there is no clue as to how long is the period between their taking-up and their reappearing.

IN THE NEW TESTAMENT

The Ascension of Jesus in Luke also falls into the general category of a rapture. Once again, we have a man loved by God, one who has walked with God, who has completed his earthly mission, taken up to heaven. His rapture-ascension was not a sudden disappearing. Like Elijah, he was seen visibly ascending into the heavens. And he has to ascend to heaven. For, although he had completed his earthly task, it remained for him still to effect the final part of the redemption plan in offering up his blood in the sanctuary in heaven to make atonement there for his people.

Now some would dispute that Jesus was 'raptured.' I'm not sure why. Perhaps they think that, as a divine man, he caused his own rising and was not taken up by God. But the event is referred to in Revelation 12:5.

[4] This 'Ezra' sees the Roman destruction in terms of the Babylonian destruction of 587 BC. The text was written probably in Hebrew and then translated, first into Greek, then into Latin, Syriac, Ethiopic, Georgian, Arabic, Armenian, and Coptic. The Hebrew original is lost, and the Greek survives only as fragmentary quotations in Christian authors. The earliest surviving edition is therefore the Latin, which is numbered as follows: chapters 1 to 2, called 5 Ezra, chapters 3 to 14 called 4 Ezra (or the Ezra Apocalypse), and chapters 15 to 16, called 6 Ezra. If the three heads of the 'eagle vision' (12:22–36) refer to Vespasian and his sons, Titus and Domitian, then the text was composed in Domitian's reign (AD 81–96). This is close to the date of thirty years after the destruction given in 3:1, though it must be remembered that the 'pseudo-Ezra' writer positions himself in time after the Babylonian destruction of 587 BC.

> She brought forth a male child who is to rule all the nations with a rod of iron; and her child was caught up (*hērpasthē*) to God and to his throne.

In this passage, the Messiah is indeed caught up; he does not float up under his own volition. So Jesus's ascension can certainly be considered as another rapture.

In fact, this particular rapture forms a core part of Christian faith the world over. It is recited in the Creed by most Christian churches: 'He ascended into heaven, and sits at the right hand of God, the Father almighty.' One can hardly be a Christian at all without believing in this particular taking-up. Nor should we disbelieve that God has the power to make such things happen. Nor should we be surprised to hear that the Lord's departure from the world is the model for ours. That is implied in several New Testament passages (John 14:1–3; 1 Cor. 15:20-28; Rom. 8:29–30). As James Tabor says,

> In the NT the ascent of Jesus to heaven is the paradigm for all those righteous mortals who follow. Just as he was raised from the dead, made immortal, and ascended to the Father, so will his followers experience the same at his return.[5]

There are other New Testament raptures, of varying kinds. Philip, after baptizing the Ethiopian by the Gaza road, is caught up bodily into the air by the Holy Spirit, but returns to earth at Azotus, that is, Ashdod (Acts 8:39). Paul testifies to being caught up to Paradise in the third heaven, but does not know whether the catching-up was bodily or not (2 Cor. 12:2–4). He too returns to earth. John, after seeing heaven opened, receives a heavenly summons to 'come up here' (Rev. 4:1), and stands before the heavenly throne. But he too returns to earth to tell what he saw. Then there are the two witnesses who ascend to heaven in a cloud (Rev. 11:12), though there is no agreement on who these two witnesses are. And there are the saints who rose at the resurrection of Jesus (Matt. 27:52–53). For, unless they died again, or are still wandering the earth – both of which seem unlikely – they must have been caught up to God.

Finally, outside the New Testament, there is the Assumption of the Blessed Virgin, attested by all the most ancient traditions of the church. Some may wish to dispute it. But they must explain why no tomb was ever built for the veneration of her mortal remains, as was done with all the apostles.

[5] Tabor 2011.

In the Olivet discourse

Turning from New Testament narrative to New Testament teaching, Jesus speaks of the rapture of the saints within the context of his Olivet discourse in Matthew 24.

Matt. 24:30–31 & Mark 13:26–27. In this first pair of parallel passages, Jesus, sitting on the Mount of Olives, facing the temple, says to his disciples,

> 30Then will appear in heaven the sign of the Son of Man, and then all the tribes of the earth will mourn, and they will see the Son of Man coming on the clouds of heaven with power and great glory. 31And he will send out his angels with a loud trumpet call, and they will gather his elect from the four winds, from one end of heaven to the other. (Matt. 24:30–31)

It has been debated since ancient times whether Matthew's 'sign of the Son of Man' is Jesus himself or a sign preceding him – perhaps a cross or a star. The Apocalypse of Elijah, for instance, says, "He will walk upon the heaven's vaults with the sign of the cross leading him" (3:2). And the *Didachê* speaks of more than one sign.

> And then shall appear the signs of the truth: first, the sign of an outspreading in heaven, then the sign of the sound of the trumpet. And third, the resurrection of the dead, yet not of all, but as it is said: "The Lord shall come and all His saints with Him." Then shall the world see the Lord coming upon the clouds of heaven. (§16)

Mark's shorter version omits the sign.

> 26At that time men will see the sign of the Son of Man coming in clouds with great power and glory. 27And he will send his angels and gather his elect from the four winds, from the ends of the earth to the end of the heavens. (Mark 13:26–27)

While he is still in the sky, he will send his angels to gather his elect to him. They will be gathered not (as we might have expected) from the four corners of the earth, but instead "from the four winds of heaven." That is, his elect are taken up in the air and gathered to him there. Since Jesus is appearing in the clouds, they too will be caught up into those same clouds.

We should be very clear that this is not a secret appearing. It is indubitably a public appearance. All people of all nations will see him and "will mourn," when he comes to gather his people in.

Matthew 24:37–40 & Luke 17:26–35. The next pair of parallel passages comes later in the same Olivet discourse. In Matthew, it follows six verses after the passage above. Jesus compares the time of the future 'taking' to the days of Noah and the Flood.

> [37]As it was in the days of Noah, so it will be at the coming (*parousía*) of the Son of Man. [38]For in the days before the Flood, people were eating and drinking, marrying and giving in marriage, up to the day Noah entered the ark; [39]and they knew nothing about what would happen until the Flood came and took them all away. That is how it will be at the coming (*parousía*) of the Son of Man. [40]Two men will be in the field; one will be taken and the other left. [41]Two women will be grinding with a hand mill; one will be taken and the other left. (Matt. 24:37–40)

In Luke's parallel version of the same teaching, Jesus compares the event not only to the time of Noah and the Flood but also to Lot and the overthrow of Sodom and Gomorrah.

> [26]Just as it was in the days of Noah, so also will it be in the days of the Son of Man: [27]People were eating and drinking, marrying, and being given in marriage, up to the day Noah entered the ark. Then the flood came and destroyed them all. [28]It was the same in the days of Lot: People were eating and drinking, buying and selling, planting and building. [29]But on the day Lot left Sodom, fire and sulphur rained down from heaven and destroyed them all. [30]It will be just like that on the day the Son of Man is revealed. [31]On that day, let no one on the housetop come down to retrieve his possessions. Likewise, let no one in the field return for anything he has left behind. [32]Remember Lot's wife! [33]Whoever tries to save his life will lose it, but whoever loses his life will preserve it. [34]I tell you, on that night two people will be in one bed: One will be taken and the other left. [35]Two women will be grinding grain together: One will be taken and the other left. (Luke 17:26-35)

The Greek word *parousía*, which we meet in Matthew, means literally 'presence.' But, as in our text here, it can also mean 'coming to be present.' Jesus has already used it this way a few verses before. He says that the Messiah will not appear secretly, in the desert or in an inner room (Matt. 24:26). Instead, his *parousía* will be public and visible.

> For just as the lightning flashes from the east to the west so will be the coming (*parousía*) of the Son of Man. (Matt. 24:27)

So his *parousía* is when Jesus comes to be visibly present in the world. And he speaks of one *parousía*. There will be only one. Not two.

In both passages, Jesus implies that the rapture will immediately precede a cataclysmic judgement. As Noah and his family entered the ark just before the Flood, as Lot was led from Sodom just before the fire fell, so a catching-away will save the faithful from an imminent outpouring of divine wrath. There is no question of those left behind having time to repent, or to rejoice over the spoils, or to be converted and witness, or anything else. Their destruction follows immediately.

However, some say these passages are not about a rapture at all. They say that Jesus, in the same context, speaks of those 'taken away' in judgement in the Flood (Matt. 24:39). So they say these passages refer to the same thing. The people are not being taken away to safety, they are being swept away in a cataclysm such as befell Jerusalem in AD 70.

But I think not. Jesus has already said plainly that he is coming to gather his elect in the air (Matt. 24:31). All that follows must be read in the light of that. So the elect are those taken, and they are saved, just as Noah and Lot were taken to save them from the coming destruction. Further, if these passages were about sinners being taken away in judgement, then it would not be 'one taken and the other left,' for the times of Noah and Lot were marked by the total destruction of all the unsaved. So these passages do speak of the rapture.

1 THESSALONIANS 4:15–17

The apostle Paul speaks of the Rapture in the fourth chapter of his first letter to the church in Thessalonica.

> [15]According to the Lord's own word, we tell you that we who are still alive until the coming (*parousía*) of the Lord, will certainly not precede those who have fallen asleep. [16]For the Lord himself, with a loud command, with the voice of the archangel and with the trumpet of God, will come down from heaven, and the dead in Christ will rise first. [17]Then we who remain alive will be caught up together with them in the clouds to meet (*apántêsin*) the Lord in the air. And so we will be with the Lord for ever.

Paul says that, when Jesus appears in the sky, he will first raise the "dead in Christ," that is, believers in Jesus who have died. They will be raised to life and will rise to meet Jesus in the air. Then living believers will be caught up, along with the resurrected dead, also to meet him in the air.

It is not said that this process will be instantaneous. Yes, the transformation of bodies, whether dead or living, will take place in 'the twinkling of an eye' (1 Cor. 15:52). But if the dead are raised first, and the living caught up later, then this process will take time. Perhaps only seconds or minutes, but maybe longer. But it all takes place at the one public *parousía* of the Lord.

There's another Greek phrase which requires our attention; that is, "to meet the Lord" or, more accurately, "to the meeting (*eis apántêsin*) of the Lord." This Greek verb has a well-defined meaning. It means to go out to meet a visitor and accompany that person back to the place one has come from. For instance, if a foreign ruler arrives in a city to stay at his national embassy, the ambassador will go to the airport, welcome him, and bring him back to the embassy. This is how this phrase is used at its two other New Testament occurrences. First, when Paul arrives at Puteoli, the Roman believers travel a distance of some 50 kilometres (30 miles) to meet him and accompany him back to the city.

> 14And so we came to Rome. 15From there the brothers, having heard about us, came out to meet (*eis apántêsin*) us as far as the Forum of Appius and the Three Taverns. (Acts 28:14–15)

Second, in Matthew 25, the bridesmaids are called to go out and meet the approaching bridegroom and bring him back with joy to the banquet.

> At midnight, there was a cry: "Behold, the bridegroom. Go forth to meet (*eis apántêsin*) him." (Matt. 25:6)

So the expression "to meet the Lord in the air" really means "to go to meet the Lord in the air and accompany him back to earth." Those who want to believe that the raptured saints are being taken away to heaven dispute this. They claim that *eis apántêsin* does not always mean this. But that is what the phrase always means in the New Testament.

So Paul's description of this appearing of the Lord echoes Jesus's own words in Matthew 24 very closely. There is the same appearing in the air, the same one-time *parousía*, the same angelic involvement, the same sounding of a heavenly trumpet, the same taking-up of saints into clouds of glory that surround the Lord. And if Paul distinguishes the taking of the dead and the living in turn, Jesus's gathering of all 'his elect' does not deny the same thing.

So one has to say that all these New Testament passages agree pretty well on the nature of this future event. And one does have to say it. For those who teach a Pretribulation Rapture claim that these passages speak of two separate events. They say that in Matthew 24:30–31 (and Mark 13:26–27), Jesus speaks of when he will come publicly to judge the world, when he will raise the Old Testament believers and Tribulation saints. But, they say, 1 Thessalonians 4 speaks of a different event, a secret coming of the Lord, invisible to the world, to gather the church many years before his public *parousía.* So, they say, there will be two distinct comings of the Lord, one secret and one public; and two distinct raptures, one for the church saints, and one for what they call the Tribulation saints. (They prefer to call this second rapture by another name, but in reality they are certainly proposing two separate raptures.)

Surely this is a strange view. As I said, everything looks the same – Jesus appearing in the air, *parousía*, angels, trumpet, saints caught up into clouds. If 1 Thessalonians 4 describes a secret appearance, why is it announced with trumpet and command and the voice of archangel? That doesn't sound secret. Those who hold to this 'secret appearing' must reply that in one case this loud summons is heard by all the world, but in the other case, it is heard only by the raptured church. But if he is appearing secretly, why does he come with the clouds? Throughout the Bible, Jehovah's coming with the clouds signifies his coming in power and glory to save (cf. Ps. 18:10; Dan. 7:13). And if 1 Thessalonians 4 speaks of a secret appearing, then why does Paul call it his *parousía*, for that is certainly his one-time visible coming to the world? At face value both passages refer to the one momentous occasion. Those who make them separate events are basing their interpretation not on the Bible texts but on their own preconceptions.

Other New Testament texts speak of the rapture (1 Cor. 15:50–57; Col. 3:4; 1 Thess. 1:10; 5:9; 2 Thess. 2:1–3). But since we will discuss them in the following chapter, we will briefly look at the rapture in patristic and rabbinic literature.

In Patristic literature

The early church fathers speak of the taking-up in the same way as does the New Testament. Irenaeus speaks of the tribulation as the last trial of the righteous, not as a thing they will be saved from before it begins.

> And therefore, when in the end the church shall be suddenly caught up hence, it is said, *There shall be tribulation such as has not been since the*

> *beginning, neither shall be* [Matt 24.21]. For this is the last contest of the righteous, in which, when they overcome, they are crowned with incorruption. (Against Heresies 5.29.1)

Tertullian spoke of how those facing death in the time of Antichrist would be caught up at the Lord's coming, as Paul taught.

> Now the privilege of this favour [i.e., being clothed with immortality] awaits those who shall at the coming of the Lord be found in the flesh, and who shall, owing to the oppressions of the time of Antichrist, deserve by an instantaneous death, which is accomplished by a sudden change, to become qualified to join the rising saints; as he writes to the Thessalonians: *For this we say unto you by the word of the Lord, that we which are alive and remain unto the coming of the Lord shall not precede those who are asleep. For the Lord Himself shall descend from heaven with a shout, with the voice of the archangel, and with the trumpet of God: and the dead in Christ shall rise first: then we too shall ourselves be caught up together with them in the clouds, to meet the Lord in the air* [I Thess. 4. 15–17]. (On the Resurrection of the Flesh 41)

In Rabbinic literature

Likewise, the rabbis speak of the rapture. Of course, they, publicly at least, rejected the teaching of Jesus and the apostles. (There are questions as to how far the teaching of Jesus and the apostles influenced them covertly.) But their testimony on the rapture suggests the idea existed among the Israelites long before the time of Jesus.

Perhaps unsurprisingly, their clearest teaching on the subject is given in relation to the sons of Korah and their psalms, which, as we saw, speak about a time when the righteous will be caught up. Remember, Korah rebelled, the earth melted, Sheol swallowed him alive, and his followers were consumed by fire. Yet the sons of Korah did not perish. Instead, says rabbinic tradition, they were caught up in the air above the earth.

> The sons of Korah said to the righteous: "Fear not; we saw all the miracles which he wrought for us. As it is said, *And the earth opened her mouth, and swallowed them up, and their households* [Num. 16:32]. And where were we in that hour? Up in the air." As it is said, *The sons of Korah died not* [Num. 26:11].
>
> According to R. Nehemiah, when the earth opened and the two hundred and fifty men were swallowed up, the Holy One, blessed be he, made them [the sons of Korah] to stand like the mast of ship. Thus it is said, *They became a sign* [Num. 26:10].

> Thus the sons of Korah said: "Ye righteous, fear not the terror of the day of judgement, for ye shall not be taken with the wicked, even as we were not taken with them." (Midrash on Psalms 46§3)

When R. Nehemiah says they were made "to stand like the mast of a ship," he means that they were lifted upright high in the air above the surging liquefaction of the earth.

A teaching in the Talmud, perhaps from the third century, connects the same idea with Korahite Psalm 46.

> And should you ask, in those years when the Holy One, blessed be he, is about to renew his world, as it is written, *And the Lord alone shall be exalted in that day* [Isa. 2:11], *What will the righteous do?* [Ps. 11:3] – The Holy One, blessed be he, will make them wings like eagles', and they will fly above the water, as it is written, *Therefore we will not fear when the earth melts and the mountains fall into the heart of the seas* [Ps. 46.2]. (B. Sanh. 92b)

Again, in a commentary on Korahite Psalm 48, the early fourth-century rabbi Naḥman bar Yaakov taught:

> R. Naḥman said, *The thing that hath been, it is that which shall be* [Eccl. 1.9]. Even as the Holy One, blessed be he, lifted up the children of Israel in clouds of glory, and wrapped them around and bore them up, as it is said, *And I bore you on eagles' wings* [Exod. 19:4], so will he do again, and it will be said, *Who are these that fly as a cloud* [Isa. 60:8]. (Midrash on Psalms 48§4).

Summary

The roots of the rapture lie in the 'taking' of Enoch and Elijah. The Korahite psalms foretell that such a 'taking' will one day be the destiny of all the faithful in a combined resurrection-rapture. The same idea appears in the Sibylline Oracles and 4 Ezra.

Jesus and Paul, like the Korahite psalmist, spoke of a time when all the faithful will be taken up to meet the Lord in the air at his *parousía.* But there is no indication at all that there is more than one rapture of the faithful. In particular, there is no support for the idea that Christian believers will be raptured first and then Old Testament saints will be resurrected later. There is one catching-up: the dead in Christ rise first, then living saints will be caught up also. Paul's use of *apantao* suggests that they rise to meet the Lord and escort him back to earth. They are caught up to be saved from the judgement to be poured out upon the earth, a judgement anciently foreshown in the salvation of Noah, of Lot, and of the sons of Korah during Korah's rebellion. The caught-up saints will remain in the air until the judgement poured out upon the earth is complete. Then they will return to earth with the Lord, as it is said, *The meek shall inherit the earth* (Matt. 5:5).

14

When is the Rapture?

NOWADAYS, then, there are two streams of premillennial (or chiliastic) belief: the historic premillennialism of the Ante-Nicene Fathers and the dispensational pretribulationism of J.N. Darby. The former hold that the faithful will be raptured after the Antichrist's tribulation. The latter hold that they will be raptured before that tribulation. This is the main point of disagreement between the two views. Apart from that – and Darby's notion of different "dispensations" for Israel and the church – they have much in common. Let's expand this a bit.

Darby's dispensational premillennialism believes the Messiah will come, invisible to the world, *before* the tribulation, and catch the faithful away, by the rapture, to heaven. In that case, Christian believers will be taken away before the Antichrist begins his persecution of the church and they will not suffer in the tribulation. In this view, the rapture happens years before the public coming of the Lord and the resurrection of the righteous, which take place after the tribulation. In this view, the Messiah could come any time, even today; his coming, as pretribulationists say, is imminent.

Historical premillennialism, on the other hand, sees the Messiah coming *at the end* of the tribulation. In that case, Christian believers on earth must endure the trials of the tribulation. This view also sees the catching-up or rapture of the church as happening at the same time as the coming of the Lord and the resurrection of the righteous, not years before. And those who are caught up – the transformed living and the resurrected dead alike – are not taken to heaven, but remain in the air, and there meet the Lord and return with him to earth. In this view, the Messiah cannot come until after the Antichrist has been revealed. So Jesus cannot come today, for the Antichrist has not been revealed.

So the key issue here is the timing of the rapture. Is it pretribulation, with the Messiah coming secretly to rapture the church before Antichrist takes power, and then coming again, years later, visibly and in glory, to resurrect the righteous (the view of dispensational premillennialists)? Or is post-tribulation, with the Messiah coming once only, visibly and gloriously, to raise the righteous dead and catch up the church in one appearing (the view of historical premillennialists).

The Scriptural Evidence

Let's begin with the scriptural evidence, for scripture must always be our firm foundation. What is the evidence there? A classic modern defence of the pretribulation rapture view is Mark Hitchcock's *The End.* Hitchcock says there are three "main passages" in the New Testament that refer to the rapture, but there are also "many others," which he lists later.[1] Let's look at his passages in order.

1. *John 14:1–3.* The first of Hitchcock's three main passages is the beginning of John 14.

   > [1]Let not your hearts be troubled. Believe in God; believe also in me. [2]In my Father's house are many rooms. If it were not so, would I have told you that I go to prepare a place for you? [3]And if I go and prepare a place for you, I will come again and will receive you to myself, that where I am you may be also.

   Hitchcock says, "Jesus briefly introduced the doctrine of the rapture in John 14:1–3," and he points out verbal parallels between this and 1 Thessalonians 4:13–17. It is possible that Jesus speaks here of the rapture. But "receive you (to myself)" (*paralêmpsomai*) is not the same as being "snatched" or "caught" up (*harpagêsometha;* 1 Thess. 4:17). And where are these many rooms? Pretribulationists say they are in heaven. But that is not said. And other rapture texts speak of being raptured into the "air" or "sky" (1 Thess. 4:17; Matt. 24:31),

[1] Hitchcock 2012: 122 with the fuller list on p. 150.

rather than heaven. So perhaps Jesus is speaking here not of rapture, but of coming for his disciples at their death. In that case, the "many rooms" might be the dwelling places of paradise. Or perhaps his words cover both rapture and taking-at-death. But there is not the wisp of a shadow of a hint that he speaks here of a *pretribulation* rapture. So rapture, perhaps. Timing, undefined.

2. *1 Cor. 15:50–57.* Hitchcock's second main passage is from Paul's first letter to the Corinthians. Here's the core of it.

> 51Behold! I tell you a mystery. We shall not all sleep, but we shall all be changed, 52in a moment, in the twinkling of an eye, at the last trumpet. For the trumpet will sound, and the dead will be raised imperishable, and we shall be changed. 53For this perishable body must put on the imperishable, and this mortal body must put on immortality.

Paul says that our bodies, that is, the bodies of Christian believers, will be transformed in the twinkling of an eye "at the last trumpet." The last trumpet is the final trumpet. There is not another trumpet to follow it. So it can only be the same trumpet that sounds when the Lord returns visibly on the clouds of heaven in glory, with a loud command, and the tribes of the earth mourn (Matt. 24:30–31; 1 Thess. 4:16). Therefore, when this last trumpet sounds at the visible coming of the Lord, the church will still be on earth (not taken away). That can only mean that they will not be transformed or raptured before his visible return. So rapture, yes. Pretribulation rapture, no. Post-tribulation rapture, yes.

3. *1 Thess. 4:13–18.* Hitchcock's third main passage is from Paul's letter to the Thessalonians.

> 14For since we believe that Jesus died and rose again, even so, through Jesus, God will bring with him those who have fallen asleep. 15For this we declare to you by a word from the Lord, that we who are alive, who are left until the coming of the Lord, will not precede those who have fallen asleep. 16For the Lord himself will descend from heaven with a cry of command, with the voice of an archangel, and with the sound of the trumpet of God. And the dead in Christ will rise first. 17Then we who are alive, who are left, will be caught up together with them in the clouds to meet the Lord in the air, and so we will always be with the Lord.

All agree this is the clearest of all rapture texts. The Lord will come publicly, in glory, with command, archangel shout, and the trumpet of God. The dead in Christ will be raised first and the living raptured straight after. Pretribulationists say the Lord appears here secretly, unseen by the world. But, if it's so secret, why the shouts and trumpeting? Pretribulationists reply that these sounds are heard only by believers. But it looks much more like the public rapture of Matthew 24:31. So rapture, yes. Post-tribulation, very likely.

So in Hitchcock's three "main passages" about the rapture, the first one is not too clear on the rapture and offers no clue as to timing, the second speaks clearly of a post-tribulation rapture, and the third most probably of a post-tribulation rapture. Now let's turn to Hitchcock's many other passages. He lists Rom. 8:19; 1 Cor. 1:7–8; 16:22; Phil. 3:20–21; 4:5; Col. 3:4; 1 Thess. 1:10; 2:19; 5:9, 23; 2 Thess. 2:1–3; 1 Tim. 6:14; 2 Tim. 4:1, 8; Titus 2:13; Heb. 9:28; Jam. 5:7–9; 1 Pet. 1:7, 13; 5:4; 1 John 2:28–3:2; Jude 1:21; Rev. 3:10. This makes twenty passages, depending on how we join or divide them. The majority of them, as we shall see, are not relevant. But let us begin with those which are. They add four more to those we saw above.

4. *Col. 3:4. When Christ who is your life appears, then you also will appear with him in glory.* This does allude to the rapture. The faithful will be gloriously transformed when Jesus comes, as in 1 Cor. 15:53. But is there any hint as to whether this is a secret or a visible appearing of Jesus? Yes, there is. When he appears in glory, we also shall appear in glory. To whom shall we appear in glory? To ourselves or to the unfaithful who have despised us? Surely it is to the unfaithful that we shall appear in glory, to vindicate our faith in the Lord they despised. So this is a public revelation of the Lord and his glorified saints to the world when he appears on the clouds of heaven at the end of the tribulation. Rapture implied. Pretribulation, no. Post-tribulation, yes.
5. *1 Thess. 1:10. To wait for his Son from heaven...Jesus who delivers us from the wrath to come.* Which wrath is this? Is it the human wrath of the Antichrist's persecution? Or is it the wrath of God's judgement which shall follow the tribulation? Well, the noun "wrath" (*orgê*) appears 36 times in the New Testament. In 86% of cases it means divine judgement; in the other 14% it means anger between Christian believers.[2] It never refers to the persecution of believers. Within this

[2] God's wrath (31): Matt. 3:7; Mark 3:5 (Jesus); Luke 3:7; 21:23; John 3:36; Rom. 1:18; 2:5 (twice); 2:8; 3:5; 4:15; 5:9; 9:22 (twice); 12:19; 13:4, 5; Eph. 2:3; 5:6; Col. 3:6; 1

same epistle, 'wrath' refers only to God's judgement (2:16; 5:9). And it's clear that this verse (1:10) is not speaking of anger between believers. So there's no ambiguity here at all. It is from the wrath of God that Jesus will deliver us when he comes in judgement to end the Antichrist's rule. He is not coming to save us before the Antichrist's persecution begins, but after it. Rapture implied, but post-tribulation.

6. *1 Thess. 5:9. God has not destined us for wrath, but to obtain salvation through our Lord Jesus Christ.* Once again, as earlier in the same letter, Jesus is to save us from a future 'wrath,' meaning the wrath of God in judgement at the end of the tribulation. Once again, rapture implied, post-tribulation.
7. *2 Thess. 2:1–3. Now concerning the coming of our Lord Jesus Christ and our being gathered together to him...that day will not come, unless the rebellion* [apostasy] *comes first, and the man of lawlessness is revealed.* Here too Paul speaks of the rapture. He says the church will not be gathered – that is, caught up or raptured – to the Lord until after the Antichrist is revealed. So clearly the church is not going to be taken away before the Antichrist's reign begins. So rapture, yes, but post-tribulation.

So, of these seven passages, one speaks explicitly of the rapture (1 Thess. 4:13–18), one is marginal (John 14:1–3), and the other five imply it. But none unambiguously support a pretribulation rapture and most point clearly to a post-tribulation rapture.

The other seventeen verses that Hitchcock cites are not relevant. Here they are.

i. *Rom. 8:19. The creation waits in eager expectation for the children of God to be revealed.* This alludes to the transformation of the body, as in 1 Cor. 15:53. It says nothing about the rapture.
ii. *1 Cor. 1:7–8.* Paul speaks of waiting for the coming of the Lord. Nothing about the rapture.
iii. *1 Cor. 16:22.* Paul says, *Marana, tha* (Our Lord, come!), but nothing about the rapture.
iv. *Phil. 3:20–21.* Paul speaks here of the transformation of the body. He says nothing about the rapture.
v. *Phil. 4:5. The Lord is at hand.* Nothing about the rapture.

Thess. 1:10; 2:16; 5:9; Heb. 3:11; Heb. 4:3; Rev. 6:16, 17; 11:18; 14:10; 16:19; 19:15. Human disputes (5): Eph. 4:31; Col. 3:8; 1 Tim. 2:8; Jam. 1:19, 20.

vi. *1 Thess. 2:19*. Paul speaks of boasting in his converts at the coming of the Lord. He says nothing about the rapture.

vii. *1 Thess. 5:23*. Paul speaks of the coming of the Lord. He says nothing about the rapture.

viii. *1 Tim. 6:14*. Paul speaks of the appearing of our Lord Jesus Christ. He says nothing about the rapture.

ix. *2 Tim. 4:1, 8*. Paul speaks of the appearing and kingdom of our Lord Jesus Christ. He says nothing about the rapture.

x. *Titus 2:13*. Our blessed hope is the appearing of the glory of our great God and Saviour Jesus Christ. Nothing about the rapture.

xi. *Heb. 9:28*. Christ…will appear a second time…to save those who are eagerly waiting for him. Nothing about the rapture.

xii. *Jam. 5:7–9*. James commends patience until the coming of the Lord. Nothing about the rapture.

xiii. *1 Pet. 1:7, 13*. Our faith will result in praise and glory and honour at the revelation of Jesus Christ. Nothing about the rapture.

xiv. *1 Pet. 5:4*. We will receive an unfading crown of glory when the Chief Shepherd appears. Nothing about the rapture.

xv. *1 John 2:28–3:2*. When he appears we may have confidence and not shrink from him in shame at his coming…when he appears we shall be like him. Nothing about the rapture.

xvi. *Jude 1:21*. Waiting for the mercy of our Lord Jesus Christ that leads to eternal life. Nothing about the rapture.

xvii. *Rev. 3:10*. Jesus promises to keep the Philadelphians from the hour of trial coming on the whole world. Hitchcock means the church will be raptured from the Antichrist's persecution. But, first, nothing is said of the rapture. Second, the "trial" could mean a historic trial within the Roman Empire. (The New Testament can use "the whole world" to refer to the Roman Empire; cf. Acts 11:28.) This could refer to a local persecution of the church. Or, indeed, it could refer to deliverance from the Antichrist's future persecution by means other than rapture. So rapture, not mentioned. Pretribulation rapture, no evidence.

Therefore, among Hitchcock's list of seventeen other passages about the rapture, none of them speak of it at all. So we still have only six texts that speak clearly of the rapture or allude to it. Yet one is missing. And it is almost beyond comprehension why Hitchcock omits any discussion of what is the most important rapture text of all. Here it is.

Matthew 24:27–31 is the first teaching on the rapture in the New Testament and the clearest rapture teaching from the mouth of Jesus. We already looked at it briefly when speaking of 1 Cor. 15:50–57. Jesus speaks of his visible return, as "the lightning comes from the east and shines as far as the west" and "on the clouds of heaven with power and great glory" (vv. 27, 30). So, lest anyone think so, he is not speaking of the AD 70 judgement on Jerusalem which he alluded to earlier (vv. 24:15–25), nor of a secret coming at that time or at any other time. This is his visible coming in glory. And he says:

> 29Immediately after the tribulation of those days the sun will be darkened, and the moon will not give its light, and the stars will fall from heaven, and the powers of the heavens will be shaken. 30Then will appear in heaven the sign of the Son of Man, and then all the tribes of the earth will mourn, and they will see the Son of Man coming on the clouds of heaven with power and great glory. 31And he will send out his angels with a loud trumpet call, and they will gather his elect from the four winds, from one end of heaven to the other.

Jesus is clearly speaking here of the catching-up of the church. His angels will gather his elect from "the four winds", from "one end of heaven to the other." That is, they will gather them from the air (not from the earth), for they have been caught up into the air. He says that this mid-air gathering of the elect will take place immediately *after* the tribulation (v. 29). It also takes place immediately on the sounding of the trumpet. This must certainly be the last trumpet. For after Jesus appears in glory, no more trumpets sound, neither in 1 Cor. 15:52 nor in the Revelation. So Jesus clearly says here that the elect will be taken away (or raptured) after the tribulation, not before it. So rapture, yes. Post-tribulation rapture, definitely yes.

I said that it is almost beyond comprehension why Hitchcock omits this passage. But, of course, he has his reasons. These are that pretribulationists recognize (rightly) that this passage speaks of the public coming of the Lord at the end of the tribulation. But, according to their philosophy, this public coming takes place years after the secret coming of the Lord to rapture the church. And they think all the other rapture passages above refer to their imagined secret coming of the Lord. Therefore, Hitchcock omits Matthew 25 from discussion of the rapture since, according to dispensationalist philosophy, it cannot refer to the rapture at all, despite the fact that it obviously does.

So leaving aside the doubtful passages, which also give no hint of timing, we are left with seven New Testament passages that speak of the rapture and of its timing. Here they are in order of clarity:

Matt. 24:27–31	Clear teaching. Gathering in the air.	Post-tribulation
1 Thess. 4:13–18	Clear teaching. Caught up in the clouds	Post-tribulation
2 Thess. 2:1–3	Clear, but dependent on 1 Thess. 4:17.	Post-tribulation
Col. 3:4	Rapture strongly implied	Post-tribulation
1 Cor. 15:50–57	Rapture strongly implied, at last trumpet	Post-tribulation
1 Thess. 1:10	Rapture implied, from divine wrath	Post-tribulation
1 Thess. 5:9	Rapture implied, from divine wrath	Post-tribulation

Among these seven texts, the first two clearly establish the rapture as a teaching, and five more refer to and support that teaching. All seven, read together, speak of a post-tribulation rapture.

To these, I would add that there is one other biblical text that speaks of the dead being raised and caught up in the air. That is Psalm 49 which we spoke of in the previous chapter.

Finally, we can add a few remarks on the Revelation. In Revelation 7:9–12, we meet an innumerable multitude praising God before his throne. Pretribulationists usually identify them with the raptured church. However, it is said of them that "These are the ones coming out of the great tribulation" (v. 14). And so, if they are the raptured church, they cannot have been raptured before the tribulation.

Last of all, since no Bible text ever speaks of the church being raptured before the tribulation, pretribulationists disagree upon where in the Revelation it takes place.

Some think it happens at 4:1, when John is told to "Come up here." But it is John who is addressed, not the church.

Some think it happens at 11:12, where the two witnesses are told, "Come up here." That's maybe more likely. Following Moses's legislation that the testimony of two witnesses is required (Deut. 17:6), the witnesses might just represent the church and its testimony. Yet this can hardly be opposed to the other clear scriptural evidence that the rapture takes place at the coming of the Lord. So, since not all events in the Revelation are sequential, it may signify the rapture ahead of time. But, really, it's highly doubtful. There are few Bible verses with as many conflicting interpretations as this one. The common view throughout medieval times, for instance, was that the two witnesses are Enoch and

Elijah.[3] But there is nothing in this verse that is clearly about the rapture, nor is there anything that speaks of when it happens.

Finally, some think the rapture happens at 12:5, in the male child caught up to heaven. But the male child is certainly Jesus, not the church. His iron sceptre is an unmistakable reference to Jehovah's all-conquering messiah (*mashiaḥ*) in Psalm 2:2, 9.

So we must conclude that all biblical teaching about the rapture points to it happening at the public, visible coming of the Lord in glory, when he comes to destroy the Antichrist. Not one Bible verse supports the view of Jesus coming secretly before the tribulation, nor of the faithful being removed before the tribulation. In short, the idea of a pretribulation rapture has no basis in scripture.

[3] Mackay 1990. Cf. the teaching of Fra Dolcino in ch. 15.

15

A Pretribulation Rapture in Church History?

OLDEN-DAY pretribulationists, in the first half of the twentieth century, used to claim there was support for a pretribulation rapture in the Church Fathers. But Ladd showed clearly that neither the Didachê, nor the Epistle of Barnabas, nor the Shepherd of Hermas, nor the relevant passages of Justin, Irenaeus, Tertullian, Lactantius, and Hippolytus, offer any support whatsoever for a pre-tribulation rapture once their words are read in context. Whenever these Fathers speak of Jesus coming to save the faithful from the Antichrist, they mean that Jesus will come to defeat the Antichrist and end his reign, not that he will take the faithful before the Antichrist reigns. I discuss many of these passages in chapter nine.[1]

Therefore modern pretribulationists, when seeking support from Christian tradition, now look to obscurer texts. Four have gained special recognition, namely, the *Apocalypse of Elijah,* Pseudo-Ephrem's *On the End of the World,* the *History of Brother Dolcino,* and Morgan Edwards's *Two Academical Exercises.* Let's look at them in turn.

The Coptic Apocalypse of Elijah

We looked at this important text and its origins in chapter seven. As said there, its earliest version, probably pre-Christian, was quoted by Paul in

[1] For those, I do not cover, see Ladd 1956: 19–34. Yet some pretribulationists still think they can summon these Fathers to their cause; see Stitzinger 2002.

1 Corinthians 2:9. But the surviving Coptic text is a Jewish-Christian version dating probably from the second century AD. Here is the passage which is commonly cited about the rapture.

> [2]On that day the Christ will pity those who are his own. And he will send from heaven his sixty-four thousand angels, each of whom has six wings. [3]The sound will move heaven and earth when they give praise and glorify. [4]Now those upon whose forehead the name of Christ is written and upon whose hand is the seal, both the small and the great, will be taken up upon their wings and lifted up before his wrath. [5]Then Gabriel and Uriel will become a pillar of light leading them into the Holy Land. [6]It will be granted to them to eat from the tree of life. They will wear white garments, and angels will watch over them. They will not thirst, nor will the son of lawlessness be able to prevail over them. (5:2–6)[2]

The passage certainly speaks of the rapture. The faithful are "taken up," as in 1 Thessalonians 4:17, and by angels, as in Matthew 24:31. And a glance at verse 6, where they are freed from the power of the Antichrist, might initially suggest a pretribulation rapture. But, on closer inspection, we see that this rapture is to save the faithful from the wrath of Christ (v. 4) not of the Antichrist. And here we must remember, as we saw in our last chapter, that 'wrath' in the New Testament habitually denotes the judgement of God, but never human persecution.

The angels lead the righteous to "the Holy Land," wherein is the tree of life and angel guardians (vv. 5–6). This may mean a renewed earthly Holy Land, or perhaps Paradise. But it is a place of safety for them.

But does this take place before or after the Antichrist's persecution? If we read the context, it seems that it is after it. Earlier in the text we read that the Antichrist "will pursue all of the saints…he will kill them and destroy them" (4:21–22). Then, after that persecution, follows our passage above, where the righteous are removed and the Antichrist can no longer prevail over them (5:6). Then follows God's judgement, when the animals die, the earth dries up (5:8–9), and God and his angels burn up the earth with fire to a depth of seventy-two cubits in a true judgement (5:23–24). After that, the Messiah comes from heaven to reign on earth for one thousand years (5:37). So what we have is first Antichrist's persecution, then the rapture, followed by the fire of wrath of God's judgement, and the messianic kingdom. It agrees with what we saw in the New Testament texts above.

[2] The text is from Wintermute 1983: 750. It is cited by Hitchcock 2012: 177–78.

But what is truly interesting about the wider scenario of the Apocalypse is that the raptured saints stay in the sky for a time – long enough even for the Antichrist to fly upwards to pursue them and to meet the angels in battle – before God's fire falls on the earth.

> Then he will take his fiery wings and fly out after the saints. He will fight with them again. The angels will hear and come down. They will fight with him a battle of many swords. (5:20–21)

So this writer could conceive of a delay between the catching-up of the saints and their return to earth.

Pseudo-Ephrem: On the End of the World

Grant Jeffrey presented this text in 1995 as evidence of a pre-trib rapture, claiming, "This discovery may revolutionize the evangelical church's understanding of the history of the rapture."[3] He speaks of "Saint Ephraem" and "Pseudo-Ephraem" interchangeably, and seems to think they are the same person.[4] He claims that the text dates from the 4th century.

The text however is not by Saint Ephrem (or Ephraim) the Syrian, but is a later Latin sermon pseudonymously attributed to Ephrem called "De fine mundi" (*Of the end of the world*). Since there are many pseudonymous Ephrem texts, both in Greek and Latin, the Latin texts are conventionally attributed to a mythical person called Pseudo-Ephrem Latinus and the Greek ones to an equally mythical Pseudo-Ephrem Graecus. In this text, the references to the Persian wars and to Roman emperor-brothers suggests it was written after the reign of the brothers Honorius and Arcadius and after the Persian wars of 421 and 440, that is, in the fifth century. The passage, as cited by Jeffrey, is this:

> Because all saints and Elect of the Lord are gathered together (*adsumuntur*) before the tribulation which is about to come and are taken to the Lord, in order that they may not see at any time the confusion which overwhelms the world because of our sins.

There is no known Syriac original of this text. It is a Latin translation of a Greek Pseudo-Ephrem text.[5] What's more, the Latin translator added

[3] Jeffrey 1995: 105.
[4] Jeffrey 1995: 115.
[5] Pearse 2018.

the words "taken to the Lord," which are absent from the Greek text. The original therefore does not speak of the rapture. Nor is it even certain that the Latin text does either. For the verb *adsumuntur* ("taken to") is different from the Vulgate and all the old Latin versions of 1 Thess. 4:17 which have the verb *rapientur.* If the translator had intended to refer to the rapture in 1 Thess. 4:17, he would surely have used *rapientur.* Since that is so, this being "taken to the Lord" may mean rather that they are taken in death. A reference to the rapture here is far from clear.

But even if we do allow here a reference to the rapture in the words of the Latin translator, there is a more glaring problem, which is the order of events. For after the passage about the gathering of the saints and elect, the wicked one (the Antichrist) comes and rebuilds the temple and his reign is described. Then we read that the just are still on earth in the time of the Antichrist, so that they may be tested by the Lord.

> Then, when this inevitability has overwhelmed all people, just and unjust, the just so that they may be found good by their Lord; and indeed the unjust, so that they may be damned forever with their author the Devil (§9).[6]

No doubt, the pretribulationist might reply that these "just" are the "tribulation saints." But, of course, the text makes no such distinction, no more than the Revelation does.

Jeffrey notes the words, "We ought to understand thoroughly therefore, my brothers, what is imminent."[7] He thinks that, by these words, the author means the rapture is imminent. But if we read the context, it is clear that the author speaks rather of the imminence of the Antichrist, not of the rapture, which is not even mentioned.

> We ought to understand thoroughly therefore, my brothers, what is *imminent* or overhanging. Already there have been hunger and plagues, violent movements of nations and signs, which have been predicted by the Lord, they have already been fulfilled, and there is *not other which remains, except the advent of the wicked one* in the completion of the Roman kingdom. (§2)

Therefore, in its entirety, this Pseudo-Ephrem sermon takes the same view as the Ante-Nicene Fathers: the Antichrist must come before the rapture; his persecution will overwhelm all people, both just and unjust; and then the Messiah will come.

[6] Jeffrey 1995: 114.
[7] Jeffrey 1995: 110.

The History of Fra Dolcino

The history of Fra Dolcino of Novara was recorded in 1316 by an anonymous notary in the diocese of Vercelli, between Turin and Milan. Fra Dolcino was the leader of a religious order called the Apostolic Brethren, founded in 1260 by one Gerard Sagarello. Sagarello, having been turned down by the Franciscans, set up another order in their image, committed to poverty and itinerant preaching. But setting up new religious orders was forbidden by the Roman Church and so, in 1300, Sagarello was duly burned at the stake. After his death, Fra Dolcino – who appears to have received his ordination from Sagarello – became leader of the group. They withdrew to live in the mountains, and there they grew to number thousands. According to the *History*, Dolcino taught as follows:

> That within those three years Dolcino himself and his followers will preach the coming of the Antichrist. And that the Antichrist was coming into this world within the bounds of the said three and a half years; and after he had come, then he [Dolcino] and his followers would be transferred [*transferrentur*] into Paradise, in which are Enoch and Elijah. And in this way they will be preserved unharmed from the persecution of Antichrist. And that then Enoch and Elijah themselves would descend on the earth for the purpose of preaching [against] Antichrist. Then they would be killed by him or by his servants, and thus Antichrist would reign for a long time. But when the Antichrist is dead, Dolcino himself, who then would be the holy pope, and his preserved followers, will descend on the earth, and will preach the right faith of Christ to all, and will convert those who will be living then to the true faith of Jesus Christ.

So Dolcino taught that within three and a half years, the Antichrist would come and Dolcino and his followers would be "transferred" to Paradise. But the transfer didn't come on schedule. And feeding thousands of landless men disinclined to work is no easy matter. With the village priests denouncing them, and the peasants in no hurry to feed them, Dolcino and his horde began raiding the villages and farms for food. This made them unpopular. A crusade was decreed against them and they were attacked by the papal armies in 1307. Over four hundred of them were slain. Dolcino was tortured and burned at the stake, not at all the transfer to Paradise which he had envisaged. The remnant scattered and fled.

But what about his teaching? Well, the Latin "rapture" verb is not used, so it's not totally clear that Dolcino was thinking of 1 Thess. 4:17. In fact, "transfer" doesn't sound like any New Testament text about the catching-up of the church, and Dolcino's "transfer" is to Paradise, whereas the New Testament rapture is into the air, with nothing said of Paradise. Perhaps we can call Dolcino's "transfer" to Paradise a kind of a rapture. But it's not quite the same as the New Testament rapture.

The period of Dolcino's rapture, before they return to earth, is three and a half years, no doubt derived from the 1,260 days of Daniel and Revelation. This would make him a mid-tribber and not a Darbyite full pretribber. And the character of the prophet is worth considering. He was, I imagine, a Christian believer. But he was surely a false prophet, for his words did not come true. And he ended up more robber than saint. And so, while he taught a pretribulation "transfer" to Paradise, nothing about him gives much reason to hold him up as a model of orthodoxy.

MORGAN EDWARDS

Morgan Edwards (1722–1792) was a Welsh-born American Baptist pastor. He was one of the founders of Rhode Island College, which later became Brown University. In a short publication, *Two Academical Exercises* (1788), he wrote:

> The distance between the first and second resurrection will be somewhat more than a thousand years. I say, somewhat more, because the dead saints will be raised, and the living changed at Christ's "appearing in the air." 1 Thess. iv:17; and this will be about three years and a half before the millennium, as we shall see hereafter: but will he and they abide in the air all that time? No: they will ascend to Paradise, or to some one of those many "mansions in the father's house" John xiv:2, and disappear during the foresaid period of time. The design of this retreat and disappearing will be to judge the risen and changed saints; for "now the time is come that judgment must begin," and that will be "at the house of God" 1 Pet. iv:17. (p. 7)[8]

Edwards is clearly speaking about the rapture, for he cites 1 Thess. 4:17. He does not speak of a secret appearing of Christ, but of an appearing to resurrect, transform, and take the saints to Paradise for judgement for three and a half years before the millennial kingdom begins.

> This event will come to pass when Antichrist be arrived at Jerusalem in his conquest of the world; and about three years and a half before his killing the witnesses and assumption of godhead. (p. 21)

[8] The pages of Edwards's book are cited as given in Ice 2009.

In other words, the saints will be raptured some time after the Antichrist has taken power but before his final self-deification. So Edwards's rapture looks more mid-tribulation than pretribulation. And then,

> The last event, and the event that will usher in the millennium, will be, the coming of Christ from paradise to earth, with all the saints he had taken up thither (about three years and a half before)...millions and millions of saints will have been on earth from the days of the first Adam, to the coming of the second Adam. All these will Christ bring with him. The place where they will alight is the "mount of Olives, which is before Jerusalem on the east." Zech. xiv, 4. (p. 24–25)

Edwards believed that the age would last six thousand years, based "on a prophecy of Elias, which the Jews have among them; where they got it we cannot tell."[9] (Probably the Tanna Debe Eliyahu, cited in chapter eight.) And it would end in 1996, based on Ussher's date of creation.

John Bray has suggested that Darby came across Edwards's book in his tours of America, and that Edwards's ideas contributed to the final mix of his rapture doctrine.[10]

Summary

Pretribulationists proffer the four texts above, dating from apostolic times to the eighteenth century, as examples of the venerable history of the pretribulation rapture theory. They hope thereby to answer the charge that this teaching was devised by J.N. Darby in the nineteenth century.

The Coptic Apocalypse of Elijah, an early text, does indeed speak of a rapture. But it is a post-tribulation rapture, after the Antichrist's persecution. However, it does see a gap between the rapture and the falling of God's wrath. *The Apocalypse of Pseudo-Ephrem* again looks like a post-tribulation rapture, for the just suffer with the unjust under the Antichrist. *The History of Fra Dolcino* has a better claim to a pretrib scenario. Dolcino did think that he and his followers would be transferred to Paradise for three-and-a-half years after the appearance of the Antichrist but before the full onset of his persecution. And Morgan Edwards believed in a rapture three-and-a-half years before the Lord's coming, after the Antichrist takes power.

Fair enough. Dolcino and Edwards do seem to have expected a

[9] From the summary of Edwards's eschatology in McKibbens 1980: 123–26.
[10] So Bray 1995.

rapture – probably mid-trib rather than pretrib – three and a half years before the Antichrist is defeated. What do we learn from this? Only that others hoped that Jesus might come and take them before the Antichrist's persecution. That is natural enough. One might well wish for that. No doubt Margaret McDonald wished for that too. But, wishes aside, the scriptural evidence still points to the rapture taking place at the coming of the Lord, when he brings an end to the Antichrist's reign. Perhaps Dolcino and Edwards might not have disagreed. They only thought that certain people would be spared part of the persecution. One might well wish for that too. But I see no clear support for that either.

Further, neither of these two texts – Dolcino or Edwards – says that this pretrib rapture will be secret. And neither speaks of seven dispensations, though Edwards believes in the millennial week. So the only support they offer dispensational pretribulationists is the idea of a period of time between the resurrection-rapture and the final judgement. The Apocalypse of Elijah has that too, but is not pretribulational.

But what is puzzling in this is how pretribulationists decry any idea that Darby received his views from Lacunza or Irving or Margaret McDonald, yet they are happy to see a precursor of his views in Fra Dolcino and his robber gang of self-ordained monks. Why is Fra Dolcino to be preferred to Lacunza? If they don't like Catholics – as some don't – was Dolcino any less Catholic than Lacunza? If they reject Irving as heretical – accidental though his heresy was – was Dolcino more orthodox? If they reject McDonald as ignorant, was Dolcino more learned? I suppose the point they hope to make is that Dolcino and Edwards saw a pretribulation rapture in the scriptures and so it is a reasonable deduction from the New Testament. Yet, they insist, Lacunza, Irving, and McDonald did not influence Darby.

They want to have their cake and eat it too. They want to see in Darby a holy prophet who revealed from the scriptures the gospel of seven dispensations and the pretrib rapture buried in ages of Catholic error. At the same time, they want to show that he was no neologist, but a holder of truths that the church knew all along. It would be better if they just acknowledged that Darby borrowed his ideas from others.

16

Jewish and Gentile Dispensations?

PART of Darby's system, an essential and intrinsic part, is his idea of dispensations. Darby claimed, perhaps in an attempt to imitate the idea of the millennial week, that there were seven dispensations from creation to the messianic kingdom. They were all of different lengths, from the short period of Adam's innocence to the long period of the Church Age. There was also the short period of the Tribulation, which generally went unnumbered to achieve the symbolic seven.

> INNOCENCE: Adam's creation to the Fall
> CONSCIENCE: Adam to the Flood
> CIVIL GOVERNMENT: Noah to the Tower of Babel
> PROMISE: Abraham to Moses
> LAW-ISRAEL: Moses to Pentecost
> GRACE-CHURCH: Pentecost to Rapture
>   Tribulation: 7 years
> MILLENNIAL KINGDOM: Jesus rules on earth.

The hub of this schema is God's covenant with Israel. The Church Age, on the other hand, is a 2,000-year postponement of God's plan for Israel, unforeseen by the prophets. During this Church Age parenthesis, the divine promises to Israel are put on hold. But when the Church dispensation is complete, Christian believers will be raptured. This will bring in the times of the Antichrist, when 144,000 Jews will be converted to faith in Jesus but suffer the Antichrist's persecution. Yet, in these sufferings, they will evangelize the world and many more "tribulation saints" will be saved, until Jesus returns to slay the Antichrist.

One people or two?

At the heart of this view lies a distinction between Israel and the Church. For dispensationalists, this distinction means that there are two separate and distinct peoples of God – Israel and the Church. Israel consists of the blood descendants of Abraham, Isaac, and Jacob. The Church consists of all those, Jew or Gentile, saved by faith in Jesus between Pentecost and the Rapture. All other dispensationalist doctrines are linked in some way to this distinction and rest upon it. For instance, one of the main reasons for the pretribulation rapture is to remove the Church so that God's suspended plan with Israel can recommence and be fulfilled.

This dispensationalist view diverges from two other views of Israel and the Church, namely, replacement theology and covenant theology.

Replacement theology: The Church replaces Israel

The farthest from it is "replacement theology." This is the reverse of Darby's view. Replacement theology sees the Gentiles as God's primary project and Israel as the later, abandoned project. This was the view of, for instance, Tertullian. The law was given not only through Moses but also through Adam and Eve, Noah, and Melchizedek. For Adam, Abel, Enoch, and Melchizedek were all uncircumcised, non-Sabbath-keeping Gentiles who found favour with God before Abraham did; Melchizedek was greater than Abraham.[1] But the nation of Israel disbelieved and was rejected, and then the Gentiles took their rightful place again. Thus the Gentile church will inherit both heaven and earth.

> To Jacob, who is the type of the later and more excellent people, that is to say ourselves [the Christian church], first comes the promise of the heavenly dew, and after that of the fatness of the earth (Gen. 27:28). (Against Marcion 3:24)

But as for the Jews:

> As for the restoration of Judea, however, which even the Jews themselves, induced by the names of the places and countries, hope for just

[1] Tertullian, An Answer to the Jews §1–4.

> as it is described, it would be tedious to state at length how the figurative interpretation is spiritually applicable to Christ and his church. (Against Marcion 3:25)

Replacement theology was the standard view of the medieval church: God had rejected the Jews; any blessings they ever possessed had now devolved upon the church.

COVENANT THEOLOGY: ONE PEOPLE OF GOD

But in between replacement theology and Darby's dispensationalism lies another view, often called "covenant theology." Covenant theology teaches that there is only one people of God, not two, and there is continuity and oneness between God's people in the Old Testament and his people in the New. This differs from replacement theology in that the church does not replace Israel. Instead, the Church is the organic growth of God's Old Testament people.

This idea, that the people of God are one, and only one, is clear in several New Testament texts. In John 10, Jesus is debating with the Judahite leaders. They, he says, are hireling shepherds (10:12–13). But he is the Good Shepherd, who must gather other sheep from outside the Judahite fold, and he will shepherd them all as one flock. *I have other sheep that are not of this fold. I must bring them also, and they will listen to my voice. So there will be one flock, one shepherd* (10:16).

Then there is Paul's discourse on the future of the Jews in Romans 9 to 11. He addresses Gentile believers in proud Rome (where Peter was the chief pastor) and warns them against becoming arrogant even though they now outnumber the Jewish believers. He speaks first of the importance of Israel in God's plan.

> 4They are Israelites, and to them belong the adoption, the glory, the covenants, the giving of the law, the worship, and the promises. 5To them belong the patriarchs, and from their race, according to the flesh, is the Christ, who is God over all, blessed forever. Amen. (Rom. 9:4–5)

Then he turns to his picture of the olive tree. He says that branches have been broken off this olive tree and "wild shoots" – that is, Gentile believers – have been grafted into it (11:17). The branches broken off were unbelieving Israelites, like the Pharisees and Zadokites, for they were dead and fruitless due to their unbelief in the Messiah. Yet God has left other natural Israelite branches who were fruitful, like the apostles, and the many Israelite believers in Galilee (1 Cor. 15:6), and the thousands converted at Pentecost (Acts 2:41), and the thousands more converted later (Acts 6:7; 21:20). Then, into this recently-pruned tree, he grafted Gentiles, so that the tree now consists both of Israelites and of Gentiles. Yet, there were always Gentile branches on the tree long before Jesus, whether Jethro, or Caleb, or Rahab, or Ruth, or Naaman, or Uriah, or repentant Ninivites, or Ebed-Melech the Cushite, or others. But now there are many, many more. Paul's olive tree is all the people of God, all who believe in his Messiah. We can call it the Israel of God (Gal. 6:16), or the Church. But it is one people.

Now, if Paul had been illustrating Darby's dispensationalism, his illustration would have been completely different. Instead of one tree, there would be several trees. To start, there would be one for Israel and one (or more) for the Gentiles. But then God would plant a new tree, called the Church, and he would take Israelites from the Israel tree, and Gentiles from the Gentile tree (or trees), and he would graft them all into the new Church tree. But this is not what Paul says at all. There is one tree. Truth be told, its roots really lie in pre-Israelite times, before the Flood, with Enoch, Noah, and others. Then the patriarchs form its base, and the prophets and the faithful of Israel form its trunk. Finally, unbelieving Israelites are excised and believing Gentiles grafted in.

Paul explains this further in Ephesians. He tells the Gentile Ephesians that they used to be *separated from Christ, alienated from the commonwealth of Israel and strangers to the covenants of promise, having no hope and without God in the world* (2:12). But now everything is changed. They are now, by implication, part of the commonwealth of Israel and sharers in the covenants because they have been grafted into the one tree of God's people. Now they are *fellow citizens with the saints and members of the household of God* (2:19).

Who is the Seed of Abraham?

Dispensationalists find this hard to grasp for they continue to identify unbelieving Jews with the seed of Abraham. Some speak of Abraham's three seeds: his seed according to the flesh (the Jews), his spiritual seed (the church), and his royal seed (the Messiah).

But such a view finds little support in scripture. As Paul explains to the Galatians, *the promises were made to Abraham and to his seed,* not "to his seeds," for the promise of the seed refers to only one person, that is, to Jesus the Messiah (3:16), the son of Abraham, the son of God. It is only by allegiance to Jesus that anyone else becomes Abraham's seed and heir according to the promise (3:29). Whoever belongs to Jesus, whether Jew or Gentile, is Abraham's seed, Abraham's son or daughter. But, as for unbelieving Jews being Abraham's seed, I'm afraid I don't see that (John 8:39–44).

Now, of course, Paul uses the terms 'Israel,' 'Gentile,' and 'Church,' and speaks of ethnic Jews and non-Jews, both inside and outside the church. But he does not speak of them so as to suggest that God has two distinct peoples. In fact, he stresses that, within the church, the dividing wall is broken down: *there is neither Jew nor Greek* (Gal. 3:28). All are the one olive tree. Jesus, when he came, did not chop down the old tree, nor plant a new one. Rather, God pruned off the dead branches, left the fruitful branches, and grafted in living, believing branches into the one tree (in addition to those engrafted earlier). Nothing is replaced. Nothing is cut down. The gentiles become part of God's one ancient tree by faith in Jesus Christ.

God's main project

Dispensationalists tend to reject covenant theology. Sometimes they incorrectly label it "replacement theology." But it is not. In replacement theology, the church replaces Israel. In dispensationalist theology, Israel supersedes the church. But in covenant theology, there is one people of God, one flock of the Good Shepherd, all who believe in Jesus the Messiah, whether Jew or Gentile. Further, all who do not believe, whether Jew or Gentile, are not part of the one olive tree or the one flock or the one people.

The dispensationalist sees the Jews as still God's primary project and favourite people, and the Church as an afterthought, unknown to the prophets. Some dispensationalists even think Jews will be blessed simply by virtue of being Jews. But the New Testament view is clear: God's primary project is the one people, all who accept the Messiah and his new covenant. Jesus says:

> [11]I tell you, many will come from east and west and recline at table with Abraham, Isaac, and Jacob in the kingdom of heaven, [12]while the sons of

> the kingdom will be thrown into the outer darkness. In that place there will be weeping and gnashing of teeth. (Matt. 8:11–12)

Paul says likewise, directly equating his own salvation as a Jewish believer in Jesus with the salvation of his Gentile converts.

> [22]What if God, desiring to show his wrath and to make known his power, has endured with much patience vessels of wrath prepared for destruction, [23]in order to make known the riches of his glory for vessels of mercy, which he has prepared beforehand for glory— [24]even us whom he has called, not from the Jews only but also from the Gentiles? (Rom. 9:22–24)

> He chose us [including Ephesian Greeks] in him before the foundation of the world that we should be holy and blameless before him. (Eph. 1:4)

> [13]In him you [Gentiles] also, when you heard the word of truth, the gospel of your salvation, and believed in him, were sealed with the promised Holy Spirit, [14]who is the guarantee of our inheritance until we acquire possession of it, to the praise of his glory. (Eph. 1:13–14)

What's more, the one people was always God's primary purpose, right from the beginning. Paul even says that the events that happened to Israel happened as a sign for the people of the new covenant (Rom. 4:23–24; 15:4; 1 Cor. 9:9–10; 10:1–11).

But does that mean that God has no future plan for Jewish people, those who trace their descent from the rabbis and Pharisees of Jesus's time? By no means. He has promised not to reject but to restore them.

> [25]Thus says the Lord: If I have not established my covenant with day and night and the fixed order of heaven and earth, [26]then I will reject the offspring of Jacob and David my servant and will not choose one of his offspring to rule over the offspring of Abraham, Isaac, and Jacob. For I will restore their fortunes and will have mercy on them." (Jer. 33:25–26)

He plans yet to save many of them to faith in Jesus, as we learn from the prophetic typology of Joseph revealing himself to his brothers (Gen. 45:1–7). And from Rom. 11:26, *The Deliverer will come from Zion, he will banish ungodliness from Jacob.* And from Zech. 12:10, *They will look upon me whom they pierced and mourn for him as with the grief over a firstborn.* He promises to gather them in and renew them entirely:

> For I will take you from the nations, gather you from all the lands and bring you into your own land. Then I will sprinkle clean water on you, and you will be clean; I will cleanse you from all your filthiness and from

> all your idols. Moreover, I will give you a new heart and put a new spirit within you; and I will remove the heart of stone from your flesh and give you a heart of flesh. I will put my Spirit within you and cause you to walk in my statutes, and you will be careful to observe my ordinances. You will live in the land that I gave to your forefathers; so you will be My people, and I will be your God (Ezek. 36:24-28).

He even speaks of saving Israel from a future invasion:

> 14Therefore, son of man, prophesy, and say to Gog, Thus says the Lord God: On that day when my people Israel are dwelling securely, will you not know it? 15You will come from your place out of the uttermost parts of the north, you and many peoples with you, all of them riding on horses, a great host, a mighty army. 16You will come up against my people Israel, like a cloud covering the land. In the latter days I will bring you against my land, that the nations may know me, when through you, O Gog, I vindicate my holiness before their eyes……21I will summon a sword against Gog on all my mountains, declares the Lord God (Ezek. 38:16–23; cf. Zech. 14:1–3).

However, to imagine that such promises of future deliverance excuse all the actions of the State of Israel toward its neighbours, or to imagine that divine justice will wink at these actions, is, I fear, wishful thinking.

But when the Jewish people finally do recognize Jesus as their long-rejected Messiah, then they will indeed become part of his primary project, the one people of God.

Once we accept the biblical evidence that there is one people of God, all the dispensationalist doctrines built on the foundation of two distinct peoples of God are left without foundation and fall. Gone are the separate dispensations of Israel and Church, and gone is the need for a pretribulation rapture to allow the postponed divine plan for Israel to restart.

17

Apostasy and Antichrist

QUITE a number of New Testament texts speak of a great apostasy or falling-away from the true faith which shall take place in the last days. Jesus alludes to it first, saying: *When the Son of Man comes, will he find faith on earth?* (Luke 18:8). Then Paul speaks of it, saying, *The Spirit clearly says that in latter times some will abandon the faith to follow deceitful spirits and the teachings of demons* (1 Tim. 4:1). And again, he says the Day of the Lord *will not come, unless the apostasy comes first, and the man of lawlessness is revealed* (2 Thess. 2:3).

This apostasy is not an apostasy of unbelievers. Unbelievers cannot fall from the faith, for they never held it. It is not an apostasy of Jews or Muslims, for they never held the faith of Paul. Only those who hold the faith can fall from it. Paul is speaking of a great falling away of the Christian church from the true faith in Jesus. Lacunza speaks of this:

> The perdition and ruin of Christians shall infallibly come to pass in the days of Antichrist; so it is clearly announced in the Holy Scriptures and confirmed in a thousand ways by the Son of God himself: the Christian world shall be already ripe for that terrible chastisement, by the malice and iniquity with which it shall be full in the sight of God.[1]

When this falling-away happens, the "man of lawlessness" will be revealed. The early church soon connected Paul's "man of lawlessness" with the Antichrist of John's epistles and the seven-headed beast of

[1] Lacunza (tr. Irving) 1827: 1:178.

Revelation 13. This one, they said, will arise before the coming of Jesus and persecute the faithful church. He would be slain, said the Ante-Nicene Fathers, by the Lord Jesus at his coming. (The amillennialists could not bear the idea of Jesus touching the earth at all at his coming, so they taught instead that the Antichrist would be slain by Michael the Archangel before the Lord returns to judge the world.) In modern dispensationalist teaching the Antichrist has grown to a world ruler with total control of the global economy and media whose persecution is to reach unimagined proportions. But what foundation does this have in scripture? Let's look at the subject in the Bible, and in dialogue with the Fathers, for it was they who first formulated the teaching about the Antichrist as it has come to us.

THE ANTICHRIST IN THE EPISTLES

In the Bible itself, the word Antichrist appears only five times, all in the epistles of John, denoting one who opposes the true Christ (1 John 2:18 [twice]; 2:22; 4:3; 2 John 1:7). John also speaks of 'the spirit of Antichrist' (1 John 4:3). Yet he also says that there is an actual Antichrist to come into the world in person: *you have heard that the antichrist is coming*; but others will foreshadow him: *so now many antichrists have appeared* (1 John 2:18). So the Antichrist figure is both singular and plural. There is a spirit of antichrist, who opposes or falsifies Christ. This spirit has already manifested itself in the appearance of 'false Christs,' and more are to come until, finally, there will come *the* Antichrist. For John, these antichrists are false teachers who may arise from within the church itself, as he says, *Many antichrists have appeared...They went forth from us, but they were not of us* (1 John 2:19).

THE BEAST IN REVELATION 13

In the Revelation, by the same apostle John, the Archangel Michael drives Satan from heaven to earth. Cast down, Satan, in fury, calls forth a fearful beast from the sea who is to rule the world.

> 1And I saw a beast rising out of the sea, with ten horns and seven heads, with ten diadems on its horns and blasphemous names on its heads. 2And the beast that I saw was like a leopard; its feet were like a bear's, and its mouth was like a lion's mouth. And to it the dragon gave his power and

> his throne and great authority. [3]One of its heads seemed to have a mortal wound, but its mortal wound was healed, and the whole earth marvelled as they followed the beast. [4]And they worshipped the dragon, for he had given his authority to the beast, and they worshipped the beast, saying, "Who is like the beast, and who can fight against it?"
>
> [5]And the beast was given a mouth uttering haughty and blasphemous words, and it was allowed to exercise authority for forty-two months. [6]It opened its mouth to utter blasphemies against God, blaspheming his name and his dwelling, that is, those who dwell in heaven. [7]Also it was allowed to make war on the saints and to conquer them. And authority was given it over every tribe and people and language and nation, [8]and all who dwell on earth will worship it, everyone whose name has not been written before the foundation of the world in the book of life of the Lamb who was slain. (Rev. 13:1–8)

The language is deeply symbolic. And, as with many of the symbols in the Revelation, our key is the scroll of Daniel, which is the fountainhead of John's prophecy. In Daniel 7:1–8, we meet four beasts which also come out the sea. The sea, in Daniel and John, as elsewhere in scripture, signifies the surging turmoil of the pagan nations (Pss. 65:7; 89:9–10). Daniel's four beasts are a winged lion, a bear, a winged, four-headed leopard, and a final beast, strong and terrifying, with iron teeth. They are to rule until judgement is given for the Son of Man and the saints of the Most High to finally possess the kingdom (Dan. 7:22–27). Daniel's four beasts tally with his earlier report of the four successive kingdoms of Nebuchadnezzar's vision of the statue (Dan. 2:31–43). The golden head of the statue is the lion, the silver chest is the bear, the bronze thighs are the leopard, and the legs and toes of iron and clay are the final beast. Jewish and Christian interpreters, since ancient times, have taken these four kingdoms to be Babylon, Persia, Greece, and Rome.[2]

Now, we read, on the one hand, that the four beasts signify four kings (7:17). Likewise, the head of the statue is Nebuchadnezzar the 'king of kings' (2:37). And when we turn to his lion image in Daniel 7:4, we read how he is turned from a beast into a man, signifying his process of conversion to faith in the God of Israel (Dan. 2:47; 3:28–29; 4:34–35). But, on the other hand, in the vision of the statue, Daniel speaks of four kingdoms rather than kings (2:39–40). We see the same thing in chapter seven. The bear 'raised up on one side', signifies the ascendancy of Persia over Media, and the three ribs in its teeth signify the kingdoms of

[2] See e.g. Hippolytus, *Christ and Antichrist* 32–33.

Babylon, Sardis, and Egypt that it conquered. We see it too in the four heads of the leopard which represent the four short-lived 'kings' or divisions of Alexander's kingdom. In other words, the beasts symbolize kingdoms, but they also symbolize the kings who rule them.

Now John's beast is modelled on Daniel's, with one big difference. Whereas Daniel's four beasts ruled in turn, John's beast possesses at one time the combined traits of all four beasts. It is altogether swift, savage, cruel, strong, and all-conquering. Its seven heads are the total of the heads of Daniel's four beasts including the four-headed leopard. And seven symbolizes, as always in the Bible, completeness. This beast possesses complete power and bestial savagery.

So is John's beast from the sea a person or a kingdom? To see it as simply a person is difficult. The seven heads must represent divisions of power, as they did in Daniel's four-headed leopard. They represent, as it were, fracture lines within the beast – ethnic or religious or ideological groups – temporarily united in one dark ruling spirit. These could be any and all of the forces that have opposed the Messiah since the beginning: all the idolatry and wickedness and suppression of the truth that have always characterized human civilization. A coalition of such forces shall appear on earth, united and armed with claws and teeth of iron, to blaspheme God and make war *against the Lord and against his Messiah* (Ps. 2:2) so as to wipe the truth of Jesus from the face of the earth.

The ten horns with ten diadems must also signify ten kings or rulers. It is not clear whether these seven powers and ten kings are successive or cotemporaneous. At their first appearance, the crowns on the beast seem to exist together, and later they receive power together with the beast for one hour (13:1; 17:12). Yet we read also that the seven heads are also seven kings who rule successively (17:10–11). The mystery is veiled. But we can see John's beast as an anti-Christian federation of kings and kingdoms, holding a mix of political and ideological views, temporarily united under a single rule.

John does not actually say that this beast is the Antichrist. But since he speaks in his epistles of a coming Antichrist who will oppose the claim that Jesus is the Messiah, and since the strategy of the beast is to make war on the saints, it seems likely that this first beast does indeed signify an end-time Antichrist figure, whom we may call *the* Antichrist.

When we turn to consider other details, the picture becomes obscure. John speaks of one of the heads being wounded and having recovered

(13:3). This may be linked with "the beast" (*i.e.,* now the whole beast and not only one head) who *was, and is not, and is to come* and *who shall arise from the bottomless pit* (17:8) and with its seven heads being seven kings, *Five fallen, one is, the other not yet come* (17:10). But no hint is given in interpreting this wound, and all is buried in deep obscurity.

Yet we must not feel frustrated if we cannot discern all the details of the beast. The Revelation foretells mysteries that will become clear only in their own time. Until that time, God has wrapped them in dark veils.

Paul says the coming of this 'man of sin' will be marked by miracles, *by the activity of Satan with all power and false signs and wonders, and with all wicked deception for those who are perishing, because they refused to love the truth and so be saved* (2 Thess. 2:9–10). But for these things, we must turn to the second beast, whom John speaks of next.

THE SECOND BEAST

In Revelation 13, John sees a second beast, working wonders, rising out of the earth.

> [11]Then I saw another beast rising out of the earth. It had two horns like a lamb and it spoke like a dragon. [12]It exercises all the authority of the first beast in its presence, and makes the earth and its inhabitants worship the first beast, whose mortal wound was healed. [13]It performs great signs, even making fire come down from heaven to earth in front of people, [14]and by the signs that it is allowed to work in the presence of the beast it deceives those who dwell on earth, telling them to make an image for the beast that was wounded by the sword and yet lived. [15]And it was allowed to give breath to the image of the beast, so that the image of the beast might even speak and might cause those who would not worship the image of the beast to be slain. [16]Also it causes all, both small and great, both rich and poor, both free and slave, to be marked on the right hand or the forehead, [17]so that no one can buy or sell unless he has the mark, that is, the name of the beast or the number of its name. [18]This calls for wisdom: let the one who has understanding calculate the number of the beast, for it is the number of a man, and his number is 666.

Unlike the first beast, which rises from the sea, symbolizing the chaos of the nations, this second beast rises from the earth. The earth, of course, unlike the sea, should be firm and stable. One should be able to stand or build or rely upon the earth. And so this beast will seem reliable to many. Yet, in the fearful days of the Revelation, even the trustworthy earth has given birth to a monster of deceit. This two-horned beast is subject to the first beast. It makes the world worship the first beast by signs and wonders and delusions. And it has power to mark everyone so that those who do not receive the mark will be excluded from society, from buying and selling, from the very means of subsistence.

It has the appearance of a lamb, with two inoffensive little horns. But its speaks the words of the dragon, the ancient deceiver of the Garden of Eden (Rev. 12:9; Gen. 3:1). So, while its appearance is mild, its intent is deceit and destruction. And behind its conciliating demeanour lies the ferocious power of the first beast. The second beast prophesies and teaches that the first beast is to be worshipped and adored, which is why John later calls it the 'false prophet' (Rev. 16:13; 19:20; 20:10). As a prophet, it lays claim to supernatural knowledge, to spiritual power and authority. That is why even the medieval doctors of the church saw in these two horns the episcopal mitre of an apostate bishop working in the service of the first beast. Yet, as Lacunza says, it is unlikely that one renegade cleric could so lead the world astray. Rather, what is depicted here is the widespread corruption of the clergy of the worldwide church.

THE APOSTASY OF THE CHURCH

Only the clergy corrupt the church. If the people fall and the leaders stand, the church stands firm. But if the leaders fall, the whole church falls with them. If the shepherds stray, the flock strays after them. This is the apostasy Paul speaks of, which must come before the man of lawlessness is revealed (2 Thess. 2:3), a great defection of the faith by Christian clergy and leaders, leading their flock astray.

Some do not like criticism of the church. I understand that. The true church is the people of God, the flock of the Good Shepherd, the bride and body of Christ, the mother of the faithful (Heb. 12:22–23; Gal. 4:26; Isa. 28:9-10). We who believe are part of it. Should we not fear to judge lest God judge us? Yet the true church has, since the beginning, been sown through with human corruption. Many shall say to him, "Lord, Lord, did we not prophesy in your name," to whom he shall say, "Depart from me, you evildoers." (Matt. 7:22–23)

For the clergy have always been corrupt in varying degrees. Every heresy and false teaching and abuse has sprung from the folly, vanity, and greed of the ministers of Christ, whether Gnosticism, or Arianism, or Marcionism, or Sabellianism, or the lucrative trade in dead men's bones which the faithful were compelled to adore, or wars, slaughters, sackings, crusades, and inquisitions, or burnings of Bibles and their translators, or of imagined witches, guilty if they confessed and guilty if they didn't, and floggings and jailings of peasant preachers, and fake healings, and sex scandals, and perpetual demands for money. Every misrepresentation of the blessed Lord Jesus and his divine truth, every empty formality, every foolish excess, every vain parade and preening folly, every harsh or foolish judgement, every hypocrisy and lie, is found among the ministers of Christ. Yet the laity venerate them as holy men, and bow humbly before their vaunted authority and semblance of spirituality.

It was ever so. It was the priests and shepherds of Israel who led their people astray (Lam. 4:13; Ezek. 34:1–10), finally opposing the Messiah, plotting his death, bribing his disciple, and rousing the people to put him on the cross (Matt. 26:3–4; 27:20). They had in their hands the scriptures which told the time of his appearing. But, in hypocrisy, malice, and selfish ambition, they rejected the promised Saviour who stood before them, and brought destruction on themselves, their city, and its people.

Christian clergy, thinking themselves a second priesthood, inherited their mantle. Of course, many have served worthily. Some cared for orphans and widows in distress. Some magnified the Son of God in preaching, teaching, and praises. Some served quietly, humbly caring for a little flock, or ministering to the sick in a little clinic, or to children in a little schoolroom. Others sealed their testimony with their blood.

But in these last days, the corruption of the clergy shall grow from a trickle to a flood. They shall reject the clear teachings of the Bible and bring destruction on themselves and their flock. The laity, ignorant of the scriptures and unable to credit iniquity to persons so sacred, will regard their evil as good and emulate it. Yet others, poor sheep of Christ, harried by the first beast, shall flee for counsel to the second, who shall compel them to receive the mark of his master, the Antichrist, and to worship his image (Rev. 19:20). Thus the priesthood, long corrupt, shall in these last days fill the world with bitter fruit.

If all this seems too monstrous a charge to bring against the clergy, sadly we shall find it confirmed when we turn to the third monster of this unholy trinity, the scarlet harlot.

The Woman on the Beast

In Revelation 17, John tells of a woman dressed in scarlet who rides on the back of the first beast. She is a queen, richly dressed. She is also a *pornê* or 'prostitute' who commits adultery with the kings of the earth.

> [3]And he carried me away in the Spirit into a wilderness, and I saw a woman sitting on a scarlet beast that was full of blasphemous names, and it had seven heads and ten horns. [4]The woman was arrayed in purple and scarlet, and adorned with gold and jewels and pearls, holding in her hand a golden cup full of abominations and the impurities of her sexual immorality. [5]And on her forehead was written a name of mystery: "Babylon the great, mother of prostitutes and of earth's abominations." [6]And I saw the woman, drunk with the blood of the saints, the blood of the martyrs of Jesus.

The angel shows John that the beast she rides is the first, seven-headed beast, the Antichrist; and now the beast's seven heads signify seven hills and the woman is a city set upon these seven hills (vv. 7–9). This leaves little doubt about which city this is, for Rome boasted of its seven hills. If there were any doubt, we find that the woman's name, 'Babylon,' was indeed a code-name for Rome among Jews and Judeo-Christians, like Peter himself when he lived in the city (1 Pet. 5:13), for Rome destroyed the second temple just as Babylon destroyed the first.

The woman on the beast looks like Europa, the Tyrian princess, whom Zeus, in the form of a bull, bore westward. Having had his bestial way with her, she bore his offspring. John would have known this story. It was part of the mythology of the ancient Greco-Roman world. But he tells the sequel. The woman, now debauched, is drunk and bedecked with the beast's jewels, as she is borne from the Levant to the west to bear the offspring of the beast.

So John's Europa is the city of Rome and its world, wherein the princess, the debauched church, now rules as wicked queen. But whose Rome is this, and of which time? There are, broadly, three options. First, those who hold to the preterite view, and see the events of the Revelation lying in the past, see in the destruction of the scarlet woman the downfall of the ancient Roman empire. In that case, the prophecy was fulfilled long ago in the destruction of pagan Rome. Second, those who hold to the historicist view of the Revelation, popular in medieval and renaissance times, see it as the Roman Church which persecuted all opposition to its rule. Meanwhile, those who hold to a futurist view see it as the downfall of a future corrupt Rome. Let's look at these three options in turn.

If the prophecy was fulfilled in the ancient destruction of Rome, then no blame attaches to the Roman Church. But there are difficulties. First, in what sense did ancient, pagan Rome fornicate with the kings of the earth? Such a charge suggests ancient Rome was unfaithful to its true allegiance, that it fawned upon foreign rulers for illicit favours, and made itself shameful. But that was not the case with ancient Rome. It was not unfaithful to any pledge. It fawned on none, but conquered all, and, having conquered them, regarded them with contempt. Illicit intercourse was not the mark of ancient Rome.

Further, when we look at the sackings of Rome in the fourth and fifth centuries, we must ask which Rome did this befall? By that time, pagan Rome was long gone. The Gauls, Visigoths, and Vandals sacked a Rome whose populace had burned its idols and followed Christian rites, where prayers were offered daily for the city in the name of Jesus. It was not ancient pagan Rome that was destroyed, but Christian Rome. How can that be reflected in the judgement of the harlot on the beast? Did pagan Rome go unpunished and were its sins visited upon Christian Rome? That seems unjust. It is hard to see the fulfilment of Revelation 18 in any scenario of the destruction of ancient Rome.

Further, were the judgements described in Revelation 18 ever visited upon Rome? For the city is to be cast down and found no more, and all human activity is to cease from it (18:21–23). But these things were not fulfilled at the historic falls of Rome, not under Brennus, nor Alaric, nor Genseric, nor Totila. Nor have they happened to the city since. And so, if they are not gross exaggerations, then they point to events that must still take place. This is confirmed by the previous chapter, where the last bowl of plague is poured out on Babylon before the final completion of the divine plan for the world in the last days (Rev. 16:17–19).

So everything suggests that this is not Rome of the past but Rome of the future. But what is its unfaithfulness that leads to its destruction? Rome, of course, is the centre of the western church. Even those western protestant churches who reject papal authority are Roman at heart. They follow the Roman calendar, Roman Christmas and Roman Easter, and have imbibed much of the Roman church's Augustinian doctrine, often following some notion of the Roman hierarchy. So broadly speaking, Rome symbolizes the western Gentile church.

Now John, of course, lived before Rome became the centre of the Christian world. But his book is prophecy and so we cannot ignore the possibility that he is speaking of the Roman church or, more broadly, the Gentile church. This Rome, which will become the centre of the Gentile Christian world is represented as a harlot-queen. She is a queen because of the wealth and honour which she possesses. But she is a harlot for she is unfaithful to her husband. The only reasonable explanation is that this represents a church which has become unfaithful to its Lord. It's a picture well-known to us from the Old Testament, where Israel or Jerusalem, beloved by Jehovah (Isa. 62:4), has become an unfaithful spouse (Jer. 2:2, 20; Ezek. 16, 23; Hos. 2). In the same way, the scarlet woman on the seven-headed beast represents the church, the bride of Christ (John 3:29; 2 Cor. 11:2; Eph. 5:25–27, 32; Rev. 19:7–9; 21:9), betraying her Lord as a prostitute to worldly kings and riches. This means that, at some time, the western Gentile church will be found whoring after the illicit favours of earthly power and will suffer the consequences of this unfaithfulness.

Does this also foretell the future destruction of the city of Rome? The answer may be yes. That would be a great pity, for Rome is a beautiful and historic city. Yet the prophecy may actually point to the destruction of much of the Antichrist-worshipping world.

Protestants would be foolish to see this prophecy as being solely about the Roman Catholic Church. As said, the western church, and much of the Gentile world church, is Roman at heart. Many Protestant denominations have surpassed the Roman Church in adopting modern ideologies that are hostile to biblical truth. As for the Roman church, despite the great lapses of some clergy, there is still good in it.

The woman on the beast, like Europa, is the church borne away by the beast from her innocent origin in the Levant to debauchery in the west. The beast has decked her in riches and made her drunk with the blood of the saints and she has no concept of where she is going or of the offspring she will bear. The closest modern parallel may be the Christian west and its church, corrupted by the Antichrist and his wealth, to slay the saints.

But, sadly, the tragedy of the picture in Revelation is that the second coming of the Messiah is like a mirror image of his first coming. For, when he came to Jerusalem, it was indeed the Holy City. No idol was to be found in it, sacrifices were offered morning and evening to the true God, feasts and fasts were carefully observed, hands were washed, kosher was kept. Yet he wept over it and predicted its terrible downfall. For the priests and teachers, inflated by pride, malice, and envy, rejected their true Messiah. So shall it be in the days described in the Revelation, when the clergy of the Gentile church shall turn from the true Lord and accept in his place the Antichrist, leading their people astray, and bringing ruin on all.

The Lawless Man Enthroned in the Temple

Paul tells us the man of lawlessness will *take his seat in the temple of God, proclaiming himself to be God* (2 Thess. 2:4). Which temple is this?

Those who reject a literal interpretation of this prophecy point out that whenever Paul speaks elsewhere of the "temple of God" it is always figurative. He means either the Christian community (1 Cor. 3:16–17; 2 Cor. 6:16) or the believer's body indwelt by the Holy Spirit (1 Cor. 6:19). Peter likewise describes the church as living stones making a spiritual house to God (1 Pet. 2:5). Following this line of reasoning, then, the temple of God is the church. The Antichrist will take control of the church, proclaim himself as God, and direct its worship toward himself. That conforms well with what we have seen elsewhere and, indeed, within this same prophecy of Paul. First shall come the apostasy. Then the Antichrist – whether a man or a movement or both – shall arise from the apostate church and direct the worship of God to himself.

If the man of sin is to gain control over the church, where will he sit enthroned? Some hold that it is the papal basilica of Saint Peter in Rome. After all, Jesus said that he would build his church upon Peter the Rock, and the basilica is built upon the tomb of Peter. Therefore the Christian building with the best claim to being the temple of God is that basilica. One may object that in Paul's day this building did not exist. Neither he nor any of his readers knew of it as *the* temple of God. Yet the church existed and was, for Paul, the temple of God. And as Saint Peter's is the most important basilica in Christendom, it is possible that the apostate Antichrist would seek to be enthroned there, as pope or king or both.

On the other hand, some say that the only actual building which Paul would have called *the* temple of God was the temple in Jerusalem. That was the temple where Paul worshipped. It was famous all over the Roman world and would have been familiar to his readers. And it is, I think, most likely that Paul is speaking of this temple. A few have argued, on the basis of Daniel 9, that the Jerusalem temple would remain desolate till the end. But most interpreters, as far back as Irenaeus and Hippolytus, as we shall see, thought Paul was speaking of the Jerusalem temple. Paul, of course, knew well that Jesus had foretold the complete destruction of the temple (Matt. 24:2). And so his prophecy requires that the Jerusalem temple should be first destroyed and then rebuilt. Of course, the Jews have always sought to rebuild their temple. In the fourth century, they made a deal with Julian Caesar, called the Apostate, to rebuild the temple for them in AD 363, but it ended with Julian's sudden death in battle.[3] In the seventh century, the Exilarch Nehemiah ben Hushiel tried to rebuild it, amid much slaughter (AD 614). But that too ended in his death. Then, after the Muslim conquest of Jerusalem, they made a deal with Caliph Umar (*r.* 634–644) to build a wooden prayer house on the Temple Mount. But when Abd al-Malik (*r.* 685–705) became caliph, he built the Dome of the Rock (Kubbat es-Sakhra) in its place, to the Jews' great dismay. And since then, for well over a thousand years, any idea that the temple would be rebuilt seemed impossible. But now, with the creation of the State of Israel, and the work of the Temple Institute since 1987, the rebuilding of the Jerusalem temple no longer seems improbable. Anyone who has seen the reconstructed menorah beside the Temple Mount, and is aware of the proclamations of the Temple Institute and the Jerusalem Orthodox community, must now see the rebuilding of the temple more as an impending reality than an impossibility. And thus the fulfilment of Paul's ancient prophecy seems closer at hand than ever.

The Number of the Beast

We are told *Let him that has understanding calculate the number of the beast, for it is the number of man. And his number is six hundred and sixty-six* (Rev. 13:18). Although this number follows the description of the second beast, it is part of the description of how the second beast will compel mankind to worship the image of the first beast (13:15–18). So the number 666 seems to be rather the number of the first beast.

Before the invention of numerals, letters of the alphabet stood for numbers. The Latin system is well known: I was one, V was five, X was

[3] Julian's attempt to rebuild the temple is well documented. I discuss it in Mitchell 2015, ch. 13, on Ps. 127. Nehemiah ben Hushiel's campaign is less well known. For that, and the prayer house in Caliph Umar's time, see Mitchell 2016, ch. 11.

ten, L was fifty, and so on. The Hebrews and Greeks had similar systems and both had a well-developed philosophy of deriving meanings from the numerical values of letters. In Hebrew, it is called *gematria* and in Greek *isopsephy*. It was practised by scholars and common folk alike. A graffito found on the wall of Pompeii says, "I love her whose number is 545."

The reason why 666 is man's number is because it falls thrice short of seven. In Hebrew thought, seven is the number of completion or perfection. On the seventh day, God ceased from his work of creation and so the days of the week are completed on the seventh day. There are seven heavens. In the seven heavens are seven fixed spheres. Music, the heavenly language, has seven notes in its diatonic scales. The Revelation abounds in sevens. It has fifty-four explicit sevens, all signifying completion. Seven letters, seven churches, seven lampstands, seven stars, seven eyes, seven angels, seven thunders, seven spirits of God, seven heads, seven kings, seven hills. Divine judgement is marked by seven seals, seven trumpets, and seven bowls. The beast's seven horns, seven heads, and seven crowns represent his complete rule for a time. There are also many hidden sevens.

Seven, then, is the number of perfection, especially in the Revelation. And so eight represents what is beyond perfection. Just as the eighth day begins a new week, or the eighth note begins a new octave, so the number eight represents a new dimension. And what John does not say, but certainly implies, is to contrast the beast's number 666 with the number 888, which represents the Greek *Iēsous*, that is, Jesus.[4]

English	I	E	S	O	U	S	
Greek	Ι	Η	Σ	Ο	Υ	Σ	
Number	10	8	200	70	400	200	= **888**

[4] The numerical values of the Greek alphabet are as follows:

Α	alpha	1	Ι	iota	10	Ρ	rho	100
Β	beta	2	Κ	kappa	20	Σ	sigma	200
Γ	gamma	3	Λ	lambda	30	Τ	tau	300
Δ	delta	4	Μ	mu	40	Υ	upsilon	400
Ε	epsilon	5	Ν	nu	50	Φ	phi	500
F	digamma	6	Ξ	xi	60	Χ	chi	600
Ζ	zeta	7	Ο	omicron	70	Ψ	psi	700
Η	eta	8	Π	pi	80	Ω	omega	800
Θ	theta	9	Ϙ	qoppa	90	Ϡ	sampi	900

The letters *digamma, qoppa,* and *sampi* were obsolete in the Greek language by the mid-first millennium BC, but were retained for numerical purposes into Roman times.

John didn't have to spell it out. The Greeks were well aware of the numerology of names. His readers in Asia Minor would have understood well enough. Just as the beast is imperfect, Jesus is more than perfect. Just as Jesus rose on the day after Shabbat, the eighth day, so he initiates a new order of being altogether. Such is the number of his name – 888 – thrice pluperfect.

Now back to the number of the beast. The one called 666 is thrice imperfection. There need be little doubt that, with this number, John signifies the Emperor Nero. The Greek form of his name, Neron Caesar, when spelled in Hebrew – נרון קסר (*nrvn qsr*) – does indeed equal 666, as we see here, reading, of course, from right to left, in the Hebrew manner.[5]

English	R	S	Q	N	V	R	N	
Greek	ר	ס	ק	ן	ו	ר	נ	
Number	200	60	100	50	6	200	50	= **666**

This suspicion is confirmed by later manuscripts of the Revelation, which have the number 616, equivalent to the Latin form, Nero Caesar, lacking the second 'n' of Greek Neron.[6]

There was good reason why John should take Nero (or Neron) as the model of the dreadful first beast. The name came perhaps from a Sabine word meaning 'strong.' But in the Greek that everyone else spoke, *nēron* means 'water,' signifying instability and lawlessness, like the beast out of the sea. Everything about Nero was lawless. He killed his brother. He killed his two wives, the second of whom, Poppaea, he took from one of his subordinates. This Poppaea induced him to murder his mother with whom he was having incestuous relations. Then, after slaying Poppaea and taking a third wife, he dressed as a woman to marry a man. Then he married a castrated boy-slave, whom he dressed as a bride, who looked like the dead Poppaea. Always drunk, he set Rome on fire in order to clear land for his villas. The Roman chroniclers were united in their disgust at him. But for Christians and Jews his monstrosity was deeper still. He proclaimed himself a god. He was responsible for the first systematic persecution of Christians when he blamed them for the fires which he had started. In November 64, he banned the Christian faith and

[5] As can be seen, Hebrew has two letters for 'n', one reserved for the final letter in a word. But both have the same numerical value.

[6] Irenaeus was aware of this divergent manuscript in the late second century. He put it down to a copyist error.

unleashed a wave of persecution against the church. He sentenced to death the apostle Paul who stood innocent before him (Acts 27:24). He had Peter killed. Numberless, nameless Christians were thrown to wild dogs or crucified and lit as torches up and down the Appian Way. Then he ordered his armies to destroy Jerusalem. He died by his own hand while his legions besieged the doomed city.

So John sees Nero as the manifestation of the man of sin. But only as one manifestation. Remember, the Revelation is about things that are yet to happen (1:1; 4:1). So Nero portends the Antichrist, and the Antichrist will be a second Nero, just as Commodianus said. Whether or not Nero was still alive when John wrote depends, of course, when the Revelation was written. As we saw in chapter six, the evidence is far from clear. But patristic testimony points to Domitian's time, after Nero was dead.

But, either way, Nero is the original man of sin. Lawless and wicked, holding all the power of empire, he persecuted the saints to death. In the same way, the Beast will be a second Nero. In fact, decades after Nero's death there were myths among the pagans that Nero would return. The monster could not die so easily. And so John sees him returning as a demon-possessed beast to persecute the church. In this he resembles Daniel's wicked king who is Antiochus Epiphanes, but also points to another in the same mould still to come.

The number of the beast is Nero's number. But does that mean we will recognize the Antichrist by this number when he comes? People have sought to decode the name since the church began. Irenaeus and Hippolytus make suggestions, based on Greek numerology – Evanthas, Titan, Latinus – all now largely beside the point.[7] Nowadays, people look for it rather in Hebrew numerology. But that raises the question of which language we should be looking out for. We saw that Neron Caesar equals 666 in Hebrew, but implies the number 888 which equals 'Jesus' in Greek, which John's readers probably understood better. So are we looking for 666 in Hebrew or Greek? The simple answer is that this, like other mysteries in the Revelation, awaits its unveiling in the end-time. Yet there is one acronym which, strangely enough, equals 666 both in Hebrew and in Greek. That is the letters www for "worldwide web." In Hebrew, that would be three *vavs* – ווו. And in Greek, three *digammas* – FFF. There is no question that the worldwide web or internet has made possible the surveillance and oppression of the world's population on a

[7] Irenaeus, Ag. Her. 5:30:3; Hippolytus, Antichrist §50.

scale never before imagined. And those who control the worldwide web, if they choose to exclude anyone from it, can completely exclude them from the power to buy and sell, from the power to receive money or pay taxes, which will inevitably lead to the imprisonment or worse of those excluded. More than that, we cannot say now.

Antichrist in the Fathers

Bit by bit, the early Church Fathers took John's Antichrist and Beast, and Paul's man of sin, and connected them to form a composite picture of a coming evil king who claims to be the Messiah.

One of the earliest Christian documents after the New Testament, written toward the end of the first century, is the ancient code of church conduct and belief called the *Didachê* or 'Teaching.'[8] (Its full title is 'The Lord's Teaching Through The Twelve Apostles To The Nations.') Its final chapter speaks of the coming "World-deceiver" who shall come in the last days, working miracles, masquerading as the Son of God, and shall rule the earth, and commit unheard-of iniquities, until the Lord comes in power and raises the elect dead in the first resurrection.

> [3]For in the last days the false prophets and destroyers shall be multiplied, and the sheep shall be turned into wolves, and love shall be turned into hate. [4]For when lawlessness increases, they shall hate and persecute, and deliver up one another; and then shall appear the World-deceiver as Son of God, and shall do signs and wonders, and the earth shall be delivered into his hands, and he shall commit iniquities which have never yet come to pass from the beginning of the world. [5]And then shall the race of men come into the fire of trial, and many shall be offended and shall perish; but they who endure in their faith shall be saved from under the curse itself. [6]And then shall appear the signs of the truth: first the sign of opening in heaven; then the sign of the voice of the trumpet; and the third, the resurrection of the dead. [7]Not, however, of all, but as was said, *The Lord shall come, and all the holy ones with him* (Zech. 14:5). [8]Then shall the world see the Lord coming upon the clouds of heaven. (*Didachê* 16.3–8)

The next person to speak in this way is Justin in his *Dialogue with Trypho* (c. 155). He too doesn't use the name 'Antichrist,' but calls him rather the 'man of apostasy' (*tês apostasías anthrôpos*), meaning the man of 'lawlessness' (*anomía*) to arise at the apostasy (2 Thess. 2:3). This one,

[8] For the date, see Holmes 2006: 157–162.

he says, will persecute the church.

> The man of apostasy, who speaks strange things against the Most High, shall venture to do unlawful deeds on the earth against us the Christians ...For it is plain that, though beheaded, and crucified, and thrown to wild beasts, and chains, and fire, and all other kinds of torture, we do not give up our confession. (*Dial.* 110)

Next, Irenaeus, in his *Against Heresies* (c. 180), is the first to give John's name 'Antichrist' to the Beast of Revelation 13, whose number is 666 (5:29–30). He says this Antichrist will be a Jew from the tribe of Dan, who will arise at the end of the age, enthrone himself in Jerusalem, reign for forty-two months, and persecute the Church, before Jesus returns to kill him and inaugurate the millennial kingdom.

A little later, Hippolytus of Rome wrote an entire treatise, *Christ and Antichrist* (c. 202). He tells how the Antichrist will rebuild the Jerusalem temple (6); he will be a Jew from the tribe of Dan (14) and gain control over the Roman state (25); he shall gather the Jews to himself and direct them against the church (54, 58). Hippolytus then applies Daniel's 'seventy sevens' to the end time. At the start of the last week of Daniel's prophecy, the two prophets will preach for 1,260 days. The Antichrist shall kill them and persecute the saints (47, 49). There will follow three and a half years of tribulation until Jesus shall appear and bring a conflagration of judgement upon Antichrist and his hosts. Then he will raise the righteous dead and bring in the kingdom of the saints (64, 65).

Tertullian, in *The Resurrection of the Flesh* (c. 206), calls him 'the beast Antichrist,' who will make war against the Church before the First Resurrection.

> In the Revelation of John the order of these times is spread out to view... so that the world may first drink to the dregs the plagues that await it out of the vials of the angels, and that the city of fornication may receive from the ten kings its deserved doom, and that the beast Antichrist with his false prophet may wage war on the Church of God; and that, after the casting of the devil into the bottomless pit for a while, the blessed prerogative of the first resurrection may be ordained from the thrones. (§25)

At the resurrection, the faithful alive at the end of the Antichrist's reign shall be immediately transformed, at the coming of Christ, to their heavenly bodies and join the rising saints in a post-tribulation rapture.

> Now the privilege of this favour awaits those who shall at the coming of

> the Lord be found in the flesh, and who shall, owing to the oppressions of the time of Antichrist, deserve by an instantaneous death [*i.e.*, by transformation], which is accomplished by a sudden change, to become qualified to join the rising saints; as he writes to the Thessalonians: *For this we say unto you by the word of the Lord, that we which are alive and remain unto the coming of the Lord shall not prevent them which are asleep. For the Lord Himself shall descend from heaven with a shout, with the voice of the archangel, and with the trump of God: and the dead in Christ shall rise first: then we too shall ourselves be caught up together with them in the clouds to meet the Lord in the air: and so shall we ever be with the Lord.* (§42)

A century later, Lactantius, in his *Institutes* (c. 305) says the power of Rome shall fall and the earth shall be in tumult. Then a great prophet of God shall come forth, working signs and wonders. But a Syrian king and false prophet shall arise and slay him and claim to be Christ. This Antichrist will then rule for forty-two months, and persecute the church and fight against the truth in four wars until Christ shall come to punish their crimes and condemn them to torments (7:15–19).

Commodianus, in his *Instructiones,* says the Antichrist will be Nero raised up from Hades. Elijah shall come to seal God's beloved ones. Then the whole earth shall be shaken for seven years. Elijah shall dominate the first three and a half years, but risen Nero shall rule the second three and a half. This Latin conqueror shall claim to be the Messiah and do many wonders with the false prophet. But the Jews shall confess to the Most High that they have been deceived. Then the Messiah shall come and bring in the era of peace and healing (41–42).

So all these early Fathers – *Didachê*, Justin, Irenaeus, Tertullian, Hippolytus, Commodianus, Lactantius – say the Antichrist will persecute the Church, but will be destroyed by Christ at his coming. Irenaeus and Hippolytus expect him to be a Jew from the tribe of Dan who will set up his kingdom in Jerusalem. But Commodianus expects him to be a Latin, wicked Nero brought back to life. They say he will rule and persecute the saints for a literal three and a half years (1,260 days or 42 months) as foretold in the Revelation. None expect the church to be removed before Antichrist comes. Instead, the persecution will end when Jesus comes to catch up (or rapture) his people and slay the Antichrist.

Is the Antichrist a Jew?

Irenaeus says the Antichrist will be a Jew. He cites John 5:43, where Jesus says to the Judeans, *I have come in my Father's name and you do not receive me; if another comes in his own name, him you will receive.* And he takes the parable of the unjust judge, *who feared not God* (Luke 18:2) to mean the Antichrist, to whom the widow – earthly Jerusalem, forgetful of God – brought her plea for vengeance on her adversary. The Jews, he says, shall acclaim the Antichrist when he comes to power. Then he shall base his kingdom in Jerusalem, raise up the Jews, proclaim himself Messiah, enthrone himself in the temple and demand their worship; he shall lay Babylon waste, give it to the beast, and persecute the church until he and his kingdom are destroyed at the coming of the Lord Jesus.[9]

Of course, Jesus does not actually say in John 5:42 that the one the Pharisees will receive will be a Jew, though it could be implied in the words being directed to Judean Pharisees in Jerusalem. They would never receive a non-Jew as a leader. One could say the prophecy was fulfilled in the messianic pretender Shimon bar Kokhba, who was indeed accepted by some of the Pharisees. Bar Kokhba's rebellion against Rome, from AD 132 until his death in 135, brought slaughter to half a million people in the Holy Land, both Jew and Christian, and exile and slavery to the survivors. Yet that does not preclude a future fulfilment of the prophecy from another would-be messiah still to arise.

Some twenty years after Irenaeus, his disciple Hippolytus took a similar line. The Antichrist, he says, will raise up the kingdom of the Jews and uproot three kingdoms – Egypt, Libya, and Ethiopia; then, with tyranny, he will stir up tribulation and persecution until he is destroyed by the stone from heaven (cf. Dan. 2:34–45), who is the Son of Man. He repeats Irenaeus's teaching on the widow and the unjust judge.[10]

But there is the further issue that John says: *Many antichrists have appeared...They went forth from us, but they were not of us* (1 John 2:19). Does *from us* mean from the Christian community or from the Hebrew people? Both are possible. It could even mean that he is an apostate Judeo-Christian, or a Jew supported by Christians. Many early Christians were of Israelite descent, and some modern ones still are. But it's another piece to the puzzle.

[9] Irenaeus, *Ag. Her.* 5.25.4; 5.26.1.
[10] Hippolytus, *Antichrist* §25, 57.

Both Irenaeus and Hippolytus say that the Antichrist will come from the tribe of Dan. This is sketchier altogether. The evidence proposed for this is *Dan shall be a serpent in the way* (Gen. 49:17) and *The snorting of his horses was heard from Dan* (Jer. 8:16).[11] There is also Revelation 7:4–8 where none of the sealed of the twelve tribes of Israel are from the tribe of Dan. But Genesis 19:17 is hardly conclusive. Jeremiah 8:16 is about Nebuchadnezzar's army approaching Jerusalem from Dan in the north. It could apply to the messianic time – for enemies usually enter the Holy Land, round the Fertile Crescent, from the north – but no-one could insist on such a view. And there are many issues with Revelation 7. We read that those sealed are *of all the tribes of the children of Israel* (7:4), so Dan is not excluded. And one may ask also why the list features Manasseh and not Ephraim? None of these passages proves that the Antichrist will arise from Dan. And there is the final difficulty that the Jews, looking for a Messiah from the tribe of Judah and of David, would not receive a messianic claimant from the tribe of Dan. Further, it would be difficult to identify any Jew today as being from Dan. The few ancient Jewish genealogies that survive tend to be from claimants to the house of David or Aaron. So there is little way that a recognizably Danite Messiah could now emerge.

Some suggest the Antichrist may be a Muslim. They derive this from John's words, describing the spirit of Antichrist: *This is the antichrist, he who denies the Father and the Son* (1 John 2:22). This agrees with John's teaching that antichrists will arise from the Christian community (2:18–19). For Islam is, at root, a heterodox Christian teaching.

Finally, Daniel's fourth kingdom is to endure to the appearing of the kingdom of God. So, if the fourth kingdom is indeed Rome, there is little room for the extended rule of a non-Roman kingdom before the return of the Lord, although a Jewish Antichrist could rule through, or control, the Roman power.

So John 5:43 and 1 John 2:19 may point to the Antichrist being Jewish or an apostate Judeo-Christian. But what is clearer is that the Jews are historically the nation that has produced messiahs. From Bar Kokhba, through Nehemiah ben Hushiel, Shabbetai Zvi, Menachem Schneerson, and down to our own time, the Jewish nation have given the world over fifty messianic claimants in the last two millennia.[12] None of them has

[11] Irenaeus, *Ag. Her.* 5.30.2; Hippolytus, *Antichrist* §14–15.
[12] See Rabow 2002.

achieved the work of the messiah. But the abundance of Jewish would-be messiahs should alert us to the likelihood of yet another messianic claimant from the Jews.

Further, the first to say these things was Irenaeus. Irenaeus was, as said, a disciple of Polycarp, who was a disciple of John the Apostle, the author of the Revelation and of the epistles which speak of the Antichrist. It follows that, if any Church Father had any inside information on the meaning of the Antichrist and the Revelation, then Irenaeus was that one. Indeed, Irenaeus says that he did not make this up, but that he received it. And Hippolytus was a disciple of Irenaeus, so his teachings come from the same Johannine sources on the Revelation. And so, even if a Jewish Antichrist is not clear in the Revelation, it is possible that this was the oral teaching that Irenaeus received on the subject from John himself. According to this tradition, the Jews, though long landless and scattered, would not remain so, but would arise to regain their ancestral land, and then the Antichrist would arise from their midst, and bear away the church, like Europa, debauched, intoxicated, and corrupted, on his back.

THE END OF ANTICHRIST

It is the Lord Jesus himself who will slay Antichrist. This needs to be said against the classic amillennial view which maintained that Michael the Archangel slays him so that the feet of Christ need not touch the earth when he comes to judge in the Valley of Jehoshaphat, and so that there is a gap between the death of the Antichrist and the coming of Christ to judge from the air, this gap being for the conversion of the Jews, the burning of Gog's weapons, and so forth.[13] But, in the New Testament, it is Jesus who slays the Antichrist.

1) *Rev. 19:11–20.* The one who comes from heaven on a white horse, called Faithful and True, Word of God, King of Kings and Lord of Lords, titles given elsewhere to the Messiah and to Lord Jehovah (Ps. 2:9; Isa. 11:4; 63:2–3; Rev. 1:14–16), can be none other than the Lord Jesus himself. It is only when he appears that the beast and the false prophet are seized and thrown alive into the lake of burning sulphur.

2) *2 Thess. 2:8.* Jesus will kill the lawless man with the breath of his mouth and annihilate him by the epiphany of his coming. The breath of his mouth means, I take it, a word of command effecting his death.

[13] See, e.g., Aquinas, *Summa,* Supp. Tert. Part. Question 76, Art. 3; Question 88, Art. 4.

3) *Matt. 24:29–30. Immediately after the tribulation of those days... the sign of the Son of Man will appear in heaven, and then all the tribes of the earth will mourn, and they will see the Son of Man coming on the clouds of heaven with power and great glory.* To say that Jesus appears 'immediately' after the tribulation implies that it is his coming that brings the tribulation and the reign of the Antichrist to an abrupt end.

4) In Daniel's interpretation of Nebuchadnezzar's vision, the rock cut with no human hand strikes the statue on its feet and the statue shatters (Dan. 2:34–35; 44–45). The rock, as elsewhere in scripture, signifies Jehovah or his Messiah.[14] Therefore it is the rock who brings to an end the final earthly kingdom.

There is no contradiction between the Antichrist being slain at Jesus's word and his being seized and cast into the burning pit. It is Jesus's command which results in the Antichrist being cast into the pit, which is his well-deserved end.

[14] Gen. 49:24; Deut. 32.4, 15, 18, 30, 31, 37; 2 Sam. 22.2–3, 32, 47; 23.3; Isa. 28:16; Ps. 118:22. For the messianic interpretation of Ps. 118:22, see 2Q23 and 4Q173 (=4QpPs^{b}) frg. 5, lines 1–6; Matt. 21:42; Mark 12:10; Luke 20:17; Acts 4:11; Midr. Pss. 18; Rashi on Mic. 5:2.

18

Judgement of Fire

READING the Bible, we find that it speaks frequently about a fearful judgement of fire which is ordained for the earth. There are two sides to this judgement: one for the world in this mortal life and one in the post-mortem state. Here we are concerned only with the first of these.

In The Old Testament

By now we will be unsurprised to learn that Genesis is where the theme of a judgement of fire first appears. There we read how the cities of the plain, Sodom and Gomorrah, were entirely given over to wickedness and particularly to the sin that bears their name, sodomy. As a result, the Holy One destroyed them by fire from heaven.

> Then Jehovah rained down on Sodom and Gomorrah sulphur and fire – from Jehovah out of the heavens. And he overthrew those cities and the entire plain, destroying all the dwellers in the cities and whatever grew on the earth. (Gen. 19:24–25)

Leaving Genesis behind, we come to the period of the wilderness wanderings in the Exodus. We already saw, in chapter thirteen, the judgement that befell the Levites who took part in Korah's rebellion and were incinerated by fire that proceeded from the presence of Jehovah (Num. 16:35). One imagines that it was because of this fearful episode that Moses later said:

> Be careful not to forget the covenant of Jehovah your God that he made with you; do not make for yourselves an idol in the form of anything Jehovah your God has forbidden. For Jehovah your God is a consuming fire, a jealous God. (Deut. 4:23–24)

Then the Lord, in the Song of Moses, says:

> A fire is kindled by my wrath; it will burn to Sheol below. It will consume the earth and its harvests, and set ablaze the foundations of the mountains. (Deut. 32:22)

Then we come to the Psalms. There David writes:

> Jehovah examines the righteous, but the wicked and those who love violence his soul hates. On the wicked he will rain fiery coals and burning sulphur; a scorching wind will be their lot. (Ps. 11:5–6)

Isaiah wrote:

> Behold, the name of Jehovah comes from afar, with burning anger and dense smoke. His lips are full of fury, and his tongue is like a consuming fire. (Isa. 30:27)

Later, at the end of Old Testament times, Malachi wrote:

> Behold the day is coming. It will burn like a furnace. All the arrogant and every evildoer will be stubble, and that day that is coming will set them on fire, says Jehovah of hosts, so that it will leave them neither root nor branch. (Mal. 4:1)

And several other Old Testament texts could be cited.[1] Then, in the late third century BC, before we get to the New Testament, the high priest Shimon ben Onias prays against Ptolemy IV Philopator's demand to enter the temple's holy of holies. He speaks of the punishment of Sodom not as an isolated event but as a continual example of judgement to those who were to come after.

> You consumed with fire and sulphur the people of Sodom who acted arrogantly, who were notorious for their vices, and you made them an example to those who should come afterward. (1 Macc. 2:5)

In The New Testament

The warnings of this judgement of fire continue into the New Testament.

[1] Ps. 46:6–9; Ezek. 38:22; 39:6; Mal. 3:2–3.

We hear it first from the mouth of John the Baptist, who introduces Jesus with the words,

> He will baptize you with the Holy Spirit and fire. His winnowing fork is in his hand, and he will clear his threshing floor, gathering his wheat into the barn and burning up the chaff with unquenchable fire. (Matt. 3:11–12; Luke 3:16–17)

Then we come to the teaching of Jesus himself. Jesus does not soften what all the prophets before him have said. On the contrary, he has more to say about it than anyone else.

> I came to cast fire upon the earth, and would that it were already kindled! (Luke 12:1)

This is worth reflecting on. Jesus is not talking about the 'Holy Ghost fire' that we sing about. The Holy Ghost fire purges believers from sin. But Jesus says he has come to throw fire upon the whole earth. And he is impatient, he ardently desires that this will happen because, we must understand, he is weary of the wickedness and evil on earth. Since that time, he has waited 2,000 years for his wish to be fulfilled. Yet, since he is the Son of the Father, it will certainly be granted. And now the time rushes toward us when his wish will become reality. As he says,

> As the weeds are pulled up and burned in the fire, so will it be at the end of the age. The Son of Man will send out his angels, and they will weed out of his kingdom everything that causes sin and all who do evil. They will throw them into the blazing furnace, where there will be weeping and gnashing of teeth. (Matt. 13:40–42)

And he says,

> The angels will come out and separate the evil from the righteous [50]and throw them into the fiery furnace. (Matt. 13:49–50)

The apostles also speak about this fire. Paul says,

> The Day…will be revealed with fire. (1 Cor. 3:13)

And again he says:

> God is just: He will pay back trouble to those who trouble you. And give relief to you who are troubled, and to us as well. This will happen when the Lord Jesus is revealed from heaven in blazing fire with his powerful angels. (2 Thess. 1:6–7)

The author of Hebrews says:

> Land that produces thorns and thistles is worthless and is in danger of being cursed. In the end it will be burned. (6:8) For if we go on sinning deliberately after receiving the knowledge of the truth, there no longer remains a sacrifice for sins, but a fearful expectation of judgment, and a fury of fire that will consume the adversaries. (10:26–27)...For our God is a consuming fire. (12:29)

Peter, in his second epistle, has much to say on the subject. Like Shimon ben Onias (1 Macc. 2:5), he says that what happened to Sodom and Gomorrah was not an isolated event. Rather, their destruction by fire is a model for what will befall all the ungodly.

> He condemned the cities of Sodom and Gomorrah by burning them to ashes, and made them an example of what is going to happen to the ungodly. (2 Peter 2:6)

He further says,

> [7]The present heavens and earth are reserved for fire, being kept for the day of judgement and destruction of the ungodly... [10]But the day of the Lord will come like a thief. The heavens will disappear with a roar; the elements will be destroyed by fire, and the earth and everything done in it will be laid bare... [12]That day will bring about the destruction of the heavens by fire, and the elements will melt in the heat. (2 Peter 3:7–12).

Jude makes the same point, that the punishment of Sodom and Gomorrah happened as an example of what will befall those given over to unlawful passions. He compares their crime to that of the angels who left their proper place to pursue the forbidden flesh of mortal women, and so are bound in chains for judgement,[2]

> Just as Sodom and Gomorrah and the surrounding cities, which likewise indulged in sexual immorality and pursued unnatural desire [foreign flesh], serve as an example by undergoing a punishment of eternal fire. (Jude 7)

The Revelation also speaks in several places of the coming judgement of fire. In a moment, a third of the earth will be burned up.

> The first angel sounded his trumpet, and there came hail and fire mixed with blood, and it was hurled down on the earth. A third of the earth was burned up, a third of the trees were burned up, and all the green grass was burned up. (Rev. 8:7)

[2] These are the fallen angels, or Watchers, of Gen. 6:1–4, whom 1 Enoch calls Semjaza and his followers, who begot giants by mortal women. Michael the archangel will imprison them in the abyss of fire in torment for ever and ever (1 En. 10.11–14).

Babylon will be consumed:

> For this reason her plagues will come in a single day, death and mourning and famine, and she will be burned up with fire; for mighty is the Lord God who has judged her. (Rev. 18:8)

So will the armies of Gog and Magog:

> And they marched up over the broad plain of the earth and surrounded the camp of the saints and the beloved city, but fire came down from heaven and consumed them. (Rev. 20:9)

JUDGEMENT OF FIRE IN PATRISTIC AND RABBINIC TEXTS

With all this biblical teaching, both in the Old Testament and the New, it's not surprising that both the Fathers and the Rabbis wrote about the coming judgement of fire. Let's look at just a few examples.

The Apocalypse of Baruch, dating from just after the destruction of the temple in AD 70, says,

> For to them [the righteous] shall be given the world to come, but the dwelling of the rest who are many shall be in the fire. (2 Bar 44:15)

A little later, the Coptic Apocalypse of Elijah says,

> The Lord will hear and command the heaven and the earth with great wrath. And they will send forth fire. And the fire will prevail over the earth seventy-two cubits. It will consume the sinners and the devils like stubble…On that day, the Messiah, the king, and all his saints will come forth from heaven. He will burn the earth. (5:22–24, 36)

Irenaeus, speaking of the Antichrist, speaks of

> the number of the name of that man in whom is concentrated the whole apostasy of six thousand years, and unrighteousness, and wickedness, and false prophecy, and deception; for which things' sake a cataclysm of fire shall also come [upon the earth] (Ag. Her. 5.29.2).

And Commodianus the poet speaks likewise.

> What shall the mother do for the sucking child, when she herself is burnt up? In the flame of fire the Lord will judge the wicked. But the fire shall not touch the just… Such will be the heat, that the stones themselves shall melt. The winds assemble into lightnings, the heavenly wrath rages; and wherever the wicked man fleeth, he is seized upon by this fire… Amen flames on the nations, and the Medes and Persians burn for a

> thousand years, as the hidden words of John declare. For then after a thousand years they are delivered over to Gehenna; and he whose work they were, with them are burnt up.
>
> The whole of nature is converted in flame, which yet avoids the camp of his saints. The earth is burned up from its foundations, and the mountains melt. Of the sea nothing remains: it is overcome by the powerful fire. (*Instructiones* §43, 45)

In rabbinic literature we read,

> Fire will come down from heaven and consume Jerusalem to a depth of three cubits, removing uncircumcised foreigners and the impure from the midst of her. Jerusalem will descend, built-up and shining, from the heavens. (Mysteries of Rav Shimon ben Yoḥai 30)

And the Zohar says,

> All the kings of the world shall assemble in the great city of Rome. And the Holy One, blessed be he, will shower fire and hail and meteorites upon them, until they are wiped out from the world. And only those kings who did not go to Rome will remain in the world. (§480)

Why this Judgement of Fire?

Now this is a truly fearful scenario. But it's scriptural. The Bible, and all its tradition of interpretation, say a holocaust of fire is set to destroy the world and its people. These are the words of the prophets, and of Jesus and the apostles. We should take these words seriously.

But, you ask, "Why is this fearful judgement to come on the world?" The answer is: For the same reason it came on Sodom and Gomorrah. Remember what Peter says. Sodom and Gomorrah are a picture of what is to come. Genesis says that they were great sinners before the Lord. They were Canaanites and worshipped some form of the Baal rite. These rites involved human sacrifice. They sacrificed little children, burning them alive, to their gods. There was ritual prostitution. Men had sexual relations with cultic prostitutes, both male and female. And Ezekiel tells us that Sodom was arrogant and overfed; they did not help the poor and needy; they were proud and did detestable things before God (Ezek. 16:49–50). And then there is the sin that bears their name. When the angels arrive in Sodom, they threaten them with homosexual rape. And when Lot rebukes them for their sin, they turn on him. And so, in addition to all their vices, they rejected God's word of correction.

How like our modern world are Sodom and Gomorrah! Little children are still slain. Arrogance and greed, prostitution and lawless sexuality abound. And still they reject the word of God. These days, you can read the Bible on the internet for free, but people act like it doesn't exist. Five hundred years ago, they couldn't see it, but they honoured it. Now they can read it, but reject it. The world is going backwards. And for this, for all its sins, the long-threatened judgement of fire hangs over our head.

How will this judgement of fire happen?

How will this judgement of heavenly fire happen? The Bible doesn't say. It could be the explosion of a super-volcano. There are places where such a thing is possible, like the Yellowstone Caldera. Or it could be a meteor strike. Or it could be an entirely supernatural and divine event. But perhaps the likeliest explanation for *the elements melting in fervent heat* (2 Peter 3:10) is that it will be a nuclear event.

For a while, after the fall of the Berlin wall, we tried to reduce nuclear weapons. But nuclear arsenals are now making a big comeback. There are over 12,000 nuclear weapons stockpiled in the world. Most of them are much greater than the bombs which fell on Japan in 1945. There are enough such weapons to destroy every major city and town in the world. And one must suppose they are not created for nothing. There is a terrible purpose in their existence. It is so that the wickedness of mankind will finally manifest itself in the destruction of the habitable earth. In a final outburst of demonic madness, man himself will push the button to bring God's dreadful judgement of fire upon a world gone wrong.

As I wrote this chapter, I sat looking out my window in the quiet suburb, or *commune*, where I live in Belgium. The spring sunshine ripples on the new leaves of beeches and large, quiet, sycamores. Red squirrels run busily among the branches. Nearby, a blackbird sings. A woodpecker drums on his tree. I wonder at the radiant beauty of creation.

But, as I write, presidential strongmen around the world feel freer than ever before to openly threaten other nations with nuclear attack. If such an attack were launched, then Brussels, the headquarters of the EU and NATO, might be among the first targets, *in the day of the great slaughter, when the towers fall* (Isa. 30:25). The place of impact, perhaps the EU *quartier* at Place Schumann, or NATO HQ in Evere, would be engulfed in a flaming holocaust of millions of degrees centigrade. The rest of the city, and its surrounding communes, would be slightly cooler, perhaps hundreds of thousands of degrees.

Of course, much would depend on the size of the warhead. But some of these weapons are immense. They divide into multiple warheads as they descend, spreading out to target a whole country. Everything in the urban centres of Brussels, Antwerp, Gent, Liège, and Namur would be instantly incinerated. Gone the blackbirds, woodpeckers, and squirrels. Gone the beeches and sycamores. Gone the people, young and old. Gone the streets and buildings, large and small. Gone every mark and memento of the ancient Franco-Flemish civilisation.

There might be a few survivors, perhaps in the countryside or coming out the Metro. Suffering perhaps from horrific burns, or blinded, they would find themselves in a post-nuclear wasteland, without food or water, gas or electricity, law and order, or medical and emergency services, a landscape of molten earth, concrete, glass, and steel, swept by poisonous radioactive clouds, under the dust-heavy grey sky of an impending nuclear winter where no crops grow.

The prospect is both incredible and credible. It is incredible that everything we now know and see and hear, the whole visible world, our families, our homes, our neighbours and friends, our civilization, could be so instantly destroyed. Yet it is also perfectly credible that this could happen. For these weapons certainly exist and they can certainly be launched on the whim of one man, and the results will be as described.

So people rightly ask, "Where is God in all of this?" Or "Why doesn't God do something?" And the answer is simple: This is what God is doing. God is at the centre of this. He spoke about this time for thousands of years. By his prophets, he told mankind since the beginning that a judgement of fire is reserved for our world. And now it rushes upon us.

If the current cycle of boasting and sabre-rattling continues, it could all flare out of control anytime. On the other hand, these people, knowing that a nuclear strike would lead inevitably to their own destruction, might refrain for now. In that case, the current order of things could continue for another five or ten or fifteen years, until the demonic power finally triumphs, within the timing of God, to induce someone to strike first against his enemies, triggering the whole process. And the world we know will be engulfed by fire.

So what is the good news?

Maybe you say, "I thought the gospel was good news!" But there is indeed good news. The good news is this: The faithful will be saved.

I do not say this quickly or lightly. The Lord doesn't always spare Christians from suffering. They were persecuted in Roman times. And in every century since, they have suffered bitterly under injustice. The faithful are not always spared from persecution.

But, on the other hand, there is another theme that runs through the Bible: when the Lord himself brings judgement on a city or a nation – when he pours out upon them the wrath of God – he spares his chosen people from that wrath of judgement. For instance,

- He caught up Enoch to save him from the evil days before the Flood.
- When the Flood came, he spared Noah and those in the ark.
- When he sent fire from heaven on Sodom and Gomorrah, he spared Lot.
- When he sent the plagues on Egypt, he spared the Hebrews.
- When he slew Pharaoh's army in the Red Sea, he brought Israel through on dry land.
- When he burned the men of Korah's rebellion by fire, he spared the sons of Korah (Num 16:23–35; 26:10–11).
- When he destroyed Jerusalem in the Roman holocaust of AD 70, when people, temple, and city were consumed by fire and sword, he spared his church. Warned by prophets, they left the city, crossed the Jordan to Pella, and were saved.

The Bible says the same thing will happen in the coming judgement of fire: the faithful will be saved.

The Lord himself says so. "As it was in the days of Noah, so it will be at the coming of the Son of Man," that is, just as Noah was plucked up and saved, so believers will be plucked up and saved (Matt. 24:37). When he says, "Remember Lot's wife" (Luke 17:32) he means that some will be plucked from the judgment of fire, just as Lot was; but others will not. Yes, perhaps he is speaking of the AD 70 destruction of Jerusalem. But that destruction is emblematic of the coming judgement of the world. And he says,

> Men will faint from fear and anxiety about what is coming upon the earth, for the powers of the heavens will be shaken. At that time they will see the Son of Man coming in a cloud with power and great glory. When these things begin to happen, stand up and lift up your heads, because your redemption is drawing near. (Luke 21:26–27)

When the destruction approaches, we should not fear, for our redemption is coming. And again, Jesus says that the burning is for the wicked, not for the righteous.

> Collect the weeds and tie them in bundles to be burned; then gather the wheat and bring it into my barn. (Matt. 13:30)

> Whoever does not remain in me, he is like a branch that is thrown away and withers. Such branches are gathered up, thrown into the fire, and burned. (John 15:6)

The apostle Peter speaks about this too. He draws a parallel between the judgement of the Flood, the judgement of Sodom and Gomorrah, and the coming judgement of fire upon the whole world. He compares the coming judgement by fire to the Flood, saying,

> By waters the world of that time was flooded and destroyed. By the same word the present heavens and earth are reserved for fire, being kept for the day of judgement and destruction of ungodly men. (2 Pet. 3:6–7)

And, he says, just as Noah and Lot were saved, so the righteous will be rescued through the coming cataclysm.

> [5]If he did not spare the ancient world, but preserved Noah, a herald of righteousness, with seven others, when he brought a flood upon the world of the ungodly; [6]if by turning the cities of Sodom and Gomorrah to ashes he condemned them to extinction, making them an example of what is going to happen to the ungodly; [7]and if he rescued righteous Lot, greatly distressed by the sensual conduct of the wicked [8](for as that righteous man lived among them day after day, he was tormenting his righteous soul over their lawless deeds that he saw and heard); [9]then the Lord knows how to rescue the godly from trials, and to keep the unrighteous under punishment until the day of judgment. (2 Pet. 2:5–9)

How will we be saved?

The point that Jesus and Peter are making is this: God saved Noah and his family by giving them an escape from the Flood. He saved Lot and his family by taking them before the fire fell. In the same way, he will rescue the faithful before the day that will *bring about the destruction of the heavens by fire, and the elements will melt in the heat* (2 Peter 3:7–12).

Paul makes the same point. In 2 Thessalonians, he first speaks of the

Lord Jesus being revealed from heaven in blazing fire with his powerful angels (1:6–7). Then he goes on to say that when Jesus comes, we will be gathered together to him (2:1–3). That is, when Jesus comes in fire, the church will be gathered to him.

In other words, on the day he casts fire upon the earth, the Lord will first catch us up as he has promised. This was understood by the early Hebrew church. We turn again to our old friend the *Apocalypse of Elijah*, which makes it clear. As we saw in chapter fifteen, it tells first how the saints will be caught up "before his wrath."

> On that day the Messiah will pity those who are his own. And he will send from heaven his sixty-four thousand angels, each of whom has six wings. The sound will move heaven and earth when they give praise and glorify. Now those upon whose forehead the name of Messiah is written and upon whose hand is the seal, both the small and the great, will be taken up upon their wings and lifted up before his wrath. (5:2–4)

Then there will be chaos on earth, and the outcry of sinners. And then fire will fall upon the earth, burning the earth thirty-six metres deep.

> It will be on that day that the Lord will hear and command the heaven and the earth with great wrath. And they will send forth fire. And the fire will prevail over the earth seventy-two cubits. It will consume the sinners and the devils like stubble. A true judgment will occur. (5:22–24)

After the judgement of fire, the Messiah and his saints will reappear and set up the kingdom.

> On that day, the Messiah, the king, and all his saints will come forth from heaven. He will burn the earth. He will spend a thousand years upon it. Because the sinners prevailed over it, he will create a new heaven and a new earth. No deadly devil will exist in them. He will rule with his saints, ascending and descending, while they are always with the angels and they are with the Messiah for a thousand years. (5:36–39)

So the Apocalypse of Elijah makes clear the connection that Jesus and the apostles imply. It is the rapture which will save the church from the wrath of God poured out upon the earth in fire.

This, of course, answers the question sometimes posed by pretribbers, which goes, "If the rapture is not to save the church from the Antichrist's persecution, then what is it for?" Here is the answer: The rapture is not to save the church from human persecution, but to deliver it from the wrath of God.

SUMMARY

Therefore, in all this, we must distinguish between the persecution of believers and the wrath of God. In the time of the Antichrist, as in any evil time, believers may be persecuted. Yet, even then, they may be shielded from all or part of the persecution. They may be miraculously saved, as Daniel and his friends were (Dan. 3:27; 6:22). They may be sealed with a seal of protection even in the persecution (Rev. 9:4). They may find a refuge where they can flee, as when Obadiah hid the hundred prophets (1 Kgs 18:4). Yet some may be called to suffer for the name of Jesus. As Ladd says,

> Physical death, bodily suffering is not to be feared, fearful as it is, by those who have been redeemed by the suffering and death of Christ. Martyrdom has ever been a mark of faithfulness to Christ. Believers have been ready, often glad, to die for Christ's sake. Why should it be any different at the end.[3]

But the church will never suffer the wrath of God, for God will never pour out his wrath upon his redeemed. That is why, on that day, when his wrath is poured out in fire upon the earth, he will catch us up to him in the air, in a 'pre-wrath' rapture. And so we should not fear. *Our God whom we serve is able to deliver us from the burning fiery furnace* (Dan. 3:17).

[3] Ladd 1956: 129.

19

The Parable of the Sheep and the Goats

THE parable of the Sheep and the Goats in Matthew 25:31–46 is one of the most misunderstood passages in all the Bible. Like many others, I too spent years misunderstanding it and worrying what it meant. But once you find the key, it really makes perfect sense. Let's start at the beginning.

The Parable of the Sheep and Goats starts with the *Son of Man* seated on *the throne of his glory* (25:31). He is the King (25:34), that is, King Jesus the Messiah, just as he is depicted in Zechariah 14, when Jehovah himself descends in bodily form on the Mount of Olives and sets up his throne in Jerusalem to judge the nations (14:4–19).

All the nations will be gathered before him (Matt. 25:32). Does that mean that, say, Denmark will be somewhere to the left, and Thailand over to the right, and Mexico in between? No, not quite. This word 'nations' is a translation of the Greek New Testament word *ethnê.* But the Church Fathers affirm that Matthew's gospel was originally written in Hebrew and that the Hebrew text was preserved by the Nazarene church in their own time.[1] And so the original Hebrew word for 'nations' here would be *goyim.* This is not just guesswork. We have three ancient Hebrew versions of Matthew which survive to our own day. They testify that *goyim* is indeed the word that Matthew wrote.[2]

[1] Papias, Origen, and Eusebius (Hist. 3:24, 39), Irenaeus (Adv. Haer. 3.1.1), Jerome (Epis., 20.5), Epiphanius (Panarion 30.13.1–30.22.4).

[2] Three Hebrew Matthew texts exist to this day: Shem Tov, Münster (Quinquarboreus),

This Hebrew word *goyim* is broader in meaning than the English word nations. English *nations* means people-groups with some kind of communal or political structure. Hebrew *goyim* can also mean that. But it can also mean individuals from the nations. In that sense we could translate *ethnê* as 'the peoples.' Yet its singular form, *goy*, is the common Jewish word for a person who is a non-Jew. So when Jesus says here 'the *goyim*,' the best English translation would really be 'the heathen,' for that word can represent a group or a single person, with the implication that this group or individual is outside the community of faith.[3] After all, it wouldn't make sense to say that the nation of, say, Norway didn't visit Jesus's brothers in prison and so they are all condemned to age-long torment (Matt. 24:44–46). No doubt some Norwegians have done well in this matter and others less well, and each must be judged separately. Yes, there is a time when Jesus will judge whole nations (Zech. 14:17–19). But here, as we shall see, it is individual unbelieving people whom King Jesus will judge when he sits on his throne.

When will this happen?

When we look at this parable hand-in-hand with Revelation 20, we are faced with the question of when this judgement happens. Does it happen when Jesus comes to earth to set up his millennial kingdom? Or does it happen a thousand years later, when the "rest of the dead" (Rev. 20:5) are raised at the end of the millennial kingdom?

In favour of the first option is verse 31: "When the Son of Man comes in his glory, and all the angels with him." This is classic Bible language for the return of the Lord Jesus to earth (Zech. 14:5; Matt. 24:30–31; Jude 14; Rev. 19:14). And "he will sit on the throne of his glory" would describe his Jerusalem throne when he comes to reign, as described in Revelation 20:4 and Matthew 19:28, where the "thrones" belong to Jesus

and Du Tillet, the last having the best claim to be the original Hebrew Matthew (Edwards 2009; Howard 1986; Schonfield 1927). Ironically, the text, lost to the Nazarenes, was preserved for 1,000 years by the Jews of Rome, from whose hands it was received by Bishop Jean du Tillet of Brieuc in 1553. The passage is at Du Tillet 1555: 116 (קיו).

[3] I should forestall the objection that I am saying we can't understand the Greek NT until we know the original Hebrew or Aramaic texts that may lie behind parts of it. I'm not saying that. The Greek NT is inspired by the Holy Spirit. But, since the New Testament is in Judeo-Greek – Greek words meaning what they did to first-century Israelites – then it should be clear that *ethnê* has this broader Hebraic sense rather than the narrower Greek sense (or the even narrower sense of English 'nations').

and the apostles, echoing Psalm 122:5, whose thrones are those of the Davidic king and his ministers. So verse 31 points to the start of the millennial kingdom.

But verse 32 points elsewhere. Before him are gathered all "nations" (Gk. *ethnê*; Heb. *goyim*). As said, the "nations" are the heathen. So they must be the unbelievers who will be raised at the end of the millennial reign (Rev. 20:5–12). And King Jesus condemns some of them to "the agelong fire prepared for the devil and his angels," which is the exact description of the lake of fire which appears at the end of the millennial reign and swallows up death and Hades (Matt. 25:41; Rev. 20:10–15). In this view, the "throne of his glory" in v. 31 can now be seen as the great white throne where "the rest of the dead…great and small" are arraigned at the great judgement at the end of the millennial kingdom (Rev. 20:11, 5–12). The judge will be King Jesus (John 5:22; Acts 17:31; 2 Tim. 4:1).

The solution to this puzzle, I think, is that the parable begins at the start of the millennial kingdom and ends at its end. That is, in Matthew 25:31, we see the return of the Lord; but from verse 32 onward, we move to the great judgement after the millennium, when the "nations," the unbelievers, are raised to be judged from "the books" (Rev. 20:12–15). This telescoping of the start and end of the millennial kingdom is exactly what we see when Daniel, Jesus, and Paul speak of the separate resurrections of the just and unjust but not of the millennium that must elapse between them (Dan. 12:2; Luke 14:14; John 5:29; Acts 24:15; 1 Cor. 15:24). So this judgement is the judgement of the unbelieving dead.

The Actors in the Drama

The King separates the peoples into two groups. One group go to his right hand, the place of favour. They are called the Sheep. The other group go to his left hand, the place of disfavour. They are called Goats. Why do sheep represent the favoured and goats the disfavoured? There are several reasons. First, sheep mostly follow their shepherd, but goats don't. Second, sheep are social animals who flock together, but goats are loners who leave the herd and disappear. Lastly, sheep smell better than goats.

Now anyone who skim-reads this parable may think that there are only three actors in the drama: the King, the Sheep, and the Goats.

Figure 3. The King, the Sheep, and the Goats

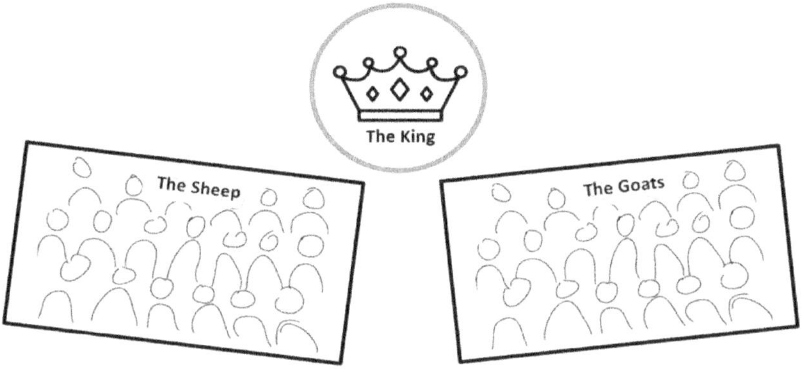

But actually, if we read carefully, we will see that there is another group. For the Sheep and the Goats are judged according to whether they did or did not help the King's Brothers when his brothers were in distress. Now the King calls his brothers, "these brothers of mine." This means that he is indicating them. And that means that they are present during the trial. They are silent, to be sure. But they are there, seated in the court-room near the King, and listening to his judgment. So the actors of the Parable of the Sheep and Goats have increased. In fact, it should now be called the Parable of the King, his Brothers, the Sheep, and the Goats, like this.

Figure 4. The King, his Brothers, the Sheep, and the Goats

No-one should imagine (as some do) that the Brothers of the Lord are actually the same as the Sheep, and that the Goats are judged for being bad to the Sheep. That is impossible. For the Sheep too are judged for how they treated the Brothers of the Lord. It's nonsense to imagine that the Sheep are judged for how they treated themselves under another name. So the Sheep, the Goats, and the Brothers of the Lord are three quite distinct groups of people.

The closer we look, the more we see that these silent Brothers of the King are real VIPs, for everything that happens to the Sheep and the Goats depends on what they did to the King's Brothers. The Sheep, who showed mercy to the King's Brothers, receive eternal life. But the Goats, who showed no mercy to the Brothers, will be cast into terrible fire. Clearly, the King thinks his Brothers are very important people indeed.

But who are the King's brothers? Some folk might reply that they are his "brothers after the flesh," that is, all the Hebrews, including the first-century Judeans. This is the view of some Messianic Jews.[4] And so, they say, Christians should support Israel. But not so fast. Many of these first-century Judeans – Pharisees and Zadokites – bitterly opposed and rejected Jesus and persecuted him to death. That's not very brotherly. And most modern Jews don't like Jesus any better. What's more, true brothers share the one father. But Jesus says of the Judeans who oppose him, "You are from your father, the devil" (John 8:44). So we can dismiss any idea that people become the king's brothers because of their claim to Judean or Israelite ancestry.

But really there's no big mystery about who the Brothers of the King are. Jesus himself tells us. When his mother and brothers want him to come home quietly, he says, "Who is my mother, and who are my brothers?" Pointing to his disciples, he says, "Here are my mother and my brothers. For whoever does the will of my Father in heaven is my brother and sister and mother" (Matt. 12:48-50).

That seems pretty clear. The King's Brothers are the ones who do the will of his Father in heaven. They are his disciples who follow his teaching. They have the same Father as Jesus, for he taught them to pray, "Our Father in heaven." They are ordinary followers of Jesus, whether first-century Galileans or modern people from every nation, scattered all through the world. And, in the parable, their Lord has come and saved them, and now, robed in immortality, they stand beside their king.

Now the important thing to note is that the King's Brothers are not being judged. The King is judging the Sheep and the Goats. But the Brothers are standing there with the King. They are not in the dock. They

[4] See Teplinsky 2008: 183; Stern 1992: 77, who also allows for the interpretation above.

are watching from the gallery. And they have total immunity. It's exactly as Jesus said: *Whoever hears my word and believes him who sent me has eternal life and will not come into judgment* (John 5:24). So the Brothers look like the blessed who were raised at the first resurrection (Rev. 20:6).

What's more, the King's Brothers aren't just bros. There are sisters there too (Matt. 12:50). Women are co-heirs with men of the kingdom of God. This is one of the marks of the divine authenticity of the Christian faith. Other religions put women on a lower rung of God's salvation. But Jesus teaches that God loves women and saves them too.

So what is the parable about?

The King's Brothers in the Parable of the Sheep and Goats are his disciples, all Christian believers, the children of the first resurrection. They are not being judged. From that we must conclude that the Sheep and the Goats who *are* being judged are not his disciples. Neither the Sheep nor the Goats are Christian folk.

This makes a huge difference to how we interpret the parable. The parable is not about how Christians may gain eternal life. It's about how non-Christian non-disciples may or may not gain life. And it all depends on how they treated the Brothers of the King. Permit me an example.

In Pakistan, Christians are not infrequently persecuted. People use the country's Islamic blasphemy laws to accuse Christians, to drive them off their land, and persecute them to death. Year on year, vigilantes kill Christians for alleged blasphemy and militias carry out attacks on Christian people and communities. Yet amidst all this, some Muslims risk their lives trying to protect Christians.

Rashid Rehman was a prominent Pakistani lawyer. When he became the defence lawyer for Junaid Hafeez, a Christian accused of blasphemy, he received death-threats. In fact, the final threats came from prosecution lawyers within the court-room itself. But Rehman refused to abandon the case. A month later, in May 2014, he was shot dead by two armed men who came to his office posing as clients.

Similarly, Salmaan Taseer, the governor of Punjab province, took it upon himself to defend Asia Bibi, a Christian woman sentenced to death for blasphemy. He soon became an object of hatred and required bodyguards for his protection. Eventually, one of these bodyguards shot and killed him inside his own car in January 2011.

Many other such stories could be brought from all round the world. But allow me one from my own experience. When I was a young teacher in southern Africa, living alone like a monk, I would come home from school every day and my neighbour, Mrs Garnie, would call to me over the garden hedge. "I just made you some curry!" Mrs Garnie came from a Hindu background but had converted to Islam when she married. And she showed me remarkable kindness over and over again. She sometimes asked me about my faith and my church, but she remained a Muslim. Then, after I'd known her three years, she became ill and was taken to hospital. I was concerned for her and prayed about this situation. I was answered with the passage above, Matthew 10:40–42. And I understood that Jesus saw her kindness to me as acts of devotion to himself.

I went to the hospital where she was in a coma. Her husband was holding back tears.

He said, "She can't move, but she hears everything we are saying."

I asked him, "Can I speak to her? It's about Jesus."

"All right," he said, and left the room.

I said to her, "Mrs Garnie, trust in Jesus and he will bring you to eternal life. Do you understand?"

Her eye blinked. And shortly afterwards, she passed away. The Lord, in his own way had already turned her heart to him, and she showed it in her acts of kindness toward the young teacher living next door. I believe she trusted in the Lord before she died. And so I trust that she, and many like her, will receive mercy among the Sheep on that day.

WHERE ELSE DOES THE NEW TESTAMENT TEACH THIS?

Such stories illustrate the teaching of the Parable of the Sheep and Goats. People who are not Christians yet who help Christians in distress – hungry or thirsty or naked or isolated or sick or imprisoned – will be counted among the Sheep (25:35–40). Yet those who show them no compassion will be counted among the Goats (25:41–45). And the reason why this happens is because the King loves his brothers and sisters.

This is not the only place where Jesus teaches this. There's a close parallel in Matthew 10:40–42.

> 40He that receives you receives me, and he that receives me receives him that sent me. 41He that receives a prophet in the name of a prophet shall receive a prophet's reward; and he that receives a righteous man in the

> name of a righteous man shall receive a righteous man's reward. [42]And whoever shall give a cup of cold water to drink to one of these little ones because he is a disciple, truly I say to you, he shall not lose his reward.

Jesus says that whoever receives a Christian because that person is a disciple of Jesus shall receive the same reward as the disciple himself. What a promise! But this is because the King loves his brothers. So whoever shows kindness to the King's brother shows kindness to the King too, and so he or she will be blessed.

Paul teaches the same thing when he writes to Timothy about Onesiphorus.

> [16]May the Lord grant mercy to the household of Onesiphorus, for he often refreshed me and was not ashamed of my chains, [17]but when he arrived in Rome he searched for me earnestly and found me—[18]may the Lord grant him to find mercy from the Lord on that day!—and you well know all the service he rendered at Ephesus. (1 Tim. 1:16–17)

Onesiphorus wasn't a Christian. If he were, Paul would expect him to find mercy from the Lord, for he saw God's mercy as a Christian's sure promise (Rom. 8:11–13; 2 Cor. 5:1–10; Phil. 1:6; 1 Thess. 4:16). So Onesiphorus was outside the Christian community, unbaptized. Yet, he saw God's goodness in Paul, and helped him. That's why Paul besought God's mercy on him and his household on "that day."

John teaches the same in the Revelation. Faithful Christians are raised at the resurrection of the righteous at the start of the millennial kingdom (Rev. 20:6). They are blessed and holy and do not come into judgement. All others are raised in the second resurrection, 1,000 years later. Those raised at the second resurrection are judged by their deeds according to the books. Those whose name is not found in the book of life are condemned to the lake of fire (Rev. 20:12–15). But those whose name is in the book of life surely receive life, just as in Matthew 25:46.

Figure 5. The millennial week

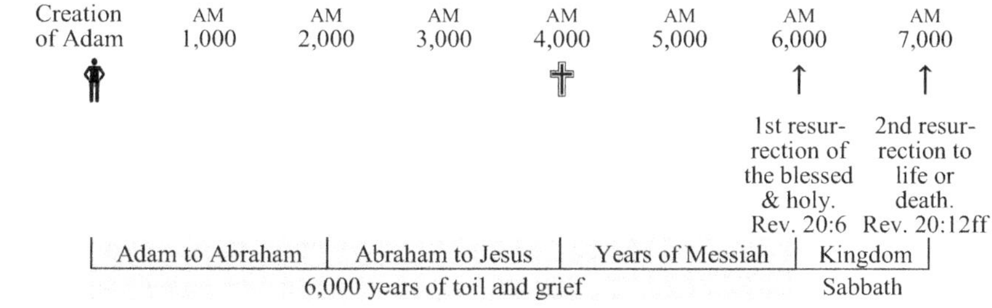

The only possible objection would be to say that there are no names in the book of life. But then it wouldn't be a book at all. So the book of life will contain the names of people who were not Christians, who did not rise at the resurrection of the righteous, yet are finally saved because of their deeds. The last judgement in Revelation 20 is not just a twofold division into saved and unsaved, but a threefold division, like the Brothers of the Lord, the Sheep, and the Goats.

Dangers of Misinterpretation

Now it's fair to add that misinterpreting this parable leads to harm. First, it leads to unbiblical ideas of justice. Second, it undermines the true biblical gospel of salvation by faith.

1. Overturning biblical justice. In 2015, the German Bundeskanzler, Angela Merkel, whose father was a Lutheran pastor, in an outburst of irrational sentimentality, and without any proper consultation with her own government, invited to her country one million Syrian Muslim refugees. They didn't need to be asked twice. Unskilled young men, and not a few violent criminals, flooded to Europe from every corner of the world, many of them having little affection or respect for their hosts. In the end, more than two million settled in Germany, and many more in the surrounding lands, getting free housing, food, health care, schooling, pocket money, and much more, with little enquiry being made into their background or record.

Many Germans objected to Merkel's decision. Leaders, after all, exist to protect and prosper their people. Yet Merkel's decision did the opposite. Levels of violent crime in Germany soared. So did taxes, to fund these hostile incomers. But other Germans counter-demonstrated, waving placards citing this parable, "I was a stranger and you invited me in."

Were they right in quoting the parable this way? Does Jesus really teach here that we must look after anyone and everyone who may wish to come to our door, from wherever they may come, even if they reject our faith and seek our harm?

The Bible's commands to do good are always set in a context of justice: justice to our community, to our family, and to our own selves. That is why the Bible sets clear rules about who we should and should not help. The Apostle Paul says we should not help those who seek to exploit us (2 Cor. 11:20–21), or who are not prepared to work: *If a man shall not work, he shall not eat.* (2 Thess. 3:10). He also says there must be evidence of Christian character and service before anyone is given material assistance, however so needy they be.

> No widow may be put on the list of widows unless she is over sixty, has been faithful to her husband, and is well known for her good deeds, such as bringing up children, showing hospitality, washing the feet of the Lord's people, helping those in trouble and devoting herself to all kinds of good deeds (1 Tim. 5:9-10).

The Apostle John makes it clear that we should not give material assistance to those who come to us and do not confess the Son of God.

> Whoever continues in the teaching has both the Father and the Son. If anyone comes to you and does not bring this teaching, do not take them into your house or welcome them. Anyone who welcomes them shares in their wicked work (2 John 9–11).

The apostles' successors also put a strong emphasis on everyone, Christians too, pulling their weight and giving no opportunity to idlers.

> Receive everyone who comes in the name of the Lord, and prove and know him afterward; for you shall have understanding right and left. If he who comes is a wayfarer, assist him as far as you are able; but he shall not remain with you more than two or three days, if need be. But if he wants to stay with you, and is an artisan, let him work and eat. But if he has no trade, according to your understanding, see to it that, as a Christian, he shall not live with you idle. But if he will not work, he is a Christ-monger. Watch that you keep away from him (*Didachê* §12).

Of course, Christians should be ready to do good and help others, with a bias toward fellow believers, as it is said:

> Therefore, as we have opportunity, let us do good to everyone, and especially to those who are of the household of faith. (Gal. 6:10)

But it is within these guidelines, and only within them, that the Bible commends assistance. It is not fair to rob and destroy our nation, our family, and ourselves in order to reward predators. Some countries in Europe opposed Merkel's hysteria. But others, wedded to a left-wing agenda hostile to family and Christian faith, are still determined to advance it. Its implications for the European Union remain to be seen.

2. A gospel of works not faith. The other danger of misinterpreting this parable is that it leads to an anti-gospel of salvation by works. That is why this parable worries so many people. After all, if it really says that you and I may be cast into countless ages of torment for not feeding the poor, clothing the naked, visiting prisoners, and so on, then we had better get up and start doing all that stuff pretty quickly. But, please sir, how many hungry must I feed, how many naked clothe, how many prisoners visit, to be saved from everlasting torment? The parable, read this way, gives no answer. Instead, it compels us to non-stop acts of service, day and night, to anyone who is in any way needy, with no assurance of ever attaining blessedness. Is this really the good news of Jesus?

Years ago, a Christian singer, Keith Green, bought into this damning interpretation of the parable. He recorded a song called 'The Sheep and the Goats,' which describes the Goats all being cast into hell, and concludes, "The only difference between the sheep and the goats is what they did and didn't do." But that's untrue. Once the parable is properly understood, the real difference between the sheep and the goats is what they did and didn't love. The sheep, deep down, loved the Lord Jesus in his people; the goats, deep down, despised the Lord in his people.

What kind of salvation does the parable teach?

So the Sheep are saved, but they are not Christians. Am I saying then that people can be saved apart from the grace of God in Jesus Christ. Not at all. Jesus said, "I am the way and the truth and the life. No one comes to the Father except through me" (John 14:6). The Sheep who are saved are saved only by the grace of Christ. They may also have believed in Muhammad or Ganesha or the Lubavitcher Rebbe. But there is salvation in none of these names. The Sheep who are saved are saved only by the grace of Jesus, in his overflowing mercy, and in the atonement of his blood, because they showed their inner love to him in coming to the aid of his servants. They honoured Jesus in their hearts, and recognized his truth, even if they remained part of the community of another religion. Only Jesus saves and, in the end, he is free to save anyone he pleases.

Likewise, the Brothers of the Lord are saved and glorified. But they did not do the feeding of the hungry, or clothing of the naked, or the prison visiting. (The Sheep did all that.) So how were the Brothers saved? The New Testament says clearly that Christian believers are saved by faith, not by works. Faith, of course, means more than mere intellectual assent. It means living allegiance and loyalty to the Lord Jesus that leads to baptism and commitment to the Christian community and good deeds. And it is that kind of faithfulness that saves the Brothers (and Sisters) in the parable. That is why they do not come into judgement.

But the compromise that some people make when reading the parable is to say, "We are saved by faith, but by works too." That may sound contradictory. In this, they may point to the Epistle of James: God gives us faith, but faith must result in good works or we are not saved. But James is making a valid point. Living faith – real allegiance and loyalty – does give rise to good deeds. But it's the faith that saves, not the good deeds. But people who misunderstand the Parable of the Sheep and the Goats are left in a position of believing that salvation is entirely by good works. But that's just what the New Testament says is the wrong approach. We are saved by the allegiance of faith. As Paul says,

> For it is by grace you have been saved through faith-allegiance, and this not from yourselves; it is the gift of God, not by works, so that no one can boast. (Eph. 2:8-9)

And Peter speaks of

> an inheritance that can never perish, spoil or fade, kept in heaven for you, who through faith are shielded by God's power until the coming of the salvation that is ready to be revealed in the last time." (1 Pet. 1:4-5)

And John says,

> God so loved the world, that he gave his only-begotten Son so that everyone having faith in him should not perish but have eternal life. (John 3:16)

And Jesus himself says (once again),

> Whoever hears my word and *believes* him who sent me has eternal life and will not come into judgment. He has crossed over from death to life. (John 5:24)

So the clear teaching of Jesus and the apostles is that we are saved by faithfully believing the gospel. If we read the Parable of the Sheep and Goats as teaching salvation by works then we oppose this clear teaching. But such a reading can only arise by ignoring the crucial role of the Brothers of the Lord within the parable.

Summary

The silent Brothers of the Lord are the key to interpreting Jesus's Parable of the Sheep and the Goats. The Lord's Brothers (and Sisters) do not come into judgment. They are saved by faith. Let no one tell you that you haven't done enough to please the Lord. All his children are saved ultimately because they love him and follow him.

It should be clear now how this fits in with the teaching in Revelation 20. The Brothers of the Lord, as said, are the blessed who are raised in the first resurrection (Rev. 20:6). The Sheep and the Goats are "the rest of the dead" raised at the end of the millennial kigndom (Rev. 20:5). King Jesus will judge them from "the books" which record their deeds (Rev. 20:12). In the Book of Life will be found the names of the Sheep and the record of their deeds. Although they were not Christian believers, their deeds will show that they respected and loved the King and his laws and his people. In the other books will be found the deeds of the Goats and the record of their deeds. These are they who hated the King and his gospel truth and his holy laws and his beloved people.

Happy all those counted among the Sheep on that day. They will pass through the fearful judgement into blessedness. But happiest of all those whom he will call "these Brothers (and Sisters) of mine." To them, salvation and mercy, without judgement, are his sure promise.

20

Sabbatic and Jubilee Cycles

UNDERSTANDING the sabbatic and jubilee cycles of ancient Israel reveals to us one of the fundamental blocks of biblical timekeeping. They are found in Leviticus and Deuteronomy, where Moses legislates a sabbatic or *shemittah* ('release') year every seventh year and a jubilee or *yovel* year at the end of every cycle of seven sabbatic years.

THE SABBATIC OR *SHEMITTAH* YEAR

The sabbatic or *shemittah* year was proclaimed in the seventh year on the first day of the seventh month, the autumn month of Tishri.

> Jehovah said to Moses at Mount Sinai, saying: [2]Speak to the Israelites and say to them: When you come into the land which I am giving to you, then shall the land keep a sabbath to Jehovah. [3]Six years shall you sow your field, and six years shall you prune your vineyard and gather its produce. [4]But in the seventh year there shall be a *shabbath shabbaton* [sabbath of sabbaths] for the land, a sabbath to Jehovah; your field you shall not sow and your vineyard you shall not prune. [5]Do not reap what grows of itself or harvest the grapes of your untended vines. The land is to have a year of rest.' (Lev. 25:2–5)[1]

After being proclaimed in Tishri, the sabbatic year ran to the end of the 29-day month Elul. As a result, when speaking of sabbatic years in our

[1] Cf. also Exod. 23:10–11; Lev. 25:1–22; Deut. 15:1–11; cf. Lev. 26:34–35.

Gregorian or Julian calendar, we must speak of, "Tishri year 959/958 BC" or "the year beginning Tishri 959 BC" or even (for short), "959t."

Four things marked the sabbatic year, three explicit and one implied. First, the land was to lie fallow and what grew of itself was for the poor. Second, the debts of fellow Israelites were to be remitted (Deut. 15:1–11). Third, at the start of every sabbatic year, at the Feast of Tabernacles, the Levite *kohanim* were to assemble all Israel, men, women, children, and sojourners, to appear before Jehovah, *at the place he will choose,* to listen to the Torah read aloud (Deut. 31:10–13). This was a necessary ordinance, in those days of illiteracy and expensive scrolls, if the people were to know the divine law for their nation. Fourth, it is implicitly taught that Israelite bondservants were to be released then from servitude (Deut. 15:12–18). That is to say, the legislation does not state explicitly that this release was to happen in the sabbatic year. But since it follows directly on the sabbatic-year teaching, it was understood that way.

Moses stresses the importance of keeping the *shemittah.* Neglecting it would result in banishment from the land (Lev. 26:33–35). Yet keeping it was difficult. And it seems the Israelites never kept it properly in the times of their kings. But we see hints of it. The law was read to the people in the third year of Jehoshaphat (2 Chr. 17:7–9), in the ninth century, and in the eighteenth year of Josiah (2 Kgs 22:3; 23:1–2), in the seventh century, and in the time of Ezra and Nehemiah (Neh. 8:1–8), in the fifth century. Isaiah, in the eighth century, speaks of ceasing from sowing and reaping (Isa. 37:30; 2 Kgs 19:29). And a release of slaves is described by Jeremiah (34:8–10) in the sixth century. But in general, the sabbatic year was not observed. And so, when the exile in Babylon finally fell, Jeremiah and the Chronicler say that neglect of the sabbatic year was a chief cause of the terrible punishment (Jer. 25:11–12; 29:10; 2 Chr. 36:21). The Chronicler adds that the seventy years of exile in Babylon are to atone for seventy neglected sabbatic cycles, that is, 490 years of non-observance. This means that it had not been properly observed since before the kingdom period. In that case, it is even less likely that it was observed in the times of the Judges, when there was no centralized rule.

Therefore, when the exiles returned from Babylon, they solemnly pledged to observe the *shemittah* (Neh. 10:31). Yet it was costly. It entailed setting aside harvest of preceding years and importing corn at greater cost from foreign lands. This would have been harder on the poor than the rich. In time of drought or bad harvest, the *shemittah* was life-threatening. In time of war, it spelt defeat. When Antiochus V besieged Beth-Zur and Jerusalem in a sabbatic year the defenders were forced to surrender because of food shortages (1 Macc. 6:48–54). The same thing happened when Herod besieged Jerusalem in 37 BC, as Josephus relates.[2] Yet the Israelites still strove to keep the sabbatic year throughout second temple times. After the Roman destruction of AD 70, it seems the few Jews left farming the land kept it as late as the fifth century. But by the middle of the first millennium, when people who identified as Jews had largely ceased from farming the land, its observance ceased.

WHICH NEW YEAR?

To understand the *shemittah* and jubilee years, we must see that Israel had more than one new year. That's not as strange as it sounds. Our own calendar year begins in January; our academic year may begin in September; some churches have a liturgical year beginning at Advent in November; and, for the British, the tax year begins on 6 April and the legal year on the first Monday in October.

In the same way, Israel had more than one new year, even in Bible times. The LORD told Moses and Aaron at the beginning of the spring month of Nisan, *This month is for you the first of months; it is for you the first of the months of the year* (Exod. 12:2). Yet the sabbatic year of rest begins in the autumn month Tishri (Exod. 23:11; Lev. 2:5). So even at the Exodus there were two new years, in Nisan and Tishri.

By the second century BC, the Book of Jubilees speaks of new years on the first, fourth, seventh and tenth months (6:15–28). In the first century AD, Josephus explains how the law of Moses counts from Nisan for religious rites, but from Tishri for commercial activities (*A.J.* 1:81). A century later, the Mishnah speaks of four new years: Nisan is the new year for kings and festivals; Tishri is the new year for the calendar and the *shemittah*; there are also new years for the cattle-tithe (either Elul or Tishri) and for trees (1 or 15 Shevat) (RH 1.1).

Throughout Israel's history there was tension between the spring new year in Nisan and the autumn new year in Tishri. The primacy of the Nisan new year was always recognised in theory, for Tishri was always called the seventh month. But there was a continual tendency for Tishri to claim the prominence. After the division of the Israelite kingdoms in

[2] *A.J.* 14; *B.J.* 1.347.

725 BC, it seems the Ephraimite kingdom kept their regnal years starting in Nisan, but the Judahite kingdom moved the regnal year to Tishri.[3] Then the Judahites were exiled in Babylon and Persia, where the new year was celebrated in autumn (Neh. 1:1; 2:1).[4] Thus the Tishri year became yet more influential among the Judeans until, from rabbinic times until now, the Jewish calendar year begins at Rosh Hashanah or 'New Year' in Tishri. Yet the ancient memory of the Nisan new year still remains in the order of the festivals and the numbering of the months.

But back in Bible times, the Israelites celebrated the calendar new year in Nisan and the agricultural new year in Tishri. The Nisan year was declared in the spring, at the first new moon after the first ripe ears of barley appeared in the warm Jordan valley. It was followed by Passover and a summer of reaping and harvesting. The Tishri sabbatic year began with the autumn harvest festivals, and was followed by a winter of pruning and sowing. Thus the calendar year and the agrarian year of the sabbatic cycle were six months apart.

Figure 6. Nisan and Tishri new years in the sabbatic cycle

<table>
<tr><td>Cultic year begins in Nisan</td><td>1</td><td>2</td><td>3</td><td>4</td><td>5</td><td>6</td><td>7</td><td>1</td></tr>
<tr><td>Agrarian year starts in Tishri</td><td>7</td><td>1</td><td>2</td><td>3</td><td>4</td><td>5</td><td>6</td><td>Shemittah 7</td><td>1</td></tr>
<tr><td>Season & activity</td><td>reap</td><td>sow | reap</td><td>sow | reap</td><td>sow | reap</td><td>sow | reap</td><td>sow | reap</td><td>sow | reap</td><td>FALLOW</td><td>sow</td></tr>
</table>

This was six-month difference was essential to the *shemittah* fallow year. If the *shemittah* year were to start in Nisan, then the crop sown the preceding fall would not be harvested, and the autumn sowing would be missed, resulting in two years without harvest, rather than the one year intended in the legislation. The result would have been famine.

The Jubilee Year

After seven sabbatic cycles they proclaimed a jubilee year, or *shnat yovel*, in the 'fiftieth' year. It was proclaimed on the Day of Atonement,

[3] So Coucke and Thiele; but Galil is more doubtful.

[4] There is a debate about when this happened. But Philo (De Sp. Leg. 1:180) and Josephus (*A.J.* 1:80-82), in the first century AD, still regard Nisan as the first month. In B. RH 2b–3b, the talmudic redactor still maintains Nisan as the first month against those who claim for Tishri. So it was well into rabbinic times that Tishri became the first calendar month.

Yom Kippur, the tenth day of Tishri, and was announced by *shofar* blasts throughout the land. In fact, its name – *yovel* – is the ram's horn from which the *shofar* trumpet was made.

> [8]And you shall count to yourself seven sabbaths of years, seven times seven years, and there shall be unto you the days of seven sabbaths of years, forty-nine years. [9]And you shall proclaim with the *shofar* fanfare on the seventh month, on the tenth day of the month; in the Day of Atonement [Yom Kippur] you shall make proclamation with the *shofar* throughout the land. [10]And you shall sanctify the fiftieth year, and proclaim liberty throughout the land to all its inhabitants; a jubilee [*yovel*] it shall be to you, and each man shall return to his possession and to his family. (Lev. 25:8–10; cf. 8–34; Lev. 27:16–25; Num. 36:4).

The rules of release for the jubilee year were similar to those of the sabbatic year. The land lay fallow, debts were pardoned, slaves were freed. But, in addition, land and property were restored to their hereditary owners, except for houses within walled cities (Lev. 25:29–31).[5]

We do not know how far the jubilee was observed in early kingdom times. But the rabbis record that it ceased after the Transjordanian tribes went into exile, in the eighth century BC, for the legislation applied only when all the tribes of Israel were dwelling in the land (Lev. 25:10).[6] Further, since the Ephraimite tribes remained in exile in second temple times, it was not revived by the Judahite returnees from Babylon in the fifth century. They swore an oath to keep the sabbatic year, but they make no mention of the jubilee (Neh. 10:31).

However, although the jubilee was not observed in second temple times, people apparently still knew of its timing. As we shall see, Ezekiel, and no doubt all the temple priests, knew when it occurred.[7] The Book of Jubilees, from the early second century BC, counts all the jubilees from creation to Joshua's entry to the Promised Land, expecting chronologists to calculate the dates from there on. The Dead Sea Damascus Document, probably referring to the same Book of Jubilees, says: "And the exact statement of the epochs of Israel's blindness to all these, behold it can be learnt in the Book of the Divisions of Times into their Jubilees and Sabbatical Weeks" (CD 16:3–4). The Melchizedek Scroll, whose text

[5] Rashi says the release of property took place at the beginning of the jubilee year, but the cancellation of debts took place at the end (on Lev. 25:28).
[6] Y. Shev. 10.3 [39c]; Sifra, *Behar* 2, 3 [107a]; B. Arak. 32b.
[7] Josephus, himself a *kohen*, comments on its significance, but says nothing about its observance or otherwise (*A.J.* 3:280–286).

dates from before 100 BC, looks forward to the coming of the heavenly prince Melchizedek in the tenth jubilee (11QMelch ii.7) – that is, in the last of the ten jubilees of the 490 years of Daniel's seventy weeks – and the writer presumes his readers will know when this tenth jubilee will be. In late second temple times, the Sanhedrin recorded a crime according to hour, day, month, year, and septennate within the jubilee; and a rabbinic comment suggests that even the number of the jubilee was known (B. Sanh. 40a/b).[8] After the fall of Jerusalem, the Mishnah preserved the *shofar* fanfare for the jubilee, suggesting that all the temple rites for the jubilee were still known in the second century AD (M. R.H. 3:5). And a third-century Babylonian sage, Rav Yehuda, was expecting the Messiah to come toward the end of the eighty-fifth jubilee from creation.

> Elijah said to R. Judah, the brother of R. Salia the pious: The world shall exist not less than eighty-five jubilees, and in the last jubilee the son of David will come. (B. Sanh. 97b)

All of which goes to say that the jubilee was counted from Moses down to late Roman times. But the modern rabbinate and the State of Israel neither observe nor count it. The rule is still cited that it cannot be kept until the twelve tribes are living in their allotted portions. And, anyway, the jubilee count is often said to be lost.

A FORTY-NINE OR FIFTY YEAR JUBILEE?

From Roman times, the Israelite sages were divided over whether the jubilee should be proclaimed in the forty-ninth or fiftieth year from the start of the *shemittah* cycle. The Bible itself speaks of sanctifying the fiftieth year for the jubilee (Lev. 25:10). As a result, some sages, from the second century on, held that the jubilee cycle took fifty years, with one jubilee year inserted after each seventh *shemittah* year. Thus the last two years of each cycle were fallow years, without sowing or reaping. Many of the medieval rabbis endorsed this view in one form or another.

But other, early sources suggest that the jubilee cycle took forty-nine years. In a talmudic dispute, R. Yehudah bar Ilay insists, "The jubilee is counted as part of the septennate." That is, the jubilee takes place at the same time as the seventh *shemittah* year, so making a forty-nine-year

[8] The Talmud's comment is ironic. Would a crime not come to court within the known jubilee? But it shows that they still knew the jubilee count in Roman times.

cycle (B. Ned. 61a). Rabbi Judah also held to a forty-nine year jubilee, although he thought the jubilee overlapped with the first year of the next sabbatic cycle (B. RH 9a).

But going back earlier, all the evidence before Roman times, supports the forty-nine-year jubilee. In the third century BC, the Book of Jubilees counts the history of the world in forty-nine-year jubilees. It numbers the 127 years of Sarah's life as "two Jubilees, four heptads, and one year" (19:7)

Earlier still, Daniel supports the same idea. Gabriel's heavenly year-count of seventy sevens, or 490 years, is not a random number. It is ten forty-nine-year jubilees (Dan. 9:24). As Wacholder says, "Although the Book of Daniel never mentions the term directly, the jubilee forms the essence of Dan. 9:24–27."[9]

2 Chronicles 36:21 also reckons history in forty-nine-year jubilees. The land will enjoy 70 years of sabbaths to compensate for seventy unobserved sabbatic cycles, that is, 490 years or 10 jubilees. We also know that the Samaritans, who kept their own calendrical traditions quite apart from the rabbinic Jews, historically observed a 49-year jubilee.[10]

To this historical evidence, one must add that the effect of a two-year fallow would have been unbearable for an agrarian society. If *shemittah* observance was hard – and it was – a double fallow year would have been intolerable. And there is no suggestion in the Bible of a double fallow year. As a result, most modern scholars see the jubilee cycle as forty-nine years, in agreement with R. Judah bar Ilay's view that the sabbatic and jubilee year in some way coincided.[11]

But how did they coincide? The key point, usually overlooked, is that Rosh HaShanah (new year) was proclaimed every year on 1 Tishri. But in the jubilee year, Rosh HaShanah was proclaimed on 10 Tishri, that is, on Yom Kippur, nine days after the usual Rosh HaShanah on 1 Tishri. In other words, in the forty-ninth year there were, in effect, two new year proclamations within nine days of each other. This is perfectly clear in Leviticus 25.

> [9]You shall proclaim with the *shofar* fanfare on the seventh month, on the *tenth day* of the month; on the Day of Atonements [Yom HaKippurim]

[9] Wacholder 1975: 210.

[10] A. Loewenstamm, "Samaritan Chronology" in *EJ* 17:732–35.

[11] Zuckermann 1857, North 1954, Lefebvre 2003, Bergsma 2005, and Mayshar 2020, all think the *shemittah* and jubilee coincided. But Bergsma (like Rabbi Judah) thinks the jubilee was a second fallow year observed on the first year of the next sabbatic cycle.

> you shall make proclamation with the *shofar* throughout the land. [10]And you shall sanctify the fiftieth year...a jubilee [*yovel*] it shall be to you.

Likewise, Ezekiel records the day on which his vision took place as Rosh HaShanah, not on the first day of the month, but the tenth.

> In the twenty-fifth year of our exile, on Rosh HaShanah on the tenth day of the month, in the fourteenth year after the city was struck down (40:1).

Since Leviticus 25:9–10 says Rosh HaShanah falls on the tenth of the month only on a jubilee year, it's clear that Ezekiel's Rosh HaShanah could only be the start of a jubilee year. Seder Olam 11 confirms this:

> *In the twenty-fifth year of our exile on Rosh HaShanah* (Ezek. 40:1). When was it said to him? At the beginning of the jubilee.

So does the Talmud:

> What year is this when Rosh Hashanah falls on the tenth of the month? Say: this is the jubilee year. (Arak. 12a)[12]

So here is the true explanation of the overlap of the sabbatic and jubilee year. On 1 Tishri of the forty-ninth year, they proclaimed the seventh sabbatic year. Nine days later, on 10 Tishri, they sanctified the jubilee year. The first nine days belonged to the sabbatic year alone, and inaugurated the *shemittah* obligations of the fallow year, remission of debts, public Torah reading, and manumission of slaves. Then, from the tenth of the month onward, the rest of that agrarian year, now called the fiftieth year, was both *shemittah* and jubilee, in which property was restored to its ancestral clans. We can depict it as follows.

Figure 7. The jubilee: two "new years" in ten days

Cultic year begins on 1 Nisan	1	2	3	4	5	6	7	1		
Sabbatic year on 1 Tishri	7	1	2	3	4	5	6	7	1	
Jubilee begins on 10 Tishri	42	43	44	45	46	47	48	49	10 Tishri 50	1
Season & activity	reap	sow | reap	sow | reap	sow | reap	sow | reap	sow | reap	sow | reap	FALLOW	sow	

[12] Cf. also Rashi on Ezek. 40:1.

21

The Pre-exilic Jubilee Cycle

WE have learned that the jubilee year was proclaimed at Rosh HaShanah on Yom Kippur, the tenth of Tishri (Lev. 25:9–10). Knowing this, we turn again to the only verse in the Bible which allows us to fix precisely the jubilee and sabbatic cycles at the time of the Babylonian exile.

Ezekiel's vision on the first day of this jubilee year was *in the twenty-fifth year of our exile* – that is, the exile of King Jehoiachin – *at Rosh HaShanah on the tenth day of the month, and in the fourteenth year after the city was struck* (40:1).

Which year was the twenty-fifth of Jehoiachin's exile? The date of Jehoiachin's capture is clear. It is recorded in a Babylonian cuneiform tablet called the Nebuchadnezzar Chronicle (BM 21946).

> In the seventh year, the month of Kislimu [Kislev], the king of Akkad mustered his troops, marched to the Hatti-land, and encamped against the city of Judah and on the second day of the month Adar he seized the city and captured the king. He appointed there a king of his own heart, received its heavy tribute and sent (captives) to Babylon.

Babylonian regnal years are securely dated on the basis of solar eclipses.[1] So we can date Jehoiachin's capture in Nebuchadnezzar's seventh year to 2 Adar (15/16 March) in 597 BC. So sure is this date that Edwin Thiele regarded it as one of the absolute dates of Old Testament chronology.[2]

[1] The Babylonian cuneiform tablets VAT4956 and BM38462 show Nebuchadnezzar's accession year began Nisan 605, and his first year began Nisan 604.
[2] Thiele 1983:173, 186.

Yet fixing "the twenty-fifth year of our exile" is less easy. Should the twenty-five years be counted from the day Jehoiachin was captured in Adar? Or should they be counted from the Nisan new year, a month after the king was captured? Or from the time Jehoiachin (and Ezekiel) went into captivity, which may have been before or after 1 Nisan? Or should it be counted in Tishri years, which was normal Judean practice at this time? And, if we count from 1 Nisan or 1 Tishri, should the part-year from Jehoiachin's capture to the new year be included in the count? (Chronographers call this 'inclusive' or 'non-accession-year' counting.) Or should it be excluded from the count? (This is called 'non-inclusive' or 'accession-year' counting.)

It would be easier too if we knew in what year "the city was struck." But that also poses problems. To this day, views differ on whether the date of the final Babylonian destruction was in 587 or 586 BC. Thiele argued for 586, and many follow him.[3] But he did so by reckoning the twenty-fifth year of the exile with a Nisan year and an accession count (*i.e.*, counting from 1 Nisan, mid-April, the month after Jehoiachin's capture). But, while a Nisan year-count was standard in Mesopotamia, it goes against known Judean Tishri-year practice in this period, as Thiele himself showed.[4]

Rodger Young has shown, in a detailed analysis, that 2 Kings, Jeremiah, and Ezekiel all reckon in Tishri years with a non-accession count (*i.e.*, they count the king's reign from 1 Tishri before he came to the throne). In fact, only such a count allows us to harmonize the various dates of these three books. Counted this way, the date of the fall of the city must have been in Tammuz (July) 587 BC, in the Tishri year 588/87, a date endorsed by many eminent authorities.[5]

The language of Ezekiel 40:1, when read carefully, seems to support this. Its first fixed point is "*in* the twenty-fifth year of our exile," counting inclusively from 1 Tishri before Jehoiachin's capture. The second fixed point, from "*after* the city was smitten," counts from Tishri after the fall of the city. Here's a diagram. Jehoiachin's capture ("our exile") on 2 Adar 597 BC is marked with a white arrow, the city's fall, in Tammuz 587 BC, with a black arrow, and Ezekiel's vision with an eye.

[3] E.g., Strand 1996.
[4] Thiele shows that Judah used a Tishri year from Solomon to Nehemiah (1983: 51–53).
[5] Young 2004. See likewise, Kitchen & Mitchell 1982: 193–200, who cite Albright and Wiseman as also supporting 587 (193). Kitchen had earlier held to 586 (1977: 103).

Figure 8. Jehoiachin's exile, the fall of Jerusalem, and Ezekiel's vision (Ezek. 40:1)

Julian BC yr	597	596	588	587	586	585	574	573
Tishri year	598t/7	597t/6	589t/8	588t/7	587t/6	586t/5	575t/4	574t/3
Events	⇩			⬇				👁
Our exile	1	2	10	11	12	13	24	25
City falls					1	2	13	14

On this basis, it seems that Ezekiel's vision was on 10 Tishri 574 BC, and that was the start of a jubilee year, which ran till 29 Elul 573 BC. From this year we can calculate all the other jubilees before and after it.

Two rabbinic texts – Seder Olam Rabbah 11 and B. Arak. 12a – say this jubilee was the seventeenth from Joshua's entry to the Promised Land. This allows us to verify the date of Ezekiel's vision. Counting back seventeen jubilee cycles from 574 BC, we arrive at 1406 BC as the date of Joshua's entry to the Land. This date can then be independently verified from 1 Kings 6:1, which says the month of Ziv in Solomon's fourth year – in spring of 967 BC – was the 480th year from the Exodus. From this, we can calculate that the Exodus was in Nisan 1446 BC and, after forty years in the wilderness, Joshua crossed the Jordan on 10 Nisan (Josh. 4:19) in 1406 BC.[6] The first sabbatic year of the first jubilee cycle in the Promised Land would have begun six months later, on 1 Tishri 1406 BC, thus confirming the date of Ezekiel's vision.

Third, for further confirmation, Seder Olam 24 and B. Megillah 14b agree that there was a jubilee in the eighteenth year of Josiah, when he initiated his reform. This was the jubilee beginning 10 Tishri 623 BC, exactly forty-nine years before the jubilee of Ezekiel's vision.

Here then is a table of the years of these seventeen jubilees, from Joshua in 1406 BC to Ezekiel in 574. Note, by the way, that the commonly-accepted dates for David's reign fall exactly in the middle of the period from the Entry to the Exile, in the middle jubilee, the ninth jubilee from the entry to the land.

This striking correspondence between Ezekiel's jubilee, Josiah's jubilee, the date

Figure 9. 17 jubilee cycles from entry to the Land in 1406 BC

1. 1406t/05–1358t/57 BC
2. 1357t/56–1309t/08 BC
3. 1308t/07–1260t/59 BC
4. 1259t/58–1211t/10 BC
5. 1210t/09–1162t/61 BC
6. 1161t/60–1113t/12 BC
7. 1112t/11–1064t/63 BC
8. 1063t/62–1015t/14 BC
9. *1014t/13–966t/65 BC*
10. 965t/64–917t/16 BC
11. 916t/15–868t/67 BC
12. 867t/66–819t/18 BC
13. 818t/17–770t/69 BC
14. 769t/68–721t/20 BC
15. 720t/19–672t/71 BC
16. 671t/70–623t/22 BC
17. 622t/21–**574t**/73 BC

[6] Based on Thiele's date for the beginning of the divided kingdom.

of Joshua's crossing of the Jordan, and the fall of Solomon's temple, not only confirms the forty-nine-year jubilee, but also testifies to the accuracy of the Old Testament and, in this case, of the rabbinic records.

Being able to identify the pre-exilic jubilee cycle with such accuracy allows us easily to calculate the sabbatic years, which fell at seven year intervals after every jubilee. When we do this, we find that every text that we identified in the last chapter as describing a sabbatic event does indeed fall in a sabbatic year.[7]

- The reading of the law in Jehoshaphat's third year (2 Chr. 17:7–9), measured from the start of his sole reign, as given in 1 Kings 22:51 and 2 Kings 3:1, was the sabbatic year starting Tishri 868.
- The eighteenth year of Josiah (2 Kgs 22:3; 23:1–2), as we saw, was the year starting Tishri 623, which was also a jubilee year, as Seder Olam 24 and Bavli Megillah 14b confirm.
- Isaiah told Hezekiah not to sow and reap in the coming year (37:30; 2 Kgs 19:29) after Sennacherib's defeat in autumn 701. The coming year, the one in which the people were voluntarily not to sow or reap, was therefore the sabbatic year beginning Tishri 700, which was 126 years, or 18 sabbatic cycles, before Ezekiel's jubilee.
- The release of slaves by Zedekiah (Jer. 34:8–10) was in the sabbatic year beginning Tishri 588 BC, two sabbatic cycles before Ezekiel's jubilee.[8]

Thus the pre-exilic jubilee and sabbatic cycle can be worked out in detail from Ezekiel 40:1. It runs from the Tishri after Joshua's entry to the land, in 1406 BC, down to Ezekiel's time. But, of course, it can also be counted back further, from Joshua's time to the day of the creation of Adam. So we may justly call it the "creation jubilee cycle." And, of course, we can continue to count it from Ezekiel's time down to our own day.

Of course, as said, the jubilee was to be observed only when all Israel was dwelling in the land. And so, when the Ephraimites were exiled in Assyria, jubilee observation was suspended, in whatever way it had ever been observed. Yet the temple *kohanim* in exile, like Ezekiel, kept a track of its years, from whom we have obtained the true date of the pre-exilic jubilee cycle.

[7] Dates from Young 2008.
[8] For the date, see Sarna 1973: 144–45.

22

The Post-Exilic Jubilee Cycle

XERXES of Persia was slain in August 465 BC by Artabanus, the commander of his bodyguard, and was eventually succeeded by his third son, Artaxerxes. The question is what happened in between. One account says Artaxerxes slew Artabanus without delay and so the first year of Artaxerxes's reign was reckoned, according to Persian custom, from Tishri 465 BC. The other version is that Artabanus seized power for seven months before Artaxerxes dispatched him, in which case the first year of Artaxerxes's reign was reckoned from the following Tishri, 464 BC.

This concerns us because Ezra and the men of the return left Babylon for Jerusalem on 1 Nisan in the spring of the seventh year of Artaxerxes (Ezra 7:7–9). If Artaxerxes's reign is reckoned from autumn 465, Ezra went up to Jerusalem in the spring of 458. But if his reign is reckoned from autumn 464, Ezra went up in spring 457. And the question of which year it was impinges on the start-date of Daniel's prophecy of the seventy sevens and on the start-date of the post-exilic jubilee cycle.

EZRA AND THE POST-EXILIC SABBATIC CYCLE

Ezra and the returnees renewed the sabbatic and jubilee cycle on their arrival in Jerusalem. The Bible tells us of their pledge to observe it (Neh. 10:31). But it was not the same cycle as in pre-exilic times, for it was reckoned from their re-arrival in the land, not from the older cycle.

> As at their arrival in the days of Joshua they reckoned sabbatic years and jubilees and consecrated walled cities, so too at their arrival in the days of Ezra they reckoned sabbatic years, jubilees, and consecrated walled cities. (B. Arak. 32b)[1]

The sabbatic cycle was kept (Neh. 10:31). But the jubilee cycle was counted but not kept in practice, for jubilees were not observed when the twelve tribes of Israel were not in possession of the Land.

> Although the Jubilee year was not observed in [the era of] the Second Temple, they would count it in order to sanctify the Sabbatical years. (Rambam, Mishneh Torah, Sabbatical Year and Jubilee 10:3)

When Ezra arrived in Jerusalem, after a four-month journey, in the summer, on the first of Ab, his priorities would have been to form his *bet-din* and proclaim the sabbatic calendar. He had no reason to delay. And so, just like Joshua, he would have ratified the sabbatic and jubilee cycle from the Tishri after their arrival. Therefore, in whichever year he arrived there in summer, whether 457 or 458, he would have proclaimed the new sabbatic and jubilee cycle on 1 Tishri in the autumn of that year.

But do we have any independent verifications of the post-exilic sabbatic cycle? In the eighteenth century, Isaac Newton, working from Josephus, identified AD 33t/34 as a sabbatic year.[2] (Newton thought the Crucifixion took place at Passover AD 34.) Then, in 1857, a Jewish Prussian mathematician, Benedict Zuckermann, working from both Josephus and rabbinic texts, released a table of sabbatic years from the Babylonian Exile to late Roman times, which agreed with Newton.[3] Zuckermann's table was endorsed by influential scholars, including Emil Schürer.[4] So when Jews began to form agricultural communities in Palestine in the late nineteenth century, they followed Zuckermann's table, and observed their first sabbatic year in Tishri 1889 (AM[J] 5649). Zuckermann's sabbatic cycle was confirmed in the Declaration of the State of Israel in 1948 , and the first Israeli sabbatic year was observed in Tishri 1951. They keep the same cycle to this day.

But in 1973, Ben Zion Wacholder proposed that Zuckermann's table is one year too early. In its place, he published a revised table of sabbatic

[1] See likewise Seder Olam 30; Rambam, *Hilkhot Shemittah veYovel,* 10:3, 5–6.

[2] See Newton 1733: 131–32. Newton and his young colleague William Whiston were both readers of Josephus. Whiston's was the first English translation of Josephus.

[3] Zuckermann 1857.

[4] Schürer 1901: 37.

cycles, running from the time of Darius I of Persia down to late Roman times (519 BC–AD 441).[5]

Both Zuckermann and Wacholder have their ardent defenders. The evidence is extremely detailed and we cannot discuss it here. So I will simply present the implications for both sets of dates. The difference between them is only one year. And both are consistent with Daniel's seventy sevens and the date of the Crucifixion. Yet they differ on one important thing:

- In Zuckermann's reckoning, a sabbatic cycle began on Tishri 457. This would be the Tishri two months after Ezra arrived in Jerusalem, if Artaxerxes's reign is reckoned from Tishri 464 BC, and fourteen months after, if Artaxerxes's reign is reckoned from Tishri 465 BC.
- In Wacholder's reckoning, a sabbatic cycle began on Tishri 456. This would be fourteen months after Ezra's arrival in Jerusalem if Artaxerxes's reign is reckoned from Tishri 464 BC, and twenty-six months after, if it is reckoned from Tishri 465 BC.

So it's fair to say that Zuckermann's sabbatic cycle fits in better with the known dates of Ezra's return and his immediate proclamation of a new sabbatic cycle.

Ezra and the Post-Exilic Jubilee Cycle

Now, as said, the jubilee was counted right through to Roman times but was not observed in practice. But can we identify the post-exilic jubilee cycle from the sabbatic cycle. Well, yes, we can. When Ezra established a new sabbatic cycle, he would have established a new jubilee cycle along with it.

> At their arrival in the days of Ezra they reckoned sabbatic years, jubilees, and consecrated walled cities. (B. Arak. 32b)

Zuckermann does not attempt to identify the jubilee cycle. But it would have begun with the first sabbatic cycle, according to his reckoning, after Ezra arrived in Jerusalem, that is, on Tishri 457.

Wacholder, on the other hand, does attempt to identify the jubilee cycle. Yet his calculation was entirely based on his presupposition that Daniel was composed in Maccabean times and its author was awaiting

[5] Wacholder 1973. His table is on pp. 185–96.

the imminent completion of Daniel's seventy sevens in the mid-second century.[6] Yet, despite that, he had a one-in-seven chance of correctly identifying a jubilee year from his sabbatic cycles, and by that chance it seems he got it pretty close – or dead right, if you prefer his dates to Zuckermann's – identifying Tishri 456 as the start of a new jubilee cycle.

So we have two options for when Ezra proclaimed the start of the new jubilee cycle. It was either in 457 BC, following Zuckermann's cycle, or in 456 BC, following Wacholder's. But Zuckermann's date is closer to the time of Ezra's return to Jerusalem, either in summer 458 or 457 – depending on when we date Artaxerxes's regnal years – and closer to Ezra's likely date for the proclamation of the new sabbatic cycle in the autumn after he arrived.

DANIEL AND THE POST-EXILIC JUBILEE CYCLE

Can we reconcile this post-exilic jubilee cycle with Daniel's prophecy of the seventy sevens – 490 years or ten jubilees – until the redemption? There are two things to be clear about here. First, Daniel's seventy sevens are certainly ten jubilees. Second, since the jubilee cycle runs from autumn, the ten jubilees cannot end exactly at the crucifixion or resurrection of Jesus in the spring. Let's deal with them one at a time.

1. Daniel's seventy-sevens are ten jubilees. This is clear from the text. Daniel, in Babylonia, gives himself to prayer, reminding the Most High of his word to Jeremiah that Israel's exile will last 70 years (9:2). Gabriel appears to him and tells him of a greater plan in the divine timetable. Yes, there will be a restoration. But, from "the going forth of the word to restore Jerusalem" until the redemption, not seventy years, but seventy times seven years are appointed until the anointing of the Holy One – the Messiah – and everlasting redemption (9:24–26). Daniel knows from the scrolls (9:2) that the exile had been a punishment for seventy unkept sabbatic years, that is, ten jubilees (2 Chr. 36:21; Jer. 25:11–12; 29:10).[7] Now he learns that there are another seventy sabbatic years to come until the Messiah, another ten jubilees.

[6] Wacholder 1975. By his "chronomessianic" reasoning he synchronizes other messianic movements, including John Baptist and Jesus, whose dates, he says, were arranged by their followers to fit into this jubilee cycle. Wacholder 1975: 207–08, 217–18.

[7] The books of Chronicles were perhaps not in their final form in Daniel's time. Yet the idea that the seventy-year exile was for seventy unkept sabbatic years is likely to have been already known among the Babylonian Jewish sages.

Some think it reasonable to split these seventy sabbatic cycles. They make the first sixty-nine run from "the going forth of the word" (9:25) to the last days of Jesus. Then they postpone the last seven-year cycle until the time of the end, from the rise of the Antichrist until the return of the Lord. Perhaps one reason they do this is because they cannot figure how to fit the 490 years into the period from the "going forth of the word" – which they take to be Artaxerxes's twentieth year – until the time of Jesus. Another reason, of course, is because they subscribe to Darby's "dispensations," which make the 2,000 years of the church age to be an intercalation within Daniel's prophecy. Presumably Gabriel and Daniel knew nothing about this intercalation, or decided not to mention it.

But the church fathers who wrote on this subject – Africanus and Athanasius – saw the 490 years as extending directly from the time of the "going forth of the word" until the time of the redemption.[8] They made no gap of any kind within the seventy weeks. And, of course, there is no need at all to do so. Many others have taken a similar line – either from 458 or 457 BC to AD 33 or 34 – including Newton, Humphrey Prideaux, Adam Clarke, and Edward Pusey.[9] Most recently, Rodger Young has shown convincingly that, it is exactly 490 solar years from 1 Nisan in 458 BC – which he takes as the date of Ezra's departure and "the going forth of the word" – to Jesus's resurrection on 15 Nisan AD 33.[10]

2. Yet ten calendar jubilees cannot end at Passover AD 33. There are two reasons why this is so. First, despite the fact that one can count exactly 490 years from a start-point in spring 458 to Passover AD 33, it is impossible for ten calendar jubilees to end in the spring, for jubilee cycles can end only on 29 Elul, in the autumn. Second, "the going forth of the word" must precede Ezra's arrival in Jerusalem, and the new jubilee cycle cannot be proclaimed until after his arrival.

So perhaps we must allow for two levels of meaning in the prophecy. First, with a starting point in spring 458 BC, the 490 years end exactly at Passover AD 33. This is possible if we accept that "the going-forth of the word," that is, Artaxerxes's command, which preceded Ezra's departure, was given in spring of that year.

Second, if Ezra proclaims a new jubilee cycle on 1 Tishri 457 BC, the tenth jubilee year of that cycle would be the year beginning Tishri

[8] See Africanus, *Chronography* §16–18; Athanasius, *De Incarnatione Verbi Dei* §39.
[9] Payne calls this "the traditional view" and cites many others who held it (1973: 387; 1962: 277–78). See likewise, Young 2022: 475n.
[10] See Young 2022: 473–89.

AD 33 and ending on 29 Elul AD 34, some eighteen months after the resurrection. Or if, following Wacholder, Ezra proclaimed a new jubilee cycle on 1 Tishri 456 BC, the tenth jubilee year of that cycle would be the Tishri year AD 34/35, ending some thirty months after the resurrection.

But it is no issue if the calendar jubilee cycle trails a year or two behind the 490 years from the "going-forth of the word." For Gabriel does not say that everlasting redemption will occur exactly at the end of 490 years. He says only that all will be accomplished within the latter part of the last sabbatic cycle or 'week' (Dan. 9:27).[11]

Summary

The Bible witnesses to two jubilee cycles in ancient Israel, which were held as fundamental measures of time by the Israelites.

We can accurately identify the first cycle from Ezekiel 40:1, where we learn that a jubilee year began on 10 Tishri 574 BC. From that date, we can confirm a recurring forty-nine-year jubilee (and sabbatic) cycle running throughout the Israelite kingdoms. It can be traced back at least to Joshua's entry to the land in 1406 BC. But there is no reason why it cannot be traced back earlier. Evidently, some sages, like the author of the Book of Jubilees, did hold to a continual cycle of jubilees from the creation of Adam continuing into the Israelite conquest. Nor is there any evidence that this ancient jubilee cycle was ever cancelled or abrogated. It can be carried forward to the time of Jesus, when we will find that a jubilee year falls in the exact centre of the period of his incarnation, in the year AD 15/16. And it can be carried forward into our own time, as we shall soon see.

However, after the exile, Daniel speaks of a new jubilee cycle to begin with the "going forth of the word to rebuild Jerusalem" and to end, ten jubilees later, after the cutting-off of the Messiah. This is the new jubilee cycle proclaimed by Ezra, as it is identified either by Zuckermann or by Wacholder. By Zuckermann's dates, the seventy sevens run from Tishri 457 BC to 29 Elul AD 34, and by Wacholder's reckoning, one year later. Yet, as some have shown, counting back 490 years from Passover

[11] Hebrew *ḥatsi ha-shabua'* means 'in a half of the week' rather than 'in the middle of the week.' For the evidence, see Young 2022: 484–87.

AD 33 takes us to the spring of 458 BC, which could have been the date of the going-forth of Artaxerxes's command or, in the view of Rodger Young, the date of Ezra's departure for Babylon.[12]

So the Bible has these two distinct jubilee cycles. We may call the first one, the older, pre-exilic one, the "creation cycle." And we may call the second, post-exilic one, initiated by Ezra, and linked with Daniel's seventy sevens, the "redemption cycle." The two cycles interlock. The redemption cycle follows the creation cycle at an interval of either eighteen (Zuckermann) or nineteen (Wacholder) years. Here are the ten jubilees of the two cycles for the period from the return from exile to the time of Jesus.

Figure 10. The post-exilic cycle: ten jubilees till the consommation.

Post-exilic Redemption cycle (Zuckermann)	*Post-exilic Redemption cycle (Wacholder)*	*Jubilee count of Daniel's seventy sevens*
1. 457t/56–409t/08 BC	1. 456t/55–408t/07 BC	Week 1
2. 408t/07–360t/59 BC	2. 407t/06–359t/58 BC	Week 2
3. 359t/58–311t/10 BC	3. 358t/57–310t/09 BC	Week 3
4. 310t/09–262t/61 BC	4. 309t/08–261t/60 BC	Week 4
5. 261t/60–213t/12 BC	5. 260t/59–212t/11 BC	Week 5
6. 212t/11–164t/63 BC	6. 211t/10–163t/62 BC	Week 6
7. 163t/62–115t/14 BC	7. 162t/61–114t/13 BC	Week 7
8. 114t/13–66t/63 BC	8. 113t/12–65t/64 BC	Week 8
9. 63t/62–17t/16 BC	9. 64t/63–16t/15 BC	Week 9
10. 16t/15 BC–AD 33t/34	10. 15t/14 BC–AD 34t/35	Week 10

My own view inclines to Zuckermann's dates. That is, Artaxerxes's command to rebuild Jerusalem was given in the spring of 458 BC, exactly 490 years before the resurrection, and Ezra then went to Jerusalem and proclaimed the new sabbatic and jubilee cycle on 1 Tishri 457 BC, which cycle terminated on 24 Elul AD 34, eighteen months after the resurrection, in fulfilment of Gabriel's word that all would be accomplished in the latter part of the seventieth septennate.

[12] Young 2022.

23

6,000 years, 123 jubilees

YOU HAVE now understood, I hope, that the millennial week is the basis of biblical eschatology. And, since we are to enter the millennial Sabbath after 6,000 years, we could calculate the long-awaited start of the Shabbat millennium from the date of creation, if only we knew the date of creation.

The Bible contains chronogenealogies from Adam to Abraham, listing the age when each son was born to his father. Theoretically, this lets us calculate how many years passed from Adam down to the period of the kings, whose reigns can be correlated with other historical events whose date is known. In this way, one can calculate, more or less, the date of the creation of Adam. This took place, according to the Hebrew text, around 6,000 years ago, give or take a few decades. Yet, although calculating the date of creation has a long history, it has never been straightforward.

THE SEPTUAGINT DATE OF CREATION

As we saw in chapter nine, the Greek-speaking Church Fathers who led the early church based their calculations upon the Septuagint Greek translation of the Bible. But the Septuagint translators, Alexandrian Jews of the third century BC, had stretched all the lifetimes of the Genesis patriarchs. As a result, the Septuagint gives a date of creation some 1500 years earlier than the Hebrew text. That is why Eusebius of Caesaria, for instance, dated creation to 5228 BC, and the Byzantine Church calendar now dates it to 5509 BC.

No one knows why the Septuagint translators did this. The best guess is that they were trying to stretch the date of creation back to fit in with Egyptian beliefs about the age of the world. But the result of this change was that the whole early church, east and west, was expecting the return of Jesus 6,000 years after a creation date of 5,500 BC. As a result, the years around AD 500 were a time of great messianic fervour in the Christian world. They got the trials of the Justinian plague. But the Messiah did not come.

The Hebrew Date of Creation

Rabbinic sages, on the other hand, possessed and read a Hebrew Bible much like our own. It is clear that they once held to a date of creation around 4,000 years before the Christian era. But the fact that Jesus came at the start of the fifth millennium of creation – exactly when the Messiah was due to come – was an inconvenient fact. So, over the centuries, the Jewish Hillel II calendar, as finalized by Rambam, moved the date of Adam's creation forward by a couple of hundred years, to October 3761 BC. As a result, Judaism is not officially expecting the Messiah for more than 220 years, although many Jews hope to see him sooner.

It wasn't until the fifth century AD that Christians began to get access to the Hebrew chronogenealogies when they appeared in Jerome's Latin Vulgate translation of the Hebrew. (Ironically, Jerome himself still based his hopes for the return of Jesus at around AD 500, based on the Septuagint dating. Old habits die hard.) The Vulgate enabled Christian scholastics for the first time to calculate the date of creation according to the figures of the Hebrew text. One of the first to do so was Bede who, like Jerome, thought the Hebrew text was more reliable than the Greek. From the Vulgate, Bede dated creation to the year 3952 BC.[1] This, of course, went against the received learning from Augustine, and resentful monks reported his heretical views to his bishop, Wilfrid.

By the sixteenth and seventeenth centuries, as the Hebrew text became available in the universities of Europe, the question of the date of creation engaged the attention of the greatest minds of the age. Kepler proposed a date of 3977 BC. Newton proposed 3998 BC. Ussher, whose

[1] De temporum ratione (AD 703), Chapter 66.

conclusions made their way into the King James Bible, proposed 4004 BC. Others made similar proposals, mostly lying in a seventy-year time-frame between 4020 and 3950 BC. The reasons for their divergences are few. But they are thorny. They revolve round questions of Terah's age when Abraham was born, of when Abraham entered the Promised Land, and of the length of the Exodus. Despite great advances in our knowledge of the dates of ancient history, these questions still hamper an exact calculation of the biblical date of Adam's creation to this day.

Another approach

But there's another way to approach the problem. We saw in chapters four to eight that, in the age of six thousand years, the Messiah comes at the beginning of the fifth millennial day of creation.

> The world is to exist six thousand years. Two thousand: chaos. Two thousand: Torah [from Abraham]. Two thousand: days of the Messiah. (Sanh. 97a/b)

Therefore, since the Messiah cannot be late, the time when he came must be at the change from the fourth to the fifth millennium. And, of course, we know he was not late, for he was revealed at the time the angel told Daniel, in the seventieth septennate from the command to restore Jerusalem. He was born probably in late 2 BC and died at Passover AD 33. Therefore it is within this short lifetime that the transition from the fourth to the fifth day of creation must occur.

We saw also, in the last chapters, that the Bible counts the ages of the world not only in millennia but also in jubilees. Since that is so, we have to calculate these six millennia also in jubilee periods. It's a fairly simple calculation. Twenty forty-nine-year jubilees are twenty years short of a millennium. Forty jubilees are forty years short of two millennia. So the best way to reconcile them is to add one jubilee for every two thousand years. That way, we arrive at a compromise of two millennia being composed of forty-one jubilees, totalling 2009 years.

In the last chapter, we spoke of the creation jubilee cycle, identified from Ezekiel 40:1, which runs back to Joshua's crossing the Jordan in 1406 BC. If we work out all the dates of this cycle, back to creation and forward to our own time, we find that it falls exactly into three 2009-year periods of 41 jubilees from creation until our own time.

Figure 11. The creation jubilee cycle: 123 Tishri cycles in Julian/Gregorian years

1st and 2nd millennial days *Adam to Abram*	3rd and 4th millennial days *Abraham to Messiah*	5th and 6th millennial days *Messiah to the Sabbath*
1. 4003t/02–3955t/54 BC*	42. **1994t/93–1946t/45 BC‡**	83. **AD 16t/17–64t/65**
2. 3954t/53–3906t/05 BC	43. **1945t/44–1897t/96 BC‡**	84. AD 65t/66–113t/14
3. 3905t/04–3857t/56 BC	44. 1896t/95–1848t/47 BC	85. AD 114t/15–162t/63
4. 3856t/55–3808t/07 BC	45. 1847t/46–1799t/98 BC	86. AD 163t/64–211t/12
5. 3807t/06–3759t/58 BC	46. 1798t/97–1750t/49 BC	87. AD 212t/13–260t/61
6. 3758t/57–3710t/09 BC	47. 1749t/48–1701t/1700 BC	88. AD 261t/62–309t/10
7. 3709t/08–3661t/60 BC	48. 1700t/1699–1652t/51 BC	89. AD 310t/11–358t/59
8. 3660t/59–3612t/11 BC	49. 1651t/50–1603t/02 BC	90. AD 359t/60–407t/08
9. 3611t/10–3563t/62 BC	50. 1602t/01–1554t/53 BC	91. AD 408t/09–456t/57
10. 3562t/61–3514t/13 BC	51. 1553t/52–1505t/04 BC	92. AD 457t/58–505t/06
11. 3513t/12–3465t/64 BC	52. 1504t/03–1456t/55 BC	93. AD 506t/07–554t/55
12. 3464t/63–3416t/15 BC	53. 1455t/54–1407t/06 BC	94. AD 555t/56–603t/04
13. 3415t/14–3367t/66 BC	54. 1406t/05–1358t/57 BC	95. AD 604t/05–652t/53
14. 3366t/65–3318t/17 BC	55. 1357t/56–1309t/08 BC	96. AD 653t/54–701t/02
15. 3317t/16–3269t/68 BC	56. 1308t/07–1260t/59 BC	97. AD 702t/03–750t/51
16. 3268t/67–3220t/19 BC	57. 1259t/58–1211t/10 BC	98. AD 751t/52–799t/800
17. 3219t/18–3171t/70 BC	58. 1210t/09–1162t/61 BC	99. AD 800t/01–848t/49
18. 3170t/69–3122t/21 BC	59. 1161t/60–1113t/12 BC	100. AD 849t/50–897t/98
19. 3121t/20–3073t/72 BC	60. 1112t/11–1064t/63 BC	101. AD 898t/99–946t/47
20. 3072t/71–3024t/23 BC	61. 1063t/62–1015t/14 BC	102. AD 947t/48–995t/96
21. 3023t/22–2975t/74 BC	62. **1014t/13–966t/65 BC⸸**	103. AD 996t/97–1044t/45
22. 2974t/73–2926t/25 BC	63. 965t/64–917t/16 BC	104. AD 1045t/46–1093t/94
23. 2925t/24–2877t/76 BC	64. 916t/15–868t/67 BC	105. AD 1094t/95–1142t/43
24. 2876t/75–2828t/27 BC	65. 867t/66–819t/18 BC	106. AD 1143t/44–1191t/92
25. 2827t/26–2779t/78 BC	66. 818t/17–770t/69 BC	107. AD 1192t/93–1240t/41
26. 2778t/77–2730t/29 BC	67. 769t/68–721t/20 BC	108. AD 1241t/42–1289t/90
27. 2729t/28–2681t/80 BC	68. 720t/19–672t/71 BC	109. AD 1290t/91–1338t/39
28. 2680t/79–2632t/31 BC	69. 671t/70–623t/22 BC	110. AD 1339t/40–1387t/88
29. 2631t/30–2583t/82 BC	70. 622t/21–**574t**/73 BC†	111. AD 1388t/89–1436t/37
30. 2582t/81–2534t/33 BC	71. 573t/72–525t/24 BC	112. AD 1437t/38–1485t/86
31. 2533t/32–2485t/84 BC	72. 524t/23–476t/75 BC	113. AD 1486t/87–1534t/35
32. 2484t/83–2436t/35 BC	73. 475t/74–427t/26 BC	114. AD 1535t/36–1583t/84
33. 2435t/34–2387t/86 BC	74. 426t/25–378t/77 BC	115. AD 1584t/85–1632t/33
34. 2386t/85–2338t/37 BC	75. 377t/76–329t/28 BC	116. AD 1633t/34–1681t/82
35. 2337t/36–2289t/88 BC	76. 328t/27–280t/79 BC	117. AD 1682t/83–1730t/31
36. 2288t/87–2240t/39 BC	77. 279t/78–231t/30 BC	118. AD 1731t/32–1779t/80
37. 2239t/38–2191t/90 BC	78. 230t/29–182t/81 BC	119. AD 1780t/81–1828t/29
38. 2190t/89–2142t/41 BC	79. 181t/80–133t/32 BC	120. AD 1829t/30–1877t/78
39. 2141t/40–2093t/92 BC	80. 132t/31–84t/83 BC	121. AD 1878t/79–1926t/27
40. **2092t/91–2044t/43 BC‡**	81. 83t/82–35t/34 BC	122. AD 1927t/28–1975t/76
41. **2043t/42–1995t/94 BC‡**	82. **34t/33 BC–AD 15t/16**	123. AD 1976t/77–2024t/25

* t is Tishri. "In Tishri the world was created" (B. Rosh HaShanah 10b). Each jubilee cycle begins on 1 Tishri; each jubilee year (last year of each cycle) begins on 10 Tishri (Lev. 25:9–10) and ends on 29 Elul.

† Ezekiel's jubilee year in Tishri 574 BC (Ezek. 40:1) from which the table is calculated.

‡ Avram: birth 2056 BC (AM 1948); birth of Isaac 1956 BC (AM 2048); death 1881 BC (AM 2123) (Seder Olam Rabbah §1).

⸸ The central jubilee cycle: at its centre is the reign of David.

The accuracy of the jubilee cycles in the table above rests on three points of confirmation.

(1) Ezekiel 40:1 allows us to calculate the exact dates of every jubilee cycle before and after Tishri 574 BC, just as they appear in the table.
(2) Ezekiel's jubilee was the seventeenth jubilee from Joshua's entry to the Promised Land (Seder Olam 11; B. Arak. 12a). This gives a date of 1406 BC for the entry. This is the same date arrived at independently from 1 Kings 6:1, where the month of Ziv in Solomon's fourth year – that is, spring of 967 BC – is the 480th year from the Exodus, from which we likewise deduce that the Exodus was in 1446 BC and the Entry in 1406 BC.[2]
(3) The Rabbis tell us there was a jubilee in the eighteenth year of Josiah (Seder Olam 24; B. Meg 14b), when he initiated his reform and there was a public reading of the law, as in jubilee years (2 Kgs 22:3; 23:1–2). This was the jubilee year beginning 10 Tishri 623 BC, exactly forty-nine years before the jubilee of Ezekiel's vision.

The overlap of the six millennia and the 123 jubilees rests upon four points of confirmation.

(1) Since we know the dates of the life of the Messiah, and since he did not come late, we know that any jubilee year of the pre-exilic cycle that falls in his lifetime must be the end of the fourth millennium. The only relevant year is the jubilee year Tishri 15 AD to Elul 16 AD, which falls right in the middle of his incarnation, sixteen years or so after his birth and sixteen and a half years before his death. This must be the last jubilee year of the 82nd jubilee and of the fourth millennium. From it, we can count back 82 jubilee cycles to Adam, who is now seen to be created at Tishri 4003 BC.[3] Thus the birth and youth of Jesus fall in the 82nd jubilee, but his public ministry and redemptive work are completed early in the 83rd jubilee, in the fifth millennium, just before the end of the tenth jubilee of the post-exilic cycle, as stated in Daniel's prophecy.
(2) Calculated this way, our date for Adam's creation is only one year after Ussher's calculation from the Masoretic text. Since Ussher did

[2] Based on Thiele's date for the beginning of the divided kingdom.
[3] Calculating this way also bypasses the question of whether the prophetic clock began at the creation of Adam or one year before, as some kabbalists say. For the four millennia of 82 jubilee cycles to the life of Jesus count back to their natural own start-point.

his work very carefully, this is reassuring.

(3) With the life of Jesus at the transition from the 82nd to the 83rd jubilee, the life of Abraham falls into place. According to Seder Olam Rabbah, he was born in AM 1948 (2056 BC) and called by God in AM 2022 (1982 BC). His son Isaac was born in AM 2048 (1956 BC) and Abraham died in AM 2123 (1881 BC). So his long life extends over four jubilees, from jubilee 40 to 43, straddling the transition from the second to the third millennium, exactly as B. Sanhedrin 97 and Ramban (see below) teach.

(4) The reign of David, the picture and prototype of the messianic kingdom, appears exactly halfway between Abraham and Jesus, bridging the transition from the third to the fourth millennium, in the middle of the middle jubilee of the six millennia.

The extra nine years at the end of each two millennia in no way displace the alignment of events with the calendar. On the contrary, they function as the transition period, as they should. As Ramban said,

> Know that from the time twilight falls it is already considered as the following day. Therefore, the subject of every "day" begins somewhat before it, just as Abraham was born at the end of the second thousand years. And you will see similar examples for each and every day. (Ramban on Gen. 2:3)

But why 123 jubilees? Is it not an arbitrary number? As I said, it's the simplest way to reconcile the millennial week with the jubilee cycle. It forms a "long millennium" of 2009 years, rather like the short cubit and the long "royal cubit" which Egypt, Babylon, and the Hebrews all used. But, more significantly still, once we add to these 123 jubilees another twenty-one jubilees for the Sabbath millennium, we find that it totals exactly 144 jubilees. This number, twelve times twelve, represents fullness and completion, as it does in the Revelation (Rev. 7:4; 14:1). So seven millennia will complete the perfect number of jubilees.

Finally, the last jubilee of this calendar began in autumn 1976. Its jubilee year falls on Tishri, in the autumn of 2024 and will finish on 29 Elul, in the autumn of 2025. According to current rabbinic calculations, 10 Tishri 2024 (the beginning of the 123rd jubilee year) is at sunset on 11 October 2024. But, over the last 2,000 years, the rabbinic astronomical calendar has decalated from the biblical calendar, whose Nisan new year began on the first new moon after the first ripe ears of barley were seen in the Jordan valley. It is therefore possible that the biblical 10 Tishri fell a month earlier, at sunset on 12 September.

The first year of the seventh millennium will fall on 1 Tishri 2025. According to rabbinic calculations, this will be at sunset on 22 September. Since the rabbinic Nisan is early in 2025 – at sunset on 29 March – the calculations for 2025 are probably correct.

THE END OF THIS AGE

If you are of a sceptical nature, you may look at the above table and say "Mitchell just made that up." But if so, I invite you to look at it carefully. Knowing the dates of the jubilee cycle, from Ezekiel, and the times of Jesus, it cannot be constructed any other way. To do so, one would have to re-date radically the lifetime of Jesus, which is not possible. Further, see how all the dates of biblical history fit the timetable without the least forcing or bending. All unfolds naturally from the pre-exilic jubilee cycle and encompasses the whole of Bible history, with every major event in its correct place. I suggest that this is the divine plan of the ages, not made up, but made plain.

If that is so, does that mean that the year autumn 2024 to autumn 2025 will see the cataclysmic end of the age? With the events now unfolding in the Middle East, that might not come as much of a surprise. But I'm not saying that. The year Tishri 2024 to 2025 is the turn of the page on the sixth millennium. Yet there is always a transition period between the ages. Jesus didn't die and rise until seventeen years into the fifth millennium. And, as we saw, scripture says the Antichrist must come before he returns. To allow for this, I suspect there is a transition period still to come. This will be the period that the post-exilic "redemption" jubilee cycle (inaugurated by Ezra) lags behind the pre-exilic "creation" cycle which we learn from Ezekiel. As we saw, this was the lag between the mid-point of Jesus's incarnation and his work of redemption. This would be a lag of up to eighteen years.

24

Final Words

ZOOMING on, let's conclude. Long before the time of Jesus, even from Moses himself, the sages of Israel read the creation account of Genesis as meaning that the world-age would last six divine 'days' – that is, 6,000 years. After these six 'days' would come the Sabbath age, which would be one thousand years of peace and plenty under the reign of the Messiah. They believed that this was a truth implied in the Genesis text. This view was early and widespread among the sages of ancient Israel. We find it in pre-Christian texts like the Book of Jubilees, the Targum on Hosea, and 2 Enoch. There is no evidence of any other view.

When Jesus came, the faith of ancient Israel split into Church and Synagogue. They parted, of course, in accepting or rejecting Jesus as the Messiah who will come again. But in most other things, New Testament eschatology resembles that of the Pharisees and their followers, the rabbis of the Talmud.

The New Testament teaches that Jesus, on his return, will set up an earthly kingdom. In John 2, Jesus himself teaches that there is a divine plan of days, when Israel's temple will be restored on the third 'day' after its destruction. Hebrews 4 and 2 Peter 3 also speak of millennial days and the millennial Sabbath. The Revelation says that Jesus's sabbatic, earthly kingdom will last one millennium and be superseded by a glorious Age to Come, with a new heaven, a new earth, and a new Jerusalem (20:4–7; 21:1–2). Paul too teaches that the messianic age will yield to the Age to Come, when Christ will hand the kingdom to the Father (1 Cor. 15:24).

Likewise, early Talmud teachings, not later than the second century, speak of the six millennial days being two days without Torah (Adam to Abraham), two days with Torah (Abraham to the Messiah), and two days of the Messiah (yet the Rabbis lament that he has not come.) These six days will be followed by the 1,000-year messianic kingdom which will, in turn, be followed by the Age to Come, the *Olam HaBa.*

In Orthodox Judaism this teaching persists unchanged through two millennia. The Messiah, they say, did not come on the fifth day, but they still hope for his coming on the seventh. Indeed, many hope for his coming in our lifetime, despite the fact that the Hillel II Anno Mundi calendar still has more than two centuries to run of the sixth millennium. When the Messiah comes, they say, he will rule the earth from Jerusalem.

In the church, all the Fathers of the first two centuries, when speaking of eschatology, testify unanimously to the millennial week and its millennial Sabbath. The earliest such teaching, the Epistle of Barnabas, says the millennial week is a teaching that Barnabas received personally from Jesus. Likewise, the Apocalypse of Elijah, Papias, Justin, Irenaeus, Clement of Alexandria, Tertullian, and Hippolytus all testify to belief in the matter.

This happy consensus was overturned by the neoplatonic teaching and allegorical interpretation of Origen. For him, it was unthinkable that the Messiah could ever return to rule a carnal kingdom on earth. The saints were promised a spiritual resurrection into a heavenly kingdom of souls. Some opposed Origen's teaching – particularly Nepos, Commodianus, Methodius, and the great Lactantius. But still it spread. The Council of Nicaea rejected Origen's worst errors – his denial of bodily resurrection and his tritheism. But they did not reject his denial of the Messiah's earthly reign. Dionysius of Alexandria endorsed Origen's views, saying the Revelation was written not by John the apostle, but by another John, and that its earthly millennium was a fable of the gnostic heretic Cerinthus. Eusebius, Jerome and Augustine followed, the latter systematizing this amillennial belief. The millennium, he said, is the current Church Age. The true future hope of the righteous is to die and go to the neoplatonic heaven of souls. Christ will not return to reign on earth. Instead, he will come only to judge the world in a single universal judgement from the air, condemning the wicked to everlasting torments and taking the righteous to the heavenly kingdom. But, when Christ did not reappear 1,000 years after his birth, the millennium became merely symbolic, and the same doctrine was carried into the second millennium. Augustine's influence ensured that Origen's heterodox teaching became the universal church's orthodoxy for some 1,500 years. In time, this morphed into what we now call postmillennialism, a modified version of Augustine's amillennialism, with a glorious finale of glorious worldwide gospel triumphs before the return of Christ for the universal judgement.

The first dent in this system appeared in the sixteenth century. Ribera and Alcázar, both Jesuits, were eager to turn aside Protestant charges about the Pope being the Antichrist. Alcázar proposed what we call Preterism, that the prophecies of the Revelation were fulfilled in the first century. This later mutated into Idealism, so popular with Anglicans since the twentieth century. Ribera, on the other hand, who had drunk deep of the early Fathers, reasserted the view we now call Futurism, that the prophecies of Revelation foretell the period immediately before Jesus returns to set up his 1,000-year earthly kingdom. He was followed in various ways by Mede in the seventeenth century, and Lacunza in the eighteenth.

Inspired by Lacunza, Edward Irving, in nineteenth-century London, taught the imminent arrival of Christ to set up his millennial kingdom. He gathered round him a group of believers who, enthused by the charismatic events in Port Glasgow, felt that the last days were imminent. J.N. Darby initially opposed Irving's teaching but later adopted and developed it. He proposed that Christ would come invisibly and secretly, seven years before his public coming in judgement, and rapture the faithful heavenward. He proposed that the Church Age was a parenthesis, unforeseen by the prophets, in God's dealings with Israel. This parenthesis would end with the rapture of the church, whereupon the Antichrist would arise, many Jews would be saved, and they would evangelize the world during the reign of the Antichrist.

In Britain, most rejected Darby's notions. But he found a more sympathetic audience in America, which was still in the grasp of postmillennialism. Soon Darby's ideas were published all over the United States and gained worldwide acclaim. They remain popular to this day, although not a few are now reconsidering them in the light of the biblical teaching that *our being gathered to him will not take place until the apostasy occurs and the man of lawlessness is revealed* (2 Thess. 2:1–3). As a result, pretribulationists have now divided into pre-tribbers, mid-tribbers, and late-tribbers.

HISTORIC PREMILLENNIALISM

The millennial week of the early Fathers is the vital underlying structure of biblical eschatology. In the seventh millennium, the Messiah will appear and catch the faithful heavenward in a 'pre-wrath' resurrection and rapture, before the judgement of God falls upon this impenitent world. Then he will set up his throne in Jerusalem and rule the world in justice and peace for one thousand years. It will be, initially at least, an earthly kingdom. Children may still need to be taught. Bodies and souls may still need healed. But the true divine law will be taught to all and mankind and the created order will flourish as never before.

The picture of a transitional kingdom between this earthly life and a heavenly eternity finds support in scripture well beyond Revelation 20:1–7. It fulfils all the Old Testament prophecies about the messianic age which we spoke of in chapters two and three. The purpose of the seventh millennium is to prepare renewed mankind to receive the immortal glory of the heavens, and sooner or later we will begin to enter upon our heavenly inheritance. As Newton says,

> But this I say that as Fishes in water ascend & descend, move whether they will & rest where they will, so may Angels & Christ & the Children of the resurrection do in the air & heavens…Thus may the whole heavens or any part thereof whatever be the habitation of the Blessed & at the same time the earth be subject to their dominion. And to have thus the liberty & dominion of the whole heavens & the choise of the happiest places for abode seems a greater happiness then to be confined to any one place whatever.[1]

Then, in the eighth millennium, God will usher in the glorious Age to Come. Then there shall be new heavens and a new earth, and the new Jerusalem shall descend from heaven to earth. Since the new Jerusalem is of such momentous size that it would throw the current earth out of orbit, we may expect that the new earth will be much greater than the current one (Rev. 21:10–16).

THE EVIDENCE FOR HISTORIC PREMILLENNIALISM

I have, I believe, good reasons for holding to this premillennialist view. At risk of repeating myself, here they are summarized.

[1] Extract from treatise on Revelation, Section 2 (Yahuda Ms. 9.2).

First, this was the standard belief of ancient Israel long before the time of Jesus, as noted above.

Second, it is agreeable with the teaching of Jesus and the apostles, as found in the second chapter of John's gospel, in Hebrews 4, 2 Peter, and Revelation 20.

Third, it was the view of the Nazarene church, as we see it in the Epistle of Barnabas and the Apocalypse of Elijah. It was the view of all the Fathers until Origen began his campaign to overthrow it.

Fourth, it was the view of the Pharisees and their rabbinic successors. The Israelite sages inherited traditions from the prophets, explaining their prophecies. And so the fact that the Rabbis held only to this view is an eloquent testimony to its antiquity and its primacy.

Fifth, the main alternative to this view – the Augustinian, amillennial view that the Messiah will not rule in this carnal world – is a thing conceived by the union of Platonism and Gnosticism, nursed at Manichean breasts, and foisted upon the world to exalt the clergy of the Roman Empire. Its authors also invented the doctrines of the immortality of the soul, the eternal torment of the damned, the condemnation of the body and of marriage and of all created things. These teachings have been a stumbling block to many through the succeeding ages.

Sixth, the Messiah must return to earth to justify, by his righteous rule, God's creation decree that all he made was very good. The earth will not be destroyed as an unclean thing, as Origen and Augustine said. *The earth is established; it cannot be moved* (Ps. 96:10). It shall be healed and restored in the Sabbath. Thereafter it shall be reborn to an existence yet more glorious, in the Age to Come, when the blessed children of God shall inherit the heavens and the earth (Rev. 21:1–2).

Seventh, it is right and fitting that the Messiah should reign in the place where he was rejected, that is, in Jerusalem, where his foes put him to an ignominious death, where they said, *We will not have this man to rule over us* (Luke 19:14), *Come, let's kill him* (Matt. 21:38).

Irenaeus or Darby

Finally, there are three main differences between the classic premillennialism of the early Fathers and the dispensationalist, pretribulation premillennialism of Darby. These are: (1) the time and events of the rapture; (2) the separate dispensations for Israel and the Church; (3) and the place of the Jews in the events of the end.

We discussed the timing of the rapture in chapter fourteen. There is no scriptural evidence for a secret rapture, but only for one resurrection and rapture of the faithful at the one glorious coming of Jesus. This will take place after the man of lawlessness is revealed.

The separate dispensations for Israel and the Church are a thing without foundation in scripture. As B.W. Newton said to Darby, "All God's people are one." All who ever served the Lord Jehovah, all who now believe and are baptised in the Lord Jesus, whether Jew or Gentile, are part of God's one chosen and beloved people, and will be saved; but all who reject Jesus, including Jews, will be condemned (Mark 16:16).

Dispensationalists see the Jews as the heroes of the last days, who will convert the whole world in the time of the Antichrist. The Fathers taught otherwise. They believed the Jews would crown the Antichrist king and persecute the church until Jesus comes and kills the impostor. Time will tell. But the prophetic typology of Joseph revealing himself to his brothers (Gen. 45:1–7), and Jesus's words that the temple will be destroyed and Jerusalem will not see him again until they hail his coming (Matt. 23:38–39) and the words *The Deliverer will come from Zion, he will banish ungodliness from Jacob* (Rom. 11:26) and *They will look upon me whom they pierced and mourn for him as with the grief over a firstborn* (Zech. 12:10) suggest that most Jews will not believe in Jesus until he appears in glory at his *parousia.*[2] But again, time will tell.

THE APOSTASY

The apostasy of the Christian church is now plain on all sides. Those of us who hold to biblical standards of behaviour feel like we have entered a crazy topsy-turvy world, as the clergy commend sexual diversity and disregard the plain teaching of Jesus, who said,

> From the beginning the Creator made them male and female, and said, 'For this reason a man will leave his father and mother and be united to his wife, and the two will become one flesh.' (Matt. 19:4–5)

Revisionist bishops and priests, in thrall to powerful advocacy groups

[2] The view too of Bruce 1963: 222 and Cranfield 1985: 283 on Rom. 11:26, who both see the same truth taught also in Rom. 11:15 (*What will their acceptance mean but life from the dead?*), that is, "that Israel's conversion will be the immediate precursor of the resurrection, to coincide with Christ's parousia" (Bruce 216).

and corporate funding, twist the Bible to condone practices that the church always called mortal sin. If you point to what the scriptures say, they say, "That's just your opinion." If you reply, you are denounced, excluded, and cancelled. Their vaunted love of diversity does not include those of us who hold that God made human beings male and female for heterosexual relations. But now what they are doing and teaching and legislating is fully in line with the practices of the Canaanites.

Shall not the Judge of all the earth do justice?

The book of Joshua is a sobering read. It tells how Jehovah commanded Joshua to enter the land of Canaan and slaughter everyone he saw, men women, and children. If you have any notions of what wounds of battle look like, what comes before your eyes as you read Joshua is fearful. Yet "all scripture is breathed out by God" (2 Tim. 3:16). So this book too has something important to tell us.

We must understand that it was God who decreed the extermination of the Canaanites, and he did so because of their wickedness. They had been given time to change. In Abraham's time, their sin had not reached its full measure (Gen. 15:16). But half a millennium later, they had not changed. The time of their judgement was ripe and Joshua was sent with the sickle. The sins of the Canaanites are no mystery. We spoke of them earlier: child sacrifice to the gods of the underworld, injustice to the poor, cultic prostitution, the sin of Sodom, idolatry, and every other sin of man. Their little children grew up to do the deeds of their fathers and mothers. They had become an offence to the Lord of the earth.

Yet, it wasn't entirely merciless. Nor was it entirely for Israel's sake. Rahab the Canaanite harlot is saved, with all her family (Josh. 2:10–14, 6:23–25). So are the Gibeonites, also of Canaanite stock (9:3–27). Saved too is Caleb, who, we learn, was perhaps never an Israelite at all, but a Kenizzite, whom the Israelites were told to conquer (14:6, 14; Num. 32:12; Gen 15:19). Yet Caleb, like the Gibeonites and Rahab, entered into Israel's inheritance through faith in Israel's God. In fact, Rahab finally becomes ancestress of the Messiah (Matt. 1:5). How's that for redemption! Meanwhile, Achan, a pure-blooded Judahite, who did not fear God, is stoned and burned, like Jericho and Ai, and buried under a heap of stones, like the king of Ai, whose forbidden luxuries he craved (Josh. 6:24; 7:25; 8:28). His heap becomes a memorial of defeat for one who, like a Canaanite, did not fear the true God. It is faith, not ethnicity, which makes a person a hero in the story of redemption.

As said, this was a decree of Jehovah the God of Israel. He gave the land to Joshua and none could withstand him (1:3–5). Before the first battle, the commander of the army of Jehovah, with drawn sword, appears to Joshua at Jericho (5:13–15). This initially mysterious figure becomes less mysterious as we look at him. He tells Joshua to remove his sandals for he is on holy ground (5:15). This is the same command Moses received when Jehovah himself appeared to him in the burning bush (Exod. 3:5). Soon, this commander of Jehovah's army is called the LORD, Jehovah himself (Josh. 6:2). (Who else would be the commander of Jehovah's army?) So we must conclude here that this mysterious man of war is Lord Jehovah himself appearing in visible form.

Jehovah appears to people visibly throughout the Old Testament. Sometimes he is called the Angel of Jehovah or Angel of God, at other times simply Jehovah. The names are used interchangeably, but refer to the visible appearance of the God of Israel. Thus he appeared to Hagar, Abraham, Jacob.[3] Thus he appeared to Moses in the burning bush as the Angel of Jehovah, and Jehovah, and the God of Abraham, Isaac and Jacob (Exod. 3:2–6). As Jehovah and the Angel of God, he led the Israelites through the Sinai in the pillar of cloud and fire (Exod. 13:21; 14:19, 24). This Angel has divine power to forgive sins, although he does not always do so (Exod. 23:20–21; Num. 20:16). This Angel is the one who drives out the Canaanites before Israel (Exod. 33:2).

The Trinity is a mystery only partially revealed in the Old Testament. But, with New Testament hindsight, we can say that whenever Jehovah appears visibly in the Old Testament, it is not the Father who is seen, but the Son, the Logos, the Word, who makes God known. As John says, *No one has ever seen God; the only-begotten God, who is in the bosom of the Father, has made him known* (John 1:18). Thus, whenever Jehovah appears visibly in the old covenant, it is Jesus who is appearing. John assures us of this, saying, *Isaiah said these things because he saw the glory of him [Jesus] and spoke of him* (John 12:41; Isa. 6:1–5).

That means that after Jehovah appeared bodily to Abraham to discuss the destruction of Sodom and Gomorrah by fire, it was Jesus who sent the all-consuming fire (Gen. 18:22–33; 19:24). When Jehovah looked

[3] Gen. 16:7–14; 21:17–19; 18:1, 13, 22; 28:13; 31:11–13; 32:24–30; cf. Hos. 12:3–4. For more on the Angel of Jehovah as the visible God, see ch. 1 of Mitchell 2021.

down from the pillar of cloud to destroy the Egyptian army in the Red Sea, it was Jesus who decreed their destruction (Exod. 14:24–28). And when the commander of the army of Jehovah appeared to Joshua with directions for the defeat of Jericho, it was Jesus who made the walls fall and the ensuing slaughter was in obedience to his command.

But Joshua's conquest of Jericho does not justify the Israeli state's attacks on the Palestinian people. Joshua's war, at Jesus's word, was made *against* a people who rejected the gospel. But modern Israel's attacks are made *by* a people who themselves reject the gospel, to kill Christians who believe the gospel, and Muslims who honour Jesus more than Israeli Jews do.

Jesus and Jehovah

This fact, that Jehovah is Jesus, is one the New Testament writers make over and over again. Mark cites Isaiah, *the voice of one crying in the wilderness, "Prepare the way of Jehovah,"* then he tells how John Baptist came to prepare the way for Jesus (Mark 1:1–9). Paul says, *God has bestowed on him…the name that is above every other name, so that at the name of Jesus every knee should bow,* meaning that the name of Jesus has surpassed the name of Jehovah (Phil. 2:9). Even at his incarnation, the angel says, *You shall call his name Yeshua* [Jehovah saves] *for he* [Jesus-Jehovah] *will save his people from their sins* (Matt. 1:21).

We must not underrate Joshua. He is one of the many Old Testament redeemers who presage the Lord Jesus. Joseph the Patriarch foreshadows Jesus's burial, death, rising, and saving rule. Moses foreshadows his rejection, exaltation, leading, teaching, and liberating. David foreshadows his rejection and royal kingdom. But it is Joshua who prefigures Jesus as conqueror and judge of evildoers. Of them all, only Joshua bears the name of the Son of God. For his Hebrew name (Yehoshua) becomes Aramaic Yeshua, the name the angel tells Joseph to give the incarnate Son, whose name we now know, via Greek, as Jesus.

But some say the Jesus of the gospels would not destroy sinners. Jesus, they say, taught us to love our enemies. Will he destroy his? Will the coming Christ act in contradiction to Jesus and his gospel? If so, the coming Christ will put Jesus in the wrong, they say. He will be someone Christians do not know.

But these people distort the Jesus of the gospels. They manufacture a

Jesus-idol from their selective reading of his words. The real Jesus spoke fearful judgement on hypocrites and foretold the utter destruction of their city (Matt. 23:33–36). He says he is the stone who will fall upon his opponents and crush them (Matt. 21:42–44). He consigns sinners to the 'outer darkness' and 'goats' to fearful punishment (Matt. 8:12; 22:13; 25:30; 25:46). The Jesus of the gospels, for all his compassion and mercy, is a judge none would want to offend. He is a perfect judge, who does not wink at evil. A judge that does not do justice is no judge at all. A judge that lets evil thrive brings grief to the innocent. Shall not the judge of all the earth do justice? (Gen. 18:25) But the Lamb shall become a Lion. The rejected, suffering servant shall become the glorious, triumphant King. We should not ignore the message of the book of Joshua. His fearful judgement of the Canaanites presages Lord Yeshua's coming judgement of the earth. All kinds of people who fear and obey him, from mighty warriors to harlots, will be blessed. He will bring his own people, the meek, into their promised inheritance (Matt. 5:5). But he will rid the earth of his enemies. And then our broken, tyrannized, demon-driven, polluted, divided world will finally know righteous rule.

He is not late

In the previous two chapters, I said that, calculating from the millennial week and the jubilee cycle, we are now turning the page from the sixth to the seventh millennium. I added that there may well be a transition period into the seventh millennium. The transition will, I suspect, be complete within eighteen years – within the overlap period of Daniel's jubilee cycle – but perhaps in much less.

Let me say here that, based on these calculations, I believe I am right. I offer them in all sincerity. But I do not guarantee them. I am not a prophet. I am only calculating from the ancient scriptural calendar. I have no heavenly word on this matter, only computations based on these old principles of the divine plan. Many have been wrong before about the time of his coming. If I prove also to be wrong, I will admit my fault and beg your pardon.

But the thing I would like you to take from this book is this: There is a calendar of the ages. It is not new. It's been there since ancient times. And, according to that calendar, he is not late. Just because he did not come in the first century, or the sixth, or the tenth, or the nineteenth or twentieth, does not mean he is late. In all these centuries, the millennial and jubilee timetable of the ages was not fulfilled. But now it is fulfilled in our own time. By early autumn 2025, the sixth millennial day of creation will have passed into history, and the Sabbath millennium will dawn upon us. Then we will witness the great unfolding. Pray that you may escape these things and stand before the Son of Man on that day. For he is not late. He is never late. He is still coming. And he will be on time. Make your peace with him and pray to be found spotless when he comes. And, if you have not done so,

> Repent and be baptized every one of you in the name of Jesus Christ for the forgiveness of your sins, and you will receive the gift of the Holy Spirit. For the promise is for you and for your children and for all who are far off, everyone whom the Lord our God calls to himself. (Acts 2:38–39).

Abbreviations & Glossary

AM, AM(J): see **Anno Mundi**.

Amidah: the central prayer of Jewish liturgy, dating from temple times. It formerly comprised eighteen blessings, from whence it is called *Shmoneh esreh* ('The Eighteen'). The ***bet-din*** of Gamliel II added a nineteenth paragraph, the ***birkat ha-minim***. Observant Jews say it three times a day, and four on Shabbat and holy days.

Anno Mundi (AM): A date measured from the creation of Adam. Thus AM 4000 is four thousand years after the creation of Adam. **AM(J)**: denotes specifically the years of the Jewish **Hillel II calendar**.

Bavli: see **Talmud Bavli**.

darshan: a midrashic interpreter.

EJ: *Encyclopaedia Judaica.*

Exilarch (Gk): the ***Resh G'lutha*** (Aram. 'head of the exile') or ***Rosh Galut*** (Heb. same), the king of David's line who ruled the Israelite community in Babylon.

gematria: biblical interpretation based on the numerical value of Hebrew words.

HaShem: literally, "the Name"; a rabbinic Hebrew circumlocution for the divine name YHVH (Jehovah).

Hillel II calendar: The modern Jewish calendar which dates the creation of Adam in the Julian year 3761 BC. It is attributed to the Nasi Hillel II in the year AD 359. But it codified four centuries of earlier Pharisaic calendar changes, and continued to be modified until at least AD 924.

isopsephy: interpretation based on the numerical value of Greek words.

Jehovah: the revealed personal name of Israel's God with the Hebrew consonants YHVH. Aharon ben Asher's 10th-century Aleppo Codex vocalizes it as Y^{e}ho**vah**. This is the likeliest pronunciation, but I keep the latinized form, Jehovah, which is more familiar. For more, see Appendix 1 in my *Songs of Ascents.*

kohen, pl. ***kohanim***: an Aaronite 'priest' offering temple sacrifices.

Masoretic text: the ancient version of the Hebrew Bible, written by the 10th century Karaite sages called the Masoretes, which is the basis of all modern Hebrew Bible texts. The foremost of these texts is the Aleppo Codex (c. AD 920) by Aharon ben Asher and Shlomo ben Buya'a. The second is the Leningrad Codex (c. AD 1008), a copy of the Aleppo Codex by Shmuel ben Ya'aqov.

mashiaḥ: 'anointed'; a divinely-appointed king or priest; the Messiah.

meturgeman: the translator of a **targum**.

midrash: a rabbinic commentary on scripture or scriptural themes.

Mishnah: a collection of Israel's temple laws and oral traditions, compiled by R. Judah ha-Nasi in the latter 2nd or early 3rd century AD. Its purpose was to save Israel's national memory from extinction, following the Roman proscriptions of 135 AD.

nasi: prince.

Nazarenes (*notzrim*): Generally, a Judaic term for Hebrew followers of Jesus (cf. Acts 24:5), in distinction to 'Christian,' which tends more to denote Greek-speaking disciples. More specifically, a Torah-observant group of Hebrew Christians, spoken of by Jerome, Letter 75, and Epiphanius, Panarion 29.

Nestorianism: The teaching of Nestorius, fifth-century Patriarch of Constantinople, in which Christ is said to have had distinct human and divine persons, joined in prosopic union rather than in the hypostatic union affirmed at the Council of Chalcedon.

Olam HaBa: The Age to Come. It is sometimes incorrectly identified with the seventh millennium, but it is really the millennium following the messianic kingdom, the eighth millennium or new heavenly age.

parousia: the Greek word for "presence," meaning the presence of the Messiah in the world at his return in glory. It is used more or less synonymously with "second coming."

Peshitta ('simple'): early Syriac Aramaic translation of the Bible, both Old and New Testaments.

Septuagint (LXX): Greek version of the Law, Prophets, and Writings (Old Testament), made in Alexandria in the 2nd or 3rd century BC.

Talmud Bavli (Babylonian Talmud): a commentary on the **Mishnah** compiled in Babylonia in the 5th century AD. It contains ancient traditions omitted from the **Mishnah** and **Tosefta**.

Talmud Yerushalmi (Jerusalem Talmud, Palestinian Talmud): a commentary on the **Mishnah** compiled in Galilee (not Jerusalem) in the 4th century. It contains ancient traditions omitted from the **Mishnah** and **Tosefta**.

tanna, pl. ***tannaim***: a rabbinic teacher of the period 50–200 AD.

tannaitic: describing the period of the *tannaim*.

targum: Aramaic for 'translation', especially the Aramaic translations of the books of the Bible.

Tosefta: supplement. Specifically, a collection of temple laws and oral traditions, compiled in the late 2nd century, supplementary to Rabbi Judah's **Mishnah**. Many of its teachings date from temple times.

yeshiva: a school for the study of Jewish texts.

Zadokite: a member of the temple priesthood of the second-temple period, who traced their descent from Zadok, the *kohen gadol* of David's time. In the New Testament, they are called Sadducees.

Bibliography

Alcázar, Luis del

1614 *Vestigatio Arcani Sensus in Apocalypsi* (Antwerp: Keerberg).

Anderson, R.

1894 *The Coming Prince: The Marvelous Prophecy of Daniel's Seventy Weeks Concerning the Antichrist* (Glasgow: Pickering & Ingles).

Bergsma, J.S.

2005 "Once Again, The Jubilee, Every 49 Or 50 Years?" *VT* 55.1: 121–25.

Black, M.C.

1991 *The Rejected and Slain Messiah Who is Coming with his Angels* (Ann Arbor, Michigan: University Microfilms International).

Blenkinsopp, J.

1990 *Ezekiel* (Interpretation Commentary; Louisville, Kentucky: John Knox).

Blomberg, C.L. & S.W. Chung

2009 *A Case For Historic Premillennialism: An Alternative to "Left Behind" Eschatology* (Grand Rapids, MI: Baker).

Blosser, D.

1981 "The Sabbath Year Cycle in Josephus," *Hebrew Union College Annual* 52: 129–139.

Bray, J.L.

1995 *Morgan Edwards and the Pretribulation Rapture Teaching (1788)* (Lakeland FL: John L. Bray Ministries, 1995).

Braude, W.G. (ed. & tr.)

1968 *Pesikta Rabbati.* 2 vols., Yale Judaica Series 18 (New Haven: Yale University Press).

Brown, D.

1887 "Personal Reminiscences of Edward Irving," *The Expositor,* 3rd series, vol. 6.3 (London: Hodder & Stoughton): 216–228.

Bruce, F.F.

1963 *The Epistle to the Romans* (Tyndale NT Commentaries; repr. Grand Rapids MI: Eerdmans).

1975 "Review of *The Unbelievable Pre-Trib Origin*," in *The Evangelical Quarterly* 47.1.

Carlson, R.

2020 'A Structure for the End of the World: 4QFlorilegium and the "Latter Days" in Early Jewish Tradition,' *Word & World* 40/3.

Charles, R.H.

1913 *The Apocrypha and Pseudepigrapha of the Old Testament in English.* 2 vols. (Oxford: Clarendon).

Charlesworth, J.H. with P. Dykers & M.J.H. Charlesworth

1981 *The Pseudepigrapha and Modern Research With A Supplement* (SSL Septuagint and Cognate Studies 75; Chico CA; Scholars).

Charlesworth, J.H.
1983 *The Old Testament Pseudepigrapha.* 2 vols. (Garden City NY: Doubleday).

Coad, F.R.
1968 *A History of the Brethren Movement* (Grand Rapids: Eerdmans).

Cockburn, H.
1856 *Memorials of his Time,* 2 vols. (Edinburgh: A. & C. Black).

Collins, J.J.
1983 "Sibylline Oracles," in Charlesworth 1983: 317–472.

Cooke, G. A.
1936 *The Book of Ezekiel* (International Critical Commentary; Edinburgh: T. & T. Clark).

Cranfield, C.E.B.
1985 *Romans: A Shorter Commentary* (Edinburgh: T. & T. Clark).

Crown, A.D.
1967 'Dositheans, Resurrection and a Messianic Joshua', in *Antichthon* I:70–85.

Darby, J.N.
c. 1848 "A Plain Statement of the Doctrine on the Sufferings of our blessed Lord propounded in some recent tracts, in extracts taken from the Author's writings," *The Writings of J. N. Darby*. Doctrinal writings, vol. 15: 98–114.
1844 "On the Presence and Action of the Holy Ghost in the Church," in *The Writings of J. N. Darby*. Doctrinal writings, vol. 3.
1830 "On 'Days' Signifying 'Years' in Prophetic Language," *The Christian Herald* (Dec. 1830).
1829 "Reflections upon the Prophetic Inquiry and the views advanced in it," *The Writings of J. N. Darby*. Prophetic writings, vol. 2.

Delitzsch, F.
1890 *Messianische Weissagungen in geschichtlicher Folge* (Leipzig: Faber). Eng. tr. of the original lectures: S.I. Curtiss, *Messianic Prophecies* (Edinburgh: T. & T. Clark, 1880).

Dodd, C. H.
1953 *According to the Scriptures: The Substructure of New Testament Theology* (New York: Scribner's).

Driver, S.R. and A. Neubauer
1877 *The Fifty-Third Chapter of Isaiah According To The Jewish Interpreters.* 2 vols. (Oxford: Parker–Leipzig: Weigel).

Du Tillet, J. (ed.)
1555 *Evangelium ex Hebraeo fideliter redditum* (Paris: Christophori).

Edwards, J.R.
2009 *The Hebrew Gospel and the Development of the Synoptic Tradition* (Grand Rapids MI: Eerdmans).

Edwards, M.
1788 *Two Academical Exercises on Subjects Bearing the Following*

Titles; Millennium, Last-Novelties (Philadelphia: Dobson & Lang).

Eisenstein, J. D.

1915 *Ozar Midrashim.* 2 vols. (New York: Eisenstein).

Fazio, J.

2020 "John Nelson Darby's Early Resistance to Pre-Tribulational Premillennialism As Expressed at the 1831 Powerscourt Prophecy Conference," presented at the National Evangelical Theological Society, *Christian History and Thought Since 1700*, Nov. 16–20.

Frere, J.H.

1815 *A Combined View of the Prophecies of Daniel, Esdras, and S. John, shewing that all the prophetic writings are formed upon one plan* (London: Hatchard).

1826 *On the General Structure of the Apocalypse* (London: Hatchard).

Friedlander, G. (ed. & tr.)

1916 *Pirkê de Rabbi Eliezer* (London: Kegan Paul, Trench, Trubner).

Friedmann, M. (ed.)

1880 *Pesikta Rabbati, Midrasch für den Fest-Cyclus und die ausgezeichneten Sabbathe* (Vienna: Joseph Kaiser).

Ford, J.M.

1995 *The Construction of the Other: The Antichrist* (*Andrews University Seminary Studies* 2:203-23).

Galil, G.

1996 *The Chronology of the Kings of Israel and Judah.* SHCANE, 9; (Leiden: E.J. Brill).

Gentry, K.

1989 *Before Jerusalem Fell: Dating the Book of Revelation. An Exegetical and Historical Argument for a Pre-A.D. 70 Composition* (Texas: Institute for Christian Economics).

Gumerlock, F.X.

2004 "Millennialism and the Early Church Councils: Was Chiliasm Condemned at Constantinople?" *Fides et Historia* 36.2: 83–95.

2002 "A Rapture Citation in the Fourteenth Century," *Bibliotheca Sacra* 159: 349–362.

Gurtner, D.M.

2020 *Introducing the Pseudepigrapha of Second Temple Judaism* (Grand Rapids MI: Baker).

Harnack A.

1883 "Millennium" in *Encyclopaedia Britannica.* (9th edition; Edinburgh: Adam and Charles Black).

Harrington, D.

2012 "Pseudo-Philo, *Liber Antiquitatum Biblicarum,*" in M. de Jong (ed.), *Outside the Old Testament* (Cambridge University Press).

Hasel, G.F.

1992 "New Light on the Book of Daniel from the Dead Sea Scrolls," *Faculty Publications* 3627. Andrews University.

Haydon, R.

2014 "The "Seventy Sevens" (Daniel 9:24) in Light of Heptadic Themes in Qumran," *JESOT* 3/2: 203–14.

Hengstenberg, E.W.

1829–35 *Christologie des Alten Testaments* (1829–1835; 2nd ed., 1854–1857). Eng. tr. of 2nd ed.; T. Meyer and J. Martin (trs.) *Christology of the Old Testament* (Edinburgh: T. & T. Clark, 1854–1858).

Hill, C.E.

2015 "Why the Early Church Finally Rejected Premillennialism," *Reformed Perspectives Magazine* 17.8. (Feb. 2015)

2001 *Regnum Caelorum: Patterns of Millennial Thought in Early Christianity.* 2nd ed. (Eerdmans: Grand Rapids MI).

Hitchcock, M.

2012 *The End: Everything You'll Want To Know About The Apocalypse* (Carol Stream IL: Tyndale).

2005 *A Defense of the Domitianic Date of the Book of Revelation* (PhD Dissertation: Dallas Theological Seminary). Available at https://www.pre-trib.org/media/k2/assets/Documents/hitchcock-dissertation.pdf (Accessed Sep. 2024).

Holmes, J.B.

2006 *The Apostolic Fathers in English.* 3rd edn. (Grand Rapids MI: Baker).

Howard, G.

1986 "The Textual Nature of an Old Hebrew Version of Matthew," *JBL* 105: 49-63.

Hulsius, A.

1653 *Theologiae judaicae: Pars prima: De Messia* (Breda: Subbingus).

Ice, T.D.

2016 "Did Edward Irving Invent the Pre-Trib Rapture View?" *The Master's Seminary Journal* 27: 57–73.

2009 "Morgan Edwards: Another Pre-Darby Rapturist," *Article Archives* 44. https://digitalcommons.liberty.edu/pretrib_arch/44.

1995 "Examining an Ancient Pre-Trib Rapture Statement," *Pre-Trib Perspectives* (The Pre-Trib Research Center, April 1995).

Ice, T. & T. Demy (eds.)

1995 *When The Trumpet Sounds* (Eugene OR: Harvest House).

Irving, E. (tr.)

1827 *The Coming of Messiah in Glory and Majesty;* see **Lacunza.**

Jacobi, M.

2007 "'In Its Time I Will Hasten It': Messianic Speculation In The Babylonian Talmud, Sanhedrin 96b-99a," *European Judaism* 40:115–119.

Jacobson, H.

1996 *A Commentary on Pseudo-Philo's Liber Antiquitatum Biblicarum.*

2 vols. (Arbeiten zur Geshichte des antiken Judentums und des Urchristentums, 31; Leiden: Brill).

Jeffrey, G.R.

1995 "A Pretrib Rapture Statement in the Early Medieval Church," in Ice & Demy 1995:105–125.

Jellinek, A.

1853–77 *Bet HaMidrash.* 6 vols. in 2. (Leipzig: Nies–Vollrath, 1853–77; photog. repr. Jerusalem: Wahrmann, 1967).

Jenks, G.C.

1991 *The Origins and Early Development of the Antichrist Myth* (Berlin: De Gruyter).

Kitchen, K.A.

1977 *The Bible in its World: The Bible and Archaeology Today* (Exeter: Paternoster).

Kitchen, K.A. & T.C. Mitchell

1982 "Chronology of the Old Testament," in J.D. Douglas (ed.), *New Bible Dictionary* (2nd ed.; Leicester UK/Wheaton IL: Inter-Varsity; Tyndale House): 188–200.

Lacunza, M.

1810 *The Coming of Messiah in Glory and Majesty,* 2 vols. Tr. E. Irving (Thames Ditton: Seeley, 1827) from *La venida del Mesías en gloria y majestad* (Cadiz, 1810).

Ladd, G.E.

1956 *The Blessed Hope* (Grand Rapids, MI: Eerdmans).

Landes, R.

2005–24 "Millennialism," *Encyclopaedia Britannica* online: https://www.britannica.com /topic/millennialism

de Lange, N.

2007 "Jewish and Christian Messianic Hopes in Pre-Islamic Byzantium" in Markus Bockmuehl and James Carleton Paget, *Redemption and Resistance: The Messianic Hopes of Jews and Christians in Antiquity* (London: T&T Clark, 2007), 274–284.

Lefebvre, J.-F.

2003 *Le Jubilé Biblique: Lv 25 – Exégèse et Théologie* (Göttingen: Vandenhoeck & Ruprecht).

Leiman, S.Z.

1974 "The Inverted Nuns at Numbers 10:35-36 and the Book of Eldad and Medad," *Journal of Biblical Literature* 93: 348-55.

Mackay, T.

1990 "Early Christian Millenarist Interpretation of the Two Witnesses in John's Apocalypse 11:3–13," in J.M. Lundquist and S.D. Ricks (eds.), *By Study and Also By Faith* (Salt Lake City, UT: Deseret Book Company, 1990), 1:222–331.

Mather, I.

1669 *The mystery of Israel's salvation, explained and applyed: or, A discourse concerning the general conversion of the Israelitish nation* (London: John Allen).

Mauro, P.

1928 *The Gospel of the Kingdom with an Examination of Modern Dispensationalism* (Boston: Hamilton).

Mayshar, J.

2020 "The Jubilee Calendar," *Vetus Testamentum* 71.2:1–14.

McGregor, G.

1950 "The Row Heresy," *Harvard Theological Review* 43:281–301.

McKibbens, T.R.

1980 *The life and works of Morgan Edwards* (New York : Arno Press).

McPherson, D.

2000 *The Rapture Plot.* 2nd ed. (Millennium III).

1975 *The Incredible Cover-Up* (Medford, OR: Omega Publications).

1974 *The Late Great Pre-Trib Rapture* (Kansas City: Heart of America Bible Society).

1973 *The Unbelievable Pre-Trib Origin* (Kansas City: Heart of America Bible Society).

Mitchell, D.C.

2021 *Jesus: The Incarnation of the Word* (Glasgow: Campbell).

2016 *Messiah ben Joseph* (Glasgow: Campbell).

2015 *The Songs of Ascents: Psalms 120–134 in the Worship of Jerusalem's Temples* (Glasgow: Campbell).

Monnickendam, Y.

2013 '"I Bring Death and Give Life, I Wound and Heal" (Deut. 32:39) - Two Versions of the Polemic on the Resurrection of the Dead,' *Henoch* 35:90–118.

Montgomery, J.A.

1907 *The Samaritans: The Earliest Jewish Sect: Their History, Theology and Literature* (Philadelphia: John C. Winston Co.).

Murphy, F.J.

1993 *Pseudo-Philo: Rewriting the Bible* (Oxford: University Press).

Murray, I.H.

1971 *The Puritan Hope* (London: Banner of Truth).

Neuffer, J.

1968 "The Accession of Artaxerxes I," *Andrews University Seminary Studies* 6.1.

Newton, I.

1733 *Observations upon the prophecies of Daniel, and the Apocalypse of St. John* (London: Darby & Browne).

1670–80 *Untitled treatise on Revelation* (Yahuda Ms. 1, National Library of Israel, Jerusalem).

1680–90 *Treatise on Revelation* (Yahuda Ms. 9, National Library of Israel, Jerusalem).

North, R.

1954 *Sociology of the Biblical Jubilee.* (Rome: Pontifical Biblical Institute).

Oliphant, M.

The Life of Edward Irving. 2 vols. (London: Hurst & Blackett, 1862).

van Oort, Johannes

2020 Mani and Augustine: Collected Essays on Mani, Manichaeism and Augustine (Nag Hammadi and Manichaean Studies 97; Leiden-Boston: Brill).

Parvis, S.

2006 *Marcellus of Ancyra and the Lost Years of the Arian Controversy 325-345* (Oxford University Press).

Payne, J.B.

1973 *Encyclopedia of Biblical Prophecy: The Complete Guide to Scriptural Predictions and Their Fulfillment* (New York: Harper & Row).

1962 *The Theology of the Older Testament* (Grand Rapids: Zondervan).

Pearse, R.

2018 "Did Pseudo-Ephraim believe in the Rapture? Some notes on the manuscripts, the passage and its Greek origins," https://www.roger-pearse.com/weblog/2018/10/27/ (accessed Apr. 2024).

Rabow, J.A.

2002 *50 Jewish Messiahs: The Untold Life Stories of 50 Jewish Messiahs Since Jesus and How They Changed the Jewish, Christian, and Muslim Worlds* (NY: Gefen Books).

Ribera, F.

1592 *In Sacrum Beati Ioannis Apostoli, & Evangelistiae Apocalypsin Commentarii* (Lyon).

Roberts, A. and Donaldson, J.

1867-85 *Ante-Nicene Christian Library: Translations of the Writings of the Fathers* (Edinburgh: T. & T. Clark).

Robin, C. & A. Al-Ghabban

2017 "Une première mention de Madyan dans un texte épigraphique d'Arabie," *Comptes rendus des séances de l'Académie des Inscriptions et Belles-Lettres* 161.1: 363–396.

Rowdon, H.H.

1967 *The origins of the Brethren, 1825-1850* (London: Pickering & Inglis).

Rydelnik, M. & E. Blum (eds.)
2019 *The Moody Handbook of Messianic Prophecy: Studies and Expositions of the Messiah in the Old Testament* (Chicago: Moody).

Sandeen, E.R.
1970 *The Roots of Fundamentalism: British and American millenarianism, 1800-1930* (Chicago: University of Chicago Press).

Schaff, P.
1858–90 *History of the Christian Church.* 8 vols. (New York: Scribner's).

Schonfield, H.
1927 *An Old Hebrew Text of St. Matthew's Gospel* (Edinburgh: T&T Clark).

Schürer, E.
1901 *Geschichte des jüdischen Volkes* (Leipzig: Hinrichs, 1901).

Smith, R. L.
1984 *Micah-Malachi* (Waco, TX: Word).

Spurgeon, C.H.
1874 "Darbysm and its new Bible," (London: Macintosh).
1869 "Mr. Grant on 'The Darby Brethren'," (*Sword and Trowel:* June).

Stern, D.H.
1992 *Jewish New Testament Commentary* (Jewish New Testament Publications, Inc.: Clarksville, MD).

Stitzinger, J.F.
2002 "The Rapture in Twenty Centuries of Biblical Interpretation," *The Master's Seminary Journal* 13.2: 149-171.

Stökl, J.
2006 "A List of the Extant Hebrew Text of the Book of Jubilees, Their Relation to the Hebrew Bible and Some Preliminary Comments," *Henoch* 28: 97–124.

Stott, J.
2001 *The Incomparable Christ* (Leicester: Inter-Varsity Press).

Strand, K.A.
1996 "Thiele's Biblical Chronology as a Corrective for Extrabiblical Dates," *Andrews University Seminary Studies* 34.2 (1996): 295–317.

Tabor, J.
2011 "If I Ascend to Heaven … Paul's Journey to Paradise," https://www.biblicalarchaeology.org/if-i-ascend-to-heavenpauls-journey-to-paradise/

Teplinsky, S.
2008 *Israel's Anointing* (Grand Rapids MI: Chosen).

Thiele, E.R.
1983 *The Mysterious Numbers of the Hebrew Kings* (3rd ed.; Grand Rapids: Zondervan/Kregel).

Thomson, J. E. H.

1919 *The Samaritans: Their Testimony to the Religion of Israel* (Edinburgh and London: Oliver and Boyd).

Ulrich, D.R.

2014 "How early Judaism read Daniel 9:24-27," *Old Testament Essays* 27/3: 1062–1083.

Ulrich, E.C.

2000 *Discoveries in the Judean Desert* 16. *Qumran Cave 4.XI: Psalms to Chronicles* (Oxford: Clarendon).

Wacholder, B.Z.

1973 'The Calendar Of Sabbatical Cycles During The Second Temple And The Early Rabbinic Period' *HUCA* 44 (1973) 153–196.

1975 'Chronomessianism: The Timing of Messianic Movements and the Calendar of Sabbatical Cycles', *HUCA* 46 (1975) 201–218.

1983 'The Calendar of Sabbath Years during the Second Temple Era: A Response', *HUCA* 54 (1983) 123–133.

Walvoord, J.F.

1976 *The Blessed Hope and the Tribulation: A Historical and Biblical Study of Posttribulationism* (Zondervan: Grand Rapids MI).

Wintermute, O.S.

"Apocalypse of Elijah", in Charlesworth, *The Old Testament Pseudepigrapha* I:721–753.

Wright, N.T.

2001 "Farewell to the Rapture," Bible Review (August 2001), also at https://ntwrightpage.com/2016/07/12/farewell-to-the-rapture/

Young, R.C.

2022 "The Theological Problem Presented by the Exactness of Daniel's 70 weeks," *JETS* 65.3: 473–89.

2008 "Evidence for Inerrancy from a Second Unexpected Source: The Jubilee and Sabbatical Cycles," *Bible and Spade* Jan. 2008.

2006 The Talmud's Two Jubilees and their Relevance to the Date of the Exodus. *Westminster Theological Journal* 68: 71–83.

2004 "When Did Jerusalem Fall?" *JETS* 47: 21–38.

Yuan, Q. et al.

2023 "Moon-forming impactor as a source of Earth's basal mantle anomalies," *Nature* 623: 95–99.

Zuckermann, B.

1857 *Über Sabbatjahrcyclus und Jobelperiode*, in Jahresbericht des jüdisch-theologischen Seminars 'Fraenckelscher Stiftung' (Breslau, 1857). Eng. tr. A Löwy (tr.), *Treatise on the Sabbatical Cycle and the Jubilee* (New York: Hermon, 1974).

Printed in Dunstable, United Kingdom

70170802R00180